Contrary to popular academic opinion in the United States, the author found that those countries with the most liberal laws on deviance (i. e., the least punitive sanctions) are those that are the highly economically developed—and least totalitarian (U. S. A. and Italy). But, when public opinion is considered, he found that the public favors harsher punishments than the law provides. In contrast, in the developing countries of India, Iran and Indonesia, where penal sanctions are more severe, public opinion is much more liberal. The crucial question is what role criminal law plays in the process of modernization: whether law is a stable cultural influence, round which public opinion wavers in a startling fashion, depending on the stage of modernization.

These, and other issues that are discussed will interest social scientists in many fields, especially anthropologists, sociologists of law, conflict theorists, criminologists, attitude theorists, moral philosophers, opinion pollsters, and labelling theorists.

Graeme Newman
COMPARATIVE DEVIANCE

Graeme Newman
COMPARATIVE DEVIANCE
Perception and Law in Six Cultures

PREFACE BY MARVIN E.WOLFGANG

ELSEVIER

New York/Oxford/Amsterdam

ELSEVIER SCIENTIFIC PUBLISHING COMPANY, INC.
52 Vanderbilt Avenue, New York, N.Y. 10017

ELSEVIER SCIENTIFIC PUBLISHING COMPANY
335 Jan Van Galenstraat, P.O. Box 211
Amsterdam, The Netherlands

Library of Congress Cataloging in Publication Data

Newman, Graeme R
    Comparative deviance: perception and law in six cultures.

    Bibliography: p.
    Includes index.
    1. Deviant behavior—Case studies. 2. Social
control—Case studies. 3. Criminal law—Case studies.
I. Title.
HV6030.N48   364'.092'6   76-19782
ISBN 0-444-99026-7

Manufactured in the United States of America

Designed by Loretta Li

To my parents

Contents

Preface

It is difficult to say where research begins and ends, especially with a research undertaking of this magnitude. Data has been collected from people in six countries scattered around the globe. Respondents have been interviewed in crowded cities, isolated peasant villages, sprawling suburbs and high-rise apartments. Many different languages and dialects have been used. We have collected enormous amounts of information all of which has been reduced to one language—the columns on a computer card. Naturally, much of the atmosphere and quality of content in the respondents' answers to our questions is lost: A university student interviews a peasant in a quiet Iranian village by the communal well; an Indonesian psychology student steps over an open sewer on his way to interview a householder in a crowded suburb of Djakarta; test-wise Americans self-administer the questionnaire; Sardinians in Orani at first refuse to answer until they find that the young interviewer is also of their village; professional marketing interviewers systematically interview selections of respondents in high-rise apartments of Belgrade; interviewers in Bombay switch from Hindi to English, back to Hindi. The contributions to this research have been extremely diverse. It could not have been conducted without the work of scores of people in the field, and the many people involved in the massive job of organizing the conduct of our social survey in six countries, ever mindful of maintaining comparability of research design.

From each country I have to thank many people for their very kind hospitality and for their expertise in carrying out the research: In India: Dr. J. J. Panakal, Head, Department of Criminology and Correctional Administration, Tata Institute of Social Sciences; Clarence Dias, Reader in Law, University of Bombay. In Indonesia: Dr. Assad Hassan and Mrs. S. Sadli, University of Indonesia. In Iran: Parvis Saney and Assaud Nezami, University of Teheran. In Italy: Giuseppe di Gennaro and Eduardo Vetere, United Nations Social Defense Research Institute. In U.S.A.: Professor Jack Kress, School of Criminal

Justice, State University of New York at Albany. And in Yugoslavia: Milan Milutinovic, Director, Institute of Criminology at Belgrade along with Doctors Davidovic, Sotic and especially Helena Spadyer-Zinic.

My thanks also go to Carol Trilling who assisted with the preparation of Chapter 3, and to Eduardo Vertere who assisted with Chapter 10. The data analysis could not have been completed without the assistance of Donald Articolo. Hans Toch also helped to keep me on the straight and narrow during my hours of weakness!

It goes without saying, of course, that my greatest debt is to Marvin Wolfgang and Franco Ferracuti whose original idea spawned this study, and who obtained the early funding from Ford Foundation. Basic ideas for the project were first discussed at a meeting held at the United Nations Secretariat in New York. Those who participated were Simon Dinitz, Franco Ferracuti, Robert Merton, Gerhard Mueller, Walter Reckless, Leslie Wilkins and Marvin Wolfgang. The study was later expanded considerably with additional support provided by the United Nations Social Defense Research Institute at Rome and by a small grant from the Committee on Institutional Funds, State University of New York at Albany. I am grateful to all these institutions. I am especially appreciative of Dr. Peider Konz, Director of the United Nations Social Defense Research Institute, for his constant support of the study through many difficult periods.

Chapters 3, 6 and 7 draw upon articles previously published in *The Journal of Cross-Cultural Psychology, Criminal Justice and Behavior,* and the *European Journal of Sociology.*

My final debt is to Dean Richard Myren and my colleagues of the School of Criminal Justice, the University at Albany, where I have found a near perfect research setting. This includes the nothing less than fantastic work of my secretary Jo Anne DeSilva.

Albany, March, 1976

GRAEME R. NEWMAN

Foreword

As a professor, there are few rewards more satisfying than having a former student to publish and still to become a colleague and remain a friend. This is not Graeme Newman's first appearance in print, but it is his first major work—one that deserves a wide sociological, legal and criminological audience.

In this volume are years of prodigious labor and careful field investigation in a variety of cultural settings, insightful conceptualization, thoughtful and well executed research design, and conclusions firmly rooted in the empirical data. Moreover, analyses internal to the data collected in each country have been interpretively linked in two ways: by cross-cultural comparisons and contrasts, and by a unifying theoretical structure. In short, the author has provided a fascinating intellectual enterprise—synthesizing an amazing amount of material, in the form of responses from diverse persons and peoples.

But, it might be said, any reasonably "trained" person could handle data analysis from binary responses congealed on computer cards or tapes. The author somewhat apologizes for this reductionism. It is true, of course, that in any large-scale research, data inputs (however cherished they may be in their original colorful forms of response) are displayed in aggregates, for science requires classifications, operational definitions, hypotheses—logic in analysis and techniques that transform a spoken language to the universalism of a number system. However, this study benefits from uncommon breadth of erudition spread on collected data. Passed through the prism of the author's mind, the data take on a lively linkage with directly relevant sociological and social psychological theory. Interpretations do not suffer from the gaps between data and conclusions, common to many studies.

The treatment of cultural relativism in this work is worthy of attention by anthropologists as well as criminologists. Neither Marxian nor general conflict theorists will be comforted by the findings, but scholars will *not* be able to dismiss easily these orientations. The labelling literature is enriched by this work—as is measurement and scaling theory and methodology. Because of my research interests in this latter area, I am especially attracted to the processes by which subjective perceptions in various cultures were obtained, as well as in the finding of considerable consensus about crime. What should be of further interest to legal scholars, as well, is the innovative and provocative findings. about public perceptions of how society *should* respond to deviant behaviors. Here is an investigation that singularly displays notions of the seriousness of crime and of the severity of sanctions. Lessons are to be learned from this work that contribute to a more rational penal policy, whatever the particular legal or communal norms that may be in a given jurisdiction.

The author may overstate my contribution to the design model and other aspects of the study. If I functioned as inspiration, I am gratified. But the scholarship and social utility of this study lie within the scope of the author's own capacity, and I am honored to have participated in this undertaking—in whatever way I might have helped.

MARVIN E. WOLFGANG

Professor of Sociology and Law
University of Pennsylvania

Graeme Newman
COMPARATIVE DEVIANCE

one

PARADIGMATIC ORIGINS
OF THE RESEARCH

In the beginning, the aim of this research was to examine the relationship between law and opinion concerning deviance in cross-cultural perspective. At the time when the research was planned, such a study was obvious. The "liberation" of social deviance by the labelling theorists in sociology was at its peak. The call for the decriminalization of many victimless crimes was strong (Schur, 1965). Criminal lawyers, as well as sociologists, suggested that laws that were not in step with public opinion were detrimental to the image of the criminal law (Morris and Hawkins, 1972) and were unfairly selective or repressive of "minority" groups. The ideology of the right to be different, a fundamental theoretical premise of American individualism, was forced into the forefront of policy (Kittrie, 1971).

Was it? The liberalization of laws concerning victimless crimes has occurred slowly. Abortion has been decriminalized in some states of the United States, but it teeters on the brink of criminalization once again. No substantial liberalization has occurred in relation to homosexuality, prostitution, alcoholism, or the taking of drugs. Indeed, in the latter case, penalization increased substantially in New York State (Newman and Trilling, 1974). One concludes, therefore, that the liberation of social deviance was confined to the ranks of academic research and theory, especially that of labelling theorists. If there is a relationship between the criminal law and public opinion as those who advocated decriminalization implied, then one concludes that the public as a whole was not in agreement with theorists' liberalizing attitudes toward victimless crimes. This is, of course, assuming that the criminal law shifts according to the weight of public opinion, and this assumption has not been demonstrated. In any case, in 1969, research into the relationship between law and opinion seemed a pressing need. Therefore, the question that it was hoped this research project would answer was the extent to which there existed gaps between public opinion and criminal law.

Other themes of fashionable sociology influenced the inception of this research. Three major premises about deviance had been advanced by the labelling theorists: 1) that there was no consensus in society concerning moral values or what was deviant and what was not; 2) no behavior could be either bad, wrong, criminal, diseased, or abnormal in and of itself (it had first to be socially defined that way); and 3) the means by which such definitions of differentiation were applied were through the agents of institutions of social control: mental health workers, police, teachers, doctors, et al. These assumptions were represented by Erikson (1962), Kitsuse (1962), and Becker (1964).

This rampant relativism was of the extreme that it led some theorists even to deny the existence of "disease," turning a blind eye to the more challenging kinds of traditional crimes—crimes of violence.[1] Indeed, most research on labelling theory was conducted in the realm of victimless crimes, only occasionally with traditional crimes.[2] This narrow focus on victimless crimes was the product of a myopic politic: the deviants had been "liberated" by identifying all "agents of control" as potential if not actual—gaolers and oppressors. The diagnostic and selection procedures of these agents were subjected to merciless scrutiny, with the view to demonstrating the ritualistic and arbitrary nature of these procedures. But, according to the "new theft" sociologists, this was a weakling's approach; a partisan politic, not an ideological politic (Gouldner, 1966). Nevertheless, evidence was accumulated to show that rates and forms of deviance were closely related to the activities of official control agents of the various institutions of social control.[3] This recognition has been influential in the research design as we will see. This does not mean, of course, that deviance is *only* the product of the activities of social control agents. What became clear, as a result of the focus of labelling theorists, was that all societies are structured and organized in a way that maintains the social control of individuals and classes of individuals. This observation had been made many years before by sociologists and social control theorists of different kinds (e.g., Parsons, (1951), and by cul-

---

[1]Even the strongest critical statement on labelling theory by Gibbs (1966) did not consider this relativism a severe limitation of the theory. It was left to the social theorist Gouldner to begin the attack upon the superficial ideology of the labelling theorists (Gouldner, 1968). Yet he did not criticize the relativism itself, but rather the partisan politic which grew out of it.

[2]The notable exception has been Sudnow (1965) where the full range of crimes dealt with in a prosecutor's office is treated.

[3]The basic works were those of Erikson (1966) who dealt historically with religious deviance; Kitsuse and Cicourel (1963) who dealt with the generation of crime rates, and Scheff (1964), studying the psychiatric screening of mental patients.

tural anthropologists such as Malinowsky (1964), and Hoebel (1954).[4] In many ways, it was the focus and method of the anthropologists that labelling theorists applied to their study of the defining of deviance by the institutions of social control.

Some difficult questions were asked about labelling theory. What of "secret deviance," that by definition could not have been labelled? (Gibbs, 1966). How could labelling theory explain the motivation of individuals to become deviant?[5] Where was the hard evidence that a label itself actually produced the self-identification of deviance? (Gove, 1970).

Gradually, at the micro and macro level, attempts at answers emerged. The answers were confusing. Lemert (1972), on whose work most had relied for evidence that the label actually produced a self-identification of deviance, in a confusing reformulation of his theory of primary and secondary deviance, ended by developing an individualistic psychology of motivation. For example, he explained stuttering by an analysis of a person "interacting" with his own symptoms. Secondary deviation in this case became the organization of one's behavior around one's "primary" deviation (i.e. original physiological symptoms), virtually nothing to do with the way these symptoms were "labelled" by others. This appeared to be a complete withdrawal from the interactionist labelling perspective. Before this, the secondary deviant had been understood as "a person whose life and identity are organized around the facts of deviance" (Lemert 1972:41), but the word "facts" here was formerly understood as the reactions of *others* to one's symptoms.

Meanwhile, theorists argued that deviants "negotiated" with others for their deviant status (e.g., Scheff, 1968). These theorists ended only with the commonplace observation that control agents are more powerful than the deviants, and so the deviants are only the *subjects* of negotiation, unable to negotiate as equals. There ensued the microanalysis of interactions by the enthnomethodologists, and the endless repetitions of Goffman in observational studies of deviants interacting

---

[4]Parsons (1951, 1965) wrote extensively on the role of social control and socialization, with many detailed examples of the former in relation to medical practice. Malinowsky's approach centered upon the instrinsically functional relationship between the roles of primitive peoples, firmly based on economic necessity, which accounted for the bulk of law and obedience to it. He observed, however, that the use of force as a show of strength by the village chief was also an instrumental function of the "criminal law." Hoebel concentrated more on the customs of primitive groups that appeared to control behavior more effectively than formal criminal law as we know it.

[5]Schur (1971:34) recognizes this problem, and answers it by equating the "how" with "why" of deviance.

with others. It became apparent that a theoretical crisis had been reached: labelling theory had been unable to explain individual motivations to deviance. It had stereotyped deviants into passive, amorphous victims of labelling without a will (Taylor, et al., 1974).

Disillusionment set in.[6] As the paradigm broke, there were attempts to show, using "hard data" that the labelling perspective either did or did not apply.[7]

Yet, Schur (1974) admitted (or should we say, "recognized") that there might be a consensus concerning the deviance of some kinds of behavior ("homicide, incest and so on . . .", Schur, 1974, p. 21). This was a far cry from the early statements of Becker (1962) and Erikson (1962) who argued that deviance was the product of the powerful groups, imposing their definitions or labels on the less powerful. In making this admission, Schur paved the way for the return of the once "radical" sociology of labelling theory into the bosom of the "social order," *a la* Talcott Parsons. In *Labelling Deviant Behavior,* Schur tried to demonstrate how labelling theory was a logical extension—a part of traditional sociological theory.

A new paradigm was raising its ugly head. Conflict theory, a traditional area of study in sociology, became relevant to the study of crime. The works of Turk (1969), Quinney (1970, 1973) and Chambliss (1971) popularized the application of the conflict paradigm to criminology. These theorists explicitly denied the validity of a consensus view of society, arguing that deviance *and* crime are products of conflict over norms. Not vice-versa. The consensus view has traditionally been that there is basically a broad agreement in society about what is deviant and what is not, what is criminal and what is not. Deviants are seen as the *creators* of conflict rather than the *product* of conflict. The most recent critics of the consensus view are the "new criminologists," Taylor, Walton and Young (1974). The evidence which these conflict theorists present in support of their model is to point to the various

---

[6]Manning (1973) in a review of several of the influential books on social deviance concluded: ". . . the quasi-paradigmatic setting work of Lemert is now in the process of disintegration . . ." (p. 127).

[7]This state of affairs culminated in the exchange of papers between Scheff (1974), Gove (1974) and the series of indignant letters involving these authors and Gwyn Nettler in the *American Sociological Review* of that year. The papers were shallow conceptually and methodologically. Indulgences included the use of arbitrary definitions of "psychiatric" and "societal reaction;" extremely distorted use both conceptually and methodologically of the concept of social class; and the "totting up" of empirical studies "for" and "against" each view, as though there were only two sides to the problem.

pressure groups, and repressed classes who, they argue, carry on their activities in conflict with other groups in society. Persons in authority, as Turk argues, are perpetually in conflict with their subjects. Yet it has not been shown unequivocally that all these groups are actually in conflict where basic beliefs are concerned. None of these conflict theorists have ever thought to survey the people upon whom they have imposed the conflict model. They have ignored the fact that considerable consensus may exist among the people about a variety of issues and values, which has been well documented (Dahl, 1967), and that consensus exists alongside of, or as well as, conflict. As we will see, our research in many ways explores the relationship between these key concepts of conflict and consensus.

In criminology, it has been the subcultural theorists, the bastion of establishment criminology, who have shown empirically that certain groups in society have different life styles, and on occasion, delinquents and criminals from various subcultures display different values and norms, compared to society at large. Yet, at the same time, a number of studies have also failed to find differences in value structure between the two groups (Matza, 1968; Ball-Rokeach, 1973). The debate is, therefore, clearly not resolved. But for the subculture theorists there is an implied valuation of the subculture as being wholistically deviant from the major culture—i.e., a deviation from the consensus. Thus, although traditional subcultural theory argues a differentiation in values between culture and subculture, it is a consensus perspective. Later, more explicitly, the Marxist subculture theorist Fanon (1968) saw the subculture as the product of consensus—not a product of conflict.[8]

Yet, it seems commonsensical that people *will* agree that such crimes as robbery, murder, assault, etc., should be punished by the law. The work of Sellin and Wolfgang (1967) insisted that there was a consensus concerning the severity of crime, which cut across all classes, and this work was replicated many times.[9] Yet the Sellin-Wolfgang work was severely criticized (Walker, 1970; Rose, 1970), and the results either never accepted or ignored by conflict theorists.

---

[8]The question is much more complicated than space allows. The difficulty lies in the definition and meaning of the term "conflict," which we will consider in the final chapter. The Fanon work is concerned mainly with the symbiotic relationship between culture and subculture, and an inevitable course of events which issues from the core values of the major culture being internalized by the subculture, thus producing a "consensus," yet at the same time the basis for deep conflict.
[9]See Chapter 3 for a review of these studies.

Thus, two other crucial questions might be answered. First, we could examine the extent to which there is a consensus concerning traditional crimes and deviances not only across different national samples, but also across different substrata within a society. Thus, a range of acts from traditional crime to borderline deviance was chosen. For the same reason, the range of countries with diverse political, economic, and social development backgrounds was chosen. Second, the range of questions asked could be extended beyond those asked by Sellin and Wolfgang. The structure and organization of deviance perception might be investigated more deeply, so that the question of cross class similarity could be tested more thoroughly, and more meaningfully. We shall see that the word "consensus" can be interpreted in many different ways, especially when dealing with what are basically abstract psychological and sociological phenomena (i.e. "perceptions" of "norms").

Modern conflict theorists, however, such as the "new criminologists" have argued that it is basically the question of economic class differences that is at the root of the crime problem. A revision of Marxist theory has recently been attempted to show that even traditional crimes such as robbery or "murder with intent" are products of a bourgeois criminal law which is at its base class biased, designed to keep the lower class in submission (Quinney, 1973). At first bite, one might predict that we should therefore expect to get differences in perceptions of crime according to class background. Yet, Marxists would argue that if no differences are found, the reason is "false consciousness." There is little one can do with this claim. If Marxists dismiss findings of "no differences," it follows that they should also dismiss findings of "differences," as false consciousness. It would seem that empirical research is irrelevant to this theoretical view. Regardless, Marxists could reinterpret them to suit themselves. However, since we have included a communistic country in our sample, it will be possible to test aspects of this theory.

A final theme which affected the inception of this research was that of deviance and social change. A difficulty with "consensus" or social order theory, so conflict theorists have charged, is that it is unable to explain social change, or at least social change becomes categorized as "abnormal" or certainly as dysfunctional. Social order theorists generally have viewed social change as gradual and incremental, especially insofar as norms, values and laws are concerned. In fact, the massive study of the evolution of criminal laws and human values by Sorokin (1957) provides much evidence for this view. Revolutions are

6

pointed to as evidence that laws may change rapidly, yet it is difficult to draw conclusions here. It is more likely that the outward forms of criminal justice alter after revolutions, but that certain traditional crimes remain the same—such as murder with intent, robbery, and so on. Furthermore, if one takes a long time period, such as that taken by Sorokin, revolutions take up only a very minor portion of the time span, so that many of the apparently drastic changes which occur as a result of the revolution, may be seen as temporary. For example, the death penalty was abolished immediately after the Russian Revolution of 1910. It was reintroduced in the 1920's, and still remains.

The question of continuity and change was addressed in another related field of research, reaching a crescendo at the end of the 1960s: the cross-national study of modernization. Questions were raised: Whether modernization as a result of technological advance and introduction of mass communications in developing countries was affecting religious, family, and village life, and the extent to which it affected individual personalities and aspirations (e.g., Lerner, 1958). The cross-cultural aspects of the present research seemed, therefore, timely. We could, indirectly, test some of these ideas about the effects of modernization, deviance and social change. Although it would have been preferable to conduct a time series or trend study to measure changes in perceptions of deviance, this would have been beyond our financial capabilities. The cost of cross-national research is phenomenally high. We could afford one splash at it and no more. However, there were indirect ways in which we could gain measures of change. Studies of modernization suggested that modernization is often accompanied by a liberalization of values. Such differences should, therefore, be observable in comparisons between rural and urban groups within each country, and between our most modernized and least modernized countries. Age differences should be important pointers of current and future change. If the premises of modernization are valid, older persons should be less tolerant of deviance than the younger. On the other hand, these differences should be discernible only for those crimes which are not traditional. The consensus theory argues that perception of traditional crimes changes only very slowly.

I have tried to show how the basic questions addressed by this research grew out of the ethos of then currently dominant theoretical paradigms. It is now five years since its beginning. Responsibility for the final product, of course, rests entirely with the writer. But the cultural-theoretical origins of the research should be recognized.

7

In summary, the basic questions and sub-questions addressed by this research are:

1. Are there any gaps between law and opinion about deviance? How can they be identified; how can they be measured?
2. Is there a broad consensus about what is deviant and what is not? Over what classes, or sub-classes of a society might consensus or conflict apply?
3. Can a consensus across cultures and nations be shown to exist? In short, is there anything approaching universal values or taboos?
4. How are individual perceptions of deviance organized and structured, and how may they be measured?
5. To what kinds of acts might consensus or dissensus apply? Can the assumed dichotomy between deviance (dissensus) and crime (consensus) be empirically supported? Is there no basic division? Or is a more complex classification appropriate?
6. What is the relationship between modernization, perceptions of deviance, and social change? Is there a discernible movement in perceptions of deviance? Do the developed countries show significantly different perceptions of deviance to the less developed countries? Do those subclass categories such as urban/rural background and age display any signs of a changing value structure?

two

DEVIANCE, THE PUBLIC AND THE CRIMINAL LAW

Five key conceptual areas need to be reanalyzed or defined to translate the research questions into empirically usable terms. These areas are the nature of deviance, the social content of the criminal law, structure of the public, the measurement of deviance perception, and the definition of culture. Of course, the point of the research is to examine the interrelationships among all five areas. Here we will examine the first three conceptual areas.

THE NATURE OF DEVIANCE

Since we were going to measure people's perceptions of deviance, it seemed reasonable that we should have some idea about what was the nature of deviance, suggesting to us how to structure our questionnaire and what questions initially to ask. Although it is often argued that tests and questionnaires are best developed phenomenologically rather than logically (Hogarth, 1971), one doubts whether a purely phenomenological construction is possible. "Intelligence is what a test says it is" has been a popular defense of this view. Yet it is clear that tests developed on this assumption are still dominated by a particular theoretical premise, whether intended by the test constructor or not. Popular I. Q. tests, for example, have been demonstrated not to measure divergent and creative thinking as an aspect of intelligence (Getzels and Jackson, 1962). But in addition to this, one has to start somewhere, and it seems more straightforward to establish a theoretical premise for development of one's questionnaire, rather than to allow "the data" to speak to the researcher. The type of questionnaire, therefore, was dictated by certain theoretical assumptions we were prepared to make in advance about the nature of deviance. These assumptions, derived from then current literature and research, are as follows.

9

The work of the labelling theorists has suggested that there is a close relationship between the forms and rates of deviance, and the activities of social control agents and agencies. Evidence for this has been found in the area of mental illness (Scheff, 1964, 1967), traditional crime, though less often (Sudnow, 1965; Kitsuse and Cicourel, 1963), victimless crimes (Becker, 1964), physical illness and deformity (Goffman, 1963, Scott, 1969), and mental defectiveness (Edgerton, 1967).

Notwithstanding the above, there are what one might term "functionally objective" forms of deviance. The activities of definers of deviance are historically determined by the same forces that act on those who are defined.[1] Thus, while the outward cultural forms of, say, physical and mental illness change slowly over time, as far as an actor in any point in time is concerned, these forms of deviance are relatively static. Indeed, as far as a one time, cross-sectional research as the present one is concerned, they may be treated as such. However, since the idea of universal values (let alone objective "truths") is currently out of favor in social science, one is not prepared at this juncture to extend this observation across cultures. It is, however, one of the points that this research will shed light on. It is often insisted that psychiatrists are unable to agree on classifications of mental illness. This criticism, one suspects, has been rather hysterically overstated. The empirical data to support that view is over-interpreted to apply to *all* mental illness. There is evidence that psychiatrists and psychologists can reach reasonable agreement in clinical diagnosis.[2] The criticisms often rely on an arbitrary division between physical and

---

[1]The work of Foucault (1965, 1975) makes this clear. The illness of "melancholia" in the 19th Century, for example, was "real" in its symptoms, and clearly diagnosable. Foucault shows how this and other mental illnesses become diagnosable as illnesses as a result of the continually evolving process of social history. Although the doctors do a lot of "labelling," the patients do a great deal of self-labelling—not merely because the doctor labels them, but because of a continually evolving cultural process. Thus, although definitions of health and illness do change over long periods of time, given a person's lifetime the chances are that they will appear as relatively static.

[2]The major criticisms by sociologists against the psychiatric model of deviance have not been that psychiatrists disagree. On the contrary, labelling theorists and other interactionists have been pleased to identify the ritualistic and stereotypical bases for the diagnoses (e.g. Scheff, 1963; Goffman, 1961). It follows that if these aspects of diagnosis are dominant, there should be considerable *agreement* concerning the diagnosis of mental illness among psychiatrists and other professionals. Unfortunately, the extensive research on psychiatric diagnosis has centered mainly around the *validity* of classification systems. Of the 20 or so studies conducted, inter-rater agreement in classification has been found to vary from 50 to 70 percent, depending on the conditions and classification system being used. However, none of these studies have analyzed the reliability of diagnoses relative to particular mental illness. This would seem to be crucial, especially when most critics of psychiatric diagnosis assume that they are far less valid or reliable than diagnoses in the main stream of "non-mental" illnesses. To

mental illness.[3] There are many "mental" illnesses, diagnosible and classifiable, just as there are many "physical" illnesses, difficult to diagnose and classify. An example is that of depression, the forms of which can be diagnosed with reasonable precision and some treated effectively with anti-depressant drugs. (Is this a physical or mental illness?) Another example is that of catatonic schizophrenia. Again, the criticism against diagnosis of this illness is that it occurs only in mental institutions, and therefore, supposedly, is not a true "illness." It is, however, a clearly identifiable *form* of behavior, the diagnosis of which psychiatrists have little difficulty in agreeing regardless of its supposed cause. Whether it is an illness or not (i.e., the *validity* of the diagnosis) is a separate question to the *reliability* of its diagnosis.

Although some of the above points suggest that deviance is the product of an application of socio-historical definitions upon a person, it does not follow that a person cannot be deviant *per se,* as Kitsuse and other labelling theorists have argued. Many aspects of behavior or merely outward anatomical appearance are ascribed automatically an inferior deviant status in our society. For many years, to be born black in the U.S.A., for example, was to be born deviant, with no possibility of change of anatomy or status: i.e., anatomy was destiny, or if you like, a static category of deviance. The same observation may be applied to being born female, or, more complicated, born a Jew. There are many fixed categories of deviance in society which are not attached to people by a specific control agent, but which people are born into.[4] In a more complicated fashion, this is the point made by subculture theories of crime and delinquency.

Deviance is a morally disapproved status. Although it is occasionally argued that outstanding persons, persons of genius or saints are "exceptional" or "deviant," (e.g., Wilkins, 1964:46) the fact is that such persons are rarely the subjects of modern sociological study of

---

my knowledge, no study has been conducted to make such a comparison, yet there are many "physical" illnesses for which very low inter-rater agreement has been found (Reisner and Semmel, 1974: 775). A comprehensive review of psychiatric diagnosis is Frank (1975). The most recent study which found a 65 percent inter-rater agreement in psychiatric diagnosis is by Kendell (1973).
[3]Again, much of the criticism levelled against psychiatric diagnosis is directed at the use of a physical illness model to diagnose a mental illness (Szasz, 1961). Yet this argument itself assumes a clear cut demarcation between physical and mental illness that cannot be supported, and in addition it overlooks the fact that the diagnosis of physical illness can be and has been subjected to the same merciless scrutiny of the interactionists who have found ritualism and stereotyping to abound. See, for example, Mechanic (1968), Freidson and Lorber (1971), and Roth (1963).
[4]"Anatomy is destiny" is an old cornerstone of psychoanalysis which has recently been reassessed. See, for example, Miller (1973).

11

deviance. The exceptions in the past have been Terman's studies of genius, and the various psychological profiles of famous persons such as Freud on Michelangelo and Da Vinci, Erikson on Gandhi and Luther. The only study conducted by a criminologist concerning genius as deviant was that of Lombroso (1896) whose hypothesis was that genius was a product of mental degeneration.

The sociological study of deviants as a *class* has always focused upon those considered by society or the researchers as "bad," "criminal," "delinquent," "crazy," "deformed," "immoral." One can think of no clear exceptions in sociological research. In spite of the relativistic protestations of labelling theorists that deviants are not "bad" but merely labelled that way, they do not conduct their voyeristic research upon those who are "good."[5]

The history of ethics provides considerable evidence that there are and have been at least since Homeric times enduring images of the "good man" and the "evil man." Depending on the cultural conditions at the time, these images of the good may be transposed into certian forbidden and sanctified forms of behavior, most often rationalized complex and forceful systems of argument, and, in Western civilization, inextricably tied to Judeo-Christian religion. The relationship between these outward forms of deviance to crime is complicated by the intermittently close and conflicting relationship between Church and State throughout history. The relationship between religious beliefs and the forms and rates of deviance has been researched only rarely in the sociological literature (Erikson, 1966), yet it is most likely that many of the early processes and formal procedures for identifying and dealing with deviants in Western society have their origin in early religious tenets, especially Canon Law. Witches, perhaps the earliest

---

[5] A possible exception to this observation is the work of the Polish school of sociologists, originating with Podgorecki, published in various bulletins of The Centre International De Criminologie Comparee, Universite de Montreal. This school argues that there is both "positive" and "negative" deviance. Deviance is first defined as the deviation from a norm, and then it is argued that a deviation may be either positive or negative. Positive deviance is when one is rewarded for deviating from a norm. Negative deviance is when one is punished for deviating. Examples of "positive" deviants might be outstanding athletes. But again, the moral overtones that are attached to the word "deviant" make it a severe distortion to attach the word to such persons, unless it can be shown that they are negatively sanctioned in some way. In addition, excellent athletes are deviations from the *normal* rather than a norm. Kojder and Kwasniewski (1975:23) define positive deviance as behavior which is approved of by 70 percent or more of respondents. But if this is the case, then what is normative? One would have to argue that it is behavior that is neither approved nor disapproved, which is a contradiction in terms. For a discussion of Wilkins' definition of deviance and of the difficulties with defining norms in relation to deviance, see Newman (1970).

and "simplest" form of deviance, were not identified by the arbitrary application of the tyranny of the church. Elaborate procedures were developed for their "objective" identification, as is clearly demonstrated in the *Malleus Maleficarum* (Summers, 1969). All religions, no matter what the culture, espouse a right way to live. We should expect, therefore, that religiosity will be a major discriminating variable in perceptions of deviance in all countries.

Finally, many theorists argue that the ascription of deviance to another is intrinsically a moral act (Douglas 1970:3–30)—the interactional situation of deviant and non-deviant is intrinsically a moral encounter (Goffman, 1963). The argument is that the ascription of a label onto another is an act of *judging* the other, necessarily arbitrary; in that sense moral. The extreme view is that all social encounters are *moral* encounters. The ascription of deviance to another is argued to be a moral act because it a) implies that there is something "wrong" (either with the deviant himself, or the situation), b) because it decreases the person in status (both in terms of stigma and subsequent life chances), and c) it is an act of oppression, in the sense that the definer uses power to the "detriment" (i.e. removal of rights) of the other (see Erikson, 1962). This does not imply that such defining should or should not be carried out, or that the deviant does not "deserve" to be so defined, or that he is not "in fact" bad. One simply notes that the use of power to decrease the rights and freedom of another is a moral act—justified or not. Were it possible to define people as deviant in our society without subsequent loss of rights and freedoms, this act would not seem "moral." But so far not at any stage of Western civilization has this been achieved. The fact is that the official definition of deviance often carries with it a critical outcome.[6] Various theorists have attempted to explain why this is so. Erikson (1966) pointed to the need to classify rules and define boundaries, others suggested that it reinforces solidarity of the group (Durkheim, 1933, 1938; Coser, 1962). Fanon (1968) identified psychomoral factors in the sense that the colonialist needs a mirror image (the evil native) of what he is not—i.e. the rationalization of one's own goodness. Nietzsche (1966), identified this motive underlying Christian thought—that Christians could define saintliness only in terms of sinfulness. Ancient moral dualism underlies our images of deviance and crime. There are "us," and there are "them." Labeling theorists have

---

[6]This aspect of deviance definition is discussed further in relation to the removal of deviants by Newman (1975).

13

tried to eradicate crime and deviance by pretending that all there is to deviance is the "label." But the cultural burden which those labels represent is enormous. The labels exist as evidence of the moral images in the minds of men. Men die; images go on. This observation has important implications for the measurement of deviance perception as we will see.

So, it has been argued that there are four central ingredients of social deviance. First, static or functionally objective forms of deviance are not only possible but are easily identified. Second, apart from various primary anatomical attributes that contribute to static forms of deviance, the existence of enduring cultural images of deviance of which all people partake adds to the static nature of deviance. The latter probably applies especially to traditional crimes such as murder with intent and to traditional deviances, such as incest. Third, the rates and forms of deviance are also closely related to the activities of official agents of control. This observation especially applies to such crimes as victimless crimes and some mental or physical illness. This class of deviance might be termed "system-related deviance" in contrast to the culturally related deviance of traditional crimes. Fourth, deviance is both the product and reaction to derogatory moral judgment by society on a class of individuals. To be a "good" deviant is a contradiction in terms. Saints are exemplary, even exceptional. Only sinners are deviant. Of course, some sinners may be vindicated in another era. This usually occurs several generations or more after the sinner's lifetime, which may benefit the sinner's soul, but is irrelevant to his life as he actually lived it.

The comparative extent to which each of these areas contributes to the nature of deviance has not been researched. The construction of our questionnaire will provide an assessment. Before doing so, we must look at other conceptual areas, closely related to the problem of the nature of social deviance.

THE SOCIAL CONTENT OF THE CRIMINAL LAW

Criminal law textbooks draw the distinction between two types of criminal acts: *mala in se,* and *mala prohibita*. Social scientists have especially been critical of this division, holding, of course, to the secular view that acts *"mala in se"* are logically impossible because they assume absolute values. *Mala in se* are the criminal law remnants of early religious influence: the idea of deviation from the "natural law."

Considering our foregoing discussion concerning the nature of deviance, however, the distinction is worth reconsideration.

The secular or "objective" perspective that social scientists and some modern legal philosophers (e.g. Hart, 1963) have brought to bear upon the criminal law has led them to try to avoid directly facing the question of *mala in se*. The relativism underlying much of social science as a result of the work of the cultural anthropologists and as a result of the labelling theorists' dogma, has focused upon *mala prohibita*, which the theorists of criminal law have rarely claimed to be "morally wrong" acts. The recognition that some crimes may be universally punished has been sidestepped. Barbara Wooton (1963) tried to dispose of the problem by identifying acts *mala in se* as merely acts *mala antiqua*. But, one may ask whether functionally there is substantial difference. Whether, for example, intentionally killing one's neighbor is a sin against God (or the Natural Law) is beside the point. The antiquity of the rule surely has the effect of embedding the prohibition deeply into our culture, and therefore into the minds of men. All that is needed, is to demonstrate that such acts are universally morally disapproved of by the people, and this would be sufficient evidence to suggest that such acts are, as far as the realities of everyday life are concerned, *mala in se*. That is, the badness of the act is self-evident, self-emanating. Thus, to call *mala in se, mala antiqua,* merely changes the name. It does not alter their cultural significance. Devlin (1968) calls these acts of *mala in se* "real criminal law" in comparison to *mala prohibita,* acts of "quasi-criminal law." If one accepts the definition of *mala in se* as equivalent to *mala antiqua,* this means that the "real criminal law" is almost entirely social in content, whether or not the ultimate source of morality is God, since it rests upon the *universal* (both current and historical) acclamation of the people.

Consensus theorists have never argued this point, because it is currently not fashionable to argue universal values. Instead, they usually use such vague terms as "anti-social conduct" (Eysenck, 1964). Conflict theorists refuse to recognize the possibility of any universal acclamation: they deny the category of *mala in se* or *mala antiqua,* arguing that all criminal law is *mala prohibita*—all criminal law is merely quasi-criminal law.

Of course, one must not lose sight of the fact that many kinds of criminal laws have evolved as a result of class-based action. Property laws, especially, as Hall (1952) shows, have their historical source in capitalist based economic activity. However, this cannot be shown to apply to all crimes, especially murder. Yet, it is sometimes argued that even murder is selectively legislated in that the State deems it just to kill enemies in war. This seems nonsensical. Every state reserves the right to kill in its own interest. There is no state that has abrogated that right. It is neither hypocritical nor tyrannical for any state to punish its citizens for killing under unacceptable circumstances, those circumstances being a universal abhorrence by the people of killing under particular conditions. The argument assumes that all killing is the same. But killing with state license is an entirely different situation to killing without a license. In many ways the state is the final arbiter, yet the final arbiter of the state is also the people, as we will see later. This argument applies equally to the supposed "injustice" of the class bias of the criminal law having to do with property often sermonized by social scientists. It is only unjust if one compares it to a utopian classless society. The only tyrannies of the criminal law, if they could be called tyrannies, are those of its domination by history, and the extent to which it is currently subject to the tryanny of the masses as Tocqueville characterized the American middle class. It is, therefore, a matter of personal taste as to whether class-based criminal laws are just or unjust. Again the extent to which such crimes are popularly sanctioned by the masses may be taken as an indicator of the extent to which the crimes are functionally *mala in se*. To say, as do some conflict theorists, that "all crime is political" is merely a cursory observation of one aspect of the criminal law; nothing more. If it turns out that 90 percent of the masses consider stealing from one's neighbor to be a crime, then it seems far-fetched to call this "false consciousness." It boils down to a question as to whether the judgment of the masses may be taken as "just" in contrast to those of the conflict theorist.

In recognition of these views of the various types of criminal law, we tentatively classified the types of crime or deviance into five categories, the validity of which we hoped subsequently to test, and if necessary, to develop a new classification based on the responses to our questionnaire. We needed to adopt some preliminary way of classifying criminal law so that we could select one or two acts from each category to ensure that the range of deviant acts to which we would elicit responses would be sufficient. Since we were severely limited in the number of acts we could use, this preliminary analysis was essential. All other studies conducted concerning perception of crime have allowed themselves the luxury of presenting large numbers of crimes to the respondent. (The Sellin-Wolfgang study (1964) used 103 crime descriptions, which meant that only one question ("how serious?") could be asked for each act.) For reasons to be stated in Chapter 3, we wanted to ask more than one question for each act. Therefore, we limited ourselves to 9 acts, and classified them as follows:

1. *Mala in se:* The act most widely considered a universal taboo, and certainly an anathema to most religions we considered was incest. Although there is much to suggest that this act also has deep cultural origins not necessarily religious (e.g., the Oedipus myth), in recognition of the claims to *mala in se,* we placed it in this category.

2. *Mala antiqua:* We chose the act of robbery to represent this category, since it is an ancient crime, and a crime which we suspected would elicit near universal disapproval.

3. *Mala prohibita:* This category was further subdivided into two groups:
   a. "QUASI-CRIME": We chose the act of appropriation of public funds to represent this category, although bribery was substituted for it in Iran. We had in mind here more the "quasi-crime" closely linked to "white collar crime," where we could expect the wide acclamation that this crime was not a moral wrong, but that it nevertheless was a crime worthy of punishment. We could not expect universal accord concerning this act.
   b. "VICTIMLESS CRIMES": We chose the acts of abortion at two months, homosexuality among adults, and taking drugs. It should be emphasized, however, that traditional Western criminal law theorists such as Devlin would classify these acts as *mala in se.* However, because of the known legal variations in tolerance of these acts, we placed them in this category. For example, abortion is legal in Yugoslavia, and at the time of conducting the research was also in New York. We know that homosexuality is much more legally tolerated in Italy, but that abortion is severely punished.

4. *Mala nova:* This was a new category which we added to examine the effects of modernization. Thus, the newly created crime in the U.S. of environmental pollution was included here. Factory pollution was the pollution act chosen for this category.

5. *Mala ambigua:* The acts we included here were two acts which we considered might truly lie on the borderline of deviance and non-deviance, but which represented two different spheres of deviance. The first was "not helping a person in a dangerous situation," an act about which the Western criminal law has

never been able to make up its mind. This is an act of ambiguous "moral" deviance. The second was public protest about one's government. Here also, governments tend to wax and wane in their criminalization of this act. This is an act of ambiguous "political deviance."

Thus, we began with a range of acts from the borderline deviant to the intrinsically deviant. A central question for our research to answer was: Would this classification hold up in comparison to the responses of the public?

One final problem remains to be considered concerning the social content of the criminal law, and that is the distinction that must be drawn between the criminal law as it is written and the criminal law as it is practiced. Because it was our aim to compare public opinion to the criminal law, it was important that we be able to assess the level of functioning of the criminal law. This presented us with a serious methodological problem, which was eventually resolved by a series of compromises (See Chapter 7). When one considers that some of the countries in which we conducted our survey have a number of different layers and systems of law, this becomes an even more challenging problem. For example, in Iran, Islamic courts traditionally conducted the business of the criminal law, but this was then overlayed by the importation of French criminal codes. The influence of Islamic law in Indonesia continues strongly, overlayed itself by the law introduced by the Dutch. We know much more about the differences in the application of the criminal law in the United States than in any of the other countries studied. However, from discussions with the criminal lawyers in each country of the study, we are able to draw one very general conclusion: that in all countries the criminal law is enforced at a level far below that which is allowed for by the law as it is written. In other words, there exists in the written criminal law of all countries studied a vast arsenal of laws and sanctions which are not enforced to the maximum.

STRUCTURE OF THE PUBLIC

In the United States, it seems logical enough to sample public opinion about the law with a view to measuring the gap, if any, between such opinion and the criminal law. Opinion polls have become an increasingly important part of the American political and legislative process,

18

even though on occasion they have been grossly misused. All Presidents since John F. Kennedy have used polls to guide their policies and campaigns. Bogart's study (1972) of the use of law and order as a major campaign issue is most informative here. The violent anti-war demonstrations in the sixties led pollsters to survey people's main concerns. Bogart argues that people placed crime high on the list because they had generalized to all crime the violence which occurred during political demonstrations. Subsequently, election campaign platforms inserted the "law and order" cry in an effort to appeal to the crime fears of the masses. It must be said that for a time it worked, certainly through to Nixon's landslide victory in 1972.

Lest it be assumed that the public is "fickle," it should also be realized that it was most likely the weight of public opinion that finally brought Lyndon Johnson's presidential career to a close. Johnson constantly consulted the results of the polls. Some may argue, of course, that it was the press that brought about Johnson's downfall by "brainwashing" the American people. It may also have been the vociferous demonstrations. Clearly, a host of factors may have been involved. For the moment, however, what concerns us is that public opinion in America is taken seriously by politicians. It can, therefore, have an effect upon the legislation of new laws. However, we must see it as a two-way process, with the public influencing the leaders, and the leaders in turn influencing the public. It is often argued that the more power one has, the more influence one has. But a leader is not by definition more powerful than his followers, since he depends on their acquiescence for his survival as leader. Weber (Gerth and Mills, 1946), Simmel (1959) and many other sociologists have noted this symbiotic relationship between the leader and his followers.[7] The only situation in which such symbiosis is not necessary is when the leader dominates completely by force: a political structure variously known as tyranny, reign of terror, or totalitarianism.

Weber noted two other sources of power, one of which is of particular interest to our research. The first, and less relevant, is the notion of charisma which appears to be some kind of magical or mystical quality of a person which invokes a blind devotion of its followers. Such a

---

[7]The concept of power is, of course, a topic to which many pages could be devoted. The concept appears to defy definitive definition and seems only indirectly related to the concept of "influence," which one would have thought is synonymous with power (Dahl, 1957). Dahl suggests that both terms can only have meaning in an operational context, and current research in experimental social psychology supports this view (Tedeschi, et al., 1973).

19

situation Weber argues is only temporary, and gradually becomes transformed into the second major source of power to a leader: authority. Thus, we should expect a country that is steeped in tradition to display much greater acquiescence to authority. The church or prevailing religious order should figure prominently in the definition of what is deviant, and the severity with which deviance is dealt. We should therefore attend closely to the public as it is structured according to intensity of religious belief. As we will see, our focus was on intensity rather than type of religion because there are so many different religions involved in a cross-cultural study, comparability of which is extremely difficult to determine.

But in the United States the relationship between public opinion and legislation is often blithely assumed to reflect a simple one-one relationship. The reason for this is the popular vision of democracy held in America, the idea of a mass of middle class, with minimal social structure. Certainly a lower class is perceived to exist, but it is mostly classified as a poverty or sub-lower class, rather than a true working class in the European sense. Those above the poverty level are assumed to blend into the common value systems of the masses of middle Americans.[8]

In contrast, other countries are heavily structured according to economics and tradition. A major distinction in distribution of power in less developed societies we expected would be the urban-rural dimension.

However, highly dynamic interest and pressure groups operate on the American political scene which may cut across the mass of public opinion. Although it has been suggested that public opinion has helped remove presidents from office, the role of well-organized vociferous pressure groups cannot be ignored. In America, such lobby groups may represent an enormous variety of issues and interests—gun control, right to life, milk producers, Blacks, Jews, meat producers, etc. The number is practically endless, to say nothing of professional associations such as the A.M.A. and extensive trade union organizations. In America, the distribution of influence is therefore spread horizontally, and may also arise spontaneously as a result of particular issues which may excite public opinion.

---

[8]Dahl (1967), after reviewing many opinion polls in America, concludes that there are no clearly consistent class divisions, but that differentiation in opinion shifts according to the dimension used to break up the respondents.

In a socialist country, the number and type of pressure groups tend to be more formally established as part of the direct governing system in the form of peoples courts, workers communes, and so on.

A similar condition exists in Iran and Indonesia where the local governance structure was established basically according to early Islamic law. The village chief and his advisers, the local arbitration council, or the larger municipal council are local groups whose role is to oversee informally the social and other relationships among the people. Although these institutions are becoming more and more secularized, they operate effectively as social control mechanisms.

An important additional ingredient to our research design would have been the inclusion of a sample of these local leaders or pressure group members to gauge the extent to which they coincide with the opinion of the masses. In this way we could have specified more accurately the process of opinion and law formation. However, financial restrictions made this impossible.

We did make a special effort purposively to sample rural respondents, upon the presupposition that the rural peasants are usually those with the least power in a society. On the other hand, the urban educated and business people are usually believed to carry much more sway with the politicians. Since the conflict theorists would hold that it is the purpose of the criminal law to keep the poor in subjection, we would expect that the educated and urban business respondents in all countries will be more intolerant of deviance.

However, if one could not sample those persons in intermediate positions of social control and influence, we could at least examine the extent to which the public viewed such persons as influential. To do this, it was necessary for us to specify more clearly what we meant by the identification of these influential persons, and furthermore to develop a model which allowed for cross-cultural comparability. The result was the resurrection of a very old concept in sociology: the concept of social institutions, and the interpretation of these as agencies of control and influence.

The proposition that major social institutions such as the family, education, religion, economic system and law are major agencies of social control was established almost as a "social law" by American sociologists in the pre-World War II era. Hertzler (1929:27) proposed that ". . . institutions cultivate in the individuals the habits of conformity and understanding, embody the organized force of the community, and, with the group opinion that is behind them, are prepared to compel obedience and punish disobedience. They are the most stabilizing and the best organized of all forms of social control in operation." Many other sociologists of that period made similar assessments of institutions, emphasizing that embodied in them were the accretions or accumulations of a culture's mores, folkways and wisdoms (see: Sumner and Keller, 1927; Ballard, 1936; Panunzio, 1939; La Piere, 1946 and 1954). In the years that followed, sociology became divided into different specialty areas to study each institution. The exception to this was, of course, Talcott Parsons who tried to construct the grand picture of the functions of social institutions. Even he, however, tended to specialize in his use of examples (e.g., the medical or health system, Parsons, 1951).

A re-examination of the functions of institutions as agencies of social control did not occur again until the labelling theorists, in their study of the sources of deviance, "discovered" that people are processed by highly organized and ritualistic agencies (e.g., "the theory of the office," Rubington and Weinberg, 1968). And, as we saw in our previous discussion on the nature of deviance, it was argued that it was the processing itself which produced the deviance. The works of Quinney (1970) and of Kittrie (1971) have also emphasized the role of various institutions, especially law and medicine as agencies of social control. What none have specifically attended to, however, is the role of public opinion, to which Hertzler referred in 1929, in providing the power base for these agencies to act. A number of studies have shown that public opinion, pressure, or attitudes towards deviant behavior can have a decided effect upon the rate at which deviants are removed to total institutions (e.g., Kaplan, et al., 1956; Wanklin, et al., 1955; Cumming and Cumming, 1957).[9]

Social institutions are structured ways in which social control is maintained. The formality of the structure may vary from the highly informal (the family) to the highly formal and ritualistic (the criminal law). However, each of these institutions plays the traditional role of

---

[9]Most of the empirical work on the relationship between public opinion and social control has been done in the area of mental illness. The idea of public opinion providing the power base for the legitimacy of law has been examined theoretically by such classic theorists as Timasheff (1939), who argues that logically there can be no gap between law and opinion since law is only a mechanism that describes relationships in society, and is not a structural part of the society. Petraczycki (1955) and Sorokin (1928) hold a similar view, suggesting the law is but an outward expression of individual psychology. Podgorecki (1974) disagreed with these theorists, arguing that law does have a structure of its own, although essentially sociological in nature.

order maintenance. Every society has such institutions through which social control is administered (Parsons, 1966). One of the key questions on our questionnaire elicited responses in terms of control agents or the institutions to which respondents would report deviant behavior. Since all societies have institutions of social control, such a question, it was hoped, would maintain the comparability across cultures, yet allow for considerable intracultural adaptation.[10]

It should be pointed out, however, that institutions of control may or may not be in close agreement with the requirements of the State. Depending upon the political and historical conditions of the society, each institution may or may not attend to the control of types of behavior in accordance with the State. In general, however, it may be suggested that the fact that they do promote behavioral control is beneficial to the State. One may also argue that any one of these institutions also has reflexive potential in the sense that it may become a vehicle for controlling the behavior of those who govern. The current role of the press in America may perhaps be considered as an extremely ambivalent example. Certainly, the role of the education system has often been to attempt to influence the view of those who govern. It is apparent that some of these institutions may be directly controlled by government, while others are not. For example, since the introduction of compulsory education, education becomes more and more an affair of the State. The institution of religion, on the other hand, with a well established tradition of its own is not formally an affair of the State in America—though it may be so in other countries, for example, Iran.[11] On some issues religion becomes more of an interest or lobby group rather than an institution—such as the fight against liberal abortion laws currently led by the Catholic Church in America. On the other hand, the church may act in collusion with the government such as its early support of America's fight against communism. The church does, however, reinforce much of the State's requirements for the control of behavior, which is not surprising when one considers that much of the ideology of criminal sanctioning probably has its origins in Judeochristian law. We need not go into all the ramifications of the relationship between the church as an institution of control and the State, for it is enough for us to assert that as an institution its function is to control behavior whether for the specific purposes

---

[10]See Chapter 4 for a full discussion of the comparability problem.
[11]But as we will see in Chapter 4, the relationship between religion and the Shah in Iran is ambiguous, constantly bordering on conflict.

of the State or not. However, because we argue that the primary requirement by the State is the *control* of behavior in a very broad sense, religion may be seen as an important institution in this regard.

The press is another clearly reflexive institution of social control. It fights strongly for its independence from State control—the catch-cry of the "free press." In this case its relationship to government becomes much more covert, and more complex. In countries without a "free press," the press is more clearly a mechanism of social control. The institution of health is an important institution for any society that is geared toward a work ethic, as Parsons, among others, has noted (Parsons, 1951). A production conscious economy must have healthy workers. Further, because of the moral overtones in a work ethic society of the importance and goodness of work in itself (Weber, 1958), the institution of health is strongly tinged with overtones of moral judgment and authority. The relationship between the institution of health and government also remains problematic. It is apparent that the A.MA. is closely aligned with the moral outlook of government, in the sense that it passes judgment on those who do not seek health care, jealously preserves its domain for treating illness, and is imbued with the right to excuse people from working. But the A.M.A. also remains separate from the formal government, and opposes attempts to socialize medicine, which would result in health systems becoming more clearly formal arms of the State.[12] The institution of health, therefore, is both an institution for control and a lobby group, as are religion and the media. The same may be said for the institution of work, where we may identify 1) the growing body of professional civil servants who are direct instruments of the State, and an increasingly powerful force in government, and 2) the trade unions which occupy a curiously ambiguous position of both controlling workers and pressuring government. Again, all of these are topics of study on their own.

It is apparent, however, that the two formal and strongest arms of the State are the institutions of law and the institutions of the military. The direct relationship between the military and the State is, of course, obvious, but we must once again be cognizant of the always tenuous relationship between the two. Military coups have become commonplace in the last 20 years. Further, because of the secrecy involved, it is difficult at any time to know what is the precise power relation between military and government.

---

[12]See Quinney (1970) for a review and bibliography of the role of interest groups in the making and implementation of law.

But the main arm of the State of relevance to our research is the criminal law and the criminal justice system, as Beccaria, among others, said many years ago. Its relationship to government may more easily be studied because most of its proceedings are public in character or made public after a comparatively short duration, and because the passage of laws or legislation is usually publicized and indeed may be the result of direct campaigning either by the people or their leaders. Although the extent of independence of the institution of criminal law from government will vary depending upon the political and social structure of a society, it is surely apparent that the laws with which jurists and prosecutors and police work are the legacy of only partly the present and mostly of former regimes.[13] No doubt some jurists may argue that the law has become an authority unto itself because of its great tradition and the cumulation of wisdom from case to case—the most eloquent and earliest argument was made by Sir Edward Coke. But this authority and tradition is certainly not independent in origin. It is deeply rooted in the economic and social history of any society, and in that sense, the criminal law is clearly a political instrument. This means that it may, and will, be used against certain groups that are less powerful. However, this observation does not only apply to capitalist countries. It clearly applies to totalitarian or communist regimes where the role of the criminal law (and other institutions of control, such as health) becomes explicitly one of enforcing the State's ideology.[14] The rule of law by analogy in Russia for many years (now abolished) allowed for social control of the tyrannical proportions required by Stalin. Crimes against property (i.e., against ideology) were categorized as crimes against the State. Similarly, as stated earlier, the State reserves the right to decide what type of killing is acceptable, and, it would seem, that it is able to remain outside the domain of the criminal law. If this is so, the criminal law is a direct instrument of the State regardless of its content. It is an instrument because it applies to the subjects, not to the rulers.[15]

---

[13]This rule applies even to such countries as Iran, occupied several times by foreign countries, and which has a king who in theory is above the law, and upon whom the law relies for its ultimate justification. But the content of the Iranian criminal code is a complicated mixture of Adat (customary) law, Islamic law, and French law.

[14]This is well documented by Solzhenitzyn in his *Gulag Achipelago* (1973) as far as crime is concerned, and in his *Cancer Ward* (1968) as far as health is concerned.

[15]This is, of course, an observation which has been made many times by students of criminal law from Beccaria (1968) who sought to curb the tyranny of judges, acting in the name of the State; to Quinney's emotional attack upon America's legal order (Quinney, 1973). Care should be taken not to overstate this observation. The State

In summary, it has been argued that by identifying the institutions of social control in a society we identify the type of deviance, and the subsequent classification of deviance is a "social system" classification. The institutions of control may be ranged from highly formal to highly informal means of control. A highly informal (but probably the most effective) institution of control is that of the family. A highly formal institution of control is that of the law.

One should again hasten to add that a classification of deviance in this way does not mean that persons are defined as deviant *only* as a result of the various activities of the institutions of control. The way in which various persons come to be inducted into the various systems of control is a complex process involving many factors, such as the type of behavior the person presents; the extent to which his behavior is or is seen as a problem by those around him; the person's perceptions of his own behavior; and many more.[16]

The major institutions of control, their mechanisms or sanctions for maintaining control, and the definitional categories relating to them may be seen in Chart 1.

So social institutions may be identified by the following pertinent criteria:

1. They have a well established tradition;[17]

---

remains outside the criminal law only insofar as it enjoys a legitimacy by the people. The only other way it may remain outside the criminal law is through a reign of terror. Marxist critics of the U.S. system, such as Quinney, either fail to take account of the people's acquiescence, or try to portray the U.S. government as a reign of terror, which when compared to other countries of the world rather than to an abstract ideal, is an absurdity. However, the problem of the legitimacy of the State to remain outside or above the law has become a pressing problem in America since the Watergate crisis, and now more importantly concerning the activities of the C.I.A. Classic sociologists have viewed authority as having accrued some kind of immanent legitimacy (Gerth and Mills, 1946). It is immanent in the sense that the legitimacy is attached to the *status* or bureaucratic position of the person or institution which represents the State. Thus, most often, the activities of authority are seen as legitimate, even if they break the laws that apply to the common people. The majority of the people, for example, would have countenanced the State's assassination of Russian agents during the Cold War. The situation is much like the parent who says to his child, "Don't do as I do, do as I tell you." A crisis of authority results.

[16]The writer has looked more closely at this question in Newman (1975). Not many institutions of control actually solicit clients. They must wait for them to be referred—much has gone on by the time the client finally presents himself at the doctor's office. See, for example, Blackwell (1963). For a rare example of the dynamics of reporting behavior in the area of the criminal law, see Bickman and Green (1975).

[17]The various works of Genet, especially *The Balcony* (1966) display the deepest insight into the importance of tradition in the establishment of institutions of social control. "We waited two thousand years to perfect our roles . . ." (p.78) says the Judge. And in

CHART 1
Institutions of Control and Types of Deviance

INSTITUTION	LEVEL OF FORMALITY	DEVIANT TYPE	EXAMPLES OF ULTIMATE SANCTION
Military	High	"Traitor"	Prison, exile
Law	High	"Criminal"	Prison, fines
Health	Medium	"Sick." "mentally ill"	Hospital, drugs
Education	Medium	"Failure" or "drop out"	Separation into special schools
Religion	Medium	"Sinner"	Expulsion, fines
Work	Medium	"Malingerer"	Refusal of welfare
Mass-media	High	"Villain"	Muck-raking
Family	Low	"Black sheep"	Referral for treatment or punishment
Village	Low	"Village idiot"	Expulsion or exclusion from social life

2. They have formally designated offices of high status and authority;[18]
3. They are bureaucratically organized;[19]
4. They have the power to sanction behavior punitively (Hertzler, 1929);
5. Each uses a system of stereotyping labels with which to identify persons to be controlled (Scheff, 1967, and other labelling theorists).

---

relation to the immanent authority of the position, "The Queen attains her reality when she withdraws, absents herself or dies." (p. 85)

[18]See, for example, Simmel (1959).

[19]The work of Weber (1966) is extensive in this area in terms of the social institutions in society which are closely related to economy and law. However, the extent to which the family is bureaucratically organized is a challenging question. Certainly there are established roles and statuses within the family, and, until recently, a clearly recognized "right" way for the family to be politically organized. The power relations of the family as *political* relations were recognized early in the writings of Reich (1971), but the dynamic rather than bureaucratic aspects of family relations have been the main focus of attention (e.g., Laing and Esterson, 1972). The recent application of systems theory to family therapy has moved a little more in the direction of studying the family from an organization point of view (Minuchin, 1974). On the other hand, one might easily interpret Laing's work on *Knots* (1972) as an exploration of the puzzles provided by a bureaucratic (i.e. immovable) structure of social relationships.

three

FOUNDATIONS OF DEVIANCE PERCEPTION

Here we will deal with a basic dimension of the measurement of deviance perception, our fourth problem area: the nature of the response process or mechanism which we expected to sample from our respondents. Only with a clear understanding of this process, could we construct a questionnaire in which every question (apart from filler questions) would have meaning or theoretical significance.

ATTITUDE OR PERCEPTION?

Both these terms have been defined in scores of different ways (see, e.g., Allport, F., 1955; and Allport, G. W., 1935), but for the purposes of this study I have chosen the term "perception" over "attitude" mainly because it has a much broader meaning. Historically, one of the earliest notions of attitude was included by the Wurzburg School of Psychology as the dynamic imageless component of perception, *einstellung* (Allport, 1955). Because the study of perception in the early years was more closely tied to cognition, attitude developed into a concept in its own right. Its early usage in American psychology was as an affective internal state variable that predisposed a person to act. In 1935, Allport defined attitude as "a mental or neural state of readiness, organized through experience, exerting a directive or dynamic influence upon the individual's response to all objects and situations with which it is related." (Allport, 1935). In the forty years since that time, attitude has undergone a series of redefinitions, ending with the current view of attitude as a more cognitive, information processing concept (see, e.g., Calder and Ross, 1973; Fishbein, 1967; Anderson and Fishbein, 1965). It has thus moved more closely to notions of perception, cognitive orientation and organization of mental processes. Since the main difference between the questionnaire constructed and the traditional attitudinal questionnaires is that we included a question requiring the respondent to organize and classify stimulus material, the term attitude as it is currently used could just as well have been used in this study instead of the term "perception." However, since the information processing aspects of attitude are comparatively recent, and as yet not widely used cross-culturally, we considered it prudent to stick with "perception," embracing the perceptual processes as well as the attitudinal. As we see below, previous research on attitudes to deviance has not often taken into account this perceptual factor. We will return to this aspect shortly. First, let us consider the aspects of attitude theory and research which are relevant to this study.

The Structural Components of Attitude

Allport proposed that the main ingredient of attitude was "affective." However, over the years two other important components were proposed and empirically supported. These were the "cognitive" and the "dispositional." While all items on our questionnaire probably tap responses that are composed of all three aspects, an attempt was made in constructing questions to use those which seemed *prima facie* to favor each area. This was important, since it was intended to construct an overall summarizing scale of person perception of deviance. The three components should be defined.

The affective component was originally seen as an "imageless" state of readiness, and was characteristically measured by various physiological devices (e.g., GSR, pulse rates, etc.) as well as self-report, a popular method thirty or forty years ago. Aside from this hypothesized vague "emotional" feeling, it was argued that the manner of response was one of bipolarity, positive-negative. This theorization gained even more support by the discovery that the firing of neurons in the brain was an "all or none" process in which neurons had to reach a particular state of readiness before impulses could be transmitted across the synaptic gap.

At the same time, a serious problem had been raised by the classic study of LaPiere (1934) who demonstrated that peoples' attitudes to Asians were different from their actual behavior. Thus, the relationship between attitude and behavior became seriously doubtful, and most studies even up to present have experienced difficulty in predicting behavior from attitudes (see: Brehm, 1960; DeFleur and Westie, 1958; Warner, 1967; Fishbein, 1967; Steiner and Fishbein, 1965 and Calder and Ross, 1973, for a review of these studies). Although this is a problem for this study, it will be taken up at the conclusion of the book. For the present, we are interested in the internal components of attitude. In 1947, Doob, in an influential paper, challenged the assumption that there was a direct relationship between attitudes and behavior. Doob argued that the affective component had been allowed to overshadow the "action-tendency" that came to be termed the "conative" component. This proposal was put forward at a time when drive theory was in its heyday, and the notion of goals, especially anticipatory behavior toward goals, was in close focus. Thus, questions which required the respondent to state his intentions to act in a certain way toward an object or to prefer certain forms of societal action were seen as comprising the "conative," or as it is known today, the "dispositional" approach. (See: e.g., Newcomb, 1964; Fishbein, 1967; Sherif and Sherif, 1967).

The next important change came with Chein (1948) who criticized previous theories of attitudes, especially those of Allport and Doob, for paying insufficient attention to the cognitive elements of attitude. Although Chein accepted that attitudes were dimensional or bi-polar, he argued that this dimensionality was more a product of a cognitive evaluation of the stimulus material, and of the differential selective manner in which persons perceived the world. Thus, the notion of a person's belief system came to be seen as an important ingredient of attitude (see: e.g., Fishbein, 1967).

Dimensionality

The large majority of attitude scales (but not all) have made the assumption that the attitudinal response is unidimensional, so that typical response categories are "good-bad," "agree-disagree," or in the case of a Guttman scale, a series of items which logically form only one dimension. The assumption of undimensionality has been a particular criticism of the seriousness scales developed by Sellin and Wolfgang (1967) in their construction of a crime index. For the present research, this was a particularly difficult problem, especially when seriousness was used to measure reactions to deviance where a much more diverse range of stimulus material was presented. Although considerable evidence has been amassed by the Osgood semantic differential scales (Osgood, 1965, 1967) that people do indeed respond consistently according to unidimentional sets, even across cultures (e.g., good-bad, heavy-light, bitter-sweet, etc.), it is still a matter for conjecture that each of those response categories is typical of an overall, generally bi-polar set on behalf of the respondent. In measuring perceptions of deviance, the difficulty arises in an acute form because it becomes apparent that a general unidimensional response requires to some extent that apples and bicycles be compared along one dimension. While this may be possible at one level (e.g., size, weight) it would not be possible using another dimension such as taste since bicycles are not edible. The dimension must be made multi-dimensional, or relative to each type. The same may apply to deviant behavior. How does one rate the comparative "seriousness" of, say, the catatonic schizophrenic, to the bank robber? It is apparent that the definition of the word "serious" must be changed to suit each case. The natural question is "serious in what terms?"

Yet, the original conception of attitude was that it was a "dynamic," "imageless," internal state. I also suggested earlier that a generalized dichotomous moral response to crime was embedded in Western culture. Along a general moral scale, catatonia and bank robbery can be conceived of as differently "serious" along the same dimension, if we tie the word serious not to the specifics of the act (thus ignoring such problems of harm done, serious to himself or others? etc.) and conceive of it as a general evaluative response with a strong moral basis which will override the specifics of the act characteristics. We will see shortly, for this and a number of reasons, the descriptions of acts presented to the respondent were kept as general as possible.

An additional argument in support of the generalized moral response of seriousness is that the definition and classification of deviance is difficult. Although the range of behavior covered under the rubric of "deviance" is broader than that covered under "crime," all these classes of behavior are, nevertheless, by definition, a "class unto themselves"—different. We may be comparing apples to cabbages, but we are not comparing apples to automobiles (though no doubt one could make comparative *moral* statements about these!). It was apparent therefore that we should develop a special item, allowing us to check on the categorization that the respondent applied to the stimulus material.

Methods have been developed that allowed respondents to classify stimulus material into the categories of their own choice (e.g., Sherif and Sherif, 1967), although these also have tended to interpret the responses as dimensional.

The question that we developed was one which provided the respondent with a set of categories and he was requested to choose the one he saw as most appropriate to the act description. Thus, we would obtain information as to whether he defined the act as "criminal,"

31

"sick," "non-deviant," and so on. In this way, it was possible to cross-check the respondent's overall ratings of seriousness with the way in which he classified the acts presented to him.

Level of Response

Parallel to the constant argument concerning the relationship between attitude and behavior, another question was brought strongly into focus during the 1950s—the relationship of attitudes to personality. Attitudes came at times to be seen as personality traits, as indeed was the case with the enormous work conducted on the F scale. In this work, although the construct of the "authoritarian personality" was developed first, then validated by a personality test, the test included standard attitude statements, requiring the usual bi-polar, positive-negative response (see: Adorno, et al., 1950). However, although the choice of many of the questions for the F scale was ordained by psychoanalytic theory to a very large extent, Adorno and his co-workers attempted to develop a clustering of items around particular "traits" or "components" of authoritarianism relying upon rather primitive correlation techniques. There was, however, no attempt to differentiate the level of complexity of these item clusters. It was assumed that each question elicited the same level of response. However, in Britain, Eysenck (1954), in a study of "tough-mindedness," proposed that responses were organized roughly on three levels. The lowest level was that of opinion, changeable from day to day—the level usually trapped by public opinion polls. Using factor analysis, Eysenck showed that these superficial opinions were in no consistent way directly expressive of the individual's personality. Rather, it was necessary to group these opinions into clusters to form "habit opinions" that he argued were more stable and could be taken as more typical of an individual's personality. A grouping of these sets of habits produced the second level of response, which he termed attitudes. Thus, an attitude of ethnocentrism may be made up of a number of sets of habitual responses (operationally, responses to items on a questionnaire). Finally, the "super level" was that of ideology, which was composed of a number of attitudes. For example, conservatism was composed of ethnocentrism, strict child-rearing, patriotism and, religiosity.

The question as to whether a person's attitudinal response on a questionnaire is related to his personality is basically the same question as to whether it is related to his behavior. So far we have discussed the importance of including items that are behaviorally oriented (i.e., "dispositional"), those which are cognitively oriented, and those which are affectively oriented, Eysenck's work suggests that the "habit opinion" level should also be included. Questions to tap this level should be very general, requiring a simple, superficial response. Their importance should not be underrated since questions of this type are used most commonly in opinion polls.

The Organization of Attitudes

Since the Eysenck work, a great deal of research has been conducted in the area of attitude organization, even to the extent that it has been argued that an attitude can have little meaning unless conceived of within a theory of attitude organization (Scott, 1968). The most recent and influential work is that of Fishbein (1967, 1973; Fishbein and Ajzen, 1972) who has developed an "expectancy-value" model, in which not only are the cognitive aspects of attitude taken more into account, but also the normative beliefs which the respondent perceives in other people. These additional components were included by Fishbein in an attempt to predict behavior from attitudes. His full equation is:

$$B \approx Bl = \begin{bmatrix} A_{act} \end{bmatrix} \ W_0 + \begin{bmatrix} \sum_{i=i}^{m} (NB_j)(Mc_j) \end{bmatrix} W_1$$

Where:

B	= overt behavior
Bl	= the intention to perform that behavior
A_{act}	= attitude toward the act
m	= number of normative beliefs
NB_j	= normative belief about what other people think the individual should do
Mc_j	= the motivation to comply with expectation j
W_0, W_1	= empirically derived weights that raise or lower the extents to which the attitudinal or normative component affect the prediction of behavioral intention.

These additional components could not be included in the present study for a number of reasons. First, they are of comparatively recent origin and have not yet run the full gamut of experimentation. Most of

33

the experimentation conducted is culture-bound to American subjects. Second, the heavy emphasis upon cognitive-evaluative aspects we were not sure about since the reaction to deviance in the then current sociological literature had come to be characterized as anything but "rational." Indeed, even the standard sociological term used often characterizing the societal reaction to deviance, that of "moral indignation," is very difficult to analyze in these terms. Usually it is defined as "a dispassionate predisposition to punish" (Ranulf, 1938). The response would seem to be inextricably both cognitive and affective.[1]

Thirdly, the very important addition which Fishbein made was that of the respondent's perceptions of the normative beliefs of others, and his motivation to comply with others' beliefs. This would have been a very useful additional component especially in the Asian samples in which considerable response bias was expected. However, it was considered too complicated to introduce into this broad study, without means of assessing which (or how many) reference groups the subject deferred to in making his response. With so many countries involved, this would have required a massive additional survey. But a related question derived from labelling theory was the respondent's perception of the official defining agents. If the labelling theorists' arguments are valid, in that deviants are the product essentially of the activities of defining agencies, we might expect people's perceptions of the activity of these defining agencies to be closely related to their perceptions of deviance. Thus, although we could not account for the respondent's perception of the normative beliefs of others, his perceptions of the actual activity of the "other" (i.e., society's general social control process) could be considered.

The Perception of Deviance

For our purposes, we may conclude that the perception of deviance is composed of the following hypothetical elements:

1. A general bi-polar reaction, either positive or negative, to the object (i.e., deviant, deviant act, description or pictures). This we will term *intensity of reaction*. This reaction is basically an internal, imageless response which may be composed either of affective or cognitive aspects.

---

[1]A recent study suggests that the response to deviance is a more cognitive-evaluative one, and that the affectual component is minimal. See: Newman, et al. (1974).

34

2. The individual's own normative beliefs, i.e. his *knowledge* of the law.
3. A perceptual reaction in which the respondent classifies or defines the deviant, deviant act, or descriptions of both, in a particular way. This will be his *definition of the act*. This response is not imageless and may be related directly to the stereotypes[2] that he holds about types of deviance, or the way in which deviants are dealt with in society.
4. A dispositional reaction, in which the respondent states what he would do with or about a particular deviant act or deviant person, or additionally recommends specifically what society should or should not do about the deviance. This will be termed the *societal reaction*.
5. The general level of habitual response, usually called *opinion*. This superficial level is important since it is from many public opinion polls that legislators characteristically are guided.
6. The respondent's perceptions of the activities of the official agencies dealing with deviance. This is not seen so much as an integral component of deviance perception, but rather as a mediating or intervening variable.

We may now review the literature to establish the extent to which each of these areas have been covered in previous studies on perceptions of deviance. Because there is much overlap, we will concentrate on four key areas: opinion, intensity, definition, and societal reaction. With the exception of the work on crime seriousness, most of the pioneering research on perceptions of deviance has been conducted in the area of mental illness, where the importance of lay perceptions of deviance to the study of referral systems (Friedson, 1961) and deviance reporting systems (Mechanic 1962, 1969; Newman, 1972) has long been recognized. The pioneering work was begun by Starr (1955) who used case descriptions of various "types" of mental illness and elicited respondents' reactions to them. By and large, this has been the technical procedure adopted for most studies, although occasionally some have used pictures, video tapes, or films as stimulus.

Research on public perceptions of mental illness will be reviewed first, followed by a review of the perceptions of criminal behavior.

---

[2]Recent research conducted by the writer suggests that sterotypes are related weakly, but in a complex way to perceptions of deviance. See: Newman, (1975).

PUBLIC PERCEPTIONS OF DEVIANCE:
MENTAL ILLNESS

General Opinion

One of the first studies to assess the public's attitudes towards mental illness was conducted by Starr in 1955. She concluded that ". . . mental illness is a very threatening and fearful thing and not an idea to be entertained lightly about anyone. Emotionally, it represents to people the loss of what they consider to be the distinctly human qualities of rationality and free-will and there is a kind of horror of dehumanization. As both our data and other studies make clear, mental illness is something that people want to keep as far from themselves as possible."

Lemkau and Crocetti in a 1962 study in Baltimore failed to support these conclusions. Respondents verbally expressed sentiments of understanding and tolerance for the mentally ill. The sample was on the whole, poorly educated, 40 percent black, median income of $4,730.00, median age in the low thirties, approximately 55 percent owned their own homes with the median value being $9,700.00. It was also found that there was no tendency on the part of the general public to "deny" mental illness, and that there was no overall pervasive tendency to isolate and reject a person who had been mentally ill. These findings are contrary to the claims of labelling theorists who suggest a conspiratorial attitude on the part of the audience toward the deviant (e.g., Lemert, 1962; Kitsuse, 1962).

Other studies, however, provide support for the labelling perspective. A section of a study conducted by Nunnally (1961) concerned itself with assessing the public's attitudes towards persons labelled mentally ill. Using a form of Osgood's semantic differential scale, Nunnally asked respondents to rate terms such as old man, neurotic man, insane man, on a series of seven-point scales such as wise-foolish, unpredictable-predictable, bad-good, dangerous-safe, etc. The analysis of these ratings indicated that "public attitudes are relatively negative towards persons with mental health problems." (p. 17). Compared to normal persons, the respondents rated the mentally ill as worthless, dirty, dangerous, cold, unpredictable, insincere. On the basis of this, as well as other sections of his study, he concluded that the public's conception of the mentally ill was not directly related to knowledge about the nature of mental illness.

The above conclusion is supported by a study conducted by Freeman and Kassebaum (1960). This study was specifically designed to test the hypothesis that attitudes towards mental illness and mental health are related to the level of education and knowledge of psychiatric concepts. The questionnaire used in this study included 31 items regarding the etiology and prevention of mental disorders, knowledge of psychiatric terms, and social characteristics of the respondents, including their level of education. The results indicated that opinions regarding the etiology and prevention of mental illness were weakly related to the level of formal education and knowledge of the technical vocabulary of psychiatry. The authors concluded that "the association between knowledge and opinion in the area of mental illness is very weak indeed and that mental health education programs are unrealistic in assuming that giving people the facts alters their opinions about the mentally ill." (p. 44).

Crumpton (1966) and Crumpton, et al. (1967) administered a 20 scale semantic differential to junior college students and hospitalized psychiatric patients to assess the difference in attitudes toward mental illness held by normal persons, as opposed to mental patients. Both samples viewed the mental patient in unfavorable terms.

Levine (1971) reported data that suggested there was a relationship between opinions about mental illness in a community and the social-political climate of that community. This study questioned students, physicians, and nurses on their opinions about mental illness, using British, Czechoslovakian, and West German samples. The study found that attitudes towards mental illness seemed to be part of a general orientation shared by various occupational groups in the community— cross-national differences were also found. These differential attitudes, it was suggested, appeared "to be part of a person's general orientation to social issues, rather than a narrow function of his concept of mental illness."

The classic study, Hollingshead and Redlich (1958), examined the attitudes of members of different social classes toward the mentally ill. They found that far more "abnormal behavior is tolerated by the two lower classes . . . without any awareness that the motivations behind the behavior are pathological even though the behavior may be disapproved of by the class norms." (pp. 172–173). Support for this statement came from the fact that lower-class patients are most likely to have been referred to "treatment" by the police, while upper-class patients were mostly referred by family or friends. This was held to be indicative of the fact that in the lower-class, behavior is tolerated much more, up to the point where outside intervention is required.

Benz and Edgerton (1970) conducted a study on 418 community leaders and 1,045 of the general public. The groups were matched on rural background, stability of residence, age, and marital status. Both groups had realistic attitudes toward the mentally ill. They differed in that the general public often ascribed "cause" to moral strength and hereditary factors, whereas the community leaders did not.

Intensity of Reaction

As we have seen, most of the studies concerning perceptions of the mentally ill are centered around the issue of their rejection by society. In a study of some of the factors contributing to the rejection of the mentally ill, Phillips (1963, 1964) presented to respondents case descriptions of paranoid schizophrenic, depressed neurotic, simple schizophrenic, phobic compulsive, and normal individuals. Applying the interview method, Phillips sampled 300 married white females. Each interview consisted of presenting the respondent with five cards on which descriptions of behavior patterns characteristic of the above psychiatric diagnoses were recorded. Following each card presentation, the respondents were asked a uniform series of questions which constituted a social distance scale "indicating how close a relation the respondent was willing to tolerate with the individuals in the case abstracts." Phillips used this scale to measure his dependent variable of rejection. The case abstracts included information about the type of help-source the described individual was using. The help categories were mental hospital, psychiatrist, clergyman, and no help. By varying the help-source purportedly used by each individual, Phillips was able to assess: 1) the influence of different types of behavior in determining rejection; and 2) the influence of different help-sources in determining rejection. His findings indicated that no matter what the nature of the case behavior, individuals were increasingly rejected as they were described seeing a clergyman, a physician, a psychiatrist, or being institutionalized in a mental hospital. It would seem, therefore, that the perceptions of official defining agencies is closely related to perceptions of deviance. Another very early study supporting this view was conducted by Cumming and Cumming (1957) who investigated respondents' reactions to behavioral descriptions of "pathological behavior," using case histories. The respondents were requested to fill out a 23-item questionnaire. This was analyzed and yielded two scales: social distance and social responsibility scales. The results were that the average respondent, even after being given a six-month education course on mental illness was neither willing to get closer to the mentally ill, nor to assume more responsibility for the problems of mental illness. Very low levels of tolerance for the mentally ill were also reported. These low tolerance levels were found to be in direct contrast to the results of the interview on the case descriptions. Thus, they concluded that public attitudes towards behavior deviations depended on whether it was identified as mental illness. The average person had a high rejection for those labelled mentally ill and placed a negative valuation on their behavior. On the other hand, the interviews with the case histories revealed that the same average person was quite tolerant of a very wide spectrum of behavior as being reasonably close to normal.

Definition of Behavior

From the studies that have been conducted to determine how the public classifies behavior, it has been shown that the public does not readily use the mental illness label to describe behavior deviations that a mental health professional would diagnose as mental disorder, and that the ordinary citizen is willing to tolerate and accommodate extensive behavioral deviations without attaching a deviant lable to them.

A study producing such results was conducted by Dohrenwend and Chin-Shong (1967). They employed the "case" descriptions to study attitudes toward pathological behavior on the part of community leaders in contrast to ethnic cross-sections in an area of New York. Following the presentation of each case abstract, the respondents were asked whether they viewed the behavior as a sign that something was wrong, and if so, whether they thought that the person described was mentally ill. Their findings indicated that only the "paranoid schizophrenic" description was viewed as serious mental illness by a large number of the respondents (87%). If this assessment as "serious" could be presumed to precede rejection of specified conduct, then the study would permit the inference that the public would probably not reject a person whose conduct would be characterized by a professional as being symptomatic of mental illness.

The study by Cumming and Cumming (1957) suggests similar findings. They concluded that their case interviews indicated that the average person seemed to perceive a much broader range of normal behavior than did mental health workers, and the *definition* of mental illness was much narrower in the minds of the lay people than in the minds of the interviewers.

The study by Nunnally (1961) addressed this issue. He used a questionnaire, supposedly describing the nature of mental illness, asking his respondents to indicate the extent to which they agreed with each statement. The following statements illustrate the type of items used: "Women have more emotional problems than men;" "Mental illness can be helped by a vacation;" "The insane laugh more than do normal people." Using factor analysis he obtained 10 factors that represented a set of generalized attitudes towards mental illness. He found that the public agreed more with these factors than the mental health professionals, although the differences between the responses of the average lay person and the average professional was not significant.

Societal Reaction

Since those labelled mentally ill have been categorized as sick, the preferred societal reaction is usually treatment, rather than punishment. One study that specifically attempted to examine the sanctions which the public felt ought to be directed towards particular forms of behavior was carried out by Woodward (1951). The study consisted of providing respondents with the original Starr case descriptions, but without identifying them as psychiatric cases. Each respondent was asked to indicate his recommendations as to the source of help appropriate to the person described in the case abstract. The results indicated that the sampled population did not view the described behaviors in psychiatric terms, and thus did not support psychiatric help. This finding again indicated that lay people were often not inclined to think in psychiatric terms about behaviors that would be considered indicative of mental pathology by the professionals. It may be recalled at this point that the previously mentioned study by Phillips (1963, 1964) also utilized type of help-source in defining attitudes towards particular behaviors.

In the study done by Phillips (1963) on rejection, it appears that rejection was influenced by the visibility of the behavior when it deviated from the customary role-expectations, rather than the "pathology" of the behavior as viewed from a mental hygiene perspective. Phillips noted that:

It is not necessarily the severity of the illness that leads others to reject mentally ill individuals, but rather the social visibility of their behavior. The more marked an individual's deviation from the norms of his society, the more visible is his behavior.

Bord, et al, (1971) replicated the Phillips study on the influence of knowledge of help sources on the rejection of the mentally ill. Like Phillips, they concluded that increased awareness of psychiatric perspective does not lead to decreased rejection of the mentally ill. For example, 76 percent of the respondents judged the simple schizophrenic's behavior to be very serious as compared to 43 percent for the depressed neurotic, but the latter was generally rejected more than the former. The findings were interpreted as showing that rejection increased as behaviors were perceived as both unpredictable and threatening. Thus, the crucial variables were perceived threat and unpredictability, rather than social visibility of the behavior, as Phillips maintained.

Another interesting study in this area was by Dohrenwend and Chin-Shong (1967), already mentioned. They measured attitudes of community leaders and members of the community toward mental illness. There appeared to be a strong tendency for the more poorly educated to recommend hospitalization, rather than out-patient care for those they perceived as mentally ill. On further investigation and measurement with social distance scales, community leaders expressed less social distance from mental patients than the cross-section of respondents of all educational levels. Of the cross-section, only the college graduates were found to exhibit lowered social distance acceptance. They were found to extend acceptance of ex-mental patients to "child-marry," and/or "child-care" situations. It was found that there was a "strong generalized disposition by the low-status members of most groups to reject what they defined as deviant." (p. 431).

PUBLIC PERCEPTIONS OF DEVIANCE: CRIMINAL BEHAVIOR

General Opinion

Several studies have discussed "fear of crime" as the basis for the societal attitude towards it. The American Institute of Public Opinion #709 (1965) surveyed this issue by questioning respondents as to their fear of walking in particular areas in their own neighborhoods at night. Seventeen percent of the men and 49 percent of the women responded affirmatively. The same question was asked again in 1972; a substantial increase in the number expressing fear was evidenced. Twenty percent of the men and 58 percent of the women now expressed fear of walking in their neighborhood at night. The respondents were classified according to sex, age, race, religion, political affiliation, occupation and community size. Those expressing greatest fear of crime were nonwhite, poorly educated and of low SES; no significant difference was found by the religious or political variables.

In a study by Furstenburg (1971), which used data from a Harris Poll, the author examined two hypotheses to explain the recent rise in the public's concern over crime. The first was that this concern reflected a reaction to unwanted social change, and the second was that the crime rate was in fact rising and the increased concern was justified. Fear of crime, in contrast to the above study, was not shown to result from personal fear of victimization. Rather the first hypothesis was believed to contribute to the increasing concern.

Another dimension in this section is the individual's willingness to resort to crime, as indicative of an attitude towards crime. The study by Blumenthal, et al. (1972) developed a baseline on the American's willingness to resort to violence. Using a national survey of American males, aged 16–64, N = 1374, a majority indicated a willingness to tolerate fairly high levels of police violence. On the other end of this continuum, a minority supported violence as an instrument necessary for producing social change. The major factor used in explaining violence was the individual's "basic values." This included attitudes towards retribution, self-defense, how property and people are relatively valued.

Individual guilt has also been used to assess willingness to resort to criminal behavior. McConnel and Martin (1969) devised a questionnaire enumerating 35 different behaviors, ranging from felonies to bad taste. This was presented to groups of judges and laymen. The former were requested to rank the items in terms of guilt the respondent would feel if he were caught committing the act. A comparison of the official and societal views showed the emergence of a fairly homogeneous moral code.

Another dimension used to gauge the public's opinions about crime has concentrated on attitudes towards offenders.[3] T. E. Dow (1967)

---

[3]The distinction between acts and actors is particularly difficult to maintain in research on perceptions of deviance. Tentatively, it would seem that respondents do not change their perceptions markedly whether the deviant behavior is presented in the form of an actor, or as an abstract act. See Newman (1974).

hypothesized that the negative attitude of the public towards offenders results from a failure in identification between the two. He tested this assumption by measuring the ability of 549 students to identify with delinquent and adult criminality. He found their ability to do so was severely limited. Another study examining attitudes toward offenders was conducted by T. Fris (1968), who presented a sample with a Likert-type attitude scale and found that more than 50 percent of the respondents had *no* well-defined attitude toward people who had been incarcerated. Unlike the study carried out by Dow, Fris found three independent dimensions relevant to attitudes towards criminals: 1) different ideas on treatment, 2) differences in concepts of causation, 3) differences in mistrust. The sample was composed of 112 members of a social work organization. A shorter version of the questionnaire was presented to 167 high school students, whose average scores were found to be quite similar to those of the social workers.

Still another study conducted along similar lines was the Harris survey, "The Public Looks at Crime and Corrections," (1967). The sample was composed of 1,000 adults and 200 juveniles. The Harris findings indicated that "rehabilitation" was perceived as punitive, and that acceptance of ex-cons was difficult for most of the community in hiring practices and social and personal contacts. Another study using a similar approach was conducted by Goffin (1969) in Belgium. This produced similar results both for a random sample of 500, and for another sample of magistrates and lawyers.

A Harris survey, using a national sample of 1,600 and conducted in 1969 (*Time,* 1969) found that public attitudes were becoming more permissive, especially among those with higher status occupations. The so-called common criminal, political radical, and sexually promiscuous, were regarded more favorably than "white-collar" criminals such as trust violators. For example, "A businessman who fixed prices is worse than a burglar."[4] In the area of white-collar crime, Smigel (1956) conducted a study to determine attitudes towards stealing from three different categories of organizations: small businesses, large businesses, and the government. The size of the sample was 212. Respondents were asked to approve or disapprove of fifteen hypothetical situations dealing with stealing from these organizations. Most respondents indicated a disapproval of stealing, regardless of the organization's size. Overall preference of the victim in decreasing order was: large business, government, and small business.

---

[4]There are, however, serious methodological problems in asking questions of this sort. See Newman (1972).

Affirmation of the increasing permissiveness concerning crime was also found by Wright and Cox (1967a, 1967b) using a sample of 2,278 seventeen- and eighteen-year old boys and girls. However, contrary to the 1969 findings of Harris, they found considerable consensus concerning all criminal behaviors relating to property and the rights of others. Lack of consensus was found only for such mildly crime-related behaviors as gambling, premarital sex, and drinking.

There have been several attempts to evaluate public attitudes toward homosexuality. An English survey, the Social Survey (Gallup) Poll Ltd. (1964) conducted a survey with a sample of 2,211, sixteen years of age and over. Twenty-six percent of those surveyed thought homosexuals should be punished by law, 27 percent thought they should receive "moral condemnation" and 36 percent thought they should be "tolerated." The survey also questioned people's attitudes towards prostitution: 39 percent felt prostitutes, not their customers, should be punished by law, 24 percent felt they should be morally condemned and 31 percent felt there should be societal tolerance. Studies of homosexuality producing similar results have been conducted by Meilof-Ooonk (1969) in Holland, and by Havelin (1968) in Norway.

A study by Kutschinsky (1970) was conducted in Denmark to describe public attitudes towards sex crimes and pornography. It was also concerned with the reporting of sex crimes, as it was hypothesized that this would be indicative of changes in attitudes. The sample size was 398; a face-to-face interview was used and the interviewers were of the same sex as the respondents. Kutschinsky found a distinct tendency for respondents to report fewer sex crimes to the police than they would have ten years previously; he also found a general liberalization of attitudes toward sexual deviance. These findings were interpreted as a response to the decriminalization of pornography in Denmark.

Perceptions of drug crimes have been studied internationally. In Belgium (a stratified sample of 460) and Holland (representative sample of 1,987) Von Houtte and Vinke (1973) found that the use of drugs deserved disapproval and punishment. In addition, in Belgium a majority also disapproved of abortion and adultery (only a minority of the Dutch disapproved of these forms of behavior) but most felt that there should be no judicial penalty attached to those engaging in such behavior. The Australian Attitude Poll of 1971 (*The Age,* 1971) with a sample size of 1,000, indicated that Australians are a highly conformist nation. They were found to be extremely rejecting towards many forms of deviant behavior. Respondents showed much antipathy towards marijuana use and users; they were somewhat less vehement against homosexuals, abortion, and capital punishment. The older respondents were generally less tolerant than younger ones. Finally, Linsky (1970), using a representative sample of 305 of the adult population of Vancouver, found that there was more acceptance, *per se,* as well as a greater belief in the therapeutic value of treatment, in the younger and more educated segments of the sample. In terms of control, 65 percent felt medical and psychological treatment to be the most beneficial alternative.

Attitudes towards political crime have also been studied. A study by Robinson (1970) found that despite sympathetic media coverage of the anti-war demonstrators in Chicago in the 1968 civil disturbances, public opinion was largely unsympathetic. A lengthy questionnaire designed by Slesinger (1967, 1968) attempted to uncover the opinions and attitudes of Milwaukee residents toward the 1967 civil disturbances in that city. The sample size was 387, of whom 259 were white and 128 were black. Although information on a number of issues was elicited, the most outstanding finding in the survey was the tremendous difference between black and white respondents as to the "cause" and the effectiveness of the disorders. Spaeth (1969) took a sample of the U.S. population and interviewed it prior to the 1968 Columbia University protests. Education and race strongly correlated with attitudes towards college student protests. Blacks, and those generally better educated had more favorable attitudes towards the protesters. Among the more educated of each race, the younger held more favorable attitudes towards the protesters than the older members.

Intensity of Reaction

Of primary concern in this section is the "morality" of the act—the perceived rightness or wrongness of particular behavior. Rettig and Pasamanick (1959) attempted to assess changes in severity of moral values by comparing their data with a study by Crissman (1942). They used identical questionnaires that consisted of fifty different behaviors, ranging from very serious crimes through slightly "immoral" behaviors, each of which was to be evaluated in terms of rightness or wrongness. The sample population was composed of students at Ohio State University, 204 men and 285 women. They found a general increase in severity of moral judgment, and that respondents made distinctions between acts that were "conventionally wrong" and those that were "intrinsically or deeply wrong." In 1961, Rettig and

Pasamanick compared students' moral evaluations of a wide range of matters with blue collar workers. They found the relationship between severity of moral judgment on general and economic issues to be generally curvilinear, reaching a peak with skilled or upwardly mobile workers. However, on matters of family and religious morality, the lower class was highest in severity of moral judgment.

Hindelang (1974) used interviews and a questionnaire on a sample composed of incarcerated urban adolescents, mean age 15.9; a sample from a rural school, spanning grades 6–12, mean age 14.6; and two samples of high school students from a large urban city, mean age 16.3 years. He asked respondents to report how they felt for each of a variety of illegal acts. The responses ranged along a continuum from strongly approved through strongly disapproved. The respondents were also asked to report how they thought their best friend felt about each act. A large majority of those engaging in various illegal acts perceived their best friends as evaluating the acts the same as themselves, or as being less approving of the acts than themselves. There was no tendency for the perceived discrepancy between self-approval and friend's approval scores to decrease with age. Hindelang found that for a wide variety of acts, those reporting involvement in a particular illegal act were substantially more approving of that act than those reporting no involvement.

Sellin and Wolfgang (1964) in an attempt to develop a measurement of delinquency based on seriousness as well as frequency of the act, developed a new means of scaling offenses. A wide range of offense descriptions was presented to various groups of people who were presumed to represent the morality of the community. Those who judged the seriousness of these offenses were university students, line police officers, juvenile division officers, and juvenile court judges. The intensity of reaction to the act was similar across all groups. There have been a number of replications supporting these findings (e.g., Velez-Diaz and Megargee, 1970; Kutschinsky's SIKOL, 1969; Kaupen and Werle, 1969). A recent work by Riedel (1972) also reaffirms the scale's validity. Riedel demonstrated that people assess the seriousness of criminal behavior regardless of whether or not the offender acted with intent to inflict harm. Thus, the external aspects of the event would seem to be the only ones of importance. This is in contrast to the criminal law that takes into account mitigating circumstances and "mens rea," in assessing seriousness of an act. A study conducted in Taipei by Hsu (1973) also underscored the usefulness of the Sellin-Wolfgang index, although unlike other studies, substantial sex differences were found in assessments of seriousness. This study was noteworthy as it utilized the index in the study of international crime statistics. Akman and Normandeau (1968) replicated the Sellin-Wolfgang study using samples of Canadian students. This study affirmed the heuristic value of using a grading system based on community values, rather than legal penalties. Rossi, et al. (1974) applied the Sellin-Wolfgang scale to a wide range of acts presented to a probability sample from Baltimore and once again corroborated the many studies which have found close similarity across disparate groups (social class, education, age, race, profession) in perception of seriousness of crime. Finally, using a scale of "wrongness," rather than seriousness, Walker and Argyle (1964) conducted a study directed towards identifying any differences between those who knew the law had changed and those who did not. They found no difference, and concluded that generally, people's pronouncements on the morality of an act were unrelated to whether or not they knew it to be a violation of the criminal law. In a recent study conducted by Newman, Articolo and Trilling (1974), strength of religiosity was demonstrated to be a very important discriminating factor, with the religious as much more punitive. The study of Kaupen in Podgorecki, et al., 1973 also found extensive differences according to type of religion, and between "believers" and "non-believers." Protestants were generally more punitive, as were believers in comparison to non-believers.

Definition

Very few studies have been conducted which have allowed the respondents to define or categorize the criminal acts according to their own frame of reference. Most of this work, apart from that concerning mental illness, has been conducted in the area of social deviance (e.g., Simmons, 1969; Gussfield, 1969; and Lippman, 1970), where it was found that people do make general categorizations of various kinds of deviant behavior (e.g., "sick," "depraved," "criminal.") No studies have been found, however, that have specifically attempted to allow the respondent to categorize the acts in the same way as the studies of perceptions of mental illness have done.

Societal Reaction

There have been various attempts to study attitudes toward the severity of legal sanctions for particular crimes. One such study was conducted by Gibbons (1969). Utilizing a questionnaire, he elicited from 400 subjects information on criminality, corrections and the degree of punishment that was considered appropriate for 20 different crimes. The most visible and coercive offenses received the most severe penalties. These were crimes which actually had severe sanctions in the state in which the survey was conducted. He found there were some discrepancies between the public's preference and the penalty currently imposed, and stressed the need for more research on the relationship between punitive sanctions directed at the offender and public sentiments about the appropriateness of such penalties.

In a *Newsweek* article ("Hard Line"–1971) the findings of a special public opinion survey showed 78 percent felt that the criminal justice system's most serious failure was that criminals received insufficient punishment. The size of this sample was 1,717.

In a study by Hindelang (1973) the results of different surveys of the American Institute of Public Opinion are noted. Study #856 (1972) found that white men with a grade school education, over 50 years old and Republican favored tougher sentences for law-breakers. An earlier study, #774, found that on a national basis 58 percent favored harsher sentences for armed robbers. AIPO also surveyed attitudes on the death penalty in study #704. In 1953 a national response was yes—68 percent, no—25 percent, no opinion—7 percent, but a series of surveys from that date through 1972 showed a gradual reversal of this trend, with 50 percent favoring the death penalty, 41 percent against and 9 percent no opinion. The 1972 study showed a significant difference between white and non-white respondents. Fifty-three per cent of the white, but only 24 percent of the non-whites favored the death penalty. In another survey conducted by AIPO, the respondents were questioned on their opinions on the severity of the present marijuana laws. The non-whites, the better educated, the higher SES and the younger respondents appeared to favor decreased penalties for the possession and use of marijuana. On the question of sale, however, only half the respondents favored decreasing the penalties. The profile of those favoring a reduced penalty for sale closely resembled the profile of those favoring a decreased penalty for use and possession.

In a survey conducted by Rose and Prell (1955), a significant discrepancy was found to exist between the law and popular judgment as to how the law should be applied in the assignment of punishments. Punishments for 13 felonies were studied and the discrepancy was thought to reflect a "cultural lag" in the law as compared to popular opinion. It was also found that many respondents were willing to be deliberately non-equalitarian in punishing convicted criminals who came from different classes in the population.

Similarly, Blom (1968) conducted a study to measure the punitive demands of the respondents. He used a hypothetical situation in which a certain offense took place in which a person of a distinct population group was accused of committing the offense. The task of the respondent was to evaluate whether the received punishment was too severe, correct, or too lenient. The sample size was 570. By and large, punishment for the rich was viewed as too mild, while for the ordinary citizens, it was considered too extreme. Thus, class-biased thinking in the differentiation of punitive demands was clearly shown.

In contrast to the above study, Makela (1966) measured sanctions preferred by judges and other groups. He found that the differences in the severity of the demands for punishment of different groups in the general population were small. There was, however, a sex difference. Women were in favor of more severe penalties for offenses against persons, and more lenient in their suggestions of penalties for offenses against property. In general, however, Makela found that the demands for punishment by the public corresponded quite closely with judicial practice, although there was a small tendency for more stringent sanctions on the part of the public.

Kutchinsky (1966) compiled several Scandinavian studies regarding attitudes towards punishments, criminals, etc. The different studies were examined and compared on the basis of sex, and more importantly education. The major findings were 1) ". . . a higher level of education is accompanied by a rising tendency to wish for higher rate of jail-sentence and less waiving of prosecution for young delinquents; 2) a tendency to consider punishment too lenient clearly increased with the level of education; 3) somewhat contradictorily, the higher education level, the greater is the tendency to believe treatment should be particularly stressed by the courts." This contradiction goes unexplained other than mentioning that "the only category which clearly increases with a rise in the educational level is the category of persons who are both in favor of treatment and consider punishment too lenient."

Boydell and Grindstaff (1971) used a choice of sanctions ranging from no penalty, to a fine, to imprisonment, to the death penalty, in order to elicit attitudes on drug and abortion offenses. Using a mailed questionnaire on a sample of 451, they found that older people were generally more severe. The sale of drugs was considered the more serious offense, but there was little difference between groups with different education levels on this act. A variable of religiosity was also measured, and it was found that those who never attended church were far less likely to assign serious sanctions for either behavior. In another study (1974), these researchers found considerable consensus concerning the appropriate sanctions for traditional crimes. Where there was consensus, religiosity accounted for the major portion of the variation, thus providing further support for Newman, et al. (1974).

CONCLUSIONS

Consensus and Dissensus

The relationship between social class and perceptions of mental illness has long been recognized in the literature, with the lower class tending to perceive less behavior as deviant. (Hollingshead and Redlich, 1958; Levine, 1971; Bentz and Edgerton, 1970; Dohrenwend and Chin-Shong, 1968). Differences according to this variable are not so discernible in perceptions of criminal behavior. The bulk of the studies reviewed have found that there exists a very broad consensus across class, educational, and age categories concerning the severity and criminality of the traditional crimes such as crimes of violence and property theft. As one moves away from traditional crimes into the realm of "quasi-criminal" acts such as white-collar crimes and various "victimless crimes," (e.g., homosexuality), considerably more variation in responses is found. However, the evidence is very contradictory. Some studies have shown that those of higher education are less tolerant of crime; others have shown that those of lower class are less tolerant. Older persons (those more likely to be victimized) tend to fear crime more than other groups. In the absence of studies that have sought to control for the interaction of these variables, one cannot draw any definite conclusions. One variable that has produced clear and consistent findings, however, is that of strength of religious belief: the stronger the religious belief, the more punitive and indignant is likely to be the response.

General and Specific Perceptions of Crime

It was noticeable that the variations according to background factors were found mostly in relation to questions eliciting preferences for legal sanctions, rather than for general reactions of intensity or opinion. Certainly, background differences in perceptions of the seriousness of crimes have rarely been found. This supports the hypothesis of general unidimensionality of seriousness, or wrongness, that taps a broad cultural response of moral indignation. However, when it comes to specific sanctions (especially concerning acts not traditionally criminal and those whose visibility depends on enforcement by the agencies of social control, such as homosexuality), class and other differences come into play. In general, it would seem that there is much less consensus concerning the criminality of victimless crimes.

Perhaps the most challenging conclusion is that a clear social consensus exists concerning "traditional crime." Those labelling and conflict theorists who hold to a relativistic conception of deviance in the sense that deviance is the product of class conflict over acceptable norms of behavior surely cannot ignore these facts. The findings reviewed herein would support conflict theory only in regard to "fringe" crime such as victimless crimes, which incidentally is the area in which most labelling theorists have researched. Furthermore, where there is a lack of consensus concerning traditional crimes, it is related to *religious* rather than *social class* differences. Conflict theorists in criminology have rarely considered religiosity as a source of conflict, since they have mostly adopted a Marxist view of society as divided into warring economic classes. One might hypothesize that since religiosity has been found to be an important discriminating variable concerning perception of traditional crime, and social class has not, that religiosity cuts across class lines. Although it is currently fashionable to view our society as secular, it would seem that a revision of this conception in relation to crime perception, may now be appropriate. In the analysis of our results, we will examine closely this question.[5]

---

[5]The reader may have realized that the words "consensus" and "dissensus" are words whose meaning is highly adjustable, often used in almost contradictory senses. A more detailed analysis and definition of them, based upon the research findings, is presented in Chapter 11.

four

MEASURING PERCEPTIONS OF DEVIANCE CROSS-CULTURALLY

QUESTIONNAIRE CONSTRUCTION

The cross-cultural requirements of the study largely dictated the level and type of stimulus material to be used. Our main problem was to select stimulus material that would be equivalent across all cultures, since without such equivalence, comparison of results is severely restricted. Previous researchers have provided a number of techniques by which equivalence may be enhanced, although many problems remain.

It is clear that absolute equivalence in stimulus presentation is an impossibility. Two possible approximate solutions present themselves, however. In the first case, it is possible to address the problem directly by using stimuli that lend themselves to individualistic interpretation. Non-verbal techniques have been suggested along these lines. However, certain sophisticated concepts are not easily handled by non-verbal treatment. In the presentation of criminal acts, as in this study, some crimes render themselves to a more graphic representation by pictures than by simple act descriptions. The interpretations of pictorial presentation are also culturally determined, so that although pictures may appear to be superficially the same across cultures, they may be open to even greater cultural bias than presentation in the respondent's own language.

When such devices appear inappropriate for the area of inquiry, one must accept the inevitability of some degree of non-equivalence but nevertheless make an effort to minimize its effect as much as possible. Careful translation is a suggestion that one finds mentioned repeatedly in this area. A commonly used technique is "back translation" in which items are translated, say, from English into the foreign language and then translated "blind" back into English by different interpreters. The two English versions (the original and the back-translated) may then be checked for comparability. This and other techniques are described by Schachter (1954). Marsh (1967) suggests a more elaborate form of standardization. He calls for the cross-cultural researcher to put emphasis on translating the cultural context of words. He observes that several factors affect meaning equivalence in translation—the lexical meaning of words, the syntactical context of words, and the availability of translated terms (p. 272). Lexical meaning can influence how citizens of different countries react to abstract terms such as "democracy" or "the law." In the case of developing countries, certain languages have no functional equivalents for the generalized Other. This must be taken into consideration when testing in such countries. Syntactical context can cause distortion when, for example, the grammar of some languages requires specification of the sex or social status of the speaker. Differences in availability of words in different languages may also influence results. However, according to Jacobson (1954). "If we have to dig far down into low frequency words in the second language to get equivalence, the stimulus of the words may differ enough though the meanings are the same."

In the present study, the "back translation" method was used. After small exploratory studies, we settled upon a structured interview with closed questions, though some free responses were permitted if the subject requested (but, as it turned out, this was rare). Again, we felt that in a first attempt, so that we could be sure of comparability across cultures, we should build in the structure beforehand, or we would otherwise collect a lot of information that would later be difficult to organize for cross-cultural comparison, much of which would possibly not be used. It was always our aim to construct an instrument which would be efficient and simple.

It is recognized that a preconceived model has been imposed upon all subjects of all cultures with the result that one is open to charges of ethnocentrism. This presents certain difficulties, especially as the preceding chapters have explicitly expounded a model for approaching deviance. The criticism is related to a general theoretical tension that underlies the study of societies as units, and cross-cultural research in general.

Cross-cultural research in any discipline involves the discovery of a common ground between differing cultures on which to base meaningful comparisons. Among the social sciences, this problem becomes a greater concern as one moves from the more impressionistic disciplines, such as history, to those with a greater empirical orientation. Until the work of Max Weber (1949), one finds little concern among social scientists or historians with the difficulties involved in transcending cultural biases when studying or writing about societies which differ· from their own either geographically or temporally. Although early anthropologists such as Tylor (1889) were instrumental in calling into question the existence of what were assumed to be universal experiences and responses, Whiting (1961, p. 693) observed that following Tylor's introduction of cross-cultural methodology in 1889, cross-cultural research was almost completely neglected as a method for 50 years. When it was revived, it passed quickly from the domain of the anthropologists to the psychologists and sociologists. Writing in 1961, Whiting said: "In the last fifteen years, the cross-cultural method has not only become more popular, but has changed in its theoretical orientation. It has drawn upon the theory of general behavior science rather than that of cultural evolution." (Whiting, 1961:523). Indeed, in sociology, the cross-cultural method seemed more like a natural outgrowth of the discipline. Durkheim wrote:·

> One cannot explain a social fact of any complexity except by following its complete development through all social species. Comparative sociology is not a particular branch of sociology; it is sociology itself, insofar as it ceases to be purely descriptive and aspires to account for facts (1938, p. 139).

Marsh (1967) also emphasized the method of covariation as being almost synonymous with cross-cultural research:

> Durkheim distinguished three applications of the comparative method or the method of covariation: 1) the analysis of variations within one society at one point in time, 2) the comparison of societies generally alike but differing in certain aspects (these may be different societies or the same society at different periods, 3) the comparison of societies generally dissimilar yet sharing some feature, or different periods in the life of one society showing radical change (1967, pp. 6–7).

Yet it was also at the same time that Talcott Parsons published works arguing for an evolutionary perspective upon societies. Although this seemed surprising at the time, it is not so remarkable when one considers that his major theoretical works on the *Structure of Social Action* (1968) viewed the theoretical structure of the classic social theorists as evolving towards a general theory, which he took it upon himself to build. Sociologists have largely ignored the evolutionary work of Parsons, since it is too "embarrassing" to the ideology of relativism.

Although it is not necessary (and probably premature) to take an evolutionary view of societies in this study, it is still important to make clear that this study is *not* a culture-free study, although one might argue that it is "objective." A model of deviance has been posited, and that model issues directly from Western sociological theory. An attempt has been made to clarify what the implications of that model are, and how they should be understood. The "objective" aspect of the study is preserved since it is possible to compare all cultures (including the U.S.) according to this standard. Hidden standards, which so often predominate relativistic models are therefore hopefully avoided.

The reply to the criticism made by the cultural relativists (i.e. every cultural view has equal value) is that although in ideal theory this may be the case, in reality, it is not. Furthermore, even philosophically a strong case can be made for the view that certain cultural precepts are superior to others both morally, economically, and politically. Full agreement would never be reached, to be sure, as to which was the superior culture. But it is surely a much more extreme view to claim that all cultures are of equal value. The fact that societies and cultures can be classified and ordered according to a number of basic dimensions (e.g., social and economic development, religion, political and social structures) means that they are not "equal."

But one need not argue that cultures have different value. If cultural relativists insist that one must conduct cross-cultural research without an ethnocentric view, what is the substitute? The position implies either an incessant series of meaningless comparisons of cultures, since there could be no structural standard by which to compare them, or it implies that there is ultimately only *one* standard, a transcultural, or more specifically, an acultural perspective. The latter is a view strikingly similar to the belief in an objective truth. It is also a contradiction since relativists would argue that truth is culturally specific.[1]

We need, therefore, not be concerned that we have developed a structural model of deviance, based largely on American and Western theories of deviance and culture. To do so, turns to advantage the charge of ethnocentrism advanced by cultural relativists. We are all prisoners of our own culture. It would be impossible to develop an "objective" or acultural research design. Therefore, we may as well design a research, clearly tied to one's own cultural perspective, so

---

[1] This problem and the general question of universals will be examined in the final chapter.

that at least one knows what one is dealing with. It is surely clear that the classic work of anthropologists, such as Mead and Benedict, unashamedly used the cultural perspective of the West to dissect and understand the societies of the Pacific Islanders. The payoff in knowledge about our own culture and that of the Islanders has been immense. The ethics of "interfering" with those cultures is, of course, a separate question.

In our own case, an effort was made to involve all participating researchers from each country in the early design of the study. Many questions for the questionnaire were designed and discarded. Although basically designed in English, after meetings with the various country experts, questions were rephrased time and time again in an effort to overcome ambiguities in one or other of the languages. This process went on about 12 months, both in individual meetings and in conferences attended by all country representatives together. In this way, we attempted to establish equivalence of stimulus material and to remove any glaring examples of cultural bias—to be distinguished from the basically broad cultural perspective of the West within which the total research was designed.

The items and scales developed for the questionnaire were not only dictated by the cross-cultural requirements of the study, but were also intended to represent quite closely the six conceptual categories of deviance perception expounded in the previous section. These were, it will be remembered, habitual opinion, knowledge or belief, definition of the act, intensity of reaction, a dispositional reaction, and the perception of official reactions to deviance. Although all six are probably components of responses to all the items we finally settled upon, we attempted to establish at least some face validity for the representativeness of each item of its category.

But the items also had to be constructed with a view to meeting the requirements of cross-cultural equivalence. In addition to attention to problems in translation, the use of concrete rather than abstract concepts is generally considered an aid to achieving comparability. This rule does, however, depend on what is being measured. In the present study, both types of items were used, the reason being that it was argued that the concept of seriousness was a generalized abstract response for all countries. As will be seen, by and large both abstract and concrete items worked well, although the concrete item generally accounted for more of the variance than did the abstract item. Much argument has also gone on as to whether descriptions of acts presented to subjects should be general or highly specific (e.g., see Rose, 1970; and for an attempt to measure the effects of general versus specified act descriptions, Newman, 1974). In the case of crime, the only possibility to maintain comparability is to provide very general act descriptions, since detailed act descriptions cannot be found to apply across all countries, because the laws vary so much.

When working with several languages one must often be prepared to sacrifice subtlety for comparability. Scales which reflect degrees of approval or disapproval or strong or weak agreement must often be collapsed or dichotomized to positive or negative poles if one is to overcome the inconsistencies which arise from cultural biases with respect to the use of "extreme" language. The use of base questions in which real intensity of opinion is known may also be an aid to scaling such items. Open-ended questionnaires, while often useful in this regard, cannot be used cross-culturally since the analysis and interpretation of responses are far too cumbersome. (For additional work concerning stimulus equivalence, see: Hudson, et al., 1959; Schuman, 1964; Przeworski and Teune, 1966/7; Converse, 1964; Ramsey and Collazo, 1960; Bruce and Anderson, 1967; Duijker, 1955; Almond and Verba, 1963). The following specific questions were eventually settled upon:

Question 1: "Do you think (this act) should be prohibited by the law?" (Theoretical component: Habitual Opinion).

Question 2: "Is (this act) prohibited by the law?" (Theoretical component: habitual level of belief, or knowledge of the law).

These two questions are taken as superficial measures of the "habit" level of response outlined by Eysenck (1954). We take on face value that the respondent means what he says in answer to a simple question, just as it is assumed in a referendum, where a person's vote or opinion has political significance. In addition, it is a common assumption in the criminal law that it is people's knowledge of the law that guides them to avoid criminal acts. We should, therefore, expect that a person's knowledge as to whether an act is prohibited by the law should have something to do with his perception of an act as criminal or deviant.[2]

Question 3: "How active do you think the government is in stopping this act?" The theoretical component here is perception of official "defining" agencies. As we noted earlier, labelling theory suggests

---

[2] As we saw in Chapter 3, the studies by Walker and Argyle (1964), Kutschinsky (1969), and Von Houtte and Vinke (1973) failed to support this assumption.

that the activity of defining agencies is closely related to the definition of deviance. Thus, if the police, for example, are very active concerning particular behaviors (e.g., homosexuality) we would expect that behavior to be definied more as criminal by the public. There are many other possible variations. We could have asked for the amount of personal contact with the police, for example, but because of cross-cultural requirements, and because it is deviance as well as crime we are studying, we tried to keep to a general question concerning government activity.[3]

Although these three questions may appear very simple, considerable difficulty was experienced in agreeing upon the wording *even* of these, since the key words often had no direct translation in other languages. "Prohibit", for example, was chosen in preference to "punish," because it seemed more general, and the word punish had many more specific or unique meanings in other languages. For similar reasons, "government" was used instead of "police" in #3, since it was more general, and enhanced stimulus equivalence.

Question 4: "To whom, if any, would you report this act?" The respondent was provided with a list of control agents from which to choose.[4] The theoretical components of response covered by this question are several, although it is intended to emphasize two. First, it elicits responses at the behavioral or dispositional level, since it asks a person to state his intended actions. Second, it invites the respondent to fit the stimulus act into a field of deviance within the range of choices provided him. Thus, we are obtaining his definition of the act. As the Gestalt school demonstrated years ago, the definition of a "figure" depends to a very large extent upon the "ground" against which it is presented. Thus, in our efforts to elicit the subject's definition of an act as a type of deviance such as sick, criminal and so on, it was necessary for us to provide an appropriate "ground" that would not only allow a breadth of definitions but also ensure that it could be interpreted cross-culturally. A serious difficulty in asking subjects to define an act is that the definition is often inextricably related to the individual reaction to the action in question. Thus, to ask a subject whether a particular act is "criminal," "sick," "immoral," etc., runs the risk of confounding his response with stereotypical reactions, which may be both culturally specific and difficult to interpret. For example, we have no

---

[3]See Newman (1972) for further details of alternative questions considered.
[4]The complete questionnaire and list of control agents from which the respondent was invited to choose may be seen in the Appendix.

idea what a person means when he says an act is "criminal" because it is often unclear what behavior is criminal even to jurists. When one considers that the official definitions of crimes vary enormously from one culture to the next, it can be seen that to ask such questions may be meaningless.

The most effective form of the question to elicit definitions follows logically from the outline of deviance theory presented in Chapter 3. If one considers that deviance is partly a function of the interaction between interpersonal process and institutional process, and that types of deviance are the outcomes of the institutions of control, then we may construct a simple question: "To whom would you report this act?" The question focuses upon the referral aspect of deviance in its relationship to the institutions of control. Depending upon the country, the subject was invited to choose from a number of major agents of control. In general, these ranged from "no one," "family only," "police," "doctor," "religious leader," "party official," "village chief," "mayor," and so on. Thus, from the respondent's choice of the agent of control, one may infer his definition of the type of deviance. For instance, if he says he would report the act to the police, we infer that he is defining the behavior as criminal; if he would report it to the doctor, we infer that he is defining the behavior as "sick."[5] Because every culture under study has a system of institutions for the control of deviant behavior, provided we have information about the systems (easily observable in action), we are able to make meaningful cross-cultural comparisons of subjects' definitions of deviance. In addition, it was possible to arrange these agents of control in each country into five levels of formality of control, constructing a scale to measure an inferred intensity of reaction. Thus, this question accounts for both stimulus equivalence and equivalence of meaning in advance. The question can be changed to suite each country's system of social control.

---

[5]Naturally, there are many other factors that may influence the audience to refer a deviant to an agent of control, such as proximity of the offense, the length of time the audience may have to spend in relation to the deviant, the relationship of the deviant to the audience (e.g. family). These are discussed more fully in Newman (1972). Recent studies on this topic are Bickman and Green (1975) and Hackler, et al. (1974). The difficulties in framing the precise language of this question are described in Newman (1972). Some difficulty was experienced in deciding whether the question should be so clearly directed towards "reportability" rather than to ask "who should be concerned?" However, mindful of the arguments advanced by the social psychologists concerning attitude, it was thought that a direct question requiring a person's statement of his intended behavior should be asked. To ask, "who should be concerned?" would have been to aim the question more at the opinion level.

Question 5: "How serious do you think this act is?" (For details of the mode of presentation of this act, see the full questionnaire, in Appendix). The theoretical component measured by this question is that of intensity of reaction. This aspect of perceptions of deviance represents the most challenging area, because it is here that we need to measure the *intensity* of a person's reactions to deviance. The nature of this intensity is, however, open to question and has been very little researched. By introducing this question separately, one may test an exploratory hypothesis that intensity of reaction may not necessarily be directly related to definition of the act as deviant. That is, a subject may consider an act "very serious," or "very bad," but will not necessarily choose the police as agents of control; he may choose a priest.[6] The question as to whether another is reported to an agent of control because of the emotional reaction he elicits in the audience, or whether it is a more "cognitive" assessing of the other's behavior as "serious" enough to warrant referral has been rarely researched. Thus, if we ask a person, "How serious is this act?", we do not know the psychological processes which underlie his response. They may be emotional; they may be cognitive. Recent research suggests that it is largely a cognitive or evaluative response (Newman, et al., 1974). For present purposes we have chosen the question, "How serious is this act?", and provided a 12-point scale including a zero. But if we do not know what psychological processes are involved, are we able to make any sense out of responses to such a question?

We consider the answer to be "yes" for three reasons: first, as we saw in Chapter 3, the question has been used widely in the U.S. and other countries with many different samples of social class and occupation, and consistent response patterns have emerged. The scales have also been found to relate closely to some psychophysical scales, though there has been some criticism of this. (See, e.g., Rose, 1970, Walker, 1970.)

Secondly, it is our theoretical proposition that dualist conceptions of morality (and, by inference, deviance) are deeply embedded in Western culture, that they form the general image against which deviance is perceived. The structural anthropologists have also argued for the existence of such polar "images" in most societies as well as Western

---

[6]For details of the mode of presentation of this question, see the Appendix. In general, a vertical ladder was used, rather than the usual horizontal scale, to avoid a left-right bias of the English language, and also to make it a little simpler for the illiterate respondents, since the "up-down" dimension seems more concretely related to evaluation than the left-right dimension.

civilizations, arguing that it is "the analogical elaboration in all spheres of social concern, of a *structural principle* of complementary dualism . . ." (Needham, 1969:106). Although this particular brand of structural anthropology is not without critics, it should be pointed out that, as a first attempt at cross-cultural study of perceptions of deviance, this approach falls well within an established school in social science. One may add that the Osgood semantic differential, based even more explicitly upon dualist conceptions has been applied extensively cross-culturally, not without success (Osgood, 1965).

Thirdly, research has been conducted which suggests that the addition of qualifying circumstances in relation to the actor in performance of a possibly deviant act has little effect upon the perception of seriousness. Age of the actor has been found to have no effect (Sellin and Wolfgang, 1967) as have stereotypes of "good" or "bad" persons performing the same act (Newman, 1974, Newman, 1975). Therefore, it seems reasonable to propose that the question of seriousness may provide a measure of generalized response to deviance, and that there is at least some theoretical and research support for supposing that seriousness is unidimensional in the sense that it is highly generalized and polar. Our research will enable us to test this hypothesis because, a) we should expect there to be only an indirect relationship between assessment of seriousness and type of deviance, and b) we provided a further "scale" question: Question 8: "How dangerous do you think this act is?" One would expect that if the polar or dualist response is dominant, any general question regardless of the wording that asks for responses along a continuum joining two opposites should elicit the same or very highly correlated response patterns.

And so, a tentative hypothesis is that seriousness is unidimensional and that there is a general image of deviance that may be tapped by a general question of "how serious," which will not necessarily be related to types of deviance. For example, a person may consider a particular act as very serious, but may choose a priest as the most important person to deal with it. There are very likely gradations of seriousness within each deviant type, but these gradations are usually officially established gradations of seriousness (such as those established by the criminal law or the church) and may or may not be related to the person's perception of the general seriousness.

The type of scale chosen was the category scale after that used by Sellin and Wolfgang (1967) as being the simplest and easiest both to administer and for subjects to understand. Cantril's self-anchoring scale was also considered, since it enables the use of a standard scale, but at the same time allows a highly individualistic response.[7] However, since the instrument had to be economical and highly compact, the Cantril scale would have required extra questions that time and space would not allow. Since Sellin and Wolfgang found evidence that the category scales resembled psychophysical magnitude scales quite closely, the category scale seemed a reasonable choice. There was considerable difficulty in deciding what size scales to use, as there had been some discussion in the literature as to the most effective. Sellin and Wolfgang used an 11-point scale without a zero in their measurement of seriousness ratings of criminal behavior, but Kutschinsky (1970) had suggested that a 7-point scale was preferable to avoid clustering of responses in one part of the scale. We were also worried that peasant respondents may have difficulty with a large scale. Finally, we settled for an 11-point scale plus the zero. The reason for the zero was that we wanted to give the respondent the possibility to say that the act was not serious at all. We kept to the larger scale because it was our hope that variations in response to the scales, especially the distribution and spread of responses over the scale could be a much more important measure in this study. We expected a great deal of disagreement among subjects about many of the act descriptions which were not necessarily criminal, indeed may even be seen as not deviant. Thus the measurement of dispersion might well provide us with a measure of the potential "political" nature of the general perception of deviance. For example, if we find that the mean rating of seriousness for an act is 5.5, but that the distribution of responses is split with half in the 10 and 11 and half in zero and 1, we may infer that perceptions toward this act are potentially "inflammatory" in that we have two opposing groups with very strong feelings.

---

[7]Cantril (1965) in his exemplary cross-national study of the "Pattern of Human Concerns" developed the self-anchoring scale which is a highly subjective rating scale. The respondent is provided with a scale (say 10 points) and asked to state the "worst" situation he might imagine, and the "best" situation. Then, depending upon the dimension being measured, he may be asked "Where are you on the scale right now?" The scales are in this way self-anchoring, but because of the extreme subjectivity of this scale, one wonders about the equivalence of meaning not only from culture to culture, but from individual to individual within that culture. The radical phenomenology, underlying this scale, is that a rating can only have meaning when anchored to the individual who made that rating, and any forced choice applied to that rating will necessarily distort the individual's response. Although Cantril tries to answer this and other critiques, there seems to be no way out of this dilemma. Although Cantril retains superficial equivalence in terms of the same scale points for each subject, the subjective meaning of the response cannot be equivalent. Of course, it may be argued that this also applies to a fixed category scale, so that the distinct advantages of the Cantril scale may be that one can gauge the extent of difference in subjective meaning in the self-anchoring scale, whereas for the fixed scale, one cannot.

With a larger scale, we stood a better chance to identify such response patterns.

Question 6: A social distance scale was constructed in an attempt to get a little closer to the "emotional" basis of reactions to deviance. A standard Guttman type scale was used. Again, this is an attempt to measure the intensity of reaction in "emotional" terms. The item was of little use in cross-cultural analysis because it failed to discriminate among the acts and was subsequently dropped.

Question 7: "What do you think should be done with a person who performs an act of this kind?" Again, this is a direct attempt to tap the dispositional or behavioral level of responses, by getting the respondent to nominate the societal sanction he considers most appropriate to the act. A broad list of possible sanctions was provided for the respondent to choose. However, equivalence of stimulus material was particularly difficult to establish for this question. By and large, the only standard sanction whose meaning remained similar for all countries was that of prison.[8]

CONSTRUCTION OF THE ACT DESCRIPTIONS

The majority of studies measuring attitudes to deviance have used brief verbal descriptions of the acts, as shown earlier. Some studies have used video-tape, films, and pictures (e.g., Guskin, 1962), but since our study was to be cross-cultural, envisaging a study of peasant populations, we settled on interviews with verbal descriptions. The reasons for our choice were: 1) we did not want to confound the already artificial interview situation with "novelties" such as video tape or films; 2) we felt we had more control over what was presented to the subject in the sense that one can easily adapt a verbal description to meet local cultural conditions, but one cannot do so with a picture; and 3) some of the acts we wanted to study either did not lend themselves to pictorial representation or might even have been offensive if presented pictorially (the act of incest, for example).

The descriptions were made as brief as possible, giving as little information about surrounding circumstances as we could. Our reasons for adopting this course were that we were interested in a

---

[8] However, the meaning of "prison" varies from one country to another, since there are many different kinds of prisons, ranging from maximum security with hard labor through various combinations—to open prison farms. In addition, in some countries the type of prison is also tied to the length of prison term.

stimulus which would evoke a "general image" rather than to present a highly detailed description of a specific act. Criticisms have been made against such an approach on the basis that one is unable to know what circumstances each respondent assumes are conditional to the act. However, this criticism is made usually from a legalistic point of view, assuming that people need or must know about details of surrounding circumstances of an act before they will either react or judge it as deviant. The reply to that criticism is that there is much research evidence in studies of racial prejudice[9] that demonstrates that people will react and judge others on the basis of little information; that it is problematic as to whether people assess or react to behavior in the detailed way that the law does. In our pretest sessions very few respondents requested further information of the act descriptions. Further, if respondents do not assume similar conditions about act descriptions, we should not find consistent and identifiable patterns of response, within a similar group let alone across diverse groups. On the contrary, as we have seen, the Sellin-Wolfgang study (1967) and subsequent replications (Kaupen and Werle, 1969; Akman and Normandeau, 1968; Hsu, 1973), have found consistent patterning in response across diverse groups, although Hsu did find substantial sex differences.

The only disadvantage in using very general descriptions is the difficulty in relating these descriptions to what is written in the criminal law, as, it will be remembered, it is an important aspect of our study to examine the relationship between what the law says and what the public says. However, if this study were being conducted only within one culture with only one legal code, this would be a serious disadvantage. But this study is cross-cultural and we must relate the act descriptions to a wide number of criminal codes and practices. To make the descriptions of ciminal law specific would be to make them more comparable to one or two criminal codes and less comparable to others. Furthermore, because a number of the acts are not clearly criminal acts, indeed not criminal at all in some countries, it seems an unnecessary imposition to define the act descriptions in criminal law terms.

---

[9]The pioneering work in this area was conducted by Allport (1954). The enormous amount of work in this area by the social psychologists is reviewed by Ehrlich (1973). The literature also provides strong evidence that there is considerable consensus (i.e. stereotyping) in perception of those considered "different," especially as far as race is concerned.

ADMINISTERING THE QUESTIONNAIRES

There are further problems relating to the administration of questionnaires rather than to their construction which may affect their cross-cultural equivalences.

Response Bias: Equivalence of Interviewers and Respondents

We recognized that there were many problems relating directly to the respondent and his situation that could work against maintaining equivalence. Although the researcher must strive for the creation of an equivalent situation in each cultural setting, he has little hope of realizing whether or not he has achieved his goal. The quest for equivalence is frought with problems and impediments over which the researcher may have little control. In certain countries, for example, the opinion survey may be a fairly well-known phenomenon—as in the United States, Canada, and much of Western Europe. In parts of the Middle East, however, the population of the region may never have heard of opinion surveys. This may be particularly the case when peasant populations are being sampled (e.g., Frey, 1963). Consequently, a serious problem of literacy arises, so that questionnaires and interview questions may have to be specially tailored to suit illiterate respondents. Correlatively, there can exist deep suspicions and apprehension on the part of the individual who is selected as a respondent. The interviewer may be perceived as a representative of the government and the respondent may tailor his answers according to what he or she believes the interviewer would like to hear. Distrust of strangers and unwillingness to respond candidly to questions are problems that often confound transnational surveys and which are more difficult to gauge and prepare for. In South East Asia, the problem of courtesy bias (the tendency of respondents to "agree" with the interviewer), is especially serious (Jones, 1963).

Stycos (1960) has identified five special interviewer problems peculiar to survey research in developing countries. They are:

1. Since interviewing usually requires a high degree of literacy, the interviewer in a developing country is often far removed in status from the respondents.

2. Interviewers are generally picked for personality characteristics considered desirable for interviews among highly industrialized Westerners. These same characteristics may not be conducive to successful interviewing in developing countries.
3. In countries in which status is ascribed rather than achieved, social and biological characteristics of the interviewer may have a greater impact on respondents than the researcher realizes.
4. The motivations of the interviewer can be more varied. Interviewers may feel that they are representatives of the country and must present a favorable picture of the respondent.
5. The interviewers and other nationals participating in research efforts may espouse a philosophy different from that of the researcher. He notes, for example, that ". . . many Indian social scientists quite explicitly believe that social science should not be neutral, but should serve a moral purpose." Thus they may conduct interviews in a manner contrary to the researchers' expectations (Stycos, 1960, p. 382).

Using indigenous interviewers is a common solution, but it may prove impossible in countries where there is excessive tribal and ethnic antagonism (e.g., parts of Africa, see Hanna and Hanna, 1966). Furthermore, the process of training the indigenous interviewer may itself remove the interviewer from his own cultural perspective. Nevertheless, as far as was possible, for the interviewing of rural or peasant populations, we used interviewers who were original inhabitants of the rural areas where the interviews were conducted. We achieved this in Iran, Sardinia, and Indonesia where we feared that response bias might be strongest. In addition, all training of the interviewers was conducted by the indigenous research directors. Generally, social science students were used as interviewers in India, Iran, Indonesia, and Sardinia. In Yugoslavia, a professional polling organization was used, and in the United States, the questionnaires were converted to be self-administering.

Organizational Problems

The problems of organizing and implementing cross-cultural survey research in criminology are enormous. With differences in language, even the simplest communications may become major organizational problems. A small error (for example, a misunderstanding concerning sampling instructions) could ruin a major portion of the study's equivalence.

One of the organizational problems is personnel selection and training (Jacobson, 1954). This may present an obstacle when working both at a distance from participating countries and when developing nations are concerned. Expert personnel are difficult to obtain at any time. Furthermore, the researcher is often several stages removed from the actual research operation. He must plan the overall research operation from a central base, staff must travel to participating countries to train local supervisory staff, who must train and supervise the field interviewers.

Another problem is serious differences in opinion which may arise if the research is planned without the very early involvement of intermediate level researchers from each country (see Rokkan and Duijker, 1954). There may be deep ideological and theoretical differences between the original design of the research, and those who will implement it. These must be worked out before the research design is completed. This is why we conducted a series of meetings over a period of 12 months before setting the research design and visits were made to the participating countries.

Temporal Equivalence

Organizational difficulties (including political or world events) may also affect the timing of a cross-cultural social survey. This may be especially crucial to cross-cultural surveys which are usually one-shot cross-sectional studies.

Standardization is difficult in that even if all surveys of sample nations are carried out simultaneously, it is sometimes difficult to be aware of particular incidents within a country that may influence responses. Rommetneit and Israel (1954) discovered, for example, that when they tested school children in post-war Germany using a task involving the assemblage of model airplanes, they elicited resistance from parents who were very sensitive to anything with military overtones. The study of crime, often having its sensational aspects, can be easily affected by media coverage of events occurring in a particular country.

INTERPRETATION OF THE QUESTIONNAIRES

It must be said that the cross-cultural interpretation of the meaning of responses to questionnaires provides us with the greatest challenge. This problem, usually known as the problem of equivalence of meaning, arises even though one may manage to construct a questionnaire which displays excellent equivalence of stimulus material. The difficulty arises when we must assign meanings to the responses. This is a standard problem in any social survey, but it is multiplied many times over in a cross-cultural survey.[10] How this affects results is, of course, related to the areas of inquiry. When one is dealing with systems of social control, for example, the fact that the agencies involved in such a system show great variety from country to country puts the researcher in a difficult position. Although citizens of several countries may reflect similar opinions on prisons or the police, for example, the fact that the reality of such institutions may differ greatly from one country to another has bearing on how one interprets results. In a sense, one is faced with a situation opposite to that encountered in stimulus comparability. The more the interpretations are cast in general dimensions, the greater the cross-cultural validity. Hence, the interpretation of "seriousness" as was noted above, is probably more accurate than one that reflects on the specific disposition for a particular offense.

The only way in which the problem of cross-cultural interpretation can be accounted for is to ensure that one knows the socio-cultural setting within which the research has been conducted. If one is not aware, for example, that the structure of family and kinship in Bombay does not differ substantially from that in a rural village in Maharashtra, serious errors of interpretation of urban/rural differences could follow. Similarly, if one is not aware of the strength or weakness of religion in a particular country, then interpretation of responses in relation to religiosity of the respondent must necessarily remain superficial, limited to specific samples, with little basis for generalization to other populations. Therefore, one must know one's sample and the socio-cultural setting from which the sample was drawn.

---

[10]See: Bendix, 1963; Przeworski and Teune, 1966/7; Hudson, et al., 1959; Ramsey and Collazo, 1960; Schechter, 1954; Nowak, 1962; Osgood, 1967; Michael, 1951.

five

THE SAMPLING OF CULTURES

CULTURE OR NATION?

Perhaps the most famous inclusive definition of culture is that of Tylor (1920:5):

> Culture is that complex whole which includes knowledge, belief, art, morals, law, customs, and any other capabilities and habits acquired by man as a member of society.

Since it cannot be assumed a priori that "society" is synonymous to "nation" (Etzioni and Dubrow, 1970:14), it is difficult to understand the current popular preference for the term "cross-national" over "cross-cultural." If this preference stems from the consistent lack of representativeness of samples that is common in comparative survey research, one would think "cross-cultural" would be more applicable since the samples are most often drawn from small sections or strata of a nation. Only if the characteristics of the samples are not known, does it seem reasonable to use "cross-national," provided it is understood that the samples are not representative, in the statistical sense, of the nation, although they may be categorized *nominally* as "national." This assumes, probably with reason, that regardless of what part of a country persons come from, they will exhibit certain national characteristics common to all people of that country, even though the country may be (and is most likely) internally diverse. It also assumes, perhaps falsely, that the national boundary is the same as the boundary of "society" or that group of individuals with similar cultural backgrounds. Of course, because of the political and often arbitrary ways in which national boundaries are established, this cannot be assumed.

For this, and other reasons which we will see shortly, no attempt was made to obtain samples that were statistically representative of a country. In addition, a "subculture" was also sampled (Sardinia), so that it is more straight-forward to use the term "cross-cultural" rather than "cross-national." However, with this decision, it is important to describe in detail the social and cultural background of the populations sampled. Country names have been used in the presentation of tabular data, mainly as a shorthand way of identifying the samples. It is understood that these are *nominal* labels.

SELECTING THE COUNTRIES

The countries selected were India, Indonesia, Iran, Italy (Sardinia), U.S.A., and Yugoslavia.[1] It can be seen from Table 1 that they differ according to many basic political, legal, social and economic dimensions. The categorizations in that table were developed according to the data provided by Banks and Textor (1963).[2] Of course, much has changed in the world since 1963 when their data were collected. However, the data are largely valid to our study since the surveys were conducted in all countries prior to any major crises or world developments. The Indonesian study was completed just prior to the riots which broke out in Djakarta in response to the visit by Japan's prime minister Tanaka in 1973. The Iran survey was completed long before the international oil crisis developed resulting in a sudden plummeting of Iran into the world's most important economic sphere. The India

---

[1]A frequent criticism of cross-cultural research is that it has often meant the comparison of only two cultures—a phenomenon referred to as the "Fullbright grant syndrome," for obvious reasons. At other times sampling of greater numbers of countries is based on considerations which seem unrelated to the phenomenon under investigation; there seem to be no efforts to achieve a random sample or a systematic sample designed to reflect several cultures whose different characteristics are related to the area of study. Selection of countries is sometimes dictated by political factors, but more often simply by the availability of funding. Cross-cultural research is extremely expensive involving as it does more personnel, travel, and time than other kinds of research. Additionally, funding agencies may have money available only in a particular country's currency, tied to that country. Many of these factors working towards greater selectivity of some countries therefore cannot be avoided. The availability of expert personnel is also an important selective factor. All of these factors affected the ultimate selection of the countries. However, as Table 1 shows, they reflect the wide variation necessary for our study.

[2]These classifications are based on the data provided by Banks and Textor (1965). Most of the categories are self-explanatory, and are defined more precisely in their book. Italy is included but it should be noted that the data are not relevant to our Sardinian sample which comes from a subculture largely divorced from the parent culture of Italy. The reader may disagree with some of the classifications, which is to be expected since the categories are necessarily very broad and sometimes arbitrarily applied. The reader may turn to Cantril (1965) for a discussion of this problem. The classifications have been directly applied from Banks and Textor (1965), to whom the reader is urged to refer for their rationale.

survey was completed eight months prior to the crisis over Indira Gandhi. The New York study was completed six months before the new repressive drug laws were introduced in that state—before the Watergate affair. Thus, the time of the study is generally one of pre-crisis in all countries, so that the 1963 data should not be too out of touch. Furthermore, many of the variables such as literacy and urbanization are ones that change only over long periods of time.

In addition to this data, however, it is necessary to consider the socio-cultural background of the populations sampled in each country, which must include a "little" of the social history of each country. As Cantril (1965) points out, without this qualitative knowledge, the meaningfulness of cross-cultural survey data is especially difficult to comprehend. However, space allows only thumbnail sketches of each culture. Those readers acquainted with any of the countries will find little that is new. But the sketches are necessary to allow for meaningful comparisons and to assist in defining more clearly what the sample represents.

INDONESIA

Indonesia provides us with the most glaring example of the pointlessness of attempting to obtain a representative sample of a country. Well over 100 clearly definable ethnic groups have been identified in Indonesia (Kennedy, 1962; Geertz, 1963; Wertheim, 1956) and 240 different languages are spoken. The reasons for this enormous ethnic diversity are geographic and historical. Indonesia is the largest country in all South East Asia. It is composed of 13,667 islands. Stretched across the equator, the climatic variations are considerable since the terrain varies from tall volcanic mountains giving way to low marshy lands of thick tropical growth, and when cleared, rich rice growing farm lands.

The traditional economic activity is that of wet rice cultivation in the wetter regions which form a picturesque pattern of intricate irrigation systems on the terraced hillsides. This very old form of intensive agriculture has formed the basis of Indonesia's subsistence economy up until recently. Peasants continue to make up roughly two-thirds of the Indonesian population. The majority of peasants are landless agricultural laborers, although some may acquire land by renting or share-cropping close to the more densely populated areas (Lebar, 1972:49).

Historically, ethnic differences are often accounted for by the degree

71

TABLE 1
Classification of All Countries on Selected
Social, Economic and Cultural Indicators

INDICATOR	INDIA	INDONESIA	IRAN	ITALY	U.S.A.	YUGOSLAVIA
MEAN DCS	7.86	12.10	19.97	10.44	7.78	13.92
Linguistically homogeneous	No	No	No	Yes	Yes	No
Horizontal power distribution	Yes	No	No	Yes	Yes	No
International financial status	High	Medium	Low	Very high	Very high	Medium
Economic development status	Inter-mediate	Very under-developed	Under-developed	Developed	Inter-mediate	Developed
Freedom of press	Yes	No	No	Yes	Yes	No
Literacy	Low	Medium	Low	Medium	High	Medium
"Personalismo" dominates polity	Low	High	High	Low	Low	Low
Newspaper circulation	Medium	Medium	Low	High	Medium	High
Per capital G.N.P.	Low	Low	Medium	High	High	Low
Muslim religion	No	Yes	Yes	No	No	No
Bicameral legislature	Yes	No	Yes	Yes	Yes	Yes
Role of police politically significant	No	Yes	Yes	No	No	Yes

72

Agricultural population	High	High	High	Low	Low	High
Religiously homogeneous	Yes	Yes	Yes	Yes	Yes	No
Representative character of regime is polyarchic	Yes	No	No	Yes	Yes	No
Participation of interest groups	No	No	No	Yes	Yes	No
Participation of institutional groups	No	Yes	Yes	No	No	Yes
Participation of kinship, lineage groups	Yes	Yes	Yes	No	No	No
Participation of anomic groups	Yes	Yes	Yes	No	No	Yes
Effective legislature	No	Yes	No	Yes	Yes	No
G.N.P.	High	Medium	Low	Very high	Very high	Medium
Autonomous political groups tolerated	Yes	No	No	Yes	Yes	No
One-party system	Yes	Yes	Yes	No	No	Yes
Leadership charisma pronounced	Yes	Yes	Yes	No	No	Yes

TABLE 1 (*cont'd*)

INDICATOR	INDIA	INDONESIA	IRAN	ITALY	U.S.A.	YUGOSLAVIA
MEAN DCS	7.86	12.10	19.97	10.44	7.78	13.92
Territorial size large	Yes	Yes	Yes	No	Yes	No
Population density	High	High	Low	High	Low	High
Population growth	High	High	High	Low	Low	Low
Urbanization	Low	Low	High	High	High	Low
Predominantly Christian	No	No	No	Yes	Yes	Yes
Stable party system executive political	Yes	Yes	Yes	No	Yes	Yes
Structure is presidential	No	Yes	No	No	Yes	No
Racially homogeneous	Yes	Yes	Yes	Yes	No	Yes
Political modernization	Advanced	Early	Early	Advanced	Advanced	Advanced
Date of independence before 1914	No	No	No	Yes	Yes	No
Politics historically western	No	No	No	Yes	Yes	No
Extreme sectionalism	Yes	Yes	Yes	No	No	Yes

Elitist political leadership	No	No	Yes	No	Yes	Yes
Civil law legal system	No	No	No	Yes	No	No
Muslim legal system	No	Yes	Yes	No	No	No
Indigeneous legal system	No	Yes	No	No	No	No
Homicide rate[3]	Medium	Low	Low	High	High	Low
Religious homogeneity	Yes	Yes	Yes	Yes	Yes	No

[3]From International Association of Police Chiefs: *International Crime Statistics*, 1965–1966.

to which local ethnic tribes resisted "hinduization" up to and around the seventh century A.D. The influence of the Hindus was especially important along the East coast of Java and the Moluccas, where there were the commercial centers trading in spices and other rare commodities (Legge, 1965). The concentration of power in the maritime towns led to a tension between the land-based kingdoms based on wet rice agriculture, and the commercial kingdoms of the maritime states. Eventually, the land-based village chiefs were transformed by the kings of the more powerful commercial kingdoms into an aristocratic class that ruled in the name of the coastal princes.

After the seventh century, Indonesia gradually became "Islamized," for reasons which are subject of considerable debate (Legge, 1965: 42–59). Of particular interest to us, however, is that the smaller land-based villages appeared to incorporate the Islamic religion much less quickly into their way of life than did the commercial centers. A familiar theme in Indonesian history is the conflict between religion and customary law (*adat*) of which the latter heavily dominates the smaller villages today (Jay, 1963). The result is that Indonesia represents a most unusual variant of the Moslem religion, in which there are only a minority of what one might call true Moslems, who fulfill all the devotional and ritualistic requirements of the religion (the *santri*). These are contrasted to the marjority who are peasants and called *abongan,* who do not practice all the devotional rites, but nevertheless consider themselves Moslem. In a sense, the *abongan* should not be considered Moslems, since the Islamic religion requires complete and unconditional commitment. The word Islam in fact means submission. Yet much of the social organization at the community level, so much a part of the Islamic religion, has been incorporated deeply into village life. Although many villages of some ethnic groups retain the customary chief and aristocratic households who trace their ancestry back to the early Hindu kingdoms, the basic social organization and laws are Islamic.[4] However, students of *adat* insist there are several distinct types of village community whose roots extend into the obscure past, beyond even the period of Hindu influence (Haar, 1963).

Three samples were taken from the island of Java, the population of which accounts for approximately two-thirds of the total population of Indonesia (about 119 million). The language spoken is Javanese which has an extensive literary history, many dialects and variations, and an elaborate system that requires obligatory distinctions relative to status,

---

[4]For a more detailed account of the origins of Indonesian Islam, see: Geertz (1960).

rank, age, and degree of acquaintances. In 1972 a uniform revised spelling was introduced and the language is now called *Bahasa Indonesia*.

THE RURAL SAMPLES. Two rural samples were selected. A sample of 100 was taken from a small hillside village, Sleman, with a population of approximately 3,000, whose main activity is that of wet rice agriculture. This village is located about 20 miles north of Jogjakarta, the cultural center of Indonesia, a city of 2.5 million. The second rural sample of 100 was taken from the marketing town of Djombang, located 125 miles east of Jogjakarta in East Java on the Brantas River. Situated on a broad plain, this town of approximately 70,000 is the trade center of central east Java for rice, corn, cassava, and peanuts.

THE URBAN SAMPLE. This sample of 300 was taken from the city of Djakarta which has a population of about 4.5 million. The city has, however, special features that need to be understood if we are to make inferences from the data collected from our sample.

Djakarta is basically a city of new settlers, who tend to identify themselves less as Djakartans—more in terms of the village from which their family originated (See, Heeren, 1955). Persons even born in Djakarta, when asked where they are from, will commonly give the village from which their family may have moved one or two generations previously. Commonly the village dialect or language will be spoken at home. Rapid population growth has occurred in Djakarta only since 1940, and continues now at an annual rate of 4 percent with peasants and farm laborers gravitating to the city in search of work. This is even in the face of government law forbidding immigration of unemployed new settlers to the city. Many end up living in crowded ghetto areas in small hidden pockets of the city. The occupational make-up of the urban population is basically of three types: the largest group engaged in commerce, banking, trade, etc.; the second group of civil servants, and various service industries; and the third the industrial (a growing number) and transportation workers.

Although the religion of the Djakartans is nominally 90 percent Moslem, we should note a further distinction here as we saw between the *santri* and *abongan*. In the city there is also a class termed *priyayi*, the businessmen or professionals who are usually not devout Moslems, though willing to identify themselves as Moslem. Although this "upper middle class" (i.e., *priyayi*) was once a closed class, it is now not uncommon for peasants and others through attainment of education and good civil service jobs, to enter into this social class. In general, Legge (1965) suggests that the *priyayi* class may be identified as that class which governs in the broad sense of the word. The *santri* are the truly devout Moslems who tend to dominate in the market place. The *abongan* are the peasants who profess the Moslem religion, but who may practice a variety of ancient and mystical rites.

In our survey, we can probably conclude that those identifying themselves as "very religious" were the *santri*. Additionally, we can also see why there are so many civil servants in our sample (Table 3), since this occupation makes up a very large portion of the Djakartan population.

HOUSEHOLDS. Since a basic area sampling method was used, the characteristics of the households are important. In general, rural houses and those of the poorer city dwellers are built of wood and bamboo mats, with an earth floor. In the city, a very common house is the single family detached or semi-detached house, standing on a separate lot, often constructed of brick or concrete with tiled roofs. These houses are generally those of the *priyayi* class, although the house of my taxi driver during my visit was also of this kind. Households are made up generally of the nuclear family similar to that of Western societies. Only among the *priyayi* of highest nobility does one find households of extended families. In Djakarta, housing is generally overcrowded. Slightly more than 60 percent of all households have only one room with an average of about 5 persons per household.

The motto of the Indonesia Republic is: "Unity in diversity." Legge (1965) noted that this motto reflects an aspiration rather than a solid reality. The role of the law may become extremely important in this respect. The colonial occupation by the Dutch Empire from 1870 to 1942 no doubt did much to insert a central administration and organization of the many diverse and obscure ethnic groups. Yet the Dutch had two criminal codes: one for themselves and the unwritten *adat* (customary law) itself intricately woven into Islamic law for the indigenous population. At present, the Dutch criminal codes are only applied to foreigners, and the *adat* and Islamic law continue to apply to the Indonesians. Attempts were begun in 1972 to standardize in writing the customary and Islamic law. The relationship between law and public opinion therefore takes on special significance for Indonesia. Although the administration of justice was unified in 1951, so that separate courts for separate ethnic groups were abolished, the laws themselves remained widely diverse.

INDIA

Unity and diversity, tradition and modernity, continuity and discontinuity, process and pattern—themes going back to Voltaire's eighteenth century philosophy of history—appear more and more as the dominant areas of interest in writers on modern India. Voltaire's belief that man was the same everywhere, yet culturally different, paved the way for a history of civilizations. The British orientalists, such as Charles Wilkins, Henry T. Colebrooke, and William Jones, steeped in this aura of history applied themselves to the study of Indian civilization (Kopf, 1969). Wilkins, Colebrooke, and others promoted the view of the cultural diversity of India during the nineteenth century, which led to a lack of emphasis on the continuous threads of Indian civilization. Indeed, Lord Elphinstone had announced in his extensive history of India that there seemed little sense to it: India's history was simply a succession of invasions (Spear, 1972). However, Jones sought to emphasize the continuity or commonality of human nature, and indeed his linking of Sanskrit to the European language lay the groundwork for the establishment of a relationship between early Indian and European civilizations.

India can be understood only with an understanding of its past. There is, it is true, an enormous diversity, an "ocean of cultures" (Spear, 1972) that exists in India today. Scores of different languages, religions, tribes, races, and castes divide the people of the country into almost endless categories. Yet, at the same time, a deep continuity persists, and with the rising nationalism since Gandhi and Nehru, it has become stronger. But the main sources of continuity issue from the content of culture. There is extensive evidence for the continuity of symbols, rituals and religious behavior (see for example, Srinivas, 1966; Brown, 1961; Basham, 1954); the stories of early religious folk heroes (e.g., the Mahabharata) are told and retold. The general orientation of life—the philosophical fusion of this world with the other world, a fusion so different for those who think in terms of a Western religious framework—have dominated Indian life, whether Moslem or Hindu, for many centuries.

The cornerstones of continuity (or if you like, social order) have hinged on three pivots: caste, kinship, and locality.

Caste, often mistakenly equated with social class in the West, has been a central source of order. The four great groups were derived from the early (pre-Christian) division of the Brahmans (priests), Kshatriyas (kings and warriors), Vaishyas (herders and traders), and Shudras (cultivators). Finally, a fifth category—the "untouchables" remain outside the caste system completely. Although there has always been some close relationship between caste, sub-caste (there may be several hundred sub-castes within any caste) and occupation, this should not be simply equated to socio-economic class as we know it in the West (Ghurye, 1961). The caste system is based upon two deeply religious concepts: the ideas of pollution or impurity, and of *"dharma"* (duty). The reificatory explication of these ideas occurred roughly in the fourth century A.D., with the Code of Manu. Since that time, an inordinate number of rules, requirements, abstinences, and duties concerning the behavior of each caste or sub-caste to the other have evolved, and although the system today is much eroded, it continues strongly in the south of India, especially in villages. Since the time of Gandhi, whose genius made it possible to reaffirm the old traditions of Hindu culture, yet at the same time push the people towards a greater recognition that "freedom" meant much more than just freedom from Brtish rule (e.g., the eradication of untouchability), the caste system has slowly become a more "open" system. Of course, this applies especially in the cities, where cross-caste marriages are common and the various behavioral requirements and abstinences are less recognized. But it has also in many ways become a parallel system to that of social class. It is no longer clearly the case (indeed sometimes the reverse) that Brahmans are the economically and politically more powerful. With land reform, introduced after independence, the legal prohibition of discrimination against untouchables, the reorganization of *panchayats* (the local, rural "council of five," which was once dominated by the upper-castes, but now is heavily loaded with lower castes and even untouchables), along political rather than caste lines, castes have tended to become more and more divorced from the economic and political structure of Indian society (see, for example, Ghurye, 1961; Beteille, 1965). The *panchayat*, once a council which pronounced mainly on the breaking of caste rules, now concerns itself more with questions of the economics and politics of local government.

The locality, as a binding force in the social structrue of India, is an especially contradictory aspect to analyze, and in many ways may be said to represent the fulcrum of tradition and modernity. The popular picture of India is the isolated village, closed in by mud walls, the untouchables living on the outskirts, next to a polluted pond. There is a rhythm to village life—a security conveyed to its inhabitants by an order laid down for centuries past. It is true that many villages are still isolated because of the poor roads and transportation facilities. Yet, they are more and more drawn together. The caste system does this partly in and of itself. Now, as Eisenstadt (1973) points out, castes may be united and organized nationally, or at least regionally, as communications, education, and transportation improve. The movement toward national unity brought forward by Gandhi kindled a national consciousness in all the masses, and, followed up by Nehru, this consciousness continues. It also led to what some have termed "regionalism" (Crane, 1966)—a hardening of views by various religious and language groups. The politicization of religion which Gandhi championed, also brought the politicization of traditional religious enemies; especially the Moslem-Hindu conflict. The war between India and Pakistan was the culmination of this problem. Thus, by bringing together villages and localities into one central consciousness of nationhood, the diversity of cultural and religious background was accentuated. Previously, Moslem, Hindus, Sikhs, and many other kinds lived in the ordered security of the village with minimum conflict—and an overriding sense of responsibility for each other, regardless of caste or creed—so long as the rules of tradition were followed. There are many examples of such tolerance: the stories of the Mahabharata give examples of inter-caste marriages; Moslems and other minorities often assume a "surrogate" or Hindu caste status (Barcon and Varma, 1955; Singh, 1956).

The third binding force is the kinship pattern. In the traditional village, castes would live in particular compounds. In addition, the family typically builds its house behind the wall where the women usually go about the chores of cooking and raising the children. Except for special occasions, they would rarely have any reason to venture outside this compound. Only the men, depending upon their occupation (most probably that of working the land) would leave and return. The typical extended family would all reside in this house. Over the women, the wife of the oldest male would be the supreme authority. Only when she died would the wife of the eldest son move up to take her place. Thus, the wife of a youngest son was relegated the lowliest of roles in the household. Extremely heavy dowries were often necessary (for the lower castes, the groom must pay the bride's family; for the Brahmans, the reverse); the land was divided among the sons when the father died leading to land holdings much too small to sustain a living. It can be seen that although there is much to envy in the rhythm and security of traditional village life in India, it also places great restrictions on behavior, and can become both economically and socially dysfunctional. It has lasted for centuries but due to the British influence and India's economic and political development, these life patterns have slowly changed. Education no doubt has played a major role in easing the problem in villages. Once, only the Brahman class was taught to read and write. More and more of the lower castes have begun to learn, although India's literacy rate is very low by U.S. standards. A farmer now complains that his sons who receive schooling are of no use to him on the land (Zinkin, 1966). Many young people therefore gravitate to the cities, looking for a new life. While this relieves the villages of the burden of feeding too many mouths, it produces serious problems for the cities. Since we have designed our sampling around a rural-urban dichotomy, we must look briefly at this topic.

The problem of urbanization and population growth in India was first brought into the limelight by Kingsley Davis in 1962, when he predicted the most "fantastic" increases in urbanization (rural-urban immigration) and almost equally fantastic population growth. He underestimated the population growth (21.5 percent of the 1951–61 decade), but he overestimated urbanization. The proportion of urban population to total population increased only 1 percent during that period (Bose, 1973:5), and it has increased only 1.9 percent to 1971. One should not forget however, that this one-fifth urban population amounts to 109 million! The urban population growth rate for the decade 1961–1971 has been 37.8 percent compared to 21.8 percent for the rural. Summarizing the 1961–1971 statistics, Bose concludes that the population growth rate has been phenomenal for the big cities (44 percent for Bombay) typified by migration from rural villages. In contrast, small towns have stagnated.

URBAN-RURAL DIFFERENCES. There is some disagreement as to the social or cultural differences in the characteristics of rural as against urban. This applies especially to the supposed change in the nuclear family that an urban, Western way of life ushers in. Recent studies find no evidence of this difference (Gore, 1968; Mukherjee, 1965). It seems that, if anything, there is an accentuation of large size, familial dependents, and the conformity with familial obligations does not differ from those of rural life (Gore, 1968). There is no substantial difference in divorce rates[5] (Bose, 1973:286). However, there is a higher proportion of unmarried females living in cities, especially in the 15–24 age group. The literacy rates vary considerably. In Maharashtra state, from which our samples were drawn, the urban literacy rate from the 1971 census was 58.1 percent (of total population) compared to 30.5 percent for the rural.

Eighty-three point five percent of the total population are Hindus. In the rural areas. Hindus make up 85 percent of the population, compared to 76.4 percent in the city. There are also considerably more Moslems in the city (16.1 percent compared to 9.5 percent in the rural areas). In 1961, there was a slightly higher proportion of "scheduled castes" (untouchables) in the rural areas (10 percent) compared to the cities (8.7 percent). In 1961, 89.7 percent of the scheduled casts were illiterate. Although the number of persons per household did not differ in the 1961 census between rural and urban, the number of houseless persons, especially males, was much higher for urban dwellers: 515 per 10,000 male population, compared to 314 for the rural. Since our interviewers used the household as a basic sampling unit, these persons are not represented in our sample.

THE RURAL SAMPLE.[6] The area selected is located 42 miles south of Bombay by road or 7 miles by sea. It is part of the Alibag subdistrict in the Kolaba district of Maharashtra. The district headquarters, Alibag, is 11 miles away.

Farming is the main occupation of the villagers, who cultivate rice (their staple food along with fish), although coconuts, betel nuts, mango fruits, and some vegetables are grown, and marketed in Bombay city. The economic condition of the population is generally poor; literacy is very low; and there is a scarcity of drinking water at the village wells during summer. Some local families are rich, but they have their earnings in Bombay. In addition, quite a few educated and skilled persons who are employed in Bombay or Alibag may visit their villages daily or weekly.

Drinking is popular among the people who distill locally a "toddy" tapped for palm trees. However, opium, hashish, and ganja are not

---

[5]All the following data on India are from Bose (1973).
[6]I am indebted to Dr. Panakal, Tata Institute of Social Sciences, Bombay, India, for his impressions and information on this area.

popular. Women, of course, do not drink. Almost the whole population belongs to the Hindu castes, but only the Brahmin caste is vegetarian. There are a few families of scheduled castes.

The village is well connected to Bombay by motor-launches, but the means of communication with other villages are limited to State Transport Buses which must travel roads of very poor quality, a few private taxis, cycles, and bullock carts.

The village administration and development are supervised by the *Gram Panchayat*. Every *Gram Panchayat* has at least one primary school. With a few exceptions, all *Gram Panchayats* are controlled by members elected on the ticket of the Peasants and Workers Party (PWP), a political party specially popular in this area. However, the level of district administration is controlled by the Congress, the ruling party of India.

THE URBAN SAMPLE: BOMBAY. Of all cities in the world, it may be said that Bombay is the city of the rich and the poor, a city which represents the colossal contradictions of Indian development. It contains the Indian Atomic Energy Commission's establishment, nuclear reactors, and so on; and, it also contains large sections of the population that still rely on cow-dung fuel.

According to the 1971 census, the population of Bombay was 5,970,000, having risen astronomically from a meagre 1,695,000 in 1941. Its decennial growth rate—now at 43.75 is almost twice that of all India—this when the birth rate is generally lower in Bombay because of family planning schemes. The increase is attributable in large part to immigration from the country areas.

The result is that the city is truly cosmopolitan. Half the population is Hindu, and most other sects and religions are well represented. Almost every Indian language is spoken, and those speaking the same languages tend to live in the same areas. As well, there is a significant foreign population.

Bombay also boasts the cultural center of India. The well developed Indian film industry is centered here, and there are many universities, research institutes, theaters, and so on. There are thus many well-to-do residential areas in which the patrons of these arts and professional workers live. But it is clear that such conditions pertain only to a minority.

Housing is the major social problem of Bombay. About 75 percent of the city's population lives in one room tenements; 13 percent live in unauthorized shanties or huts with no sanitary facilities; 62,000 are estimated to be homeless. It has been estimated that these one-room tenements, already severely over-crowded, will need to be increased five to six times to cater for the demand which will exist by 1980.

The bulk of the poor population of Bombay is made up of immigrants from villages who come to seek work. The pattern of immigration tends to be that immigrants will settle in the city in locations where other persons from their own village have settled. Generally, also, the man will leave his wife in the village and call for her only when he has established himself. Thus, the ratio of women to men in Bombay is only 6:10. It was once the pattern that the man stayed until he had made sufficient money to return to his village and buy some land. But with the scarcity of land, and the higher cost of living in the city making it more difficult to save, this seems to be coming less and less the case. There are also a number of immigrants who have been ostracized from their villages for one reason or another, and so they seek the anonymity and shelter of the city.

Such a contrast is made between the lives of these people and those of the educated middle classes of Bombay. Yet, for all its apparent callousness, Bombay has for many years been in the forefront of social reform, and the provision of health and social welfare services. And while the city continues to grow until it is bursting at the seams, the provision of adequate services (even necessities such as drinking water, of which there is a severe shortage), becomes more and more impossible.

IRAN

It has been said that Iran has been in a state of shock for most of the twentieth century (Frye, 1969), since it was first thrust headlong into modernization by the present Shah's father, Reza Shah. Although Iran has been occupied by foreign countries several times this century, and many times previously, the same rule applies to Iran as it does to the other countries we have described: although massive changes in the society have occurred, these have been more than outweighed by the continuity of the culture (Wilbur, 1963). This observation does not just apply to the Iranians of the twentieth century; it has been evident since the beginning of Iranian history, even from the first dynasty, the Archaemenid, which ruled for two centuries from 559 to 330 B.C., when it was conquered by Alexander the Great. At that time, there began a great fusion of Greek and Iranian cultures. The extent of the influence of each on each other is unclear. The Iranians had an "impressionable nature" (Bhirshman, 1965), but also a rebellious spirit. By the time of the Sassainan period (224 B.C. to 651 A.D.—the flowering of Iranian culture), reaction had set in against Hellenism which was accused of being unable to solve the "eternal problem of human society."

But the Sassainan period had its problems. The rigid class structure of Sassainan society was to be confronted by the teachings of Islam. Islam stressed the equality of brotherhood and the equal distribution of wealth. Sassainan society was rigidly divided hierarchically into four classes: the clerics, the warriors, the bureaucrats, and the peasant masses. Each of these classes was further divided into sub-classes, and it was a firm principle that one could not aspire to a class to which one was not destined by birth. The social system had become so brittle, and the lower classes especially so resentful, that they would not defend it against Arab attack. Even though the Persians outnumbered the Arabs almost 10 to 1 in the final battles, the Arabs won an easy victory. Thus, the Sassainan dynasty ended. The lower classes converted easily to Islam, as did the upper class for reasons of expediency (Bill, 1972). Of course, as we know, under Islam, all men did not become equal in wealth and status, as is the case in any complex society.

Why did the class structure not change dramatically? Apart from the sheer impossibility of total equality, one of the reasons lies in the deep psycho-political tradition in Iran of the *Shahanshah*—"king of kings." Traditionally, the rulers of Iran, regardless of how they came to power, have commanded an almost mystical reverence from the people—a God-like charisma (Frye, 1969). In all descriptions of class and political structure at any period of Iranian history, the Shah, or king, is always placed at the center, surrounded by a specially selected court of advisers and surrogates. It is only under these extremely privileged levels do the usual aspects of class structure expand. Today, this *Shahanshah* mentality survives, although some suggest that religious reverence for the Shah has deteriorated as a result of his cutting away some of the power of the religious dignitaries and by the sheer pace at which he has thrust Iran toward modernization (Frye, 1969). However, the small set of privileged courtiers remains an integral part of the political structure.

Although a highly differential class structure continued after the Islamic victory, the membership in these classes altered, especially among the top levels, although the peasants remained peasants. It is a fact of Iranian history that threatens each generation of landed aristocracy in Iran, that with the beginning of each new dynasty, indeed sometimes new rulers within a dynasty, the tendency has been for the reallocation of landholdings. A very deep insecurity persists in the landed upper and middle class, especially today, since the present Shah began reallocation of land to peasants. Wealthy landowners were encouraged to sell their land to the Shah and to invest their money in industry instead. The Shah would then reallocate the land—to peasant ownership. The small landowner, however, who might own one or two small villages was caught in the middle. Although the changes made here have not been substantial, the traditional, almost absolute power of administration of these villages including administration of justice, which this small landowner enjoyed has quickly been eroded by the new institutions of social administration introduced by the Shah.

Another aspect of Iranian life is that of religious tradition and practice. Although made up of a number of separate cultural groups and tribes, such as the Turk men of Azerbaijan (the largest minority group of 5 million people), or the Kurds, the nomadic herdsmen inhabiting the mountain slopes from Mt. Ararat to the Zugros mountains, the Lurs and Bakhtiaris, also nomadic herdsmen inhabiting the Zugros area, 98 percent of the entire Iranian population is estimated to practice a form of the Islamic religion (Wilbur, 1963). Of these, 92 percent practice Shiite Islam, or as it is popularly known, the "twelver" sect. Iran is the only Islamic country in which Shiism is the dominant Islamic sect.

Shiism is contrasted to the "purer" form of Islam, the Sunni or orthodox Islam. It is sometimes said that Shiism is to Sunni as Christianity is to Judaism (Frye, 1969). Briefly, the distinction between Sunni and Shiite sects is that the Sunni religion sticks steadfastly to literal interpretations of the Koran, while the Shiites believe that there were twelve descendants of Allah who were the *Imam* ("saints"), the link between Allah and people on earth. The twelfth descendant hid in a cave and subsequently disappeared, and it is believed that he will return to earth as the Messiah on the day of judgment. However, in his absence, the religious leaders of Shiite Islam (the *mujtahids*) direct the people on behalf of the hidden *imam*. There are many different sects of Shiism, also a multiplicity of "saints" of divine personages as heroes who are worshipped very emotionally on various "saints" days. Frye (1969) suggests that the everyday practice of Islam is of the "saint worship" or "folk" type. Naturally, the more intellectual clerics consider this form of Islam a deterioration of the religion, and so the Shah's underwriting of it as the national religion is seen as an attempt to undermine the spiritual basis of the "church." A very strong sect also considers that there is no hidden *imam*, but that the twelfth *imam* is in point of fact the divine king-of-kings. Thus, the present Shah has pronounced himself a direct descendant of one of the twelve *Imams*, and has invested in himself the degree of divinity fitting to a Persian "king of kings." At the same time, however, he has decreased the powers of the *Mujtahids* by delimiting their control over *waqfs* (land and resources allocated for charitable purposes, traditionally controlled by the Islamic clerics). Although the religious functionaries would deny that there was any hierarchical organization (or any organization for that matter), outside observers argue that there is a quite distinct division of labor and status among the Islamic religious leaders (Binder, 1962). At the top level of religious leaders are the *Mujtahids* who continue to enjoy great prestige, and are able, in contrast to the Sunni sect, to interpret the holy books in accordance with Shiite custom. (According to the Sunni, the holy books are closed and are not subject to any addition or amendment.) At the lower level are the *Mullahs* who have earned a bad reputation for venality and greed especially in administration of favors through the *waqf* system, and in their rigid overseeing of the education system. Understandably, the *Mullahs* have been accused by the growing number of westernized professional intellectuals of selling out the peasants and holding back the stream of progress which would only benefit the poor in the long run. Yet the *Mullahs* argue that they are the only ones who understand the masses and who are able to speak for them. Administered from Qum, the religious leaders and their aids continue to represent Islam in every village, and to preside over religious courts. However, the *gendarmerie* and various other institutions introduced by the *Shahanshah* rapidly overtake the *Mullah's* influence. The new houses of Equity and Arbitration Councils—local courts composed of locally elected officials dispense with most petty justice matters. The literary corps (army draftees who fulfill their services as teachers in remote villages) and the influx of Western methods of education slowly undermine the *Mullah's* hold over the people.

The extent to which all these changes affect the actual psychology and values of the people cannot yet be gauged—although we may get some idea from the data in this book. It is clear that the political and social structure of Iran has undergone and continues to undergo drastic upheaval and change. The one source of great stability appears at present to reside in the *Shahanshah*, who seems firmly in command. The current opinion is that this state of affairs has had a serious effect upon the Iranian's sense of security—or lack of it. Deeply embedded in his psyche, some suggest, is the mark of supreme ambivalence between good and evil, with its cultural roots in the Manicheism and Mazdakism of the ancient Zoroastrian religion which dominated Iran in its early cultural beginnings. Since that time, the Iranian has constantly wavered between the idea of good—defined in Islamic terms as brotherhood, equality and devotion to the ritual requirements of one's religion, against the idea of bad: again in Islamic terms, the feelings of inexorable fate, the pessimism that things are as they are, and will be as they will be. The early Zoroastrian roots of this duality sought for absolute evil and absolute good.

Some have suggested that this profound ambivalence has led to an often extreme fanaticism against anything foreign coupled with an extreme retreatism (Nye, 1969). The latter especially is seen as symptomatic of the deep insecurity the Iranian continues to feel about his relationship to the political structure (see, e.g., Harneck, 1965, for interesting first-hand accounts of this). Thus, the Shiite doctrine of *taqiyeh* or *kitman* has become a dominant aspect of Iranian culture. By this doctrine, the Iranian is allowed to conceal his true feelings while even perhaps doing or acting the opposite to what he thinks. This is, of course, the supreme defense against a political tyranny since, unless one writes or speaks about one's thoughts, they cannot be known by anyone else. One is reminded here of the arguments in social science concerning the relationship between attitudes and actual behavior.

For the Iranian what amounts to a complete disjunction between thought and action may have dire consequences both psychologically and socially. Such a view of life, if carried out successfully must have dire effects on social dealings. It has resulted in a language full of elaborate ceremoniousness and deference required before social intercourse occurs. The Sa'di's book of The Rose Garden, used traditionally to teach children to read, expresses the moral that it is better a white lie that brings good will than the truth that causes trouble. Simmering beneath the increasing Iranian prosperity, there lies, one suspects, strong forces for change and rebellion—forces that have risen on many occasions throughout the expanse of Iranian history. If this disjunction between thought and action is so dominant in the Iranian's psychology, problems arise which concern the interpretation of their response to our questionnaire. Careful analysis allows us to make some reasonable inferences from the data we have but the reader is cautioned to interpret the responses of the Iranians, as with all national samples, in the light of their socio-cultural background.

Now we turn to the more formal and descriptive aspects of the sociological background of our Iranian samples.

SOCIAL STRUCTURE. The Iranian society is structured according to four basic dimensions: 1) the family, 2) the village, 3) socio-economic class, and 4) the traditional class. Religion, as we have seen, has an all pervasive influence, but divisions of the people according to religious classes tend not to have serious importance. These classes overlap considerably with each other, but they also often exist side by side, competing for positions of power (Bill, 1972). In addition, there are many other types of social groups and informal organizations, but they are not at this time of crucial relevance.

The Family: Family and kinship ties underlie Iranian social relationships, and very extensive patrilineal kinship groups (traced back to very distant ancestors) are invested with many kinds of formal and informal obligations. They have led to the common practice of nepotism which only very recently have some top Iranian officials chosen to fight (Sadeg Ahmadi, when appointed the 62nd Chief Justice in 1972, denounced nepotism as one of his immediate targets: *Iran Almanac,* 1972:23). Because of their very extensive patterning, they may indeed cut across socio-economic class lines. The greatest influence of nepotism is therefore mostly in getting favors from large and growing bureaucratic classes. Kinship patterns also have their origin in the early desire of the Islamic believers for purity of patrilinealage, resulting in the practice of marrying first cousins. This, of course, also had the effect of keeping land that would otherwise be sub-divided among the sons, within the patrilineal group. The practice of marriage of first cousins is common in Iran today, especially in rural areas.

The Village: Since at the last census in 1966, 60 percent of Iran's population was engaged in the rural occupations of working the land, the village remains of central importance in the social structure of Iran. Before the Shah's "white revolution" in the sixties, the majority of peasants were landless who worked in the fields of the absentee landowner by day, and returned to their village homes (which they also did not own) by night. The owner of the village arranged the taxation of the peasants and dealt with the representatives of the Shah. In this way he was both the protector and oppressor of the peasants. Although there were many tyrants, most sought to establish a balanced relationship between the Shah, themselves, and the peasants (Bill, 1972). With the advent of the land reform introduced by the Shah, the number of such landed aristocracy has begun to dwindle. In addition, the introduction of the Houses of Equity to deal with local petty justice has undercut the landowner's absolute power position. However, it must be said that even with these changes, the majority of the peasants, although their health care and standard of living may have improved, remain landless (Bill, 1972), and without a power base. All of this instability has also contributed to a certain friction in the Iranian village, which does not conform to the idealized picture of the secure and serene village life. The villages are usually divided into quarters according to status—landowners, tenant or share farmers, and the lowliest landless farm laborers. The typical house both here and in the city is a walled-in compound, providing the maximum of privacy and seclusiveness. The typical lay-out of these villages is along the course of underground tunnels that carry water from natural springs tapped up the hill and reaching the surface below the village. Usually, the "upper" class peasants will occupy the house at the top end of the village where the water will be purest and more plentiful, and the peasants of poorest status will occupy the houses lowest down the hill where the water may be fouled and often reduced only to a trickle (English, 1966).

The former existence of predatory tribes (common as recent at the 1960s) coupled with the often harsh environmental conditions of geography and climate, tend to make life in the village an insecure, somewhat apprehensive existence. Although great strides have been made in the last two decades to increase communications throughout Iran and to extend rail and road transportation, the geography of the country (mountainous ridges and deserts which naturally cut areas off from each other) still keeps them comparatively isolated. The average village resident is distrustful of others from outside his village yet there is undeniably a steady flow of migration toward the cities.

Socio-Economic Class:[7] At the top of the socio-economic class are the economic elite, composed of foreign capitalists, the landless rentier elite (often those who were traditional landowners and who, as the result of the Shah's land reallocation, moved their investments to foreign banks), wealthy merchants, and bankers. It should be noted that this "upper class" does not bear a direct relationship to the "ruling class" which depends, as we will see, on other factors. Given the bribery system of Iranian government, however, having money obviously helps. The second or middle socio-economic class is composed of four types: the bureaucratic middle class, or the traditional state

---

[7]The following exposition depends largely upon the work of Bill (1972). Most work on social class in Iran is largely impressionistic and done from a political science perspective. There is little reliable information concerning the day-to-day activities, practices and values of these classes.

functionaries and civil servants; the bourgeois middle class of merchants and businessmen usually of the bazaar, the oldest Iranian middle class; the clerical middle class, related to the bureaucratic middle class but claiming to represent the masses, so that tension between this and the two bourgeois classes is traditional and persistent; and finally, the "new" professional middle class of foreign educated professionals—professors, doctors, lawyers.

The third class is that of the lower classes which traditionally have been composed of the peasants and tribal masses, and the traditional working classes composed of craftsmen and tradesmen. However, the industrial working class continues to grow considerably as Iran produces automobiles, mechanizes its textile industry, and develops its oil reserves.

The Traditional Class: Although mention has been made of the traditional middle class, we have in mind here the Shah-name class which depends directly upon the good grace of the Shah for its security and power. Underlying this ruling class conception is the mythical "1000 families" of Iran—said to control its body politic. Although most experts consider this to be an oversimplification (Binder, 1962), it is nevertheless agreed that probably about 300 families enjoy the favor of the Shah and occupy many key positions of state. It can be seen, therefore, that because of the extensive web of kinship linkages, this patronage by the Shah must to a large extent encourage nepotism and therefore undercut what might otherwise be a sharpening of economic class lines. It is the aura of *Shahanshah* by way of the kinship obligations through which much social control of the socio-economic classes is maintained.

THE RURAL SAMPLES. These were drawn from various villages that lie about 50 miles from Tehran, mostly to the North in the foothills of the Elzbeuz mountains. It was not possible to control the number of villages selected, since we used social work students who were indigenous to the villages to do the interviewing to ensure their acceptance by the respondents, aware as we were of *taqiyeh*. No nomadic tribal respondents were interviewed. The typical Iranian village is a walled compound of houses clustered closely together, usually along the underground water course, sometimes fortified against outside attack. Generally, each house is occupied by one conjugal family, although in the not uncommon situations of poverty, one family may live in each room of the house. This arrangement is, as one would expect, particularly common in the poorer city districts. Approximately 60 percent of Iran's population (30,820,000) may be classed as rural.

THE URBAN SAMPLE. This sample was taken from the city of Tehran according to a purposive sampling design based upon a selection of social class areas of the city. These are reasonably well defined in Tehran.[8] Urban residential setting may also be commonly divided into quarters with their own names, headmen, public bath, and ceremonial group. Urban houses, excepting the very new, are one or two story, walled in compounds, not unlike the design in villages. In modern Tehran, the streets are wide and symmetrically designed. In old Tehran, the streets are very narrow and winding, following the ancient underground watercourses.

According to the 1966 census, the population of Tehran was 2,719,720. Although Iran's population is increasing at a phenomenal 3 percent per year (higher than India), the estimated growth rate for Tehran is estimated around 6 percent. There appears to be a heavy influx of people from rural areas. Its population in 1975 is estimated to reach close to 4,000,000, causing serious water and housing shortages. In 1970, there were approximately 370,000 dwelling units, and about 40 percent of the population lived in one-room units. Now, almost 85 percent of the dwellings have piped water and electricity. The population of Iran is comparatively young, with approximately only 17 percent of the population over 40.

A note on sex roles also is of interest. Although it is the common assumption that in Islamic countries, women are kept out of public life, completely hidden from public view, some writres have disagreed with this assumption. Women are said to play an important role in the selection of marriage partners for their children (an extremely important role in Iran) and it has been a strong tradition for women of the landed aristocracy and *Shahanshah* court to be very active in welfare and charitable work. At present, the Shah's wife, Queen Sorya, leads this tradition.

YUGOSLAVIA

The inherent overlap between the terms "cultural" and "national" when applied to samples is clearly highlighted in the case of Yugo-

---

[8]E.g., North of Sipah Avenue to the suburbs of Shrinran is the residential area of the elite, whereas South of the Avenue lies the old city which gradually declines into slums.

slavia. Its population by the 1971 census was 20,505,000 people, of which Serbia and Croatia are the most populated (Serbia: 5.2 million and Croatia 4.4 million).

The nation is divided into six different ethnic groups, which coincide generally with the six semi-autonomous republics of Yugoslavia: Bosnia and Hercegovina, Croatia, Macedonia, Montenegro, Serbia, Slovenia; in addition, there are two autonomous provinces of Kosovo and Vojvodina.

Although all of our sample was drawn from the socialist republic of Serbia, most books on the culture and history of Yugoslavia would argue that not only do Serbs have special "cultural" characteristics of their own, but they also display national characteristics common to all other ethnic groups in Yugoslavia. This view was especially advanced by Brown (1954), but is generally held by most students of Yugoslavia, for two general reasons. The occupation of most of Yugoslavia by the Turks from the 15th to 18th centuries is seen as a crucial event in the evolution of the culture of the Yugoslav people. The Turks completely destroyed the Yugoslav society, and held the people in utter subjection for more than two centuries—an experience which bred a deep resistance within the people against outside oppression. This is evidenced both in the many folk tales and epics of heroes who rose up to fight the oppressive Turks (stories from the Kosovo myth) and in this century the way in which the Yugoslavs first fought the Germans through the resistance, then established their independence from the USSR—the only East European country to do it successfully during the cold war years following World War II. Again, we see the familiar antithesis and synthesis. Constant occupation by foreign reign introduced vast ethnic differences in many regions, and this interacted with the natural physical differences of the land. The Turkish occupation left behind a substantial deposit of the Moslem religion—one-tenth of the population of Yugoslavia is Moslem, mainly residing in the socialist republic of Bosnia. The Serbs—"vital Serbs," "independent Serbs"—often serve as the prototype of the Yugoslav national character. Prior to the Turkish rule, the Serbs had broken away from Byzantine influence and established a church of their own. They had no stake in the society prior to Turkish domination, so were largely culturally unaffected by the Turkisn occupation. Thus, the continuities of culture were preserved and have constantly reappeared in times of crisis.

Croatia, which encircles a large part of the northwestern boundaries of Serbia provides a further problem for the assessment of national character. Largely a Roman Catholic State, Croatia was never occupied by the Turks, but was always close and often part of the Austro-Hungarian empire. Here, historical circumstances and Croat personality appear to have been different from the Serbs. The intellectual and educated Croats for a long time deluded themselves into thinking they could both serve an alien emperor, yet also maintain country independence (Brown, 1954:55). The Croats are renowned soldiers; yet they have fought mostly for foreign rulers. Not until the liberation war of 1941–45 did they finally realize the delusion of that position. Even then, the Ustasa (pro-Nazi terrorists) were instrumental in instigating a serious and continuing conflict between the Serbs and Croats. Admittedly, in the early period of liberation, the Serbs wanted all Yugoslavia to be developed in the Serbian image—too much for the proud Croats to accept. It was not until the break with Russia, when Yugoslavia was expelled from the Comminform in 1948, that Tito and his party began to rethink their socialist ideology, especially its highly state-centralist aspects (Singleton, 1970). Slowly, it was realized that the only workable way to maintain a country made up of such diverse cultures (Serbs, Croats, Montenegrins, Bosnians, Slovenes, Macedonians) was that a larger measure of independence must be allowed each group. Today the result is a fairly loose federation of socialist republics, governed within a basically socialist model. No doubt the religious differences between the Croats and the Serbs have been a significant source of conflict. One-third of the Yugoslav population is Roman Catholic, and these are mainly Croatians. The dominant religion is Eastern Orthodox.

SOCIAL STRUCTURE. *Kinship:* Although the following remarks are based on research in Serbia, they probably apply to Yugoslavia as a whole. However, this is not important, since our sample was drawn totally from Serbia.

The ancient kinship group (more appropriately, system) was the *Zadruga,* which is "a residential kin unit composed of at least two nuclear family units, often including other relatives as well, who work and live together and jointly control and utilize the resources of the household" (Halpern and Halpern, 1972:17). In modern terms, it is now sometimes translated simply as a cooperative or partnership. The *Zadruga* in traditional peasant villages was headed usually by the eldest male—but often elected to the position on the basis of qualifications of frugality, efficiency, honesty, cleverness. It was his job to manage the *Zadruga* and deal with the outside, with marketing, taxes, and so on. The advantages of such an arrangement have been considerable: the women could be left for longer periods while the men went off on other jobs to bring in extra income. This has become necessary with the gradual overpopulation of peasant lands, so that peasants have had to get outside jobs to supplement the meagre earnings from the land. Problems, however, have arisen, both related to the process of modernization—endemic to the organization itself. A skilled craftsman would be required to turn over all his earnings to the *Zadruga* head. If one member were sent away to school, conflict would develop as to his rights of inheritance, since he was not contributing to the income of the group.

Before the process of modernization began (i.e., before 1950) the closest kin ties were between father and son, father and brother. More and more, Halpern observes, the closest ties are becoming husband and wife. The larger *Zadrugas* tend now to be declining, and nuclear kinship groups along Western lines are becoming more common. The number of households in Yugoslavia with 8 or more persons has decreased from 397,153 in 1948, to 283,798 in 1971, and this when the total number of households has increased from 3.5 million to about 5.5 million (*Statistical Yearbook*, 1974).

Although moves were made at the inception of the socialist state to collectivize the farms, this has proceeded at a very slow pace. There is a legal maximum of 10 Hectares for an individual holding, and 90 percent of farms are privately owned. Thus, half of all farms are run at a deficit, and about two-fifths of Yugoslav farms have a surplus of labor power. State and cooperative farms contain only 5 percent of the people employed in agriculture, yet they offer 56 percent of the total market production (Matejko, 1974:139). The extent, therefore, to which the introduction of "workers commune" and collectivization of farms have altered the social structure of the society is difficult to ascertain. Fisher (1966), a political scientist, argues on the basis of the analysis of a multiplicity of macro indicators, that the introduction of workers' self-government and the evolution of the communal system were decisive instruments in thwarting what seemed to be unavoidable conflict among highly developed and undeveloped areas. He suggests, however, that this decentralization was achieved at the cost of economic efficiency.

On the other hand, anthropologists seem to suggest that although the outward structure of peasant life has changed tremendously—in that the *Zadruga* is much smaller or non-existent in the village and villagers now dress the same as urbanites—the ties to the village and family are still extremely strong, so that cooperatives have not had that much effect on most villages. In fact, cooperatives hardly exist (and this is born out by the statistics as seen above).

Urban-Rural Structure: Migration from the village to the city has increased tremendously since the War. In 1940, rural to urban moves accounted for one-third of the total migratory movement within Yugoslavia. In 1961, this proportion had risen to two-thirds.

In his *Peasant Urbanites,* Simic (1973) makes a great deal of the effects of peasant life on urban life, rather than vice-versa. The ties to the village that the new migrant to the city carries with him tend to militate against the effectiveness of workers' communes, since the peasant migrants will visit their villages as much as possible, often sending their money back to the village and their family. The pattern of rural-urban migration is therefore not unduly different to that in India. The male workers of the household first leave and try to establish themselves in the city. They take with them many of the aspects of village life: they may continue to cultivate vegetables and even keep livestock. When they earn sufficient money, and get themselves established, other relatives may then join them, including their wives. The village is visited on every possible holiday; the "peasant urbanites" remain oriented to their village. Furthermore, their ways change the complexion of the city considerably. As modernization continues, urbanites begin to see in the peasant life a "romantic" way of living, and so begin to see the village as an object of relaxation rather than toil. They begin to build or buy holiday houses in the countryside. People tend their gardens in the suburbs of most large cities in the West, but the significance of this activity may vary according to the country. In Yugoslavia, at present, such persons are mostly "peasant urbanites." In America, such persons are usually migrants getting away from the cities. Thus, the important area of interest to anthropologists and sociologists nowadays is in the interaction between city, suburb, and village. The idea that the urban life overtakes or dominates village life is no longer tenable (Simic, 1973). Each has a decided effect upon the other, and each are affected by common factors such as, in the case of Yugoslavia, an increasing *national* pride in the development of their country, and thus an increasing national identity that exists side by side the vast ethnic and rural-urban differentiations in Yugoslavian society.

"Social Class": The existence of a social class structure in Yugoslavia as it is generally conceived of in the West is difficult to interpret. This is not only because a socialist state attempts to minimize or eradicate social class differences, but also because under the Ottoman rule, the middle and aristocratic classes were totally destroyed, or, if not

destroyed, completely converted to the Turkish culture (Brown, 1954). Thus, when Tito and the Partisans began to fight the Germans during World War II, simultaneously setting up a new socialist state, there was no previous class structure upon which to build. As it turned out, however, this was an advantage, as Tito's partisan movement was able eventually to appeal to all Yugoslavs, cutting across ethnic differences. This is in sharp contrast to the Ustasa, who appealed only to one ethnic group, the Croats. Tito's movement, indeed, was basically a peasant movement and has thus on occasion been likened to the Maoist revolution. The only clearly traditional class structure therefore has been the classification of peasants into the lower category compared to the rest of the society. In general, this observation still holds (Barton, et al., 1973).

It is apparent now, however, that a political elite has begun to appear (Barton and Deuitch, 1973) and that if one wants to "get on" in the Yugoslav world, joining the party is probably advisable. In addition, there is now very keen competition for jobs, and job selection tends to be carried out very much along American lines (Fisher, 1966). Within limited range some profit-taking is permissible in business, so that the sources of competition are available. This means that education has become a most important indicator of "social class." Although there are still a number of high ranking officials who may be poorly educated (Fisher, 1966) the overall tendency is to select well-educated professionals for the more important jobs.

Above the peasant strata, Lukic (1973) suggests that there are three main strata: 1) upper class which consists of political and economic officials, leading intelligentsia and well-off people in the commercial and professional fields; 2) a middle stratum of white-collar workers, performing predominantly service functions; and 3) the stratum of manual laborers. Although income varies relative to these occupational levels, Lukic is careful to point out that the differentiation among the levels is generally far less than in Western capitalist countries. Thus, the social structure must be seen as relative to Yugoslavia, and comparisons across countries must be made with caution. It cannot be interpreted alone, because one must also consider the vertical differentiation that may cut across this horizontal "class" structure. There are some geographical areas where literacy is over 90 percent; there are other areas where less than half the people can read. The cultural, religious, and ethnic differences have been already referred to, and these, Lukic observes, tend to cut across the class lines. However, this area has been inadequately studied except in the most general way.

Fisher (1960) for example, concluded on the basis of a factor analysis of macro-data that there was a very strong positive correlation between economic development and the northern or more "European" area of Yugoslavia, whereas the southern and more "eastern" areas were clearly by most economic and social indicators, much less developed. There is therefore probably a rough correlation between socio-economic status and ethnic area. However, many ethnic groups are found spread into a variety of areas (e.g., there is a sizeable Serbian minority in Croatia; Bosnia is a mixture of Moslems and Serbs; and so on).

THE URBAN SETTING: BELGRADE. In stark contrast to other cities sampled in this survey, Belgrade is the only one which does not have well established socio-economic sectors of the city. There is, it is true, a small section in which the politically elite live, but by and large, rich and poor may live next door to each other. The basic reason for this has been the government policy of housing allocations, which appears to ensure that people from very different spheres of life will reside in the same building, although there are many exceptions (Simic, 1973). In addition, the existence of high-rise apartment buildings next to dilapidated wooden barracks is not uncommon. Simic also argues that there is a close relationship between occupational mobility and quality of housing. Thus, as the peasant immigrant gradually improves his vocational setting, he is able either to afford better housing, or gains easier access to the public housing, generally of high standard and cheap. He thus is constantly moving over a period of years. This mobility also clearly militates against the tendency seen in other cities reviewed in this chapter (e.g., Tehran, Bombay and Djakarta) for peasant immigrants to reside in one small cultural ghetto. They are instead forced to spread throughout the city.

Belgrade is popularly, and probably accurately, described as the fulcrum between East and West. During the Ottoman rule, Serbs left the city and migrated to the countryside in which the Turks were little interested. Those who stayed in Belgrade were mostly not of Yugoslavian or Serbian ethnicity. The city during that period took on the appearance of a typical Eastern city—with narrow, chaotic winding streets, white minarets reaching to the sky. Virtually none of this remains today. By the end of the 18th century, the Serbs had thrown off the Turkish oppression, and the 19th century saw a fantastic change of Belgrade's cultural complexion. It became predominantly Christian (Eastern orthodox), with only a minority of Moslems, most of whom migrated south to Bosnia and Hercegovina. (There has, however, been a recent immigration of Albanian Moslems into the city from western Serbia (Kosovo)).

During most of the 19th century, Belgrade continued to grow economically after it was freed by insurgents led by Karadjardje. Belgrade became the political and cultural center of Serbia. It also copied, a little too quickly, the 19th century classicist architecture of Western Europe. Today, the city is a mixture of great contrasts between old and new. There are areas of cement and glass. High rises exist next to small houses. Cafeterias exist next to traditional Eastern style restaurants selling kabobs, peppers and native plum brandy. Cobblers and other traditional craftsmen still conduct their craft, even though the efficient factories and industries in Belgrade have taken over the major area of the market. Simic (1973) portrays vividly the very real Westernization of Belgrade, built upon a substructure of Balkan traditions and life styles. The stark contrasts of old and new exist side by side in the "intermediate society." Simic reports that Belgradians refer to their city as a "big village," and notes that they do not tend to see themselves as "European," or as within the main stream of civilization. This does not refer so much to an ideological appraisal, but rather the people have in mind images of life styles, and proximity to the main current events of the world.

If one stands on a corner of the Fortress of Kalemegdan, one sees the breathtaking view of the fork where the rivers Sava and Danube meet—once of great strategic importance, the "funnel" between East and West, the frontier between Christendom and Islam. It is no more. Across the river, now spanned by a new bridge, the satellite city of Novi Beograd has been built, a massive complex of high rise buildings, built on marshes reclaimed from the angle between the two rivers by Belgrade's first youth brigade. Beneath the Kalamegdan are the imposing modern buildings of the Federal Executive Council and the contemporary art gallery. Yet, Simic notes that from this same position, one can still hear the sound of cocks crowing in the early morning.

U.S.A.: NEW YORK

"New York is not the United States," so the cliché goes. Indeed, New York City has many unique characteristics that set it apart from the rest of America. But there are also many aspects which make the city typical of the American way of life. Its vast "suburbs" (Nassau, Suffolk, Westchester, Rockland County, Fairfield County in Connecticut, Northeast New Jersey) are typical of the urban sprawl that has surrounded most large cities in the United States during the past thirty years. A large proportion of our sample was drawn from these suburbs.

The cultural and historical background of our New York sample bears a striking contrast to those of the other countries we have so far described. In all of those, we noted a pattern of strong rural-urban migration, especially in the recent years of modernization. In addition, in all countries, the lives of rural people were seen to be dominated by the power and dynamism of the growing cities. In New York State the opposite tends to hold. Although of course many economic and cultural aspects of the State are dominated by New York City, political power lies Upstate, rather than in the city. Historically there has existed strong antagonism between "Upstate" New York, and New York City, an antagonism that remains strong. Throughout history, the State legislature has been dominated by conservative Upstate Republicans, even though in terms of numbers, New York City far outstrips the rest of the state, and is (and always has been) predominantly Democrat: the reason for this, of course, is that, until very recently, the way in which electoral districts were divided did not allow for equal representation. The districts were constructed geographically, rather than in terms of population density.

The dominance of Upstate perhaps goes back to the early beginnings of the American colony, when the Dutch settled along much of the Hudson and Mohawk Rivers and established themselves as landowners. The social structure of landowners renting to peasant farmers was well established and continued long after the British took over the State (Ellis, et al., 1967). Even after the Revolution, universal male suffrage was late in coming, and certain landholding rights were required before one could vote.

By the turn of the 18th century, New York State was just beginning to gather its momentum. The chaotic years after the Revolution (New York State saw probably twice as much action as any other state, and was torn apart far worse than others since it had such a high proportion of loyalists as to make the revolution more like a civil war) gave way to a resurgence of development. The Erie Canal was opened in 1825, and New York became the gateway to the west. In addition, many hardworking sons of the Puritans from New England began to migrate and settle in New York State. Gradually, with the introduction of public schools, the great insurgence of the patriotic Presbyterian Church, the Upstate of New York had taken on a solid, "Puritan" heritage.

In contrast, New York City's periods of rapid migration were not from New England. Rather, waves of migrants came from Europe, at first from Northern Europe, later from Southern Europe. By 1870, the census of Manhattan showed that of nearly 1,000,000 residents, almost 400,000 were foreign born. By 1920, of New York City's population of about 5.5 million, almost half were foreign born. In 1921, immigration was sharply curtailed by the Federal Government. However, migration into the city continued—not from Europe, but blacks from the Southern States. The first influx occurred during World War I, and by 1940, about 4.4 percent of the population of New York was non-white. By 1970, 18 percent of New York City's population was non-white, and this reached 20 percent of the City's borough of Manhattan. Most recently, a strong influx of Puerto Ricans has contributed to the diversity of the city, and in 1970 there were over 800,000 residing in New York City.

Yet, over this period the population of the City has remained relatively stable. Table 2 shows clearly why this is so. As fast as blacks have moved into the City, whites have moved out into the newer, sprawling suburbs. This is in contrast to the other country samples which we have described, where the movement has been clearly toward the cities. In addition, if we break down the Upstate cities into city-suburban, we find again that the cities have remained relatively stable (1.4 million in 1940, 1.2 million in 1970) whereas the numbers in the suburbs have increased steadily (from 0.6 million to 1.7 million). Thus, if we consider together the suburbs of both New York City and Upstate cities, there has been a dramatic increase of 3.5 million (from 1.9 to 5.4) since 1940 living in suburbia, compared to only .2 million in the cities for the same period.

The religious backgrounds of the respondents not only offer some-

TABLE 2
Population Movement in New York State, 1940–1970 (Millions)

	NEW YORK CITY	NEW YORK CITY* SUBURBS	UPSTATE** CITIES	RURAL
1940	7.5	1.3	2.0	2.7
1950	7.9	1.7	2.2	3.0
1960	7.8	2.9	2.6	3.5
1970	7.9	3.7	2.9	3.7

*Nassau, Suffolk, Westchester, Rockland
**Buffalo, Rochester, Syracuse, Albany-Troy-Schenectady Metropolitan areas.

thing of a contrast between New York City and Upstate, but also offer a contrast to the rest of the United States. While the Upstate rural areas are dominated by the various sects of the Protestant religion, reflecting the early Dutch, German, and New England settlements, all the cities are predominantly Roman Catholic. Approximately 35 percent of New York residents are Roman Catholic (compared to a national percentage of 22 percent) and 15 percent are Jewish (compared to a national percentage of 3 percent). In New York City itself, the number of Jews increases to 20 percent.

While New York is the second most populous of the 50 states (recently overtaken by California), it also enjoys a per capita income level 22 percent above the national figure, and 13 percent above its neighboring Atlantic States. Personal incomes have doubled since 1950, and this rate has been about the same for all urban areas, including New York City.

SARDINIA: BARBAGIA, THE SUBCULTURE OF VIOLENCE

Although D. H. Lawrence (1923) saw in the Sardinians and Southern Europeans generally, a warm-hearted, hot-blooded disposition in which lay the reservoir of raw sexual urges, the expression of which formed the basis of many of his novels, even he found it difficult to cope with the sullen, hostile attitudes of the inhabitants in the Barbagia area. (Sardinia is just east of Italy, an island in the Mediterranean). At the time of his travels through Sorgono and Nuoro, it was common to refer to the inhabitants as "ignorant." Indeed, based upon his experiences in a hotel that provided neither food nor hospitality, he described them as "a sorry lot." Even the street urchins jeered at him. The bus driver complained that the Italian government spent nothing on Sardinian roads; the carabinieri complained that the shepherds hated the land, going abroad to work for practically nothing.

Today, as one travels through the area, many of these superficial aspects are gone. The underlying problems are not. Violence continues at a very high rate, and special forces of carabinieri are intermittently allocated to track down bandits who hide in the almost inaccessible wild mountains (the Gennargentu) surrounding the main villages of Barbagia—Oristano, Orani, Oliena, Ogliastro, Gavoi and Aritzo.

The patterns of violence occur on two fronts: there is a steady killing of carabinieri and other policemen and a steady killing of shepherds by other shepherds. For example, from 1950–1954, 27 homicides of shepherds by other shepherds occurred in the small village of Orgosolo (pop. 5,000); in addition, no fewer than twelve police died as the result of ambush (Fernandez, 1967). During the same period, 21 inhabitants of Orgosolo were sentenced to life imprisonment, and 32 were deported to Ustica (the island, incidentally, to which Mussolini banished Italy's great Marxist theorist, Gramsci). The annual homicide rate for this small village has been roughly one in 600 since 1900.

The reasons for this high level of violence are often described by Italians as being intrinsic to the inhabitants' nature. They are called the "Barbaracini"—meaning barbarian. But although this might imply some kind of inherited predisposition to violence, it is also, without exception, seen as the result of a reaction against centuries of outside oppression (Macciota, 1971).

As early as 181 A.D., the Ilienses were the most fierce opponents of the Romans, and these peoples are generally considered to be the first descendents of the Barbaracini. In 468 A.D., the area was also used as a place of banishment by the Vandals for irreconcilable Moorish rebels. The Emperor Justinian appointed a military leader to control them, but this was largely unsuccessful. The fierce and inhospitable terrain was sufficient to keep most military men away. However, Pope Gregory, who observed that "they live like Beasts" did effect their conversion to Christianity. But this was as far as it went. He could never get them to pay their taxes (Bouchier, 1971).

Many argue that the Sardinians have "fought to the last to remain free" (Guido, 1964). Thus, they have displayed a deep hostility to change, so that along with their attitude, and the natural geography of the area, the people are some of the last in Europe to become "modernized." Many of the villages have remained unchanged for 300 years. The customs and folk-ways, although beginning to change, have also remained deeply embedded in everyday life.

The "Barbaracino Code" (Pigliaru, 1970) is an excellent example. Although the origins of the particular forms of this code remain obscure, it is easy to understand how an informal system of justice can develop in a subculture in which the outside system of justice is considered oppressive and unjust. Furthermore, it can be seen that the "code" itself engenders more violence. Pigliaru (1970) has "codified" the norms of the *vendetta barbaracina* as follows:

Article 1: The offense must be avenged. The man who does not perform the duty of the vendetta has no honor, unless throughout his life he has proved his virility and gives up the vendetta for a superior moral reason.

Article 2: The law of the vendetta binds all those who for any reason live and operate within the community.

These two rules express the binding, inescapable, social expectation to exact violent revenge, and the power of the dominating values to impose their own fulfillment. Wolfgang and Ferracuti (1967) point out the deep nature of these norms, and that the indoctrination is almost total. The Italian criminal code, they suggest, is accepted passively as a political, externally imposed necessity, and is discarded whenever it conflicts with the barbaracino code. An upsurge of violence occurred in the 1960s, the peak of which was reached with the murder of two Englishmen who were mistaken for police. But the code required that this error be corrected; so the shepherds themselves killed the assassins, and threw their bodies on the road.

Although custom no doubt plays an extremely important part in promoting violence, the economic structure of the region plays a central role in promoting the hostility of the peasants toward outside control. A small number of wealthy landlords rents pasture lands to the mass of shepherds, who must borrow money for the rent from the wholesalers of milk, cheese, wool, and meat. Thus, if the least accident strikes the peasant's flock, he is immediately in debt, and may be prosecuted. He may choose prison or flight. This is a stylized description of the peasant's plight provided by Fernandez (1967) and by De Seta in his film *Bandits at Orgosolo*. This view is basically one of Barbagia as a colonial possession of Italy.

There are many widows in Barbagia, and some of the more "colorful" cultural forms of the people have grown up around the grief over the deaths of loved ones. Widows have been known to wail beside the body of their husband for two to three days without a break, often then to collapse from exhaustion, and not uncommonly follow their husbands into the grave (Posse-Brazdova, 1933). Much of the improvized folk singing bears a strange resemblance to this wailing. The Sardinians have a saying: *"Dolori spingi boxi"* (Grief bursts into song").

Our sample was taken from the village of Orani, situated roughly in the middle of the Barbagia area, amidst an almost impenetrable landscape. Its population is roughly 3,000. All the interviews were conducted by a young female student who had been raised in the village, but who was currently a student at the University of Rome. Only in this way could we expect to gain the cooperation of the inhabitants, since *Omerta* (the rule of silence) also a part of the Barbarcino Code, would not permit the people to talk to outsiders about such delicate matters.

105

SAMPLING METHODOLOGY. Although it may be desirable at times to treat a country as a unit for statistical and very broad classificatory purposes (Ramsey and Collazo, 1960), we have seen that in a social survey this is both an impossibility and a fiction. Few countries are made up of one clearly defined cultural unit. Most are conglomerates of many different cultural, ethnic, and geographical groups, many of which speak different languages. To sample representatively a total country would, therefore, be extremely expensive, and of doubtful results.

A spot-check conducted by the writer of 21 cross-cultural social surveys reported from 1958 to 1969 in various journals, revealed that not one had made claims of representativeness.[9] There are two related though separate issues to be considered when sampling for cross-cultural surveys. The first is the maintenance of comparability. The second is to take into account the structure of the public.

Regarding the former, Lerner (1958) in his influential studies of the passing of traditional society has emphasized two factors. First, representativeness is not essential since the fact that samples are taken from different countries ensures differentiation among the samples. Since one is constantly involved in testing the cross-cultural generality of hypotheses, samples should be drawn from cultures which *prima facie* appear very different from each other. Thus, Lerner notes, "Instead of working from sample to total population, therefore, we were obliged to work from sample to theoretical typology." Lerner was prepared to make inferences from his sample to national characteristics only when a) the distributions of the data were so significant and so invariant, that there was a very high probability that they were typical of the population; and b) when he could compare his data to other comparable figures. Secondly, although representativeness may not be possible, Lerner (1958), along with Frey (1963), points out that the categories or demographic characteristics of the sample should be clearly stated and held constant, if possible, across cultures. In the survey of cross-cultural studies mentioned above, the writer found only 50 percent which attempted to maintain equivalence for three or more

---

[9]These studies were: David (1961), Maclay and Ware (1961), Osgood (1960), Klett and Yankey (1959), Lerner (1958), Bagby (1957), Hudson (1960), Rosenzweig (1961), Dennis (1966), Triandis and Triandis (1962), Pettigrew (1958), Greenfield (1966), Vernon (1967), Goodnow (1970), Smith and Inkles (1966), Dator (1969), Allport and Pettigrew (1957), Jahoda (1966), Segal, et al., (1963), Mundy-Castle (1966), Dawson (1967), and Weber (1967). See also Moore (1967) for a review of the sampling methods used in 50 cross-cultural studies.

sampling categories across cultures, the most common categories being age, sex, education, and urban-rural background.[10] Many other studies solved the problem by sampling within a very narrow field. (University students and school children were favorite sampling groups for the obvious reasons of their accessibility.) But the extent to which one may generalize from such samples must remain very questionable.

The second major issue (more difficult to resolve) is how to take into account the differing structure of public opinion in different countries. While one may not be able to draw samples which are representative of the total population of a nation, it has often been argued that one can easily identify those groups who hold the power in each country, so that if one wishes to gain a measure of the opinion "which counts" in a country, all one need do is to sample these groups. This had led to the emphasis placed by many cross-cultural researchers upon sampling elites (Rokkan, 1955, 1964; Converse, 1964). It is apparent, however, that once one moves away from the well established "concrete" demographic categories of age, sex, education and urban/rural, to a more theoretical category of "elite," it may be more difficult to claim a *prima facie* case for equivalence, since the social characteristics of elites may vary considerably from country to country. (This does, of course, also apply to some extent to the four variables just mentioned.)

Our attempt to deal with this problem was purposively to sample urban and rural respondents, upon the presumption that it is usually the rural class that has least power in the politics of a society. As in other studies, no attempt was made to draw samples which were completely representative of a country. Instead, a major city in each country was selected, plus a rural area as close to 50 miles distant from that city. Although we tried to sample by households, there were some serious problems in some cases. For example, in some ghetto areas in Djakarta, there are no formally designated streets, so that areas and even households cannot easily be delineated. Furthermore, the "head of household" principle so commonly employed in the United States and other Western countries becomes very ambiguous in less developed countries where extended families may commonly live under one household. Our instructions to our research experts in each country, therefore, had to be reasonably broad. Research experts in each

---

[10]These studies were: Davis (1961), Lerner (1958), Bagby (1957), Hudson (1960), Triandis and Triandis (1962), Greenfield (1966), Vernon (1967), Smith and Inkles (1966), Jahoda (1966), and Weber (1967).

country were instructed to select their sample according to an area sampling method at the first stage, but to correct this sample if necessary to ensure that a suitable cross-section of the city in occupational or social class was obtained. Also, to ensure an age and sex range, all members of the household from 18 years and up were interviewed. The resulting demographic make-up of the samples may be seen in Table 3, where it is also apparent that we were unable to maintain complete equivalence across cultures. This was usually due to problems unique to the country concerned or to organizational difficulties.

DEFINING THE DEMOGRAPHIC VARIABLES. In criminology one is often faced with the need to develop indicators of a particular social category, especially social class (see, Garofalo, 1976). The problems associated with finding cross-cultural indicators for social disorganization, for example, have been well articulated. (See: e.g., Gurr, 1968; Olsen, 1968; Merritt and Rokkan, 1966). One can readily see that when one is dealing with five or six countries, the resolution of the dilemma becomes very elusive. Indicators of social disorganization can be arrived at, but to ensure that these indicators are equivalent in all the countries studied is another question. Clinard and Abbott (1973) note, for example, that criminologists who ordinarily rely heavily on official statistics in their work are particularly troubled by the lack of official and consistent record keeping in developing countries. Even in technically advanced countries, questions relating to the use of such things as mental health facilities can be meaningless when one considers vastly different social service systems among industrialized countries.

The difficulties involved in obtaining comparable social categories when dealing with several nationalities are quite formidable. Differences in the economic structure and even the educational systems of countries makes matching subgroups extremely hazardous. Stycos (1960) notes that among developing countries even information such as age and family size is unreliable and difficult to standardize. Apart from the urban-rural sampling, the categories we chose to ensure that comparison could be made across cultures were age, sex, education, intensity of religious belief, and occupational structure.

Age: It can be seen in Table 3 that smaller percentages of the older age group were obtained from Iran, Indonesia, and India. Since our cut-off point for "old age" was 50, this is an important observation, and is explained by the fact that these three countries have a much lower life expectancy than do Italy, United States, and Yugoslavia. In addition, because of the small size of the samples taken in Italy and

108

United States, it was necessary to sample the older a little higher than usual to ensure a sufficient N for comparisons.

Sex: The proportion of males to females was much higher for the countries of Iran and Indonesia, where women still occupy a much more conservative (or "hidden") role in society, as is usual in Moslem societies. The non-response or refusal rate is therefore much higher for women in these countries.

Education: Since the literacy rate for Iran is the lowest of all countries, we would expect a high number of illiterates, but certainly not so many with higher education. The latter were sampled purposively to ensure a sufficient N for statistical comparisons. The same applies to both India and Indonesia, although one would expect a higher proportion of Indian respondents to have received higher education. The proportion of the sample is, of course, too high for the total population, and probably reflects both the current overabundance of Indians with higher education who are gravitating towards the cities in search of employment, and organizational problems encountered in interviewing illiterates in extremely overcrowded ghetto areas of Bombay. The extremely high number of illiterates in the Italian sample is explained by the special nature of the sample selected from a rural area in Sardinia, and is certainly not intended in any way to be representative of Italy as a whole.

Religiosity: Instead of collecting information concerning type of religious affiliations, of which there are so many cross-culturally, so that analysis would have been too complex, we asked for subjective ratings of intensity of religious feelings. The question simply was: "How religious are you?" It can be seen that the generality of this question was extremely useful, and allows for easy cross-cultural equivalence. The more traditional, non-Christian countries clearly display a much higher religious attachment, followed closely by the Catholic Sardinians, then by only 63 percent of the Americans, and last by a minority of the Yugoslavians most likely displaying the effects of communist ideology.

SOCIAL CLASS. We attempted to measure social class by occupational classifications, using both occupation of head of household, and occupation of the respondent. As can be imagined, however, maintaining equivalence for this variable across six widely diverse cultures was next to impossible, especially when one considers that there is often little agreement within a country as to the appropriate allocation of occupations to various levels of social class. The problems were numerous. The Yugoslavian researchers, for example, insisted upon

TABLE 3
Demographic Characteristics of the Six Country Samples
(Percentages unless otherwise stated)

	INDIA N=512	INDONESIA N=500	IRAN N=479	ITALY N=200	U.S. N=169	YUGOSLAVIA N=500
Urban	77	72	59	0	80	78
Rural	22	28	39	100	20	21
No answer	1	0	2	0	0	1
Young (18-30)	52	39	31	38	20	23
Middle aged (31-50)	40	53	40	37	43	46
Old (50+)	7	8	11	22	37	27
No answer	1	0	18	3	0	4
Life expectancy at birth*	41.3	40.5	50.0	70.6	71.3	67.7
Median age	30	33	35	36	48	42
Male	50	80	62	49	44	44
Female	50	20	37	51	56	51
No answer	0	0	1	0	0	1
Illiterate	2	5	29	65	0	7
Elementary school	6	27	24	22	0	33
High school	31	52	13	10	68	40
Higher education	58	15	33	2	32	17
No answer	3	1	1	1	0	3
Mean years of education	12.8	9.4	10.5	6.9	14.4	8.9

110

Very religious	16	15	51	10	7	4
Religious	76	80	37	71	59	24
Not religious	7	5	10	19	34	67
No answer	1	0	2	0	0	5

*Source: *Demographic Year Book*, United Nations Department of Economics and Social Affairs, 1973.

the uselessness of a category of "unemployed" since by definition in a communist country there are no unemployed. The equivalence of the category "self-employed rural" in, say, U.S.A. compared to Iran is also most questionable. Similarly, the "self-employed businessman" of Djakarta could be operating anything from a two-passenger tri-cycle taxi to a sophisticated store selling *batik* prints. The only categories which seemed to be reasonably common across cultures were those of civil servant and the professional-managerial. We have usually used these as our locus for a class classification, assigning them the "upper" category. This is, of course, a nominal identification only used for comparative purposes. There were no "upper" class, in the absolute sense, sampled in our survey.

A general comment on the method of comparison across cultures according to sociological dimensions is necessary. There are generally two ways it may be approached. First, we could retain the categories as set out in Table 3 across all countries. However, if this were done, the number of breakdowns one could develop may be limited, since some of the categories have extremely few cases (e.g., there are no non-religious rural Iranians). The second method adapts the comparison to the characteristics of each country. Thus, instead of conducting comparisons of all educational levels across cultures, where the U.S. has no cases in the two lower levels, the cut-off points are readjusted upwards. In this way, one recognizes the specificity of these sociological dimensions within each country, but at the same time must assume that their comparison across cultures can be interpreted meaningfully.[11] For example, the assumption is that even though the U.S. sample has been totally educated beyond elementary school, a differentiation between the well educated and less educated of the U.S. sample will have some equivalence of meaning to the differentiation between the well educated and less educated of Indonesia.

Although we have tried to keep this procedure to a minimum, where necessary, we have used it to establish sufficient N in each category.

---

[11]This is not unlike the problem confronted by Cantril's self-anchoring scale (1965) in which he tried to retain measures which allowed for the uniqueness of the individual, but assumed that these measures could be compared meaningfully to other's responses.

six

COMPARATIVE PERCEPTIONS
OF DEVIANCE

"There is apparently no pattern of human behavior which has not been at least tolerated in some normative structure," writes Austin Turk, the conflict theorist (Turk, 1969:10–11). Although he observes that there "do seem to be universal categories of norms (e.g. norms limiting the use of violence; . . ." he goes on to assert, referring to the work of Hoebel (1954:76–77) on matricide that there is an "absence of universal norms,"[1] These two statements appear to be directly contradictory to each other, but we will see that they are both correct. The problem turns on two critical points. First, the tolerance level of particular kinds of behavior, and second, the strictness of the definition of "universal." Now let us proceed to analyze the responses to our interviews in six countries, mindful of the different levels or areas of perception outlined in Chapter 3. We shall begin at the most general level, that of opinion.

"THE CONSENSUS OF OPINION IS. . . ."

It can be seen from Table 4 that there was clear and universal disapproval of two acts: robbery and appropriation of public funds. Incest was disapproved of in all countries except the New York sample where the proportion disapproving of it was down to 75 percent. These three

---

[1]The manner in which Turk used Hoebel was misleading. Hoebel's work concerned the practice of matricide, patricide, senilicide, and invalidicide. All the acts he described were clearly "mercy killings" or assisted suicides. There was no "evil intent" involved. These homicides are renowned for the disagreement concerning the extent to which they should be tolerated in many societies. They most likely fall into the category "*mala ambigua*." Turk clearly overstates his case: "Again, there appears to be nothing of which the human body is capable that is universally approved or disapproved." The onus should be on him to provide examples of societies or historical periods when murder with evil intent, for example, was not universally disapproved.

acts, it will be noted, were those which we originally hypothesized as *mala in se, mala antiqua,* and *mala prohibita* type 1 (quasi-crime).

The deviant acts of homosexuality, abortion, and drug-taking may also be taken together. Here, the decriminalizing opinion of the New York respondents in comparison to all other countries is indeed striking. Only 18.3 percent thought the act of homosexuality should be legally prohibited. Of the remaining five countries, only in Yugoslavia was there a clear weakening in the criminalizing attitude to this act. Interestingly enough, this weakening occurred more clearly in the most economically developed country.

The preference for decriminalization by the two more developed countries of Yugoslavia and U.S.A. was also demonstrated for the act of abortion, with the Yugoslavians showing much greater tolerance of this act than any other. The Indian respondents were also very tolerant of abortion which at first sight appears perplexing when one considers the high status which the sanctity of life enjoys in the Hindu religion. However, since our sample was taken mostly from cosmopolitan Bombay and biased heavily toward the well educated, it is not too surprising. This is especially so in the light of the heavy emphasis placed by the Indian Government on birth control and the recent abortion law making abortion permissible if the pregnancy resulted from the failure of a recognized method of birth control.

There was remarkably little variation in the generally very strong, almost universal, disapproval of taking drugs; remarkable because taking drugs, probably more than any other act, has culturally specific attributes. In Iran, taking opium was a traditional way of treating visitors and it still is for the older generation. However, it was outlawed in 1970 by Reza Shah in his rush toward the development of Iran. Similarly, in Indonesia, the act of taking hashish has generally been outlawed, especially in response to Western pressure to suppress cultivation of the opium poppy. In Yugoslavia, where at the time there was no recognized drug problem, the act was strongly disapproved. In the U.S. the act (taking heroin) was also strongly disapproved, which is no doubt related to the long history of the villification of dope addicts in that country (see Becker, 1964; Newman and Trilling, 1974; Lindesmith, 1965).

The reactions to acts of environmental pollution give an excellent chance to gauge the extent to which "deviance" produced as a direct result of industrialization (and therefore indigenous to the well developed countries) has been transported to other less developed countries. It can be seen from Table 4 that pollution has been unanimously criminalized in all six countries as though it were a traditional crime.

The acts *mala ambigua* (protest and not helping) elicited an interesting differentiation of responses. The New York respondents were clearly the "deviant" respondents of this survey, with only a negligible proportion criminalizing public protest, and less than half the proportions of all other countries criminalizing "not helping." However, if we view responses to these acts in comparison to responses to other acts *within each country sample,* we can see that these are generally the least criminalized acts in all countries. The large discrepancy between Indonesia and Iran, compared to Italy, U.S.A., Yugoslavia, and India in favoring criminalization of public protest is indeed striking, especially when Indonesia and Iran are countries usually rated as more totalitarian and probably less economically developed than the remaining countries.[2]

The act of not helping is also interesting, where the proportions of the less developed countries criminalizing this act were less than Yugoslavia and Italy, yet America was the great exception, with only 27.8 percent criminalizing the act. There was, however, considerable confusion in most countries as to the legal stagus of this act, so that this may explain the wide diversity in opinion. This does, of course, depend upon whether knowledge of the law is related to opinion, a question which we shall examine shortly. For the moment, we may summarize our findings as follows:

1. If one were to order the acts according to the proportions of each country sample criminalizing them, one would find a general consensus across all countries as to the extent that all acts should be tolerated. When one looks at specific acts, however, the consensus tends to fade, and holds only for traditional crimes of robbery, misappropriation, environmental pollution, and taking drugs.
2. Traditionally deviant acts were significantly more decriminalized by the respondents from the industralized countries of Yugoslavia and U.S.A., and to some extent India.
3. "Ambiguous" acts were more highly criminalized by the less developed, more totalitarian countries.
4. Indonesia and Iran displayed extremely high criminalizing opinions. This result, however, should be interpreted with caution

[2]The relationship between economic, social, and political variables to tolerance of deviance is examined in Chapter 8.

TABLE 4

"Do You Think This Act Should Be Prohibited by the Law?"
(Percent distribution: "Don't know" category excluded)

	INDIA (N=509)		INDONESIA (N=500)		IRAN (N=475)		ITALY (SARDINIA) (N=200)		U.S.A. (N=169)		YUGOSLAVIA (N=500)	
	YES	NO	YES	NO	YES	NO	YES	NO	YES	NO	YES	NO
Incest	94.3	5.7	98.0	0.6	98.1	1.9	97.5	2.0	71.0	20.7	95.0	0.8
Robbery	97.3	2.7	99.2	0.0	97.9	2.1	100.0	0.0	100.0	0.0	98.4	0.4
Appropriation	96.6	1.2	99.8	0.2	97.1	2.9	100.0	0.0	92.3	7.1	98.0	0.0
Homosexuality	74.1	25.0	85.9	7.2	90.3	9.7	86.5	12.5	18.3	66.9	71.6	13.6
Abortion	40.9	58.7	95.3	3.0	83.9	16.1	76.5	21.5	21.9	74.5	24.8	63.2
Taking drugs	74.9	24.6	93.3	2.4	89.8	10.2	92.0	3.0	89.6	11.8	89.2	4.2
Factory pollution	98.8	1.2	94.9	1.0	97.7	2.3	96.0	3.5	96.4	3.0	92.8	1.6
Public protest	33.3	65.8	72.3	20.9	77.0	23.0	34.5	64.5	5.9	91.1	46.2	38.4
Not helping	44.5	53.9	67.7	24.4	56.4	43.6	79.5	20.0	27.8	52.7	76.6	12.2

since experience with surveys in these countries has suggested that an element of response bias may operate in the direction of acquiescence (the "courtesy bias," Jones, 1963). Since interviewers would be seen as persons of authority, a bias towards criminalization of the acts would be expected in these countries. It did not, however, occur in India, which may again point to the higher sophistication of the India respondents.

5. We may tentatively conclude that consensus theory is supported by this data, since consensus theorists have never argued that *all* criminal acts are universally disapproved, but only the traditional ones. It has been long accepted that deviant acts (in contrast to criminal acts) are those about which there is extensive disagreement in society (see, e.g., Aubert, 1970). The point at which consensus theory is *not* supported, however, is the failure of the subculture of violence (i.e., the Sardinian sample) to display a distinctly different patterning of response. This should have been found, since subculture of violence theory argues for a consensus on the part of the major culture, but a substantial contradiction of these values by the subculture (Wolfgang and Ferracuti, 1967). Let us look at our next component of deviance perception to see if this pattern of consensus holds.

INTENSITY OF REACTION

The next most general measure of deviance perception is that of the perceived seriousness of the acts. Although some argue that for universality to be supported, only one dissenting case needs to be found, this seems like an unrealistic criterion for rejection of the universality hypothesis. Stated around the other way, a conflict theorist could hardly defend the proposition that one dissenter (unless under extremely unusual circumstances) was sufficient for a conflict situation in a total society. The more important questions to ask have to do with the comparative amount of consensus and dissensus, and, as we will see in Chapter 8, the sociological distribution of that dissensus. When interpreting the data of Table 5, we must be careful to discern three levels of the consensus-dissensus continuum.

First, there is the general international consensus. This level may be tested by ranking the acts in order of seriousness as seen within each country, then comparing the rankings among the countries. We can see that there is a very high agreement concerning the relative seriousness

117

TABLE 5
Mean Raw Category Scale Scores of Seriousness

	INDIA (N=509)		INDONESIA (N=477)		IRAN (N=479)		ITALY (SARDINIA) (N=200)		U.S.A. (N=169)		YUGOSLAVIA (N=980)	
	MEAN	s^2	MEAN	s^2	MEAN	s^2	MEAN	s^2	MEAN	s^2	MEAN	s^2
Robbery	8.10	7.22	9.62	4.02	9.95	4.60	9.62	3.69	9.28	4.24	8.95	5.46
Incest	9.70	5.24	9.21	6.88	10.71	1.78	10.03	3.68	7.95	13.05	10.30	2.65
Appropriation	8.59	6.48	9.60	4.73	10.04	5.34	9.28	3.50	8.22	9.23	9.10	5.30
Homosexuality	6.04	14.15	7.70	9.01	9.29	10.82	8.52	13.77	3.37	13.52	6.59	13.33
Abortion	3.88	14.03	8.76	7.41	9.09	11.51	7.73	11.64	3.92	18.39	3.03	12.60
Taking drugs	6.61	10.32	9.09	6.93	9.79	6.07	9.62	4.91	9.55	5.20	8.67	8.24
Factory pollution	8.85	6.57	8.85	6.95	10.20	3.39	9.18	4.20	9.32	4.22	7.68	8.37
Individual pollution	Not asked		7.07	9.92	9.15	9.39	8.28	6.60	7.80	8.16	7.56	8.28
Public protest	2.48	7.93	6.96	9.32	8.06	16.47	2.62	9.93	2.04	8.98	4.55	15.84
Not helping	6.25	10.56	7.49	9.12	9.56	9.13	9.20	4.24	6.81	11.68	6.54	9.11

of each act.[3] It can be seen that the differentiation among the acts is much clearer, although the relative seriousness with which the acts are viewed is quite similar to that obtained from our measures of opinion. The criticism is often levelled at this type of analysis that ranks are very superficial or too general. While this may be the case, this level of analysis is still important since it allows for us to take into account the possibility that the seriousness scale did not elicit equivalent responses from each country sample. For example, it is clear that the Indonesians and Iranians rated the acts at a *generally* much higher level of seriousness than did other countries. Either this is evidence of response bias, or these respondents may have seen deviant acts as more serious than other respondents.

The second level of analysis is to look directly across the ratings of seriousness, assuming that each measure is equivalent. We find here that there are considerable case-by-case variations,[4] although there is clear similarity of the seriousness ratings for the traditional crimes of robbery, incest, and appropriation. However, when it comes to the more traditional deviance (as opposed to traditional crime) of homosexuality, the mean seriousness ratings range from a low of 6.04 for India to 9.29 in Iran. The act of abortion varies even more strikingly from 3.03 in Yugoslavia to 9.09 in Iran. The acts of taking drugs and environmental pollution showed less cross-cultural variation, and were perceived as relatively serious. The acts *mala ambigua* elicited a particularly interesting pattern of response. Public protest was clearly the act about which there was widest cross-cultural variation from a low of 2.04 in the U.S. to a high of 9.56—again in Iran.

The third level of analysis is achieved by comparing the variances, assuming once again that the seriousness scale is an equivalent measure across all countries, and interpreting the variances as indicators of the amount of dissensus concerning the seriousness of the acts. Those acts eliciting the smallest variances once again were generally the traditional crimes of robbery, incest, and appropriation, although the New

---

[3]Spearman's Rank Difference correlation was applied to a matrix of the ranks for all six countries. The highest correlation was .99 between India and Iran, and the lowest was .59 between Sardinia and the U.S. All correlations were significant at better than .05 level.

[4]Analysis of variance produced an F significant for all acts. We should note, however, that because of the large N, this is not surprising. To avoid an oversimple interpretation of these differences, analysis of the variations within countries according to sociological variables was undertaken, using multiple regression and analysis of co-variance. These findings are discussed in Chapter 8, so the univariate F tests are not presented here.

York respondents, in stark contrast to all other samples, displayed an extremely high amount of disagreement about the seriousness of incest. Those acts which elicited the highest amount of dissensus were once again the traditional deviances of homosexuality and abortion, and the *mala ambiguae* of protest and not helping. The variance for the *mala nova* offense of environmental pollution appeared to hover around the average, as did that for taking drugs, with the exception of India where considerable dissensus was found.

But we must ask a further question concerning these variances and their relationship to their respective means. What does it mean when, as in some cases such as Italy for the act of homosexuality, the mean seriousness of public protest is extremely low (2.62) yet there is a very high variance (9.98)? Are the means pushed high or low by the responses of a few extremists? If we look at the frequency distributions to these acts for all countries combined, we obtain a clear picture of the structural differentiation of the acts. Although individual countries differed to some extent for particular acts, the general patterning of responses, plotted from the seriousness ratings of all country samples combined provides a framework that may be generally applied to all our samples.

In Chart 2, we see the typical response pattern to traditional crimes—the gross heaping of responses in the most serious category. Incest, supposedly the deepest of traditional crimes of immorality, is the most extreme case. These acts, it is reasonable to conclude, have elicited a broad, cross-national consensus that they are very serious acts.

Chart 3 displays the next gradation from the traditional crimes, the curves of the quasi-crimes. Here, the heaping of responses in the most serious category is not quite so heavy, and the curves rise more gradually from about 3 onwards. It may be argued that because such a large scale was used, respondents tended to respond only in one section of the scale, not using those levels of the scale below 4. However, Charts 4 and 5 demonstrate that this is not the case. The deviant acts in Chart 4 elicited responses in a U-shaped curve, but with the characteristic heaping of responses in the most serious category. Drugs may be seen as a transitional case from crimes *mala prohibita,* moving then to homosexuality, and finally the prototypical case of abortion, with a heaping of responses in the most serious category, but also a strong heaping of responses in the not serious category. The acts *mala ambigua,* display a similar distribution of responses, but much more ac-

CHART 2

Percent Distribution of Seriousness Scores for Traditional
Crimes, (Mala in Se, Mala Antiqua) All Countries Combined*

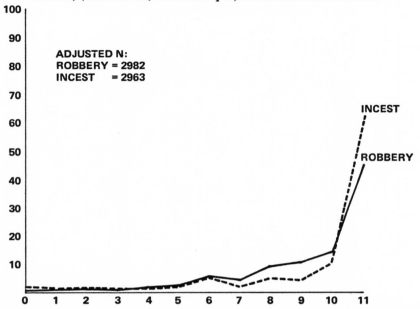

*Because of the different sample sizes, the following weighting procedure was employed in combining
the samples:

India:	.98
Indonesia:	1.0
Iran:	1.04
Italy:	2.5
U.S.:	2.96

Thus, the total sample size for Charts 1 to 4 is adjusted upwards.

centuated, and with a somewhat higher preponderance of responses in the middle of the scale.

A number of hypotheses concerning the consensus-dissensus problem now emerge.

1. One can rely upon at least one-third of all respondents placing any act of any kind into the most serious category (i.e., 11 points on the scale).
2. A typical pattern of consensus is for over 50 percent of respondents to rate acts as very serious (9–11 on the scale), and for zero percent to rate the act as not serious (i.e., less than 4 on the scale). This consensus may be said to apply to both the traditional and quasi-crimes on Charts 2 and 3.

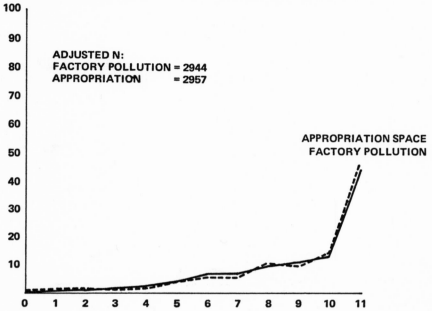

CHART 3

*Percent Distribution of Seriousness Scores for Quasi-Crimes
(Mala Prohibita and Mala Nova), All Countries Combined*

ADJUSTED N:
FACTORY POLLUTION = 2944
APPROPRIATION   = 2957

APPROPRIATION SPACE
FACTORY POLLUTION

3. Conflict may be defined where roughly equal proportions of all respondents assess an act either as very serious or as not serious. In graduated degrees, this applies to the acts of public protest and abortion, where severe potential conflict over norms may be seen to pertain; next (in the order of extent of normative conflict) comes homosexuality and taking drugs.

4. The act of *mala ambigua* (not helping) elicits a characteristic response of a generally random distribution along the scale, with a slight heaping in the very serious category. Rather than describe this pattern as symptomatic of normative conflict, it is more likely a situation of general dissensus—with no clear sides drawn. This is in contrast to conflict which involves a much more factional or divisive public opinion.

However, before we conclude that consensus "really does" exist for some acts, let us look at the extent to which these acts have been defined as criminal.

CHART 4

Percent Distribution of Seriousness Scores for Deviant Acts
(Mala Prohibita), All Countries Combined

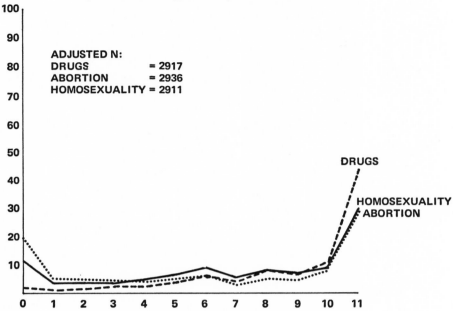

DEFINITION OF THE ACTS

"There is selective and differential perception of every element . . . of a situation involving a criminal act," writes Turk (1969:11), and he concludes, ". . . human fallibility and mendacity insure that the same behavior will sometimes be defined as criminal and on other occasions be defined as noncriminal, and that different behavior will sometimes be labelled as identical behavior."

Perusal of Tables 6 through 11 demonstrates that the definitions applied to the acts, as inferred from choice of control agent, at a general level were only roughly similar. If we rank the acts within each country according to the proportions defining them as criminal (i.e., choosing police as control agents), we find only a mild correlation of these rankings.[5] This may be because the cross-cultural equivalence of

---

[5]Spearman's rank difference correlations applied to these rankings produced correlations ranging from a low of .28 between Sardinia and Iran, to a high of .8 between

123

CHART 5
Percent Distribution of Seriousness Scores for Crimes
(Mala Ambigua), All Countries Combined

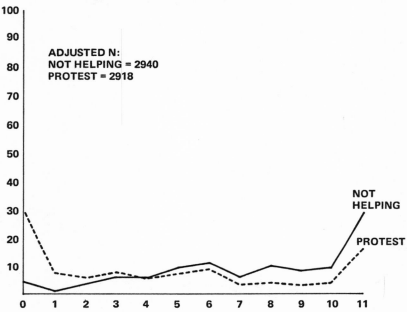

this question is in doubt since institutions of control may vary considerably, depending upon the particular country. However, of the many
social institutions from which the respondents were invited to choose
as agents of control, the institutions of religion, education, and party
politics were rarely chosen in any country. Not even did a reportable
proportion of the Sardinian sample choose religious leader for the act
of abortion, although 9.5 percent did choose religious leader ("priest")
for the act of incest. A minor portion of the New York sample chose
"political official" for the act of appropriation (7.7 percent). We may
conclude that the institutions of religion, education and party politics in
all six countries were not seen as agencies of direct social control in
the sense that people will resort to them to have others controlled. As
can be seen from Tables 6–11, the major social institutions invoked by
the respondents were police, medicine, government bureaucracy, and
the family, with the additional institution of the village chief for Indonesia.

Yugoslavia and the U.S. Of the 14 correlation pairs, 7 were not significant at the .05
level. These were the correlations of Sardinia with Indonesia and Iran, Yugoslavia
with Indonesia and Iran, the U.S. with Indonesia and Iran, and Indonesia with India.

TABLE 6

Perception of the Acts as Criminal According to Percent Choices of Police as Agents of Control

	INDIA (N=480)	INDONESIA (N=500)	IRAN (N=475)	ITALY (SARDINIA) (N=200)	U.S.A. (N=169)	YUGOSLAVIA (N=500)
Robbery	84.2	70.0	81.2	50.0	95.3	91.6
Incest	26.5	26.9	63.5	39.5	20.1	59.6
Appropriation	40.5	58.5	46.4 (bribery)	68.0	21.9	67.6
Homosexuality	12.6	19.6	54.8	18.5	4.1	34.2
Abortion	5.6	26.4	39.8	10.0	2.4	5.4
Taking drugs	22.9 ("gange")	37.7 ("soft")	49.7 (opium)	19.0 ("soft")	35.5 (heroin)	44.2 ("soft")
Factory pollution	36.9	32.2	48.7	45.0	16.0	22.0
Not helping	10.4	15.1	36.4	44.5	31.4	48.8
Public protest	20.3	46.8	43.4	5.0	5.3	35.2

125

TABLE 7

Perception of the Acts as "Bureaucratic Crimes" According to Percent Choices of "Government Official"*

	INDIA (N=480)	INDONESIA (N=500)	IRAN (N=475)	ITALY (SARDINIA) (N=200)	U.S.A. (N=169)	YUGOSLAVIA (N=500)
Robbery	1.6	7.0	4.8	0.0	1.2	1.6
Appropriation	35.6	5.2	22.4	2.0	57.4	16.0
Factory pollution	14.4	15.0	27.2	19.5	73.4	48.8

*Other acts excluded because of negligible proportions choosing a government official.

126

TABLE 8

Perception of the Acts as "Sick" According to Percent of Choices of Doctor or Social Worker*

	INDIA (N=480)	INDONESIA (N=500)	IRAN (N=475)	ITALY (SARDINIA) (N=200)	U.S.A. (N=169)	YUGOSLAVIA (N=500)
Incest	15.0	0.0	11.1	6.5	23.1	9.8
Homosexuality	16.6	.5	13.4	8.0	14.2	16.2
Abortion	16.7	1.2	10.2	1.0	4.7	10.0
Taking drugs	13.1	0.4	13.1	7.5	17.8	21.4

*Other acts excluded because negligible proportions defined these acts as sick in all country samples.

TABLE 9

Perception of the Acts as "Familial Deviance" According to Percent Choices of "Family Only"

	INDIA (N=480)	INDONESIA (N=500)	IRAN (N=475)	ITALY (SARDINIA) (N=200)	U.S.A. (N=169)	YUGOSLAVIA (N=500)
Robbery	5.2	0.4	1.3	3.5	0.0	1.8
Incest	38.0	8.9	10.3	18.0	20.1	11.2
Appropriation	1.2	0.5	2.1	1.5	1.2	0.2
Homosexuality	43.1	23.7	11.6	19.0	5.9	8.6
Abortion	26.4	16.9	18.7	12.0	10.7	4.8
Taking drugs	38.9	13.3	17.5	37.0	23.1	16.2
Factory pollution	0.5	4.4	0.8	12.5	0.0	0.2
Not helping	24.1	25.7	30.3	24.5	13.6	10.2
Public protest	4.1	5.7	22.6	17.0	1.2	2.2

TABLE 10
Perception of the Acts as "Non-deviant" According to Percent Choices of "No One"

	INDIA (N=480)	INDONESIA (N=500)	IRAN (N=475)	ITALY (SARDINIA) (N=200)	U.S.A. (N=169)	YUGOSLAVIA (N=500)
Robbery	2.2	1.8	6.1	41.0	0.6	2.6
Incest	12.9	2.8	6.3	23.5	21.9	7.6
Appropriation	7.0	6.1	19.1	20.0	1.2	9.8
Homosexuality	24.8	8.0	18.3	49.0	69.8	29.4
Abortion	49.6	4.7	23.9	73.5	72.2	72.8
Taking drugs	17.6	4.2	13.1	29.0	10.1	8.8
Factory pollution	5.4	3.0	11.0	15.0	1.2	14.6
Public protest	59.2	21.9	27.9	77.0	83.4	51.6
Not helping	46.2	29.9	19.2	18.5	29.6	28.6

129

TABLE 11

Perception of the Acts as "Village Deviance" for India, Indonesia (N=500) and Iran (N=475) According to Percent Choices of Village Control Agents

| | VILLAGE CHIEF | | | VILLAGE COUNCIL | | MUNICIPAL HEAD | |
	INDIA	INDONESIA	IRAN	INDONESIA	IRAN	INDONESIA	IRAN
Robbery	4.2	18.6	.2	1.8	.8	1.8	1.7
Incest	2.9	47.2	.2	4.3	.6	3.4	2.7
Appropriation	8.6	21.0	.8	2.9	1.1	4.7	2.9
Homosexuality	1.2	37.3	.2	4.0	.2	3.6	.2
Abortion	0.6	38.0	2.3	3.9	.2	3.9	1.5
Taking drugs	5.1	32.9	1.9	2.7	1.3	4.6	0.4
Factory pollution	24.2	31.6	1.5	6.6	1.5	13.6	3.6
Public protest	6.3	19.0	.6	2.4	.4	2.4	.4
Not helping	7.1	24.2	.8	1.1	.4	2.1	0

130

At a deeper level of analysis, it is clear that there was considerable variation across countries in their definitions of all acts. This is in contrast to the measures of opinion and seriousness where there was much less variation. We find, for example, that robbery, our traditional crime of *mala antiqua,* is by no means universally defined as criminal (although again, it tends to be defined as more criminal than other acts). Only 50 percent of the Sardinians defined it as criminal, with proportions ranging up to 91.6 percent of the Yugoslavians defining it as criminal. Many of the differences were so great as to suggest that they were not due to lack of equivalence of the measuring instrument, but rather to specific conditions of the samples. However, the variations found in definition of the act of robbery provide us with the clearest support of consensus theory. Let us consider each act separately, discovering further interesting variations.

Robbery

This act was defined as criminal by all country samples except the Sardinians, which is what the subculture of violence theory would predict: that a criminal subculture will perceive criminal behavior differently from the larger culture. Although undeniable unanimity was reached only for Yugoslavia and the U.S., the definition of it as criminal was also very high for India and Iran, and to a lesser extent Indonesia. But Sardinia is the striking exception, where only 50 percent of respondents said they would report the crime to the police. This is explained by the fact that Orani is a town in the violence area of Sardinia (Ferracuti, et al., 1970) where there is a tradition of violent crime, and also a traditional opposition against the police who are seen as outsiders, since they are usually placed there by the central administration of the Carabinieri. In terms of labelling theory, it might be argued that for 50 percent of the sample, robbery was not a crime in the sense that it would be reported to the police. This does not mean, however, that the respondents necessarily saw the act as "right." On the contrary, when asked how serious the act was, the majority considered it very serious, as we saw earlier. The inference of strong opposition toward reporting the act of robbery is even more reinforced when we see in Table 10 that 41 percent of the Sardinians would report the act to no one. No formal social institution was seen as relevant. The informal means of social control, vendetta, is the main institution of control. We also see in Table 10 that the proportions of all other samples, including Indonesia, defining the act as non-deviant were extremely low. We may conclude therefore, that although there was no unanimous definition of robbery as criminal, there *was* a unanimous view (with the exception of the special case of the subculture of violence) that the act was sufficiently deviant to require control, if not by police, then by a government official.

Appropriation

Understandably, the Sardinians, perhaps cynical towards government, saw appropriation by government officials as more criminal than robbery. In contrast, New Yorkers saw the act more as a "bureaucratic crime" to be dealt with by government officials rather than police, and to some extent this also applied to Iran (where, incidentally, there has been considerable import of American methods of law, economics and government). None of the New York, Yugoslavian, Indonesian or Indian respondents defined the act as non-deviant (by choosing "no one" to report it to) whereas substantial minorities of both Iran and Sardinia did so (Table 10). The Yugoslavians criminalized this act more than all other countries, which may be explained by the fact that the appropriation of "social funds" is considered an especially serious crime against the State in socialist countries.

Incest

How universal is the incest taboo? In practical terms, that is, the chances of being reported to an official defining agency, it seems that at least in Sardinia, New York and India, the act would have been either not reported or kept within the family by more than 40 percent of respondents in each sample (Tables 9 and 10). The act was strongly criminalized by the Iranian and Yugoslavian samples (Table 6), and to some extent also by the Sardinians. Only in New York and India was the act seen as "sick" (by choice of medical worker) by a substantial number (Table 8). Again, however, we must not lose sight of the fact that at least 80 percent of all samples considered that some form of social control was necessary for this act. It remains, therefore, close to universal disapproval.

Homosexuality

It would seem that the liberation of homosexuality from the ranks of deviant behavior has occurred substantially only in the New York

132

sample where 69.8 percent defined it as non-deviant. The act is also regarded as non-deviant by sizeable minorities within other countries except Indonesia. On the other hand, more than half of the Iranian sample would report the act to the police, as would one-third of the Yugoslavians, and roughly 20 percent each of the Sardinians and Indonesians. Small portions of each sample (except Indonesia) did define the act as "sick." However, as far as Sardinia is concerned, homosexuality was defined as non-deviant at a roughly similar rate to robbery. (The general patterning of responses within each country should be kept in mind when making cross-cultural comparisons.) The country clearly different in its response to this act was Indonesia, which predominantly chose the village chief as the agent of control (Table 9). This is understandable since in Indonesia, the village chief remains a very rich and powerful person in the community, and the organization and make-up of the people of Djakarta, continues to be "village oriented."

Abortion

Considering the deeply religious and moral debates which constantly surround this issue, the results for this act are indeed striking. Only in Indonesia and Iran would a substantial number of respondents report this act to the police (Table 6) or, with the addition of India, to the family (Table 9). The proportions who would report the act to the medical system were surprisingly small (Table 8), the largest being that of India. The predominant response for Sardinia, Yugoslavia and New York was that this act was clearly not deviant (i.e., they would report the act to no one). Again, the predominant response for Indonesia was to refer the act to the village chief. Thus, the medical system is not seen by any country sample as a significant control agency for abortion, and this does perhaps explain why "back alley" abortionists command a steady trade. In this instance, it may be that failure to choose the medical system is symptomatic of its perception as an agent of social control.

Taking Drugs

It is difficult to make comparisons across countries for this act, since the type and social meaning of drugs taken in each country varies drastically. In general, taking drugs was criminalized by substantial portions of all samples except the Sardinian and Indian samples. Of special interest was that only the New York and Yugoslav respondents showed any marked tendency to see taking drugs as an illness. Both the Sardinians and Indians strongly preferred to keep the matter within the family or to report it to no one. The predominant response for other countries was also to report it only to the family, with Indonesia in addition preferring the village chief.

Factory Pollution

Factory pollution was not seen as a family matter, but as predominantly more deviant. The Sardinian sample would report this act to the police almost as often as it would robbery. The Iranians and Indonesians were also severe with factory pollution. But rather than the police, all countries preferred to report this act to a government official (Table 7). The Indonesians and this time the Indians preferred to refer the matter to the village level, but it is important to note that the Indonesian sample chose "government official" more for this act than any other act. This is especially significant since the "government official" in Indonesia is seen more as a military or government police agent. The Indian sample saw this act almost as criminal as appropriation of public funds.

Not Helping

The criminality of this act is extremely difficult to interpret by criminal lawyers, let alone laymen. In general, all countries' preferences for control were more or less evenly divided between police, family only, and non-deviance, with a slight general tendency towards criminalization. Typically, Indonesia was the exception to this pattern, preferring to report the act to the village chief rather than the police. We may conclude that there was considerable disagreement as to how to deal with an act of this kind. India was the exception, however, with a clear majority requiring no control beyond the family—certainly no police intervention.

Public Protest

The predominant response for Sardinia and New York was clearly to define this act as non-deviant (Table 10). The other four countries appear to have been deeply divided on this issue. Although half of the Yugoslavian sample saw the act as non-deviant, 35.2 percent would report it to the police, and this applies in similar though less proportions for India, Indonesia, and Iran. One might hypothesize that it is the political and social cohesiveness of the countries that produces differing degrees of consensus. It has been suggested earlier that Orani is a tight, closed community. The response of the New York sample is typical in the wake of Vietnam war protest and government scandal. In India, Indonesia, Yugoslavia, and Iran, there is great diversity of political belief and cultures, each country displaying signs of political instability from time to time (Feirabend, et al., 1969). Thus, the deep divisions in perceptions of this act are to be expected. The strong resistance by the Indians to the social control of this act in any way was perhaps symptomatic of the political unrest which later overtook the country during the Indira Gandhi crisis in 1975. We shall look more closely at these and other socio-economic variables in relation to perceptions of deviance in a later chapter.

SUMMARY AND CONCLUSIONS

"Universal Selective Perception . . ."

The hypothesis of a universal selective perception in regard to deviant behavior was indeed supported. Vast cross-cultural differences were found in respondent's definitions of criminal, deviant and non-deviant behavior. Robbery was perhaps the only act to be consistently defined as criminal, but even this did not receive the unanimous criminalizing responses that it had received from our two prior measures of seriousness and opinion. The failure to define acts as criminal, however, does not mean that there is no consensus concerning their disapproval. As we have seen, although respondents may consider that an act should not primarily be controlled by the police, they may consider that it should be controlled by various other social institutions. It requires only a meagre step to infer that if persons favor the social control of an act, it is by definition "disapproved of" by them. Thus, the most vigorous measure of the lack of disapproval is the choice of no one to control the behavior. There may, however, be a problem in interpreting this response, as the next point suggests.

Defensive Reaction

If we can conceive of the family as an intermediate institution of social control which may be resorted to in order to prevent the intervention of the State, the choice of no one to control deviant behavior may be interpreted as an especially defensive reaction. Although labelling theorists would argue that if respondents would not report an act to anyone, then they are not defining the act as deviant (i.e. because deviance is seen as essentially the product of social control), this can only be valid at one level of analysis. It was seen, for example, that 41 percent of respondents in the Sardinian sample would report the act of robbery to no one. Yet, as we shall see, the majority countenanced severe penal punishments for robbers.

In some circumstances, therefore, the choice of no one to deal with *prima facie* deviant acts may reasonably be interpreted as a defensive reaction. It can be seen from Table 10 that the Sardinians displayed this reaction at a much higher rate than other country samples. The reason is well known by students of the Sardinian subculture: the fear of reprisals and the subsequent system of *omerta* (rule of silence). Of further interest is the finding that the Yugoslavian and Indian samples were the next most likely not to report acts of deviance to anyone. In regard to the former, it would seem that in the socialist society, although the family is used less as a defense against the formal social control of the State over the individual, yet there is considerable individual defensiveness, especially concerning the reporting of environmental pollution and various deviant acts.

In regard to India, the problem is much more complex. The *panchayat,* an ancient and well established rural institution for the conduct of the affairs of villagers (Kumar, 1965), was practically never chosen by respondents as an institution of social control.[6] Thus, intermediate controls between the family and the State appeared to be almost nonexistent, with the exception of "government officials" or the actor's employer for the act of appropriation. It would seem, therefore, that the family in India remains the pivot of social control of all behavior not defined as criminal, but defined as requiring social control. All this

---

[6]An explanation of this may lie in the fact that the *panchavat* in recent years has developed more political power (administered by Non-Brahmans: Beteille, 1965), and is devoted more to political dealings with the State, rather than criminal justice, or deviance issues.

suggests that we must look closely at the perceived role of institutions as agents of control.

Institutions as Agents of Social Control

We may conclude that the universal institutions that the public in six countries will invoke for the purpose of social control of *prima facie* deviant behavior are limited to the police, government bureaucracy, and family.

Respondents from Iran, U.S., and Yugoslavia were generally high reporters to the police. The Iranians were by far the most consistent users, not making a great deal of discrimination among the acts in their choice of police. The Americans and Yugoslavians on the other hand, showed wide discrimination from unanimous criminalization of robbery down to unanimous non-criminalization of abortion. Only in Indonesia, the less economically developed country, was there a clear and consistent preference for an "intermediate" institution of social control, that of village chief. For the two countries most economically developed (U.S.A. and Yugoslavia) the health or medical system was invoked as an "intermediate" means of social control, but even here it was only for a small number of specific acts (incest, homosexuality, taking drugs). As one would also expect, the family played a much less important role in perceptions of deviance for the two developed countries in comparison to Sardinia,[7] Indonesia, Iran and India with the family probably playing the most important role in Sardinia and India. In general, these results support the classic sociological theories concerning the effects of industrialization upon societies: the change from the "village" structure of social life ("gemeinschaft") to the more complex urban life ("gesellschaft") where there is a greater gap between the individual and the society in terms of its agencies of control. But although it is often argued by labelling theorists that the health system has assumed the intermediate position of social control, as far as the layman is concerned according to the data collected, it was not strongly seen as performing this function.

The implications of these findings for current thinking concerning the role of institutions as social control agencies are extensive, especially in relation to the position expounded by the "new criminology"

---

[7]Although Italy is, of course, a highly industrialized country, this particular area of Italy may be said to be more a "subculture" and less developed.

(Taylor, et al., 1974). These writers argue that as modern Western States have developed larger and larger welfare oriented bureaucracies, so a diverse set of massive systems for the selection and removal of deviants out of society has developed. If this is the case, the persons responding to our questions certainly do not see the institutions as performing such a role. And, since the "new criminologists" also argue that selection of deviants for social control purposes also rests heavily upon the "social psychology of social reaction" (i.e. a negotiating or interactional relationship between the definee and the definer, i.e. the public), it would seem crucial to their position that the public see those institutions as agencies of social control.

Although there was a small tendency for people in developed countries to see the medical or social welfare professions as social controllers, this was for only a small and clearly delimited number of acts. Thus, the popular view of the anti-psychiatrists toward the medical profession as tyrannical social controllers of deviance may be superficial. Rather, the work of Solzhenitzyn (1968, 1973) would suggest that massive increases in social control issue directly from great increases in police and para-police bureaucracies, and that the medical and other "helping" professions are later subjected to the power of these police organizations. From the data we have it is unlikely that the medical or helping professions will ever achieve a prominent position as social controllers of deviance, since they lack the support of public opinion. But it is apparent that there is an extensive reservoir of power for police and para-police agencies in regard to a number of deviant acts, especially those of traditional crimes and sins (i.e. robbery and incest). A fascinating contradiction arises with this observation: that those social control agencies which enjoy strong support of the public, are the very ones which, when they become excessively powerful may "imprison" the public which supports it. This is the point which Taylor, et al. (1974) recognize, as does Solzhenitzyn in his many writings. However, in their efforts to place criminological theory within the framework of general social theory, Taylor, et al. tend to lump together all social institutions as though they all perform similarly extensive functions of social control. The data presented here show that this is probably not the case.

Are the institutions of religion, education, and party politics no longer viable institutions for the control of deviant behavior, because, apparently from this survey, they lacked the support of "group opinion"? It would seem that a useful distinction could be made between institutions which are client-centered agencies in the sense that they rely upon clients either to come to them, or to be reported to them, as a result of pressures in the society to do so, and other institutions which are so much a part of the fabric of societies that they are not seen as formal controlling agencies. Rather, one might hypothesize that their work is done through socialization rather than the social control, and that it is only when the work of socialization breaks down do people report behavior to the institutions of social control. The distinction which Parsons (1951:298) made between the processes of "how to" (socialization) and "how not to" (social control) need to be closely researched in their relationship to the various forms of social institutions. Radical critics of Parsons have argued that there is no distinction between social control and socialization—that both are basically coercive. From the data of this study, it can be said that the lay person does not see it that way, and that he draws clear distinctions between those institutions traditionally seen by professionals as institutions of social control (police, government) and those usually seen as socializing institutions (religion, education). The problematic institution from the data in this study is the family.

The Family as an Institution of Social Control

The family has been seen as generally an important agent of control in all countries, especially concerning acts of deviance as opposed to traditional crime. And it was also seen as more important in countries with a more traditional or "community" social structure. The role of the family as a "buttress" between the formal controls of the State and the incipient deviant cannot be underestimated. Studies in medical sociology (Freeman and Simmons, 1961) have emphasized the strong capability of the family to contain deviance within its group, even under very stressful situations. Legally, parents are provided considerable autonomy in dealing with deviant behavior within their families. Yet it would seem from our data that as societies develop socially and economically, so the institution of the family is resorted to much less in order to confine deviance. Deviance becomes more a matter for the State and less a matter for the family unit. Further research into this phenomenon would be enlightening, especially as there is one clear exception to this rule, which is India. One might predict, for example, that the higher possibility to refer deviance out of the family in developed countries would relieve the family of considerable stress which the presence of a deviant in its midst might often generate. But there is undeniably a higher rate of dispersion of family groups in industrialized societies (with the possible exception of developing countries where rural family groups are broken up by migration to the cities). In addition, it is likely that in a traditional society, the family bonds are stronger, social attachments closer, so that it can cope more adequately with a deviant in its midst. When the bonds are weaker, when it is more acceptable for family members to live and work apart, it is more likely that a family will be less inclined to contain a deviant.[8] In this regard the closeness or tightness of the Indian family system has been commented on by many authors (Gore, 1968; Karve, 1965; Mandelbaum, 1970).

The distinction between traditional and modern society should not, however, be overdrawn. As was seen in Table 9, the family figured quite importantly in the U.S. sample for at least two acts (incest and taking drugs), possibly three (abortion), certainly more than for the Yugoslavian group which one might consider somewhat less developed than the U.S. Perhaps the reason for this is the continuing emphasis placed on the "richness" of family life in America, where a man's home is still considered his castle, and there is strong resistance to state's rights over the individual. That is, the family is the symbol in the U.S. of individual sovereignty. In contrast, Yugoslavia is a socialist state, where the society and the State are recognized to have sovereignty before the individual. It can be seen that further cross-cultural research into the relationship between family, state and the control of deviance would be especially fruitful in shedding light upon this basic philosophical rift between the socialist and American views of the individual in society.

The Preferred Societal Sanction

PUNISHMENT. At the general level of analysis, it is apparent that there was considerable agreement as to the amount of official punishment appropriate to each act (Table 12). If we rank the acts within each country according to the proportions punishing them, we find that there

---

[8]This is, perhaps, another way of stating Hirschi's control theory of delinquency (Hirschi, 1969) in terms of social development. Although this approach would emphasize, a little more than does Hirschi, the family's willingness to control the delinquent, in contrast to the incipient delinquent "controlling himself" depending on the strength of his family attachment. Both aspects are no doubt equally important, and point up the extremely complex relationship between the mechanisms of social control and socialization which operate within the family.

is general agreement in ranks across all countries.[9] In general, the acts most heavily punished by all countries were those of robbery, appropriation, and factory pollution. Incest followed closely, but with the clear exception of the U.S. sample. Perhaps the most striking finding here was the apparently inconsistent responses of the Sardinians who ranked among the highest proportions punishing robbery—an act which half of the sample had previously stated it would report to no one.

The type and severity of punishments favored in each country are also noteworthy. For the traditional crimes of robbery and incest, prison was by far the most popular punishment favored by all country samples. The Iranians displayed the most severely punitive attitude in terms of the proportions choosing prison, and also from their selection of punishments: 20 percent favored some type of corporal punishment (usually a form of mutilation) and 10 percent favored capital punishment for these acts. For the acts of environmental pollution, although prison featured quite strongly, the predominant punishments favored were heavy fines in all countries.

The differential punishment of the deviant acts is also of special interest. For homosexuality, the U.S. sample was clearly not punitive, whereas a sizeable minority for every other country did favor some form of punishment. However, when it came to abortion, the U.S. was joined by Yugoslavia and India as clearly non-punitive, in contrast to almost 50 percent of the Indonesian and Iranian samples respectively favoring punishment (usually prison, and for Iran, often mutilation).

Taking drugs was another matter, with small minorities of all samples favoring punishment. However, we should note in this regard that the drug specified for the U.S. sample was that of heroin—a "hard" drug, whereas for all other samples the cultural equivalent of soft drugs was used. Thus, the low punitiveness of the American sample is very significant, especially in the light of recent trends toward increased penalization of this behavior (Newman and Trilling, 1974).

For the deviances *mala ambigua,* we also find a generally low level of punitiveness. There were, however, some striking exceptions. For public protest, Yugoslavia, Iran, and India considered this act worthy of punishment at twice the rate than did American, Sardinian, or Indonesian samples. We can only speculate at this stage on the reasons for this finding. It is easier to explain the lower punitiveness than the

---

[9]Spearman's Rank Difference Correlation was applied to a matrix of the ranks for each country. All except one were significant at a level above .05, with the lowest correlation of .38 between Iran and the U.S. and a high of .88 between Iran and Sardinia.

TABLE 12
The Preferred Societal Sanctions*
(Percentages)

ACT AND SANCTION	INDIA (N=497)	INDONESIA (N=500)	IRAN (N=475)	ITALY (SARDINIA) (N=200)	U.S.A. (N=169)	YUGOSLAVIA (N=500)
Robbery						
treatment	6.2	0.8	5.4	7.0	16.8	0.6
punishment	85.6	89.6	87.0	92.0	79.6	94.8
nothing	8.0	5.2	7.6	4.0	0.0	1.8
Incest						
treatment	29.3	12.4	17.2	41.0	62.7	41.4
punishment	45.7	55.0	82.3	62.5	12.4	50.8
nothing	24.9	25.4	2.8	4.5	16.0	2.2
Appropriation						
treatment	2.0	0.4	4.4	4.0	6.0	0.0
punishment	93.1	87.4	82.1	91.0	85.7	90.2
nothing	4.9	7.6	13.6	4.5	1.8	2.0
Homosexuality						
treatment	26.9	14.4	26.8	65.5	33.7	58.8
punishment	20.2	21.6	60.9	22.5	5.9	17.4
nothing	52.9	57.6	12.3	9.5	60.4	13.0
Abortion						
treatment	5.6	6.4	13.5	15.0	14.9	1.0
punishment	9.2	43.8	48.4	32.0	4.0	11.2
nothing	85.1	45.2	38.1	52.5	77.5	80.8

Taking drugs						
treatment	23.0	19.8	68.9	63.0	78.1	68.4
punishment	21.4	25.4	15.8	4.0	15.4	18.2
nothing	55.8	48.0	15.1	15.0	1.2	5.6
Factory pollution						
treatment	3.0	2.6	1.1	2.0	1.2	0.2
punishment	82.3	46.8	78.2	62.5	87.0	76.2
nothing	14.7	42.2	20.8	26.5	6.5	14.8
Public protest						
treatment	1.6	3.6	5.3	1.5	3.0	0.2
punishment	19.2	10.6	22.6	7.5	5.3	21.2
nothing	79.4	73.2	71.9	85.5	91.7	60.4
Not helping						
treatment	5.4	2.4	7.1	2.5	11.6	0.2
punishment	15.2	8.4	22.6	59.0	14.7	42.6
nothing	77.3	84.0	70.1	38.0	56.2	55.4

*"Treatment" = choice of probation, mental hospital, other treatment.
"Punishment" = choice of prison, fines, corporal or capital punishment, other punishment.
"Nothing" = choice of "nothing" or "warning only."

higher. Americans have always prided themselves on freedom of speech; the Sardinians insist on their right openly to resist government from the outside; the Indonesians having experienced many occupations in their country in the last half century, and having lost a Western style democracy for Sokarno's "guided democracy" not too long ago, may understandably feel the right and necessity for public protest. The higher levels of punishment favored by Yugoslavia and Iran, may be explained by the totalitarian nature of the regime. India, a democracy at the time of the survey, is more difficult to explain, unless the results display some disquiet on the part of conservatives over public protests that were occurring prior to the Indira Gandhi crisis. In addition, India has a very long tradition of public, mass protest popularized by Mahatma Gandhi about whom there is a great deal of deep, divided sentiment.

The act of not helping also provides us with some interesting puzzles. We can see from Table 12 that 59 percent of the Sardinians would punish this act, of which the majority chose prison as the punishment (Table 13). Again, we can explain this finding by referring to specific attributes of the subculture. *Omerta,* the code of silence in the subculture of violence, encourages individuals to "look the other way," in the face of someone else in danger. The respondents' answers here starkly display the double bind in which they find themselves. The overall punitiveness of the Sardinians was almost as severe as the Iranians. It is clear that a very deep sentiment has been tapped. While the rule of *Omerta* requires that they look the other way when another is in danger, respondents nevertheless know that it is probably morally wrong to do so. The reason they do not go to help is, of course, that they are too frightened. Thus, when it comes to a choice of official societal sanctions, they strongly favor severe punishment of those who do not help.

For the Yugoslavians, on the other hand, the high punitiveness is explained by the more obvious and direct ethic of Marxism: the idea of community and of responsibility for one's neighbor requires that one should go to his assistance. However, socialist society allows the State the clear right to intervene if persons do not abide by this ethic. Hence, the harsh punishment for this act.

The mean months of prison displayed in Table 13 offer particularly interesting contrasts concerning the severity of sanction. The table is, however, difficult to interpret, since the averages are computed only on the basis of those who chose prison. If all people who did not choose prison were included (i.e. as zeros), the means would be much lower.

144

TABLE 13
Mean Months of Prison*

ACT	INDIA	INDONESIA	IRAN	ITALY (SARDINIA)	U.S.A.	YUGOSLAVIA
Robbery	13.4 N=255	14.2 N=318	20.1 N=202	101.9 N=149	51.9 N=89	41.0 N=421
Incest	57.4 N=118	30.3 N=199	93.3 N=69	162.0 N=67	120.5 N=12	100.4 N=151
Appropriation	32.6 N=179	44.3 N=259	35.4 N=121	96.7 N=145	75.5 N=58	80.7 N=319
Homosexuality	25.6 N=37	11.8 N=72	57.1 N=86	98.7 N=31	90.0 N=1	56.6 N=54
Abortion	16.2 N=20	20.9 N=171	41.9 N=77	61.7 N=52	30.0 N=1	28.6 N=36
Taking drugs	16.6 N=30	10.1 N=83	47.2 N=16	72.2 N=20	89.3 N=8	42.4 N=70
Factory pollution	21.3 N=107	20.3 N=70	43.0 N=46	68.43 N=37	74.1 N=20	44.8 N=87
Public protest	4.2 N=21	7.3 N=41	36.4 N=40	48.2 N=10	0.0 N=0	36.0 N=106
Not helping	12.1 N=13	5.1 N=15	39.8 N=38	76.7 N=90	109.2 N=5	26.1 N=98

*Responses above 20 years were recoded as 240 months, to avoid distortion of the means by extreme values. The N of those choosing prison only was used.

145

Such a measure would not accurately depict the severity of sanctioning reactions since for some countries, a sizeable proportion chose capital or corporal punishment. For the moment, however, this is not a serious problem since we are only concerned with the cross-cultural comparisons of "prison choosers." We will return to it in Chapter 9 when we consider the relationships between public perceptions and the law.

Studying Table 13, one is struck by the extremely low means of prison displayed by the Indonesians, which contrasts with their general high intolerance of deviance as displayed by other measures. This may suggest the presence of some response bias in that with measures concerned with opinion, not directly related to behavior, respondents were more likely to acquiesce. But, when required to state specifically the amount of prison term, respondents displayed much more leniency in comparison to other countries. This is in contrast to Iran, in which we also suspected response bias, where respondents consistently displayed their extremely high level of intolerance by choosing very long prison terms. In addition, it can be seen that the U.S. sample, usually the more tolerant of all countries, displayed generally very high means of prison, especially for the traditional acts of incest and appropriation. The perplexing case here is robbery, which had been so unanimously severely sanctioned by all other measures for the U.S. sample, received a mean prison term much lower than the other two traditional crimes—indeed, lower than that for homosexuality, the more tolerated act. A similar pattern of results is apparent for other countries, especially for the acts of homosexuality, abortion, taking drugs, and not helping for all countries except Indonesia. We may conclude from these observations that those people who wish to sanction deviant acts, are motivated by highly punitive feelings. According to the proportions in each country, they may be seen as constituting a group which harbors highly punitive reactions and is clearly set apart from the rest of the respondents. It is not surprising therefore that there are strong emotions when the questions about the legality of these traditional deviances are brought into public focus.

TREATMENT. The "medical model," once a dominant mode of explaining crime and deviance, has come under considerable attack over the last two decades (Hakeem, 1958; Schur, 1969:61–67; Newman, 1970) by criminologists and sociologists. Germane to the more recent criticisms has been the claim that the medical model was a self-perpetuating explanation of deviance, in that once persons were labelled as "sick" by the doctor, they more or less became that way, because others perceived them as such (Schur, 1971:60–65). These "labelling theorists," as they were called, rarely considered the process that led up to the actual official labelling by the doctor—the very complicated referral process.[10] If the treatment model is so dominant as a mode of explaining and dealing with deviance in everyday life, we should expect respondents to recommend treatment for the acts presented in our study. As we have noted earlier, the extent to which persons would report acts to the doctor was severely limited to the acts of homosexuality, abortion, and taking drugs, and this mainly for the U.S. and Yugoslavian samples.

In the choice of treatment as an official sanction, we see a generally high preparedness to do so. Treatment was favored by close to 50 percent of respondents from Sardinia, U.S., and Yugoslavia for the acts of incest, homosexuality, and taking drugs. The treatment model is indeed more dominant in the U.S. where even a comparatively high proportion of respondents was prepared to refer robbers for treatment. Of interest also was the very high choice of treatment by Iranians, suggesting that they are extreme in their desire to control deviance both punitively and through medical means. The only act to which the Iranians did not respond punitively was that of drugs, for which instead there was a very strong preference for treatment. This may reflect the Iranian government's recent introduction of medical treatment centers to which addicts may turn to avoid criminal prosecution.

The type of treatment is interesting. Although 62 percent of the U.S. sample desired treatment for the offender, the type of treatment favored was predominantly that of a mental asylum. It can be seen therefore that the control of this act is very definitely desired by the U.S. sample. This applied also to the U.S. choice of treatment for robbery. In general, country samples choosing treatment for the act of incest usually favored mental asylum. In contrast, preferences for the treatment of homosexuality were mainly for "out-patient" treatment, with the exception of Iran which again favored an asylum. All samples favored the out-patient treatment of taking drugs.

NOTHING. This category is our best measure of preferences for no control. The act of public protest was the only act which came any-

---

[10]The exceptions are: Mechanic, 1969, 1962; Friedson, 1961; Goffman, 1963; and Newman, 1975, where the problem of dealing with deviants in everyday life is discussed, and the often complicated paths to seeking doctor's help are outlined from various points of view.

where near being universally assessed as deserving no official sanctions. The main exception was the Yugoslavian sample, although indeed a majority nevertheless considered that it should be penalized. Abortion and not helping came close seconds. The Iranians and Indonesians were less favorable to doing nothing for not helping. The only other two acts that received considerable choices of doing nothing were homosexuality for the U.S., India, and Indonesia, and taking drugs for India and Indonesia. Without the extreme proportions of some other countries, India may be seen to have generally favored doing nothing for a wider number of acts. In fact, considerable proportions favored doing nothing for all acts except robbery and appropriation. The Indians were closely followed by the Indonesians, a sizeable proportion of which favored doing nothing even for factory pollution.

CONCLUSIONS. Reactions to this question may be summarized under three headings: 1) the number of acts considered sanctionable; 2) the amount of sanction favored; and 3) the severity of type of sanction. By all three of the measures, the Iranian sample closely followed by the Sardinian sample was clearly the most punitive. It has been suggested that these responses are symptomatic of deep, emotional feelings. Treatment was favored generally more by the American sample, which is taken as evidence that the "medical model" (an indigenous Western way of perceiving deviance) dominated especially for the acts of incest, homosexuality, and taking drugs.

Although the U.S. sample was almost unanimous when it perceived that nothing should be done for an act, in smaller proportions the Indian and Indonesian samples were prepared to "do nothing" about more acts than any other country sample. The act of public protest was the only act to elicit overall cross-cultural preference for nothing to be done.

Knowledge and Belief

As we shall see in Chapter 9, for a number of act descriptions, it was extremely difficult for the legal experts in each country to state categorically whether the acts were prohibited by the law or not. Such being the case, we should not be surprised if there is confusion and uncertainty among our respondents. Table 14 shows that the samples from Yugoslavia, Iran, and India displayed more lack of knowledge than the remaining countries. For Iran and India, however, the ambiguity of the law may be a major factor. The abortion law in India was undergoing a

TABLE 14
"Is This Act Prohibited by the Law?"
(Percent "Yes")

	INDIA (N=512)	INDONESIA (N=500)	IRAN (N=475)	ITALY (SARDINIA) (N=200)	U.S.A. (N=169)	YUGOSLAVIA (N=500)
Robbery	86.2	98.0	91.6	98.5	97.6	92.8
Incest	67.1*	89.5	95.6	87.5	76.9	82.6
Appropriation	88.6	97.8	86.1	94.0	85.2	94.4
Homosexuality	45.6	66.0*	81.9	77.0*	52.5	54.6
Abortion	24.3	88.7	84.9*	90.5	8.3*	24.4*
Taking drugs	53.8	80.3	87.0	73.0	97.6	72.8
Factory pollution	65.2	75.0	73.7*	72.5	69.2	56.2*
Public protest	52.4	68.8	82.1*	57.0	0.6*	57.6*
Not helping	14.2*	45.4	31.6*	44.5	7.1*	30.8

*Indicates that "yes" would be an "incorrect" legal response.

149

complex revision to make it less criminalizing at the time of the survey. In Iran it is not against the law for a woman to obtain an abortion through a doctor. However, it is against the law for the doctor to perform one unless to save the mother's life. Technically, therefore, the act described in our study is not necessarily against the law. In practice, it probably would turn out to be. The "mistaken" knowledge here may be a more realistic appraisal of the "law applied," especially for the act of public protest in Iran. It is well known that the totalitarian regime of Iran does not tolerate open criticism, let alone public protest—that is, in practice. Only technically is the act not prohibited by the law. This also most likely applies to the act of protest in Yugoslavia.

The mistake on the part of both the Iranians and Yugoslavians concerning factory pollution is an interesting case of opinion anticipating the law. Because of the pervasive mass communications, and current "crisis" concerning the environment, this act is slowly becoming criminalized around the world, and in this case, the publics of Yugoslavia and Iran anticipated the legislation. A similar rationale probably applies to the act of taking drugs in Yugoslavia, where at the time of the survey there was no drug problem, but the U.S. fight against drug traffic conducted at an international level was receiving wide attention. It is most likely therefore that the Yugoslavian respondents were anticipating legislation.

The mistaken belief in Sardinia and Indonesia that homosexuality was prohibited by the law is symptomatic of the inherent qualities of traditional deviances: they are believed to be morally wrong, and so it is assumed that they must also be prohibited by the law. The same rationale also no doubt applies to the case of incest for India, where 67.1 percent mistakenly considered the act punishable by the law. The act of homosexuality elicited the broadest lack of knowledge across all countries except Iran. At least half or more in each country either did not know or was incorrect as to whether the act was prohibited. The same also applies to the act of not helping, for which there were no exceptions. We can see that its classification as *mala ambiqua* is shown by this data: the respondents were confused to about the same degree as is the law!

Another possible effect upon belief, which has been implied to some extent so far, is the level of government activity in dealing with the various crimes and deviances. This may apply especially to acts of deviance, which, according to labelling theorists, are most commonly defined by the practices of official defining agencies. The relatively high mistaken belief that taking drugs was not prohibited by the law in India, for example, may be explained by the fact that police do not enforce the law, so that people come to think that it is therefore not illegal.

Perceptions of Government Activity

If we rank the acts according to the amount of perceived government activity, we find that there is no broad similarity across all countries.[11] There was, however, a general tendency, as can be seen in Table 15, for respondents in all countries to perceive the government as most active for the traditional crime of robbery, and least active for the ambiguous crime of not helping. The extent to which the government was seen as active in stopping all other crimes varied considerably from country to country, which is understandable since the methods and organization for dealing with crime both on a day-to-day basis, and in terms of national policy, we know vary considerably cross-nationally.

There are also variations within countries which are of interest comparatively. First, it is apparent that the U.S. sample has displayed the widest variation in perceptions of least to most active, suggesting that these respondents are either more finely discriminating in their perceptions of the acts (an hypothesis born out by their responses to other questions), or that the official agencies of control are particularly selective in their enforcement of these acts. In contrast, the Sardinians displayed very little discrimination among the acts, tending to see the government as generally much less active in comparison to all other countries. Again, this probably illustrates the rather cynical view that Sardinians have of outside government: that it is there to oppress, not to deal with deviant behavior. In contrast to Sardinia, the government was seen as generally very active in stopping all behaviors in Indonesia, Iran, and Yugoslavia: the totalitarian countries. India appears to be transitional between these and the U.S. in this regard. Further evidence for this relationship is gotten from the perceptions of government activity in stopping public protest. All samples, except the U.S., rated their governments as very active in this area.

Some puzzling responses to particular acts are interesting. The Sardinians rated the government as most active in stopping incest. This

---

[11]Spearman Rank Difference Correlation was applied to a matrix of the countries. The only correlations significant at better than .05 were India with Indonesia (.80), India with U.S. (.64), India with Yugoslavia (.89), Indonesia with Iran (.62), Indonesia with Yugoslavia (.73), Indonesia with U.S. (.85), and Yugoslavia with U.S. (.72).

TABLE 15

How Active Is the Government in Stopping Acts of this Kind?
(Percent responding "active or very active")

ACT	INDIA (N=467)	INDONESIA (N=460)	IRAN (N=475)	ITALY (SARDINIA) (N=200)	U.S.A. (N=169)	YUGOSLAVIA (N=500)
Robbery	70.8	96.1	86.3	43.5	79.9	83.4
Incest	58.2	71.7	91.3	59.0	31.4	73.8
Appropriation	70.7	84.8	58.2	40.0	60.9	81.4
Homosexuality	27.7	50.0	69.4	35.0	16.6	51.0
Abortion	35.0	70.1	76.4	58.5	24.3	41.0
Taking drugs	41.6	87.4	77.5	36.0	87.0	75.4
Factory pollution	58.0	60.5	66.5	33.0	63.9	53.0
Public protest	58.2	40.4	95.7	51.5	37.3	75.6
Not helping	25.7	42.7	60.4	39.5	10.1	50.4

seems a strange response when one considers that this act is only against the law in Italy if it creates a "public scandal," so that in practice it is rarely prosecuted. The only interpretation that presents itself is that the government is seen as "meddling" in areas of private behavior. The same interpretation may apply to abortion.

The very low proportions seeing the government as active in stopping bribery in Iran is also symptomatic of that country's long difficulty with official corruption, which is almost an everyday way of doing business, even though serious penalties have been introduced. Finally, the U.S. respondents' perception of the government as active in stopping pollution may reflect the many anti-pollution laws enacted over the past five years in the United States.

CONCLUSIONS

We have now completed a general comparative survey of the six components of deviance perception. We have seen that, depending on the level of analysis, there is a universal (i.e. cross-cultural) consensus concerning the disapproval of a number of crimes and deviances. This applies especially at the general level of opinion and intensity of reaction. A generally deep, probably emotional reaction, as measured by choice of sanctions was also found cross-culturally.

Wide variations occurred in the definition of the acts. Even here, considerable consensus could be found at the general level concerning those acts that respondents thought should be subject to social control. The variations occurred when we considered the *forms* of social control deemed appropriate to the various acts. Finally, there appeared to be only minimal cross-cultural similarity in respondent's knowledge of the law or perception of the government in stopping the described behaviors.

The question which now confronts us is: How are these components of deviance perception organized?

seven
___

THE STRUCTURE OF
DEVIANCE PERCEPTION

INTRODUCTION

The type of relativism to which many of our remarks and data analysis
so far have been addressed is that usually termed by moral
philosophers as descriptive relativism, the extreme form of which is
cultural relativism. The thesis of this position is that there is a fundamental disagreement about values, and that this disagreement is basically a function of enculturation.[1] There are many logical and definitional difficulties with this position, especially concerning the meaning
of fundamental. However, for the sake of clarity, we will reserve discussion of this and other problems relating to relativism and universality until the final chapter.

There is another form of relativism in which, according to Brandt
(1967:75), "a person might accept descriptive relativism, but still suppose that there is always only one correct moral appraisal of a given
issue." In the social sciences, the only work empirically to support this
view is that of Kohlberg and Turiel (1972) and Tapp (1971) who have
argued and demonstrated to some extent the universal existence of
stages in moral development, based upon a Piagetian model of cognitive development. There is no necsssity to embroil ourselves in the
additional ethical problems that a development model implies. But
nevertheless our data provide us with a unique possibility to test the
proposition that although particular deviant acts may be viewed superficially as different across cultures, this may merely be a function of
enculturation—that beneath this cultural encrustation may lie a common structure, or common way of organizing perceptions of deviance.
Our aims in this chapter, then, are to investigate:

___

[1]The most influential philosophical defense of descriptive relativism may be found in
Westermarck, E. A. (1906). Evidence for extreme cultural relativism is presented in
Benedict (1934).

1. Whether a meaningful grouping or classification of criminal and deviant acts according to public perceptions of them is possible. (We have already seen in Chapter 6 that there were typical patterns of response as far as seriousness was concerned, and these conformed roughly to the classification assumed at the inception of the study.)
2. The extent to which such a classification might apply cross-culturally.
3. Whether a patterning of the components of deviance perception applies to particular act classifications.
4. If such patterning, when found, applies cross-culturally.

To achieve these aims some preliminary manipulations of the data were necessary.

CONSTRUCTION OF THE NORM RESISTANCE SCALE (NRS)

As we saw in the distributions of responses to the seriousness scales, curves were skewed heavily to one or both ends of the scale, especially the "serious" end of the scale. In an attempt to take these problems into account, since they could adversely affect the statistical analysis, we decided to construct a summarizing scale that sampled only the extreme lower ends of each component of deviance perception. An additional reason for choosing the lower ends of the components was our concern of possible response bias, already mentioned. By sampling the "resistance" aspects of the component measures, it was hoped that a more valid measure would be obtained. Thus, the operational definition of norm resistance was: a reaction to a description of behavior characterized by a) *a strong decriminalizing attitude,* b) *a preference for informal or no control of such behavior over other more formal social controls,* c) *an assessment of the act as not serious,* and d) *the preference for "nothing" or "only a warning" to be given to the actor over other possibly harsher and controlling dispositions.*[2]

Mean NRS scores for each act in each country are presented in

---

[2]Methodological details concerning the construction of the NRS can be seen in the Appendix. The Spearman-Brown reliability was computed, and the scale was found to have a reasonable overall reliability ranging from a low of .55 for the act of incest in Yugoslavia, to a high of .88 for protest, also for Yugoslavia. Most coefficients were around .7.

Table 16. The means ranged from a low of .0769 for New Yorkers' resistance to the control of robbery, to a high of 6.16 for the Sardinians on protest. In general, taking all countries together, the acts eliciting highest norm resistance were protest ($\overline{X}=4.2367$), abortion ($\overline{X}=3.2254$), homosexuality ($\overline{X}=2.0868$), and individual pollution ($\overline{X}=1.1446$). The least resisted were robbery ($\overline{X}=.3783$), appropriation ($\overline{X}=.4055$) and factory pollution ($\overline{X}=.5427$). Taking all acts together, the countries displaying highest norm resistance were U.S.A. and India ($\overline{X}=2.08934$ and 2.0831 respectively), followed by Italy ($\overline{X}=1.8055$), Iran ($\overline{X}=1.6909$), Yugoslavia ($\overline{X}=1.4708$) and finally Indonesia ($\overline{X}=.0902$). However, in spite of these very broad differences among the countries, there was considerable agreement as to the general ranking of acts in terms of norm resistance, which we would expect from our previous analysis in Chapter 6. In fact, a matrix of Spearman's Rank Difference Correlations was developed for the rankings of acts for all countries, and the correlations were all significant at a greater than .05 level. The lowest correlation was between Sardinia and Indonesia (.70) and the highest between Sardinia and India (.93). We may conclude for the moment that there was universal (as far as our diverse countries are concerned) agreement as to the order in which the control of each of these deviant behaviors should be resisted. However, comparison of rank ordering is only one measure of agreement.

It may be argued that although there is evidence of general agreement across countries, this may merely be superficial and that there may be extensive disagreement within each country. Furthermore, some theorists have argued that it is the extent of disagreement about the sanctioning of behavior which separates deviant from criminal behavior.

If we take the standard deviation[3] as our measure of agreement, we find from Table 16 that agreement within each country is roughly similar across countries for the acts of taking drugs, and not helping. Disagreement concerning robbery, although generally minimal, was higher for the Sardinian, Iranian, Yugoslavian, and Indian samples, compared to the much lower standard deviations of the Indonesians and New Yorkers. This difference may be explained on the one hand by the higher resistance to governmental authority characteristically displayed by the Sardinians, because of their closed subcultural lifestyle,

---

[3]The qualitative or sociological components of disagreement will be dealt with in the following chapter. We are concerned here only with disagreement in general.

TABLE 16
Norm Resistance Scale
Raw Mean Scores for Each Act and Each Country

		INDIA (N=512)	INDONESIA (N=500)	IRAN (N=479)	ITALY (SARDINIA) (N=200)	U.S.A. (N=169)	YUGOSLAVIA (N=500)
Robbery	Mean	.4473	.148	.3716	.9600	.0769	.266
	S.D.	.8353	.4588	.9394	1.0696	.3450	.9126
Incest	Mean	1.0020	.544	.3424	.785	1.5325	.346
	S.D.	1.1845	.9043	.8628	1.1556	2.1823	.7717
Appropriation	Mean	.3711	.264	.6889	.525	.2604	.324
	S.D.	.8364	.6317	1.2615	.9075	.6924	.8369
Homosexuality	Mean	2.4102	1.288	.9937	1.685	4.7219	1.422
	S.D.	2.1095	1.3025	1.6973	1.6027	3.0744	1.8294
Abortion	Mean	4.0371	.922	1.8205	3.195	4.7278	4.65
	S.D.	2.2601	1.1483	2.5163	2.4096	2.3673	2.6171
Taking drugs	Mean	2.1660	.8720	.9123	1.345	.935	.658
	S.D.	1.7985	1.0573	1.4524	1.3949	1.736	1.1882
Factory pollution	Mean	.4063	.68	.5177	.78	.1183	.754
	S.D.	.8317	.8872	.9166	1.1481	.4200	1.2167
Public protest	Mean	5.0625	2.0680	2.7537	6.1600	5.716	3.66
	S.D.	2.9984	2.1148	2.8582	2.9611	2.0154	3.3411
Not helping	Mean	2.8457	2.228	2.1628	1.315	2.2426	1.788
	S.D.	1.8104	1.5048	1.7401	1.4719	1.9009	1.8137

and on the other hand, the high agreement shown by the New Yorkers concerning robbery probably represents the typical American and especially New Yorkers' fear of violent crime.

In general, for the acts of incest, factory pollution, and homosexuality, the New York sample differed from all other countries, where extent of disagreement was roughly similar, although again, India tended more toward the U.S. pattern. For incest and homosexuality, there was much greater disagreement among the New York respondents. Inspection of the distribution pattern of responses to this act also showed this disagreement to be factional, in the sense that there were fewer in the middle—either respondents strongly advocated resistance to the sanctioning of these acts or they very strongly advocated that they should be sanctioned. Again, we would expect this response pattern in a highly diversified society as the U.S. where it has long been the fashion for interest groups to campaign for or against various forms of deviance. The high consensus among the U.S. respondents concerning factory pollution is no doubt due to the current preoccupation of the media, legislative, and interest groups in this area. It would seem that this has to some extent spread to other countries, although strangely enough, not so much to the other industrialized country, Yugoslavia. The other major differences between countries are those of the Belgradian's high disagreement concerning public protest compared to other countries, and the very high agreement concerning abortion in Indonesia. The former may be explained by the extensive history of political and factional disagreement among the Yugoslavians, the Serbo-Croatian problem to name only one. The latter finding is most likely evidence for the more conservative view of sex-related behavior in the more traditional society of Indonesia. It will be noted also that the Indonesians displayed much less resistance to this act as deviance compared to all other countries.

What conclusion can be drawn from this data? We have seen that by rank ordering the acts in terms of norm resistance there was almost universal agreement across country samples. However, when the specific measures of the NRS were taken as equivalent measures across cultures, wide variations in norm resistance were observed. There are three possible interpretations of this data. First, that the ordering of the acts was superficial and did not really measure the extent of variation across cultures. Second, that the NRS is a more searching measure and therefore revealed gross differences not only across countries, but within countries. Third, that the NRS cannot be taken as being an equivalent measure across cultures, so that although we have uncovered quantifiable differences in norm resistance, this is simply because one sample responds in one area of the scale, and another at a different area. Indeed, it was apparent from the seriousness scale that Indonesians and Iranians tended much more than other respondents to answer only within the top three points of the scale. Thus, one might conclude that although the intensity of resistance to norms may vary from culture to culture, the patterning of perceptions of deviance may not. It was noted above that Kohlberg and his associates argued for universal structure or moral evaluation. To go further into this question, therefore, factor analysis was performed for the acts within each country.[4] Two aspects of the results of factor analysis might be considered as evidence for universalization of the structure of deviance perception: if a similar number of factors were found for each country, and if these factors grouped the acts in roughly similar categories. Table 17 displays the results of the factor analysis (after orthogonal rotation varimax solution) for each country.

The interpretation of this table is complex, so we will begin with the more obvious points. First, it is indeed striking that, with the slight exceptions of U.S.A. and India, three factors only were found to underlie reactions to deviance. Although the grouping of the acts according to these factors differed somewhat from country to country, it is possible to discern some consistent patterning across all countries.

The first factor may be identified as the *deviance-protest factor*. Although various other acts were grouped under this factor, the consistently core acts of the factor were taking drugs, abortion, and homosexuality—the three acts most commonly regarded as "deviance" in the sociological literature. The grouping of other acts with these core acts in the different countries may perhaps give a clue as to the underlying perception of deviance in each country. Protest is included in this deviance factor for U.S.A.: the study and societal image of deviance in the U.S.A. has been dominated by protest over the last ten years. Indeed, we find protest grouped in this factor for all countries. The possible exception was Indonesia, and it will be noted from

---

[4]The factor analysis was performed within each country. Since the analysis so far had displayed such culturally specific patterns of response, pooling such diverse groups of respondents would have created a highly artificial sample, and application of factor analysis to such a sample would, in the writer's opinion, have biased the results in favor of the universalization hypothesis. Undoubtedly a number of factors would have been found, but then one could only argue that they were common to the artificial sample, not to all separate samples. The successive factor analytic method adopted in this study is much more rigorous, similar to a series of replications on diverse samples.

TABLE 17

Factor Loadings* (after Rotation) for Each Act Based upon the Norm Resistance Scale

	INDIA N=512	INDONESIA N=500	IRAN N=479	ITALY (SARDINIA) N=200	U.S.A. N=169	YUGOSLAVIA N=500
Deviance-Protest	Abortion .72 Protest .31 No help .35	Drugs .32 Protest .59 Abortion .41 Homosexuality .46 Factory pollution .21 Not helping .33	Drugs .64 Protest .57 Abortion .58 Homosexuality .39 Robbery .39 Incest .40 Bribery .33	Drugs .48 Protest .40 Abortion .48 Homosexuality .68 Robbery .24 Incest .52	Drugs .24 Protest .48 Abortion .64 Homosexuality .67	Drugs .24 Protest .48 Abortion .60 Homosexuality .43 Not helping .35
Factor...	I'	II'	I'	I'	I'	I'
Percent of variation	45.6	17.0	75.6	52.0	52.8	62.2
Moral indignation	Drugs .29 Incest .23 Homosexuality .68 Abortion	Bribery .31 Incest .89 Homosexuality .25 Not helping .42	Bribery .43 Incest .36 Homosexuality .41 Not helping .38	Robbery .62 Appropriation .48 Factory pollution .34	Drugs .43 Incest .83 Homosexuality .49	Drugs .49 Incest .37 Homosexuality .36 Robbery .44 Appropriation .40 Factory pollution .21

TABLE 17 (cont'd)

Factor Loadings* (after Rotation) for Each Act Based upon the Norm Resistance Scale

	INDIA N=512	INDONESIA N=500	IRAN N=479	ITALY (SARDINIA) N=200	U.S.A. N=169	YUGOSLAVIA N=500
Factor . . .	III'	I'	III'	II'	II'	II'
Percent of variation	16.6	70.0	10.2	31.6	23.3	24.0

Social responsibility

INDIA	INDONESIA	IRAN	ITALY (SARDINIA)	U.S.A.	YUGOSLAVIA
Appropriation .48					
Factory pollution .37	Factory pollution .06	Factory pollution .59	Not helping .75	Factory pollution	Factory pollution .61
Robbery .42	Appropriation .60	Bribery .39		Not helping	Appropriation .22
	Incest .21				
	Abortion .30				
	Robbery .46				
	Homosexuality .24				

	INDIA	INDONESIA	IRAN	ITALY (SARDINIA)	U.S.A.	YUGOSLAVIA
Factor . . .	II'	III'	II'	III'	III'	III'
Percent of variation	23.6	13.0	14.2	16.4	13.1	13.8

(YUGOSLAVIA III': Factory pollution .48, Appropriation .34)

*Loadings below .2 excluded.

Table 16 that the Indonesians were more willing to allow the sanctioning of public protest. Interpreters of Indonesian personality suggest that Indonesians are milder and more acquiescent than the groups sampled from our other countries. Observation of factor II for Indonesia, however, shows that on this factor protest is grouped with the other core deviant acts. It would seem, therefore, that the factor of protest-deviance is a basic factor in perception of deviance for *all* countries, but with the qualification that for Indonesia, protest deviance accounts for much less of the variation.

The proportion of variation accounted for generally by the protest factor is interesting to note. While the protest factor accounted for only a small portion of the variation for Indonesia, for the reasons stated above, the proportion of variation accounted for by protest in other countries was quite high at least half, and in the case of Yugoslavia and Iran, much higher. Again, it would seem that the countries with dictatorships have elicited reactions to deviance based more strongly with protest.

The second factor identified was that of *moral indignation*, by far the strongest for Indonesia. This factor generally grouped together taking drugs, incest, and homosexuality for five of the six countries, the exception being the Sardinians. There were also other exceptions which require explanation. It may be noted at the outset that the moral indignation factor accounted for by far the largest portion of the variation for Indonesia in contrast to other countries. We may interpret this finding to suggest that Indonesia, being the most traditional of all countries sampled, views deviant behavior much more in terms of "moral outrage" rather than the more relativistic or "secular" view of deviance that usually accompanies diversification in a developed modern society. It is especially interesting to note that moral indignation is reserved only for the three acts of taking drugs, incest, and homosexuality in the New York sample: three acts most traditionally seen in moralistic terms by Puritan America. In contrast, although these three acts are core acts for other countries, other acts are also grouped on this factor. The appropriation of public funds and robbery—both seen in Yugoslavia as especially serious crimes against the state—are also included. Similarly, bribery, a traditional Iranian crime, and subject to a strong campaign by the Iranian government is included. It is likely that not helping another is subject to moral indignation in Iran as a result of the passing of traditional society where once in a small community setting, people relied on, and helped each other. But with modernization, people become competitors rather than helpers.

The most difficult results to explain are those for Sardinia, where one might have expected sex-related acts to be the subject of moral indignation, considering the usual influence of church morality upon small peasant communities. Instead, the acts of pollution, robbery, and appropriation of public funds were grouped on the moral indignation factor. We have noted in our previous analysis in Chapter 6 that over half of the Sardinians would not report robbery to anyone. Yet, when asked what punishment, if any, should be given to such persons, consistently harsh punishments of long prison terms were recommended. This would suggest that the respondents were morally outraged by these acts, but were unable to report them to the authorities because of the tradition of violence in this area: that they were too frightened or distrusted the ability of the authorities to deal with the acts. This may especially be the case for the appropriation of public funds and environmental pollution. Thus, moral indignation is not directed toward what one might call "church related" acts of deviance (not even abortion which is strongly condemned by the Church) but rather against criminal acts with which the authorities are impotent to deal and perhaps are themselves suspected of perpetrating. It will be noted that drug taking is not grouped on moral indignation for Iran. This is, of course, what one would expect since taking drugs (especially smoking opium), has long been a traditional social entertainment in Iran, although it is now outlawed.

The third factor identified was the *social responsibility factor*. On this factor were grouped acts in which the actor fails to display social responsibility. Thus, the core acts for this factor are factory pollution and not helping another in a dangerous situation. It is to be noted that this factor accounts generally for the smallest amount of variation for each country, with the exception of Iran. It is apparent, however, that there is really very little differentiation between the act groupings for Indonesia. Perhaps as societies become more industrialized and urbanized, so also does the structure of deviance perception become more diversified, where more different acts are "tolerated" but at different levels and according to different criteria. In contrast, traditional societies may display only a generalized diffuse moral evaluation of deviance. In a small community where each person depends closely on the other, social behavior also becomes moral behavior and vice versa. As society diversifies, an individual's behavior is less likely directly to affect his neighbor. Thus, moral indignation may become separated from behavior involving social responsibility.

A fourth factor applied only to robbery for the New York sample and incest for the Indian sample, and accounted for only a tiny portion of the variation. This finding is most likely symptomatic once again of the fear of violent crime so often evidenced by big city dwellers. However, in the absence of other acts grouped on this factor, we are unable to go beyond this speculation. Furthermore, the appropriation of government funds was not grouped on any of the factors for the U.S. sample, which means, in the light of our interpretation so far, that it was not seen as an act worthy of protest, or of moral indignation or even as relevant to social responsibility. Since this survey was conducted before the Watergate scandal, are we able to interpret this as suggestive of public indifference? At the very least, we may hypothesize that our New York sample perceived this act in very different terms to any other country sample. The acts of robbery and appropriation were grouped on the social responsibility factor for the countries of India, Indonesia and Iran, but on the moral indignation factor for Yugoslavia and Sardinia and not on any for the U.S. This suggests that such "traditional crimes" are seen more in terms of the traditional way of life—i.e., one's social responsibility to the community in the less modernized countries. In contrast, in industrialized countries, the socially responsible aspects of these acts have become divorced from the reasons for punishing them, so that a more retributive or morally indignant reaction follows. The reasons for the moral indignation and deviance protest reaction for robbery in Sardinia are, of course, not related to industrialization, but to the specific subcultural perceptions of robbery which we have discussed. Thus, the fourth factor for the U.S. might be termed the *secular-puritanical* factor in which respondents feel that the act must be severely punished because of what it is (i.e. *male in se*) rather than what it does directly to society. The grouping of incest by the Indians on a fourth factor also lends support for this view, since we may consider India to be the transitional country (as far as our sample goes) so that incest, the once heavily sanctioned act in traditional society, although now less disapproved, is still reacted to with indignation.

CONCLUSIONS

Rettig and Pasamanick (1959, 1961) found five factors underlying lay perceptions of "wrongness" (measured on a scale of 1–10) of criminal or "immoral" behavior. These were: 1) a general factor of "basic morality" (acts wrong regardless of circumstances), 2) a religiosity factor, 3) family-related factor, 4) a factor of "puritanical morality" (acts superficially wrong, but condemned), and 5) an economic factor. However, it should be noted that the range of 50 acts which Rettig and Pasamanick presented to the respondents was very wide—from girls smoking cigarettes to robbery. The present study confines itself to 10 acts and much more information concerning the respondents' perceptions of each act was collected.

No general factor, as was found in the Rettig and Pasamanick study (1959), was discovered. It is possible that this is partly a function of the fewer number of acts presented in this study. It is more likely, however, that this has resulted because of the highly developed discriminatory perceptual process on the part of the respondents. The process of differential perception of deviance has developed hand in hand with the increasing complexity of social development. Thus, one can discern more evidence for a general factor in the Indonesian sample, whereas the most extensive differentiation has occurred in the American sample.

One hesitates to make any firm conclusions concerning universality at this point. The great diversity in responses so far noted raises serious questions. Yet it must also be realized that quantified differences among cultures according to a scale does not permit the automatic assumption that agreement concerning the perceptions does not exist. Patterns of responding to questions and scales may be culture specific, as Stycos (1960) has noted. The anchoring of these responses is crucial. In the present study, since there was such high cross-cultural agreement in the ranked order of the acts, yet such vast differences when each country was compared according to each act, it is justifiable to question the cross-cultural equivalence of the scale. Yet, even if one assumed comparability of the scale, the findings do not completely contradict the universalization hypothesis. The hypothesis is contradicted only to the extent that the levels of norm resistance in cultures differ, so that if the level of resistance in say, Indonesia, is *generally* low, it does not mean that all acts will be discriminated in relation to each other in a different fashion to a culture in which resistance is *generally* high. This may explain why there was near universal ranking of the acts with wide quantifiable diversity within each act.

In addition, although the interpretation of factorial groupings is an extremely complex undertaking, it may be concluded that considerable evidence was collected to support the hypothesis of a very general agreement across six diverse cultures concerning the perception of deviance. Tentatively, the dimensions of protest, moral indignation, and social responsibility were identified in all countries, although differing in importance especially in relation to degree of modernization of the country. The taking of drugs, abortion, and homosexuality were clearly and constantly grouped together for all countries. This was also the case for the acts of environmental pollution, not helping another and public protest. These are perhaps the most interesting findings since it would seem that there was "universal" agreement concerning the classification of these deviant acts, usually considered by criminologists to be the most difficult to classify in both legal and sociological terms. On the other hand, acts usually regarded as clear cases of "crime" such as robbery and appropriation of funds were not consistently grouped together across cultures.[5] One might speculate that increased modernization has produced a basic agreement across cultures concerning those acts about which there is often much publicity—acts of deviance. However, modernization has increased the diversity with which traditional acts are perceived. On reflection, this is what one should expect, since modernization implies the eroding away of traditional values.

THE ORGANIZATION OF DEVIANCE PERCEPTION

The little previous research in this area has concentrated upon the relationship between knowledge of the law and obedience to law or perception of acts as criminal or wrong. The reason for this narrow focus is, of course, because it is a central psychological assumption of the criminal law, either in terms of a deterrence model (i.e., a person must know that an act is prohibited before he can be deterred from doing it) or in terms of the ascription of moral and/or criminal responsibility (i.e., he must know that what he was doing was wrong).

Kaupen (1973) found an inconsistent relationship between knowledge of the law and perception of the degree of "wrongness" of various acts. In addition, he found an inconsistent relationship between perceived degree of moral wrong and the sanction chosen. Kaupen concluded (as did Kutschinsky, 1973 and Walker and Argyle, 1964) that knowledge of the law was not a necessary condition for obedience

---

[5]A more straightforward explanation for the inconsistent grouping of the traditional crimes of incest and robbery may be the very low variation in response patterns to these act for particular items of the questionnaire. Although the NRS was able to overcome this problem to some extent, when in some countries the response was so overwhelmingly intolerant, the variances remained very low, as we see in Table 16.

to the law, and that the degree of wrongness with which an act was perceived was too general a measure to predict the sanction a person would choose. However, this may also have been a function of the very general question on sanctions used by Kaupen—jail or none. In addition, the crude mode of statistical analysis, especially the lack of statistical tests of significance, makes the interpretation of these findings unclear. It must be said that the general consensus of researchers is that knowledge of the law bears little or no relationship to perception of an act as criminal or wrong (see, e.g., Podgorecki, 1974; Podgorecki, et al., 1973; Kutschinsky, 1973; Walker and Agryle, 1964).

All of these studies, however, make a serious error of inference: to infer that, because no statistical relationship is found between knowledge and one other measure of "wrongness," that there is therefore *no* relationship between the two variables is to assume that *all other possible variables* have been accounted for. As Blalock (1970) points out, this is an unwarranted assumption, for it may well turn out that although A may not be related to C, it may be related to B which in turn is related to C. In the following analysis, it was therefore necessary to analyze the relationships among all components of deviance perception in relation to each other, in an effort to take into account other possible intervening variables. In order to achieve this end, we were confronted with difficult methodological decisions. To survey the relationship among the components for each act and for each country would have entailed an endless and ponderous description of a mass of data. On the other hand, it was apparent from other research that the differences among acts should be taken into account. Therefore, the procedure we adopted was to construct correlation matrices (Pearson r) among the components for each act, and each country. Then the correlations for each component pair of the matrices were averaged.[6] The result was an overall matrix for each country. Then, in a further step to reduce the complexity of the data, we excluded all correlations below .2,[7] and charted the pattern of relationships as can be seen in Charts 6-11.

These diagrammatic representations now make it possible for us to consider the way in which each component fits into the *process* of

---

[6]The method used was that described by Guilford (1956). The correlations were converted to "z" scores. summed and averaged, and then converted back to correlations.

[7]This cut-off point was chosen because the conventional .05 level of significance would have meant that nearly all correlations were "significant" mainly because of the large N. The level .2 was chosen since this appeared to provide a useful discrimination among the component measures. However, where it appeared to make sense, correlations which were slightly below the point were included.

CHART 6

Significant Relationships among the Components of Deviance Perception for India, All Acts Combined

Opinion
Knowledge
.23
.3
.28
.17
Sanction
.38
Definition
.2
.21
.24
.18
Seriousness
Activity

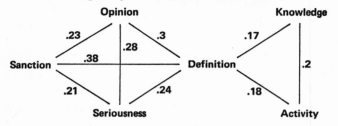

CHART 7

Significant Relationships among the Components of Deviance Perception for Indonesia, All Acts Combined

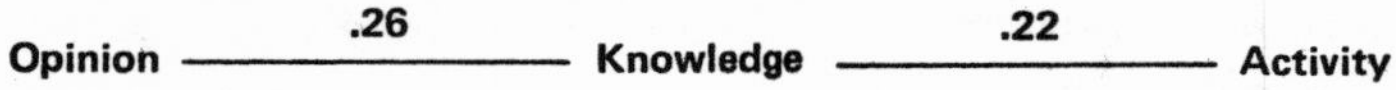

Opinion
.26
Knowledge
.22
Activity

CHART 8

Significant Relationships among the Components of Deviance Perception for Iran, All Acts Combined

Opinion
.29
Knowledge
.23
.25
.22
.45
Sanction
.34
Definition
.33
.35
.44
.24
Seriousness
.37
Activity

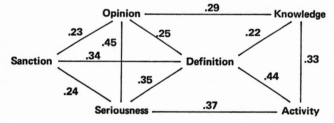

CHART 9

Significant Relationships among the Components of Deviance Perception for Sardinia, All Acts Combined

Sanction
.28
.2
Definition
.32
Opinion
.19
Knowledge
.25
Activity
.27
.31
Seriousness

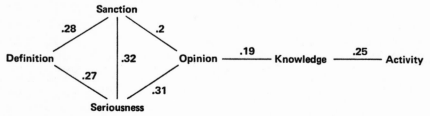

CHART 10

Significant Relationships among Components of Deviance Perception for the U.S.A., All Acts Combined

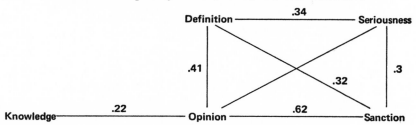

CHART 11

Significant Relationships among Components of Deviance Perception for Yugoslavia, All Acts Combined

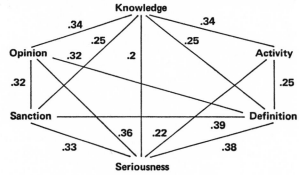

deviance perception. Before we consider the part played by each component, a number of general observations can be made.

First, there is clearly a close affinity among the four components of definition, seriousness, sanction, and opinion for the four countries of India, Iran, Italy (Sardinia), and the U.S. The components of knowledge and activity tend to be only indirectly related to these variables, especially sanction.

Second, Yugoslavia and Indonesia are two extremes, with Indonesia displaying only two significant relationships, compared to Yugoslavia where almost every component was significantly related to the other. Yugoslavian respondents, then, perceived deviance according to all six components of response and may be said to have displayed a highly cohesive process of deviance perception. The Yugoslavs were followed by Iran, India, the U.S., with somewhat cohesive patterns of response, then Sardinia, in which a highly selective process is apparent. It will be noted that the two countries displaying highest "cohesiveness" of deviance perception were those which view acts most strongly in terms of deviance-protest, whereas Indonesia reacted by far the least according to that factor. One might hypothesize that the tendency to view acts in terms of deviance-protest is more likely to "activate" the components of deviance perception, in a way which increases the consistency or similarity in response of each component. Although it is pure speculation, one is struck here by the analogy to the work in psychology on anxiety as a generalized drive (e.g., Spence, 1958): perhaps in this case, respondents are emotionally charged by acts of deviance-protest, and thus all modes of psychological behavior are affected or "blanketed" by a general emotionally based stimulus (e.g., moral indignation).

Another explanation may be that in a communist country, the activity of the government in controlling deviance is highly visible, and theoretically, at least, the government becomes the sole source of morality. We would therefore expect the components of official activity and knowledge to be more centrally involved in the deviance perception process. In similar fashion, the "Shahinshah" tradition in Iran— that the Shah (i.e., the government) is the sole source of morality in the country also explains why Iran displays such high cohesiveness, almost to the extent of Yugoslavia. On the other hand, Indonesia which is still highly diverse, although superficially a totalitarian state, lacks the integration of cultures, values, and laws. Thus, the components of seriousness, sanction and definition which were central to the deviance perception process in all other countries have played a lesser role, since they require a more selective perception of the stimulus material.

One might hypothesize here that instead of selective perception being universal in the simple sense used by Turk (1969), it rather is a trait of a more socially developed or modernized culture with not only a more complex division of labor, but a more complex division of deviances. Thus, the Indonesians have related only the most general measure of opinion to the knowledge and subsequently official activity components. One would predict that with increased modernization and unification of Indonesia, so will the other components of deviance perception (seriousness, definition and sanction) assume a more central, intervening role between opinion and knowledge. Let us now consider each component.

Opinion: According to our theory, we should expect opinion, a very general habitual measure, to be generally correlated with all other components. We can see from Charts 6–11 that opinion was indeed widely related to other acts in all countries.

Knowledge: Contrary to other research discussed, we find that knowledge of the law was positvely correlated to definition of the act as criminal in Yugoslavia, Iran, and India. For Iran and India, the definition component appears to act as a "filter" or gate through which knowledge of the law may be related to the several other components. In comparison, it was the opinion component which provided the link between knowledge and the other components in the U.S.A. and Sardinian samples.

Activity: In general, we can see that this component tended to be on the fringe of the deviance perception process. Therefore, the labelling theory view that the perception of the official defining agents' activity should be highly correlated to perception of acts as criminal or deviant is borne out in part. Significantly, for the U.S., the component was not related, according to our criteria, to any of the other measures. However, in other samples it was related to knowledge of the law and it was through it that it was related to other components. Unless one adopts a unicausal model and argues that all deviance perception begins with perception of official defining activity, one must assume that its role in the deviance perception process is indirect or auxillary. Since correlational measures do not allow for directional causal statements, the former assumption cannot be made. Furthermore, there are good theoretical reasons for not doing so, since it is most likely that deviance perception, as with any other aspect of perception, is a "give-and-take" interactional or processing model that has no one primary source.[8]

We can see that the components of knowledge and perception of official activity were generally auxillary and often grouped together. To this extent, the findings of previous research that knowledge is not a *necessary* condition for perception of acts as deviant are supported in some instances, provided one interprets necessary as meaning not directly related but possibly indirectly related to perception of acts as deviant.

Seriousness: In only one case (Yugoslavia) was seriousness related

---

[8]Thus, standardized beta weights have not been used to signify the "paths" among the variables. However, a more important reason for staying with zero-order correlations was that the extent to which each variable is exclusive of the other is considerably in question. As we saw earlier in construction of the questionnaire, although some effort was made to ensure each item represented a different aspect of deviance perception, it was also recognized that each item probably overlapped several of the theoretical categories.

to knowledge or official activity. Thus, previous research is supported in this case. On the other hand, our hypothesis that seriousness is a general measure, so should be widely correlated to other components is firmly supported.

Definition and Sanction: Next to seriousness, the sanction tended to be the least directly related to the opinion, knowledge, and activity components. However, definition of the act appeared to be the major or central component about which most other components revolved. This finding makes a lot of sense, as it was this measure that we hypothesized was the measure of perception or the perceptually *organizing* response.

As a test of the comparative weight or importance of each measure, we conducted a step-wise multiple regression analysis of each component of the NR scale upon the total scale for each act. It will be remembered that in the construction of the NR scale, the opinion, knowledge, and activity items were combined in various ways. This had the advantage of offsetting the distorting effect of the opinion question for which in two countries (Italy and U.S.) there was actually a zero variance. It also increased the disposition of directional components of the measures. Table 18 shows that the definition item was by far the most significant of all measures. The opinion, knowledge, and activity measures accounted for the major portion of the variance for far less acts. The sanction component was also important, and the most important in the U.S. sample, along with seriousness. Although the definition item did not feature strongly as the primary item for the U.S. sample, it was second in importance for six of the nine acts. We may conclude that the patterning of correlations that tended to group the sanction, seriousness and definition components which we observed in Charts 6–11 accounts for the major aspect of deviance perception, and that the knowledge of the law, perception of government activity, and habitual opinion are of peripheral significance.

Does the Perceptual Process Differ According to Different Types of Acts?

The work of Van Hautte and Vinke (1973) analyzed different components of reaction in relation to different types of acts. The acts were classified according to the factor analysis in Table 17, and the average of the correlations among the components of deviance perception was computed for each act classification and for each country. No significant differences in the organization of the components were found

TABLE 18

Number of Acts in Which Each Component Accounted for the Major Portion of the Variance in a Multiple Regression Analysis of Each Component on the NR Scale

	INDIA	INDONESIA	IRAN	ITALY	U.S.A.	YUGOSLAVIA
Opinion/knowledge	0	0	0	1	1	0
Opinion/activity	0	0	1	0	0	0
Definition	4	6	7	7	1	7
Seriousness	2	0	1	0	3	
Sanction	3	3	0	1	4	1
Range, r^2	.39 (Definition, drugs) to .64 (Definition, incest)	.39 (Sanction, drugs) to .55 (Definition, no help)	.46 (Definition, drugs) to .68 (Opinion/ activity, protest)	.48 (Definition, drugs) to .91 (Definition, robbery)	.54 (Definition, protest) to .81 (Seriousness, robbery)	.54 (Definition, drugs) to .78 (Definition, incest)

in relation to any of the classifications for the U.S. or Indonesia in comparison to that found for all acts combined. The acts of *deviance-protest* and *moral indignation* elicited no different organizational process in any sample except the Sardinian. In this case, the patterning for deviance-protest remained similar to that for all acts combined except that knowledge and activity were no longer significantly related. For moral indigantion a further attrition occurred, with the relationships of:

Seriousness ——— .20 ——— **Definition** ——— .22 ——— **Sanction**

However, the act classification that did elicit some differences was that of the acts of *social responsibility*. Quite a different pattern of relationships was found for Yugoslavia, Sardinia, Iran, and India, as seen in Chart 12. The effects on India were dramatic—the relationships among many variables disappeared, leaving only one relationship—the definition of the act to its sanction. The number of relationships was also reduced for the Yugoslav sample, producing the familiar patterning of seriousness, sanction, definition, and opinion grouped together, all related indirectly through definition of the act to knowledge and official activity. For Iran, a slight reduction occurred in the relationships among the components, mainly in the area of opinion where its relationship to definition and sanction diminished.

In the case of the Sardinian sample the reverse trend occurred, with an increase in relationship among the components of deviance perception when considered only in relation to the acts of *social responsibility*. Very noticeable is the central role which knowledge of the law came to play, being directly related to all but the seriousness component. The relationship between knowledge and sanction was particularly high.

These observations would suggest that unlike the acts of *deviance protest,* acts of *social irresponsibility* were less likely to arouse an overall, generalized reaction among all components of deviance perception, especially in the case of India and Yugoslavia. The clear exception was that of the Sardinian sample, where the effect was the opposite, especially in terms of the perception of government activity and knowledge of the law becoming much more closely related to other measures. Since the act involved in Sardinia was only not helping another—an act not generally proscribed by the *barbaricino code,* one might hypothesize that respondents would be more likely to depend upon the activities of the official agencies of control for their knowledge of the law and hence their perception of the act as deviant. In general, since the acts of this class tend to be either *mala nova* or *mala*

CHART 12
Significant Relationships among the Components of Deviance Perception for the Acts of Social Responsiblity

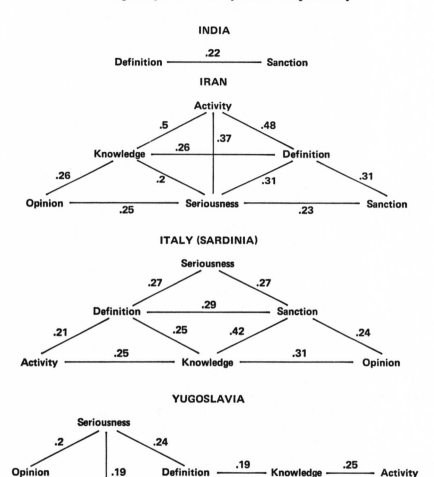

INDIA

Definition ——————— .22 ——————— Sanction

IRAN

ITALY (SARDINIA)

YUGOSLAVIA

ambigua, it is understandable that more stress would be placed on external referents such as official enforcement. In general, we can see from Chart 12 that this was the case, and that the role of the more general measures of opinion and seriousness decreased somewhat in importance. In all cases, however, the definition component remained the central organizing factor.

Summary

A very general similarity in perceptual organization was found for the country samples of India, Iran, Italy, and the U.S. in which the components of seriousness, opinion, sanction, and definition assumed a central role and were closely related. Knowledge and opinion played a peripheral role and were usually indirectly related to the other components through the definition measure.

Thus, the knowledge variable should not be discounted as unrelated to perception of crime or law, as other researchers have suggested. Rather, it should be investigated more thoroughly in relation to the several other components of deviance perception.

Proponents of labelling theory should not overstate the importance of the activity of official defining agents in its relationship to lay perceptions of deviance, especially its relationship to the seriousness or definition of deviance. However, there was strong evidence that it was closely related to knowledge of the law, and thus is indirectly related to other aspects of deviance perception.

All correlations were positive, which means that generally speaking, if persons answered that an act should be prohibited, they were also likely to say that it was criminal, that it was serious and that punishment rather than treatment or nothing was appropriate. There were, of course, some noticeable exceptions for particular acts, but *as a general rule,* this conclusion holds.[9] This does not, of course, mean that we could predict responses on other items when we had knowledge of response to one item (e.g., opinion). We have so far not addressed ourselves to the question of the amount of variance that each component accounts for. We have been interested only in the patterning of the process of deviance perception. The comparative importance or weight of each component we will consider later. However, according to our model, we should not expect a total correlation among the compo-

---

[9]There were a number of particular exceptions if one treated each act separately, and used cross-tabulation as the means of analysis. To report these findings would lead to the presentation of masses of data. In addition, since we are dealing with extremely abstract concepts, one is inclined to be cautious in making inferences from reactions to only one act. Since we are interested in general structure, and since it is really unclear as to what the one act on its own represents except in relation to other acts, it seems most prudent, when investigating the process of deviance perception to combine acts either all together, or in meaningful groups. If the reader wishes to pursue the detailed analysis of the inter-relationships among components in relation to each act, these are set out in the series of country reports prepared by the writer for the U.N.S.D.R.I., Rome, Italy (Newman, 1976a, 1976b, 1976c, 1976d, 1976e, 1976f).

nents. We hypothesized at the outset that there should be some overlap among all the components, especially because of the hypothesized generalized polar response of intensity of moral reaction. Thus, each component should tap resources unique to itself, and in addition exhibit a common relationship to the other components.

No substantial differences were found in the process of deviance perception when the acts were classified according to those of *deviance protest* or *moral indignation*. However, for the acts of *social irresponsibility,* knowledge of the law, and perception of government activity assumed a more important role for the samples of Iran, Sardinia, and Yugoslavia. May we conclude then, that the perceptual process is basically the same for all types of acts? Commonsense would suggest that this should not be so, since it is indeed possible to make logical distinctions among acts according to attributes intrinsic to them (this is what the criminal law does), and we have also seen here that they can be grouped with some consistency according to people's perceptions of them. In other words, we are hypothesizing that the process of deviance perception is not only a function of the perceiver's psychology, but also of the character of the acts themselves. To investigate this possibility, we conducted a factor analysis for each country on the correlation matrix of a selection of one act from each hypothesized act type along with each of its six component measures. The acts used for the analysis were robbery (*mala antiqua*), incest (*mala in se*), factory pollution (*mala prohibita*), abortion (*deviance*), and protest (*mala ambigua*). Thus, we had five acts with six components, making 30 measures in all. The results of these factor analyses are fascinating, raising further questions as to the role that the perception of governmental activity plays in the perception of deviance. The two rotated orthogonal factors (Varimax solution) extracted for each country may be seen plotted in Chart 13.

For the samples of Italy and the U.S., the robbery-opinion item had to be dropped, because there was zero variance, which precluded the possibility of computing communalities, and also distorted the statistical results of the factoring. Factor analysis was run on all other countries dropping the opinion robbery item, and this was found to have no serious effects upon the factor loadings.

The most striking finding is the very consistent location across all countries of the activity items in the negative portions of both factors. Yet all other groupings of items tended to be according to act classification rather than component type. The act most predominantly associated with Factor 1 (the horizontal factor) was that of protest. This

177

CHART 13

Position of Various Act/Components with Regard to Proactive and Reactive Indignation along the Act Intrinsic–Act Extrinsic Orthogonal Factors

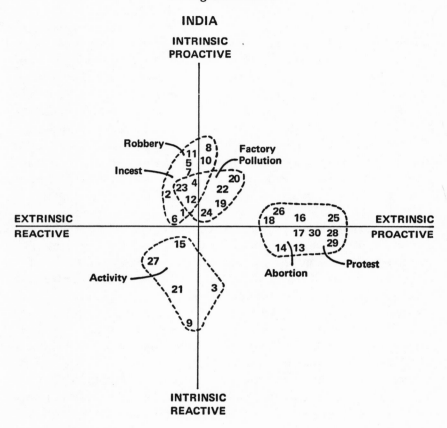

Key to Chart 13

	ROBBERY	INCEST	ABORTION	FACTORY POLLUTION	PROTEST
Opinion	1	7	13	19	25
Knowledge	2	8	14	20	26
Activity	3	9	15	21	27
Definition	4	10	16	22	28
Seriousness	5	11	17	23	29
Sanction	6	12	18	24	30

CHART 13 (*cont'd*)

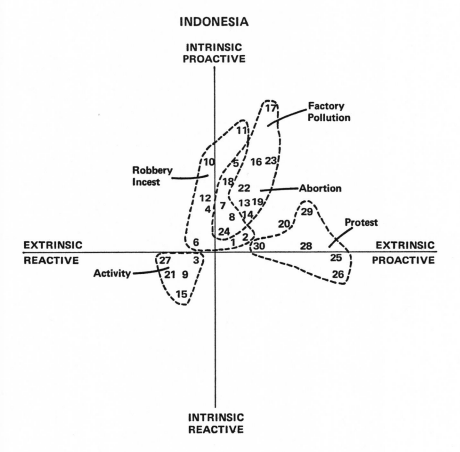

INDONESIA

applied for all countries except Indonesia where it was Factor II (the plots have been rearranged to facilitate comparison in Chart 13). Those acts in all countries except Sardinia most closely related to Factor II were those of robbery, incest, and to some extent factory pollution. We may conclude that it was predominantly the characteristics of the acts themselves that elicited the grouping of the components of deviance perception. That is, as a very general rule, deviance perception tends to be act specific. The clear exception was that of perception of government activity that cuts across the grouping of perceptual components according to the specific acts. Again, the consistency with which

179

CHART 13 (*cont'd*)

IRAN

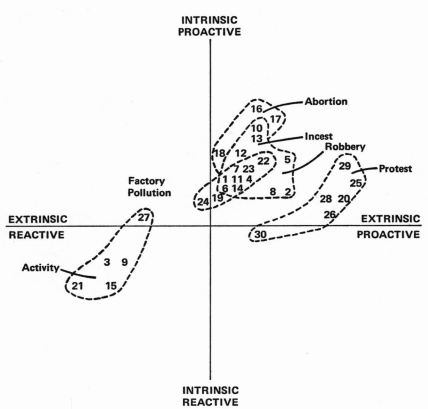

INTRINSIC
PROACTIVE

Abortion

16
17
10
13
Incest
Robbery
18 12
7 23   22   5
1 11 4
Factory
Pollution
6 14
29   Protest
25
24 19   8   2
28 20
26

EXTRINSIC
REACTIVE
27
30
EXTRINSIC
PROACTIVE

Activity
3   9
21   15

INTRINSIC
REACTIVE

this finding is presented in each of the six different countries is impressive. What is it about the perception of government activity which places it so much apart?

Our explanation lies in an understanding of the psychological reaction to the social or official control of deviance, but seen only in relation to the type of acts to be controlled. As can be seen in Chart 13, we have termed Factor I Extrinsic and Factor II as Intrinsic. Each item related to these factors is seen as being arranged along a scale of *proactive moral indignation,* to *reactive moral indignation.* By introducing this refinement of the psychological reaction to deviance we can explain the location and separation of the activity items. The four aspects of deviance perception may be defined as:

CHART 13 *(cont'd)*

ITALY (SARDINIA)

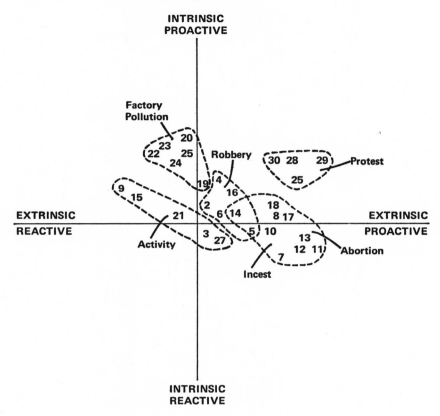

The Act-Intrinsic Factor: These are acts which because of their very nature will elicit consistent patterns of response. That is, acts which are either *mala in se* or *mala antiqua* or to some extent *mala prohibita,* provided that their criminality or wrongfulness is so deeply embedded in culture that they elicit consistent reactions—that they are to the same degree embedded in the person's psyche. Thus, the psychological reaction to these acts is unlikely to be affected by what the government or other official definers are doing. Hence, the responses are closely tied to act type, i.e., intrinsic to the acts.

Reactive Indignation: Many sociologists and social theorists have written on the contradiction of submission and superordination. In particular, both Weber (1966) and Simmel (1959) have argued that there

CHART 13 (*cont'd*)

U.S.A. (NEW YORK)

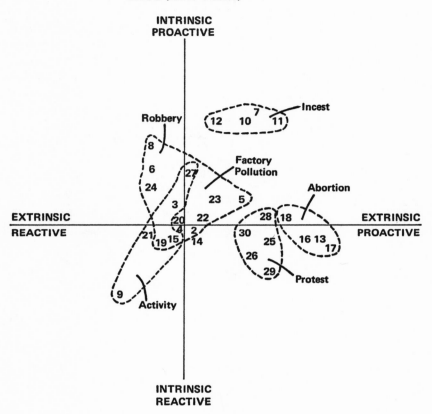

is a very deep ambivalence embedded in the submissive reaction. Even "voluntary" submission to authority, Weber argued, still implied some coercion—and by inference, some resentment. Thus, while individuals will approve (quite often very strongly) the punishment of other wrongdoers, they should at the same time harbor some resentment that the official authority is able to perpetrate this punishment on others, by way of commanding obedience. Thus, their indignation to outright control or official government activity in stopping deviance is also *reactive*. The official agencies are held both in esteem and derision, since it is their actions which may directly, and certainly indirectly, command each individual's obedience. Thus, the items concerning the govern-

CHART 13 (*cont'd*)

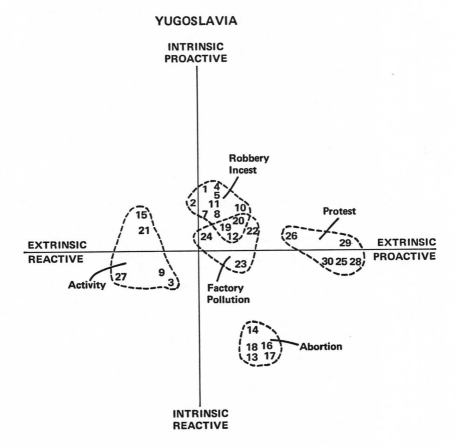

YUGOSLAVIA

ment as active are found towards the negative ends of the scales, where the government is resented for its activity as deviance controller. Only in special cases, where feeling about a particular act runs very high do other components of deviance perception become related to reactive indignation, such as the case of abortion for Yugoslavia. The contrast between proactive and reactive indignation is heightened when we look at the act-extrinsic factor.

Act-Extrinsic: These acts are those which depend for their reactions on the activities of interest groups, official agencies, and so on. The reactions to them depend much more on people's perceptions than on their culturally intrinsic attributes. The most typical act in this category is that of public protest, about which it will be remembered, there was considerable factional disagreement concerning its deviance in all country samples. Again, however, as was noted in the previous chapter, the general overall response was toward its punishment and control. The plots for every country sample support this hypothesis, with the slight exception of the U.S. sample where the overwhelming majority could not be said to have reacted with reactive indignation along the extrinsic factor, but they most certainly did according to the intrinsic factor. This may suggest that as far as reaction against the control of deviance is concerned, this is a deeply embedded reaction in American culture. This interpretation has considerable face validity.

Proactive Indignation: This term is used to refer to that conglomeration of responses which approves of the punishment or official control of others for wrongs, either criminal or social. We call it proactive because it is a response that supports the activities of the official authorities.

Variations within Countries

INDIA: The plots for this country probably illustrate our interpretations to the best. Robbery, incest, and factory pollution (all acts heavily punished by the Indians) are closely related to the Act-Intrinsic factor; whereas abortion and protest are clearly separated onto the extrinsic factor. Both sets of acts are located toward the proactive ends of the scales. The activity items are located in the reactive ends of the scales.

INDONESIA: The separation of the acts is also reasonably clear cut. It can be seen that robbery and incest are clearly separable onto the intrinsic factor, as is protest to the extrinsic factor. Factory pollution and abortion appear to be transitional between the two—a common finding for other countries. Proactive indignation is high for all acts, especially for abortion, although somewhat less for robbery. The activity items are clearly separated onto the reactive ends of the scales.

IRAN: Protest is clearly correlated to the extrinsic factor, but the acts of robbery, incest, abortion, and factory pollution are not so well differentiated, although they do all tend more toward the act intrinsic factor. The reason for this lack of discrimination may be in the observation we have made previously concerning Iran, that the overall reactions were extremely punitive for all acts except protest, without a great deal of discrimination between them. The only component which did provide considerable discrimination among acts was that of the preferred sanction, and it can be seen that these components are very closely correlated to the act intrinsic factor for robbery, factory pollution, abortion and incest. Other measures tend to be equally related to both the act extrinsic factor and the act intrinsic factor. Another reason for this may be the tendency for crimes to be defined more clearly by the *shahinshah* tradition in Iran—i.e., that what is criminal varies most directly with the edicts of the government. Thus, even culturally determined acts such as robbery are subject more to the referents of official activity and the societal reaction which they incur. Again, we see that the proactive indignation is very strong for all acts, especially abortion. A final reason for the lack of differentiation may be the forces of modernization in Iran, so that the traditional boundaries between act types or wrongs are blurred. This is in contrast to India which has also undergone modernization, but where the religious culture remains strongly intact. In Iran, on the other hand, the authority of religion has been slowly whittled away, especially as a result of specific policies of the Shah. The extent of religious influence in Iran upon perception of deviance is therefore of special interest, and it shall be taken up in the following chapter. The activity items are very clearly separated onto the reactive ends of the scales.

ITALY (SARDINIA): The results are the most difficult to fit into our model. The activity items, although grouped together, are not so clearly divorced from other items as is evidenced in other countries. Reactive indignation is confined almost entirely to incest and abortion, which it will be remembered, were acts highly resisted on the NR scale. The acts of robbery and factory pollution are grouped towards the act intrinsic factor, with abortion and incest correlated most highly to the extrinsic factor. Protest appears to be equally correlated to both factors, and strangely, there was no reactive indignation towards this act. The only interpretation that presents itself is that the Sardinians would have nothing to do with the government concerning most crimes in the sense that they do not react *against* the official agencies, but rather according to the unwritten code, they ignore it—or act in spite of it. The only acts on which there are clear reactive elements are abortion and incest—family matters not related to the Barbaracino code. Robbery and protest are also transitional between the two factors since they are both closely related to activities of the unwritten code, so are act-intrinsic to the extent that the Barbaracino code is embedded in Sardinian culture. But, these acts are subject to considerable government interference specifically because they are dealt with by the Barbaracino code. Hence, they are correlated to the extrinsic factor.

U. S (NEW YORK): Abortion and protest are closely correlated to the act extrinsic dimension as expected, as are robbery and factory pollution to the act intrinsic factor. Incest provides the exception, but this act was not very highly criminalized by the American respondents, although they were almost all quite clear that it should be the subject of formal social control. Thus, it is a transitional act correlated to both dimensions. However, the incest activity item was the most extreme subject of reactive indignation, suggesting that there also exists a strong feeling that the official agencies of control should keep their distance from family matters. As remarked previously, the majority of the components of perception of protest were clustered toward intrinsic reactive indignation, evidence of the long tradition in America of the right to political freedom and protest. Yet, strangely, the activity item for protest is located on the intrinsic-proactive axis. Maybe this is evidence of the profound tension between political freedom and political license that Americans experienced during the Vietnam War years of the 1960s, which has occurred in other periods of American history.

YUGOSLAVIA: Once again, the activity items are clearly grouped towards the reactive ends of the scale. So also are robbery and incest grouped towards the intrinsic factor, and protest on the extrinsic factor. Factory pollution remains a transitional type. Of special interest is the act of abortion that is the subject of extreme intrinsic reactive indignation, suggesting that this act should not be criminalized, although some control is necessary in terms of its extrinsic features.

CONCLUSIONS AND SUMMARY

We have seen that there is a consistent and similar structuring in perceptions of deviance across all countries.

The way in which deviance is perceived is a function of the intrinsic nature of the acts, the way in which they are dealt with by official agencies of control and the psychological make-up of the perceiver.

The central organizing component in perceptions of deviance is the definition of the act into various classes, measured in this study by the respondent's choice of control agent. The other two components closely related to this function are the assessment of the seriousness of the act, and the preferred sanction.

Opinion, knowledge of the law, and perception of government activity in stopping the deviance are peripheral factors—not central to the perception of deviance. They are, however, related to other components of deviance perception indirectly, usually through the organizing component of definition of the act.

The acts can generally be divided into two simple groups: acts intrinsic (crime) and acts extrinsic (deviance), and the general social psychological dimensions of reaction to these two groups conceived of as ranging from proactive indignation (i.e., support of official control of deviance) to reactive indignation (resentment of official control).

eight

SOCIOLOGICAL CORRELATES OF DEVIANCE PERCEPTION

Previous empirical research (Chapter 3) suggested that education, religiosity, and social class have important effects upon the perception of
deviance. However, the ability of previous studies to assess the *comparative* effects of these variables has been inconclusive. For current
theoretical criminology, the assessment of these comparative effects is
crucial, since conflict theorists, especially the "new criminolgists,"
insist that *all* crime is perceived according to one dominant factor, that
of social class. Consensus theorists on the other hand hold that traditional crimes inhere a general consensus, and that acts of deviance do
imply considerable disagreement. Only are subcultures seen to hold
different perceptions of traditional crimes. In this regard, the Sardinian
sample has been dropped from this stage of the comparative analysis,
since there is no urban sample. Sardinia will be considered later as a
special case.

In addition to the three variables of education, religiosity, and social
class, we are also able to consider the comparative effects of age, sex,
and the key variable hypothesized at the beginning of our study, that of
urban-rural background. At the same time, of course, the effects of
country or culture will be considered.

TYPES OF MEASUREMENT

The NRS scale (Chapter 5) was used which allows a summarizing
measure of deviance perception in relation to each act. However, because this scale uses the "resistance" aspects of the items, it was
considered that it should be supplemented by a measure that took into
account the controlling aspects of deviance perception. This seemed
especially important since, as we have seen, the general tendency of
our respondents was toward controlling deviance.

The Deviance Control Scale (DCS) was therefore constructed,

which skimmed off the controlling responses for selected items. However, because of the heavily skewed response distributions to the items, we did not construct a Deviance Control Scale in relation to each act, but rather sought to pool responses from items of all acts to construct an overall summarizing scale of deviance perception. In this way, it was possible to construct a scale to which responses were minimally skewed, as can be seen in Table 19. The method of constructing the scale was:

1. Responses were pooled from the six response categories of deviance perception, for eight of the nine acts (taking drugs was excluded because of its widely, varying definition across cultures). However, responses were weighted and combined according to a number of criteria, and included as follows:[1]

   a. The more superficial measures of opinion, knowledge, and perception of government activity were combined so as to give a measure of "criminalization." Specifically, a response that an act should be prohibited combined with a belief (whether legally correct or not) that the act was not prohibited, and a response that an act should be prohibited combined with a perception of the government as not active in stopping it.
   b. Choices of the control agents of "police," "government official," "doctor," or "village chief."
   c. Only the 9–11 end of the seriousness scale was included.
   d. The preference for incarceration (i.e. prison or mental asylum).

These items were differentially weighted a second time, according to each act. Since we knew the general response distributions to each act, we weighted those responses which favored controlling deviance and which were generally responses not strongly favored by the rest of the sample. For example, the choice of "police" as control agent for abortion was given double the weight compared to choice of police for robbery. There were two reasons for adopting this procedure. One was that the responses to many of the acts were highly skewed, even bimodal in some cases; this applied to each response category. Thus, it seemed sensible to develop a measure that accounted for those areas of the frequency distributions in which the N was largest, and which in general happens to be the upper end, or controlling end, of the response categories. The other reason was that by weighting responses

---

[1]See the Appendix for details of the Deviance Control Scale scoring procedure.

TABLE 19
Statistical Attributes of the Refined DCS

	INDIA	INDONESIA	IRAN	U.S.A.	YUGOSLAVIA
Mean DCS	7.86	12.096	19.97	7.78	13.92
Skewness	.858	.598	-.183	2.08	.325
Reliability*	.63	.76	.83	.71	.73
Standard error	.241	.339	.455	.372	.343
"Best 10"** Proportion of variance	.66	.83	.79	*.77*	.81

*Spearman-Brown Reliability was computed.
**The "10 best" items were: a) the definition items for homosexuality, protest, no help, abortion, incest, factory pollution, and appropriation, and b) the seriousness items for homosexuality, protest and abortion. It will be noted that the act of robbery is no longer included in the refined scale, no doubt because of its very low variation in responses. A maximum score of 30 is possible on this scale.

190

which were "deviant" according to the rest of the sample (i.e. a highly controlling response to a generally lower controlled act) we hoped to accentuate or increase the amount of variation, thereby enhancing our chances of finding differences according to the various sub-groups of our sample.

2. A total of thirty items was developed, and a stepwise multiple regression analysis was conducted of the 30 items upon the total DCS scale. The multiple regression was conducted within each country and on the scale with all countries combined. We were able to choose 10 items that were comprised only of the seriousness and the definition/ control agent questions which, when placed in a multiple regression analysis of all items with the total DCS, accounted for 70 percent, and often more, of the variation. It can be seen from table 19 that our refined DCS scale of the 10 "best" items displays quite respectable statistical attributes, with minimal skewness, and high reliability in each country. The instrument may therefore be considered statistically adequate for cross-cultural measurement.[2]

MACRO ANALYSIS

Zero order correlations were run between each of the macro indicators reported in Table 1 and the dependent variable, the mean DCS for each country. Table 20 displays the only macro indicators which were significantly related to deviance control, using the country as the unit of analysis. A clear grouping of the indicators emerges.

An authoritarian or totalitarian political structure is correlated with a high propensity to control deviance. Thus, we may expect that countries where there is low toleration of autonomous groups, where police

---

[2] It may be noted that throughout this and the following analysis, we have worked with the raw scores of the dependent variables of DCS and NRS. Previous work on the seriousness scale has employed logarithmic transformation because of the heavily skewed frequency distributions (Sellin and Wolfgang, 1964). Preliminary runs with the regression analysis were conducted both with and without logarithmic transformation of the dependent variable. It was found, however, that the regression of the independent variables on the DCS and NRS raw scores displayed a better fit. This is not surprising, since we have seen that the frequency distribution to the DCS was very close to normal. Indeed, we obtained an R^2 with raw scores of the DCS of .31 on all independent variables, but with the logarithmic transformation of the DCS the proportion explained was reduced to .19. For the NRS, the logarithmic transformation made negligible difference to the amount of variance explained, nor was the order in which the independent variables entered into the regression analysis changed in any substantial way. Therefore, for ease of presentation, all analysis has been conducted on the raw scores of the dependent variables.

TABLE 20

Significant* Zero Order Correlations between Mean
DCS for Each Country and Macro Indicators
N=5**

INDICATOR	r
Horizontal power distribution	−.82
International financial status	−.92
Freedom of the press	−.82
Newspaper circulation	−.86
Gross national product	−.92
Police politically significant	.82
Participation of institutional groups	.82
One-party system	.82
Toleration of autonomous groups	.82
Representative polyarchy	.82
Effective legislature	.82

*These correlations are significant at .05 level or better. A high r was
necessary to achieve significance because of the small N.
**Italy (Sardinia) was excluded.

play a central political role, and where there is a high participation of
institutional groups (i.e. government bureaucracies, and organizations
especially common in communist polities[3]), there will be high deviance
control.

Those indicators usually taken as exemplifying Western democracy
were negatively correlated with propensity to control deviance. Thus,
countries with a free press, a representative polyarchy, and horizontal
power distribution may be expected generally to display a greater tolerance of deviance.

The richer, better economically developed countries may also be
expected to require less control of deviance than the less developed
countries. Thus, international financial status and Gross National
Product, are very highly negatively correlated to deviance control. In
addition, newspaper circulation, a common indicator of social development and degree of modernization, was negatively related to deviance control.

An effective legislature, not necessarily typical of Western or Eastern polities, was also negatively correlated to deviance control.

[3]Banks and Textor (1963) use the following definition: ". . . legislatures, political
executives, armies, bureaucracies, churches, and the like . . ." Also ". . . all
Communist-bloc polities are classified under A." (i.e. very significant) (pp. 90–91).

Although one can only make general observations, these findings raise interesting questions. Some theorists (Dickson, 1968) have argued that bureaucratic requirements dominate the making of new laws, or that new laws result from the work of "moral entrepreneurs" (Becker, 1964). One might have thought that with an effective legislature, presumably responsive to the demands of the public, especially entrepreneurs, more laws on deviance control would be passed, and thus tolerance of deviance would be less. This would appear to be not the case from present data. On the other hand, the bureaucratic model is supported by our finding that participation of institutional groups appears to be related to propensity to control deviance.

The most developed countries in this sample are, of course, those with a capitalistic economy. One may infer, therefore, from our findings, that tolerance of deviance is higher in capitalist countries when compared to totalitarian countries.

It is abundantly clear that totalitarian regimes are less tolerant of deviance. It is unfortunate that we do not have a socialist democracy in the sample so that the effects of socialism compared with capitalism might be gauged, without the spurious effects of totalitarianism.

THE EFFECTS OF SOCIOLOGICAL FACTORS

Procedures for Assessing the Comparative Effects of the Variables

A preliminary three-way analysis of variance was conducted using country, urban-rural and religiosity, with the DCS and NRS as dependent variables. From this analysis, it was clear that the country variable accounted for by far the greatest portion of the variation in the DCS and in the NRS for all acts except appropriation.

The cases for each country were weighted as in Chart 2 to give each country equal weight in the analysis.

A step-wise multiple regression was conducted on the DCS of all independent variables of country,[4] urban/rural, education, age, social class and sex, in which the country variable was entered first, followed by a stepwise ordering based upon criteria used by SPSS.[5]

---

[4] The five country samples were effect coded into four vectors, according to the procedure outlined by Kerlinger and Pedhazur (1973).

[5] Although other criteria are used, the essential one is that variable that would add the highest portion of variation—i.e. that variable with the highest partial r. See: Nie, et al., 1975.

Criteria for the selection of independent variables as possibly having a significant relationship to deviance control were those used by Sellin and Wolfgang (1964) and by Riedel (1972): the variable must have a significant "b" (i.e. it must have a unique input into the regression equation); and it must display a significant zero order correlation to the dependent variable, so that there is at least a prima facie case for a linear relationship.[6] Variables not meeting with *both* these criteria were dropped from further analysis.

For those variables retained, a saturated regression model was adopted, and a multiple regression analysis was run which included all interaction terms.

Summarizing tables of analysis of variance were constructed, and also regression lines were plotted. Using both the regression lines and the analysis of variance tables, it is now possible to assess the comparative importance of each independent variable.[7]

Deviance Control

It can be seen from Table 21 that the background variables of country, education, urban/rural and religiosity along with their various interaction effects accounted for 40 percent of the variation. All effects were highly significant, especially those of country. However, we can see from Chart 14 that the partialled effects of these background variables have been quite different in the various countries.

EDUCATION. In general, for Iran, U.S., and Yugoslavia, as education increased, preference to control deviance decreased. India was the exception where education had no effects. However, for Indonesia, the opposite effects occurred: as education increased, so also did preference to control deviance.

---

[6]The criterion for a significant r was around .2, and for the "b" an F significant at .05 or better.

[7]A mixture of both the "experimental" and "a priori" approaches was used. As mentioned above, the five countries were effect coded into four vectors. From our preliminary regression analysis, it was possible to estimate which general ordering of the variables to use in the regression analysis using the saturated model. Thus, the country variable was forced in first, followed by the main effects (in the order provided by the SPSS criteria) followed by second order interactions (in any order), then by third order interactions (in any order). Although this method worked well for most acts, it was necessary to rearrange the ordering for the acts of taking drugs, incest, and homosexuality where it was apparent that third order interactions were accounting for a major portion of the variation. Although technically, the urban/rural variable is not a continuous variable (but rather it is dichotomous), for illustrative purposes, the use of regression lines is most suitable.

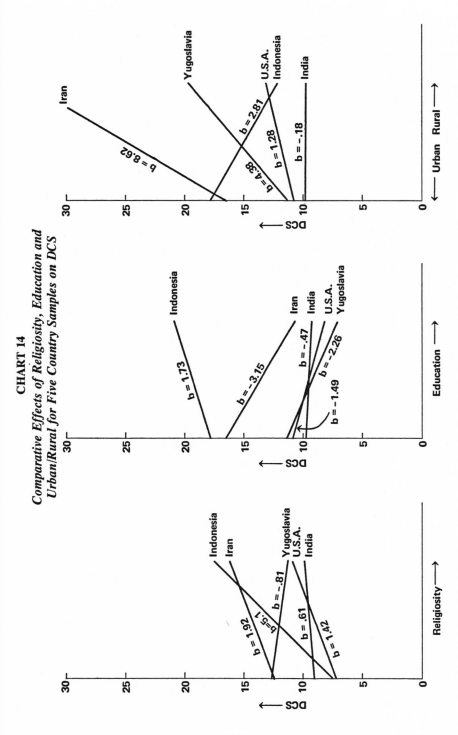

CHART 14
*Comparative Effects of Religiosity, Education and
Urban/Rural for Five Country Samples on DCS*

TABLE 21
Significant Effects of Country, Urban/Rural, Education and Religiosity on General Perceptions of Deviance (DCS)

VARIABLE	PROPORTION OF VARIATION	DF	F	P
Country	.25935	4	261.301	.001
Education	.03320	1	133.799	.001
Urban/rural	.01484	1	59.806	.001
Religiosity	.00445	1	.934	.001
County by urban/rural	.06850	4	69.015	.001
Country by education	.01857	4	.709	.001
Country by religiosity	.00433	4	.62	.01
Total	.40324	19	85.531	.001
Residual	.59676	2,405		

The most obvious explanation of the exceptional effects of education in Indonesia is that the sample was made up heavily of civil servants who, in a polity of "guided democracy" may be expected to display preferences to control deviance, or if not, to acquiesce to the interviewer if he is seen as a representative of the government, a problem which is common in interview surveys conducted in South East Asian countries. The failure for significant effects to be found in India also supports this interpretation.

URBAN/RURAL. Again, there were no significant effects in India (Chart 14), which supports the previous research that has argued for no substantial differences in values between urban and rural Indians (Gore, 1968). For the U.S., Yugoslavia and Iran the effects were basically similar: the rural respondents significantly favored control of deviance much more than urban respondents. Again, the effects in Indonesia were the opposite. The rural respondents were less controlling than the urban respondents. This finding supports the previous interpretation that educated, city dwelling civil servants are more likely to favor control of deviance in a developing country, since it supports their tenuous power position.

RELIGIOSITY. The effects of religiosity were significant in all countries, but this time, Yugoslavia was the exception. For all other countries, religiosity was positively correlated to deviance control—a relationship to be expected, and which corroborates other research. As religiosity increased in Yugoslavia, however, deviance control decreased. One can only speculate as to the reasons for this finding, but it might be that those who have clung to their religious ideals in the face of a polity, trying to eradicate religion, are more aware of the "right to be different," and thus show less willingness to control deviance.

It is important to see those effects that were found not to be significant. Social class as measured by occupation of head of household was not found significant. Nor were the effects of age and sex. Nor were any other interaction effects except those presented in Table 21. Thus, we may conclude that no easily definable group (e.g. poorly educated, religious, rural) was consistently the highest controller of deviance. This finding supports the conclusion made by Dahl (1967:270–276) from his review of the research on the effects of background variables on a wide range of political and personal values.

The findings on education are generally opposite to those of previous research: education generally had a liberalizing effect. Thus, the theories of reaction to deviance as a function of middle class indignation (Ranulf, 1938) are not supported. If we take education as a rough indicator of social class, the orthodox Marxist interpretation is also not supported, since it would be argued that the bourgeoisie (i.e. better educated) would strongly favor the control of deviance. This analysis applies only for Indonesia, where we have hypothesized that there may exist a group of "bourgeoisie," if one defines this class as comprised of upwardly aspiring persons, clinging tenuously to their social and economic power.

Norm Resistance

Significant effects of background variables were not found for all acts. As can be seen from Table 22, only a tiny proportion of the variation was accounted for by background variables for the acts of robbery, appropriation, factory pollution, and not helping. According to the theory outlined in Chapter 2, these are the results one would expect. For these acts, the major portion of the variation was accounted for by the country variable, although the act of appropriation was a possible exception. For this act, whereas the country variable accounted for 3 percent of the variation, the interaction effects of country and urban/rural accounted for 5 percent. However, because such a small proportion of variation was accounted for overall, interpretation of this finding should be made cautiously.

It was suggested in Chapter 2 that reactions against traditional

TABLE 22
Proportion of Variation* Explained by Background Factors for DCS and NRS on Each Act

	PROPORTION OF VARIATION (R^2)
DCS	.40
Robbery	.06
Incest	.21
Appropriation	.10
Homosexuality	.39
Abortion	.43
Taking drugs	.18
Factory pollution	.08
Not helping	.08
Public protest	.29

*These proportions are based upon a stepwise multiple regression analysis which used a saturated model of the country variable (effect coded), with the background variables selected according to the criteria outlined previously. The proportion only includes main and interaction effects if they were significant.

crimes are culturally embedded in the psyche of all individuals. If this is true, We should expect little or no variation in background variables, and the bulk of the variation should be explained by factors *within* individuals. This was the case with the acts of robbery and appropriation, if we take the residual of the regression model to represent the "within" variation.

The act of not helping is a particularly interesting one. We saw in Chapter 6 that it elicited a frequency distribution which supported our hypothesis that it was an act *mala ambigua*. It is a striking finding that even though there was wide variation in responses, so little of this variation was accounted for by any background variables. We may conclude that in cases of *mala ambigua* or of "moral dilemma," perceptions are almost entirely a function of personal idiosyncratic factors.

The lack of differential norm resistance to factory pollution poses a challenging problem of interpretation. We saw earlier that it was certainly not an act *mala ambigua,* but elicited responses more like the traditional quasi-crime of appropriation; responses were very similar for these two acts. Since factory pollution cannot be considered as a culturally embedded crime as is appropriation, perhaps the similarity of the acts is better seen in terms of "white collar crime," especially in the sense that both these acts could be perpetrated only by persons in positions of authority or of relatively high status in society. If this were the case, one would expect to obtain differences according to social class variables. These were not found. One can only assume therefore that "property" crimes (appropriation) and "environmental" crimes (factory pollution) are viewed similarly across social and class categories within all countries. Perhaps we are here tapping an aspect of the univeralization of norms as a result of increased communication.

Incest

The New York respondents were clearly highest in norm resistance to control of this act, with a mean NRS of 1.5325. The New Yorkers were followed by Indonesia, Iran, Yugoslavia, and finally India. It can be seen from Table 23 that age, religiosity and education and certain interactions among them had highly significant effects on norm resistance to this act. Although the country variable clearly accounted for the major portion of the variation, the interaction of country with other variables was highly significant. Chart 15 shows that education had a basically similar effect across all countries. As education increased, there was the tendency in all countries (except Indonesia) for the NRS to increase. The effects of age were considerably greater for India than any other country, with a decrease in norm resistance as age increased. In lesser degrees, this correlation was found in Iran and Yugoslavia. However, for the U.S. the relationship was the opposite—as age increased, so did norm resistance. There appears to be no explanation for this, since it is popularly assumed that the young are more liberal than adults. The explanation of the differential effects of religiosity is also challenging. As religiosity increased, norm resistance also decreased, as one would expect, but only for the countries of Indonesia, Iran and the U.S. The reverse effects occurred with India and Yugoslavia. The difference for Yugoslavia is consistent with our explanation for the DCS—the religious people in Yugoslavia are more likely to favor resistance to government control. There is also some evidence that this also is the attitude of religious Indians (See: Newman, 1976) toward official control of family affairs. The emphasis is for containment of deviance within the family.

Why were differences found for this act, when we earlier argued that it was an act *mala in se,* and should be explained by factors entirely within the individual? The data forces us to reconsider the long accepted view of the anthropologist of the universal incest taboo. Indeed, the law

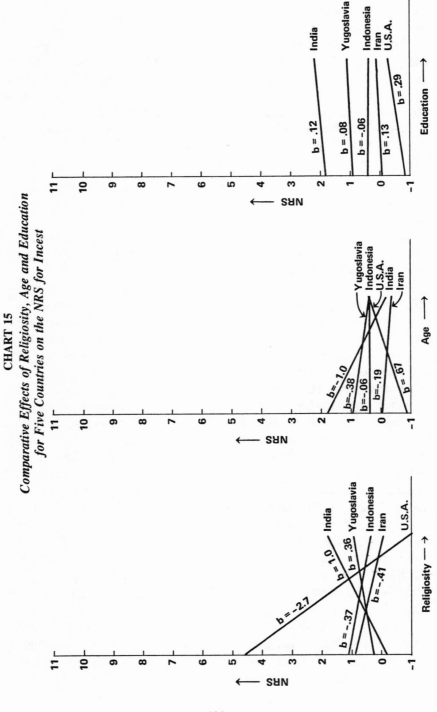

CHART 15

*Comparative Effects of Religiosity, Age and Education
for Five Countries on the NRS for Incest*

200

TABLE 23
Significant Effects of Country, Age, Religiosity, and Education on Norm Resistance to Incest

	PROPORTION OF VARIATION	DF	F	P
Country	.11215	4	81.928	.001
Age	.02545	1	74.368	.001
Religiosity	.00679	1	19.841	.001
Education	.00209	1	6.107	.01
Country by age	.03426	4	25.028	.001
Country by religiosity	.00577	4	4.215	.01
Country by education	.00422	4	3.083	.05
Country by religiosity by age	.02285	4	16.693	.01
Total	.21358	26	24.004	.001
Residual	.78642	2,298		

on incest is not at all clear, and its application generally rare in most countries. Although most religions on the surface forbid various kinds of incestuous relationships, so also are limited incestuous relationships permitted: for example, the tradition of marriage between cousins in Iran. It is rather fascinating to speculate on the significance of age for norm resistance to incest. Are older New Yorkers less puritanical than younger New Yorkers? Has the wheel of liberalization of the post-industrial society begun to turn back? Low norm resistance displayed by the older respondents is what one would expect, especially in developing countries. Yet perhaps there are limits to modernization and that now we see in the New York sample a glimmer of a return to traditional moral values by the young.[8]

DRUGS. As Table 24 shows, apart from the country variable, the factors of religiosity, education, and age had significant influences on norm resistance concerning the taking of drugs. Since the drug described in each country differed considerably, it is difficult to interpret. The effects of religiosity appear to be extremely inconsistent, as in Chart 16. With increased religiosity, norm resistance increased in both India and Iran—countries where the use of hashish is established in the

---

[8]Earlier surveys, such as that by Rettig and Pasamanick (1959), found that there was a strengthening of moral values held by the young.

CHART 16

*Comparative Effects of Religiosity, Education and Age
for Five Countries on the NRS for Taking Drugs*

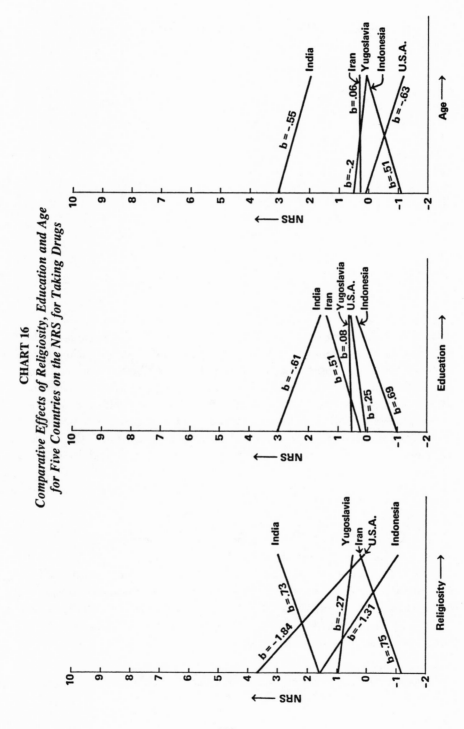

TABLE 24

Significant Effects of Country, Religiosity, Education,
and Age on Norm Resistance to Taking Drugs

	PROPORTION OF VARIATION	DF	F	P
Country	.11778	4	82.154	.001
Religiosity	.01839	1	51.309	.001
Education	.01070	1	29.853	.01
Age	.00495	1	13.811	.01
Country by religiosity	.00681	4	4.760	.05
Country by education	.00854	4	5.956	.05
Country by age	.00538	4	3.752	.05
Country by education by religiosity	.00353	4	2.462	.05
Total	.17607	23	21.359	.01
Residual	.82393	2,298		

culture, and where legislation has outlawed their use. On the other hand, one would have expected the same for Indonesia, yet the responses were similar to the U.S. sample: the more religious were much less resistant, which is what one would expect in the U.S. Religiosity was not an important variable in Yugoslavia, a predictable finding.

The effects of education were similar across all countries except India. The dominant pattern was for the better educated to display higher norm resistance to this act. The reverse was the case in India.

Age had rather inconsistent effects. While it had little effect in Iran or Yugoslavia, its effects in India and U.S. were very similar: as age increased, norm resistance decreased. This we would expect, since both countries have a tradition of official disapproval of taking drugs, and it is the young who question this resistance. In contrast, age in Indonesia had the opposite effect. The older were much more resistant, suggesting that they upheld the traditional use of hashish in Indonesia.

It can be seen that third order interaction effects were also found for country, education, and religiosity. A look at the cell means of NRS broken down by these variables reveals a consistent finding: in all countries (except Yugoslavia where there were no significant differences), the most extreme resistance was displayed by the well educated, non-religious respondents.[9]

---

[9]The means for these groups were: India: 3.548 (N=31); Indonesia: 2.00 (N=14); Iran: 1.976 (N=42); and U.S.: 1.615 (N=13).

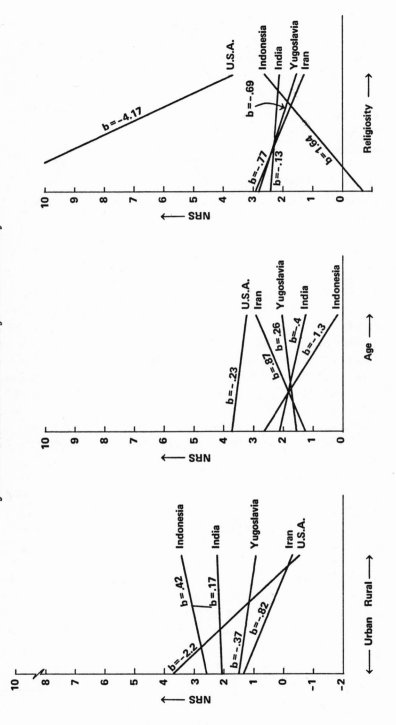

CHART 17

*Comparative Effects of Urban/Rural, Age, and Religiosity
for Five Countries on the NRS for Homosexuality*

204

HOMOSEXUALITY. The massive effects of the country variable along with the significant effects of religiosity, age and the urban/rural factors, are displayed in Table 25. Religiosity was by far the more important factor, but its effects were rather chaotic as Chart 17 shows. While the general tendency was for increased religiosity to be correlated to a decreased norm resistance, this was demonstrated in the extreme for the New York sample, yet in the opposite extreme for Indonesia, where increased religiosity was related to increased norm resistance. There is no ready explanation for this finding.

The effects of age were also of considerable interest. It can be seen from Chart 17 that for the U.S., India, and Indonesia, as age increased, norm resistance decreased, suggesting again that the older were more conservative in their views of homosexuality than the younger. The opposite relationship was found for Iran and Yugoslavia, in which the older of these countries displayed greater resistance.

The effects of the urban/rural factor appeared to have a rather steady interaction effect with each country. The rural U.S. was less resistant, in Iran somewhat more resistant, and successively Yugoslavia, India, and Indonesia became clearly more resistant.

Third order interaction effects were also obtained among the variables of country, religiosity, age and, urban/rural. The cell means after the NRS was broken down within each country according to these variables revealed a highly culture-specific grouping of respondents. In the U.S., the middle-aged, religious rural respondents were clearly the lowest norm resisters ($\overline{X}=2.538$, N$=13$). In India, it was the middle-aged, non-religious urban group which was the highest resister ($\overline{X}=3.923$, N$=13$). The Iranian non-religious urban respondents were the highest resisters to control of this act ($\overline{X}=2.125$, N$=8$). And in Yugoslavia, it was the old, non-religious rural who least resisted control ($\overline{X}=0.222$, N$=9$).[10]

ABORTION. Table 26 displays the significant effects of the background factors of country, urban/rural, religiosity, and education.

We see in Chart 18 that the urban/rural factor interacted considerably with the country variable, in the same direction for all countries except Indonesia. For the former, the urban were high resisters to

---

[10]These means and those reported in footnote 9 above, should be compared cross-culturally, taking into account the precautions outlined in Chapters 6 and 7. The initial comparison of most interest here is to compare these means to those for the entire sample of each country as displayed in Table 16. The means should also be considered only as roughly tentative because of the rapidly reducing N.

abortion, and the rural low resisters. In Indonesia, it was the rural element who were again high resisters.

The effects of education, although not all that great, tended in the direction of the better educated to be higher on norm resistance. The slight exception was Indonesia where the opposite relationship was found. Education was not a significant factor in the U.S.

TABLE 25

Significant Effects of Country, Religiosity, Age and Urban/Rural on Norm Resistance to Homosexuality

	PROPORTION OF VARIANCE	DF	F	P
Country	.29923	4	284.873	.001
Religiosity	.02289	1	87.167	.001
Age	.00949	1	36.139	.001
Urban/rural	.00634	1	24.143	.001
Country by religiosity	.00892	4	8.492	.001
Country by age	.01542	4	14.680	.001
Country by urban/rural	.01048	4	9.977	.001
Country by religiosity by age	.0095	4	9.044	.001
Country by urban/rural by age	.00351	4	3.342	.01
Total	.38578	27	54.410	.001
Residual	.61422	2,339		

TABLE 26

Significant Effects of Country, Urban/Rural, Religiosity and Education upon Norm Resistance to Abortion

	PROPORTION OF VARIANCE	DF	F	P
Country	.32714	4	343.968	.001
Urban/rural	.04695	1	197.461	.001
Religiosity	.02500	1	105.144	.001
Education	.00719	1	30.239	.001
Country by urban/rural	.01685	4	17.717	.001
Country by religiosity	.00275	4	2.891	.05
Country by education	.00396	4	4.164	.01
Total	.42983	19	95.145	.001
Residual	.57017	2,398		

206

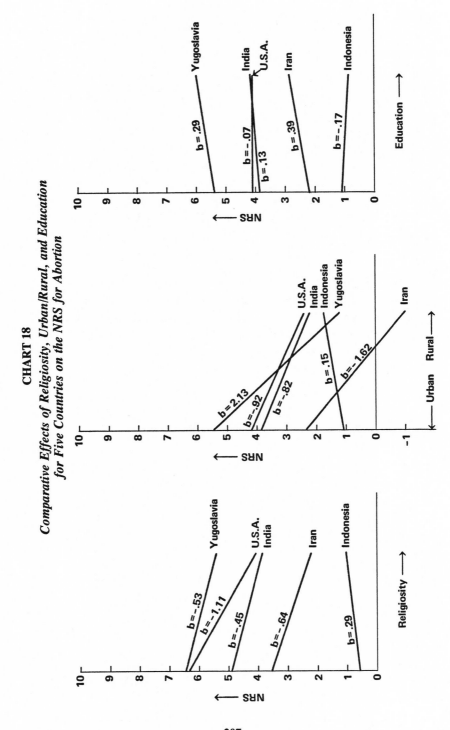

CHART 18

*Comparative Effects of Religiosity, Urban/Rural, and Education
for Five Countries on the NRS for Abortion*

207

Religiosity was generally negatively correlated to norm resistance for all countries except Indonesia, where the relationship was positive, and there is no explanation for this.

PROTEST. It can be seen from Table 27 that education, religiosity, and urban/rural factors had significant effects on norm resistance to this act.

Education accounted for the highest portion of variation apart from the country variable, and we can see from Chart 19 that the effects were generally in a similar direction for all countries: as education increased, so did norm resistance. This relationship was especially accentuated for Yugoslavia and Iran.

The urban/rural factors had widely differing effects specific to the various countries. The rural of Indonesia and the U.S. were high norm resisters, but they were low norm resisters in Yugoslavia, Iran, and India.

Religiosity had clearly similar effects across all countries: as it increased, so norm resistance decreased. One might interpret this to mean that the general, cross-cultural effects of religiosity were strongly correlated to political conservatism: clear support for the Marxist interpretation of religion.

TABLE 27

Significant Effects of Country, Education, Religiosity and Urban/Rural upon Norm Resistance to Public Protest

	PROPORTION OF VARIANCE	DF	F	P
Country	.20304	4	170.844	.001
Education	.04393	1	147.856	.001
Religiosity	.01668	1	56.14	.001
Urban/rural	.00754	1	25.377	.01
Country by education	.00794	4	6.665	.05
Country by religion	.00128	4	1.077	NS
Country by urban/rural	.01385	4	11.654	.001
Total	.29423	19	52.001	.001
Residual	.70577	2,370		

208

CHART 19

Comparative Effects of Religiosity, Education and Urban/Rural
for Five Countries on the NRS for Public Protest

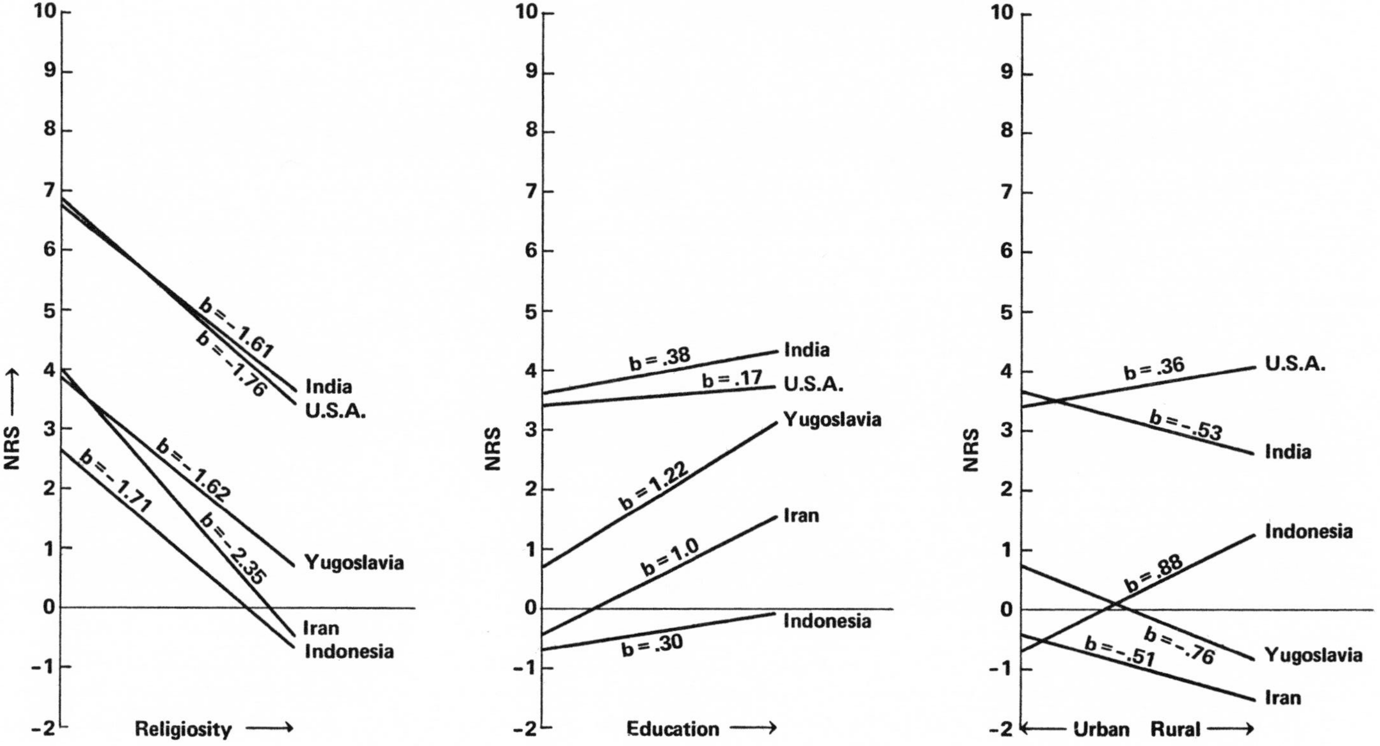

SUMMARY AND CONCLUSIONS

Extensive cross-cultural differences were found in the perception of taking drugs, homosexuality, abortion, incest, and public protest, as measured by the NRS. Minimal and probably insignificant differences were found for the remaining acts of robbery, appropriation, factory pollution, and not helping. The summarizing measure of the DCS also displayed considerable cross-cultural differences. In general, the countries most favoring control of deviance were Iran, Indonesia, and Yugoslavia, and these countries tended also to be those that had totalitarian polities and were less economically developed.

While taking the cross-cultural differences into account, it was apparent that religiosity played a consistently more important part in affecting perceptions of deviance or norm resistance than any other variable. It was positively correlated to deviance control for all countries except Yugoslavia, an exception explained by the religious respondents of Yugoslavia being more aware of the "right to be different." In general, it was negatively correlated to the NRS for most acts for most countries. The one exception in this regard was Indonesia where religiosity was positively correlated to the NRS for homosexuality and abortion. This finding is difficult to explain except to suggest that the Indonesian sample displayed other "deviant" response patterns according to other independent variables.

The urban/rural factor was also found to be a very influential factor. It was generally positively correlated to deviance control, and negatively correlated to norm resistance for all acts for which it had a significant effect (the deviant acts of homosexuality, abortion, protest), for all countries *excepting* Indonesia where the relationship was the reverse.

Education, next in importance to religiosity in its impact upon deviance perception, was negatively correlated to deviance control and positively correlated to norm resistance of all acts in which it had a significant effect (all except homosexuality) for all countries. Again, the only clear exception to this rule was the Indonesian sample, where the direction of the relationship was reversed for the DCS, and the NRS on abortion.

Age was only of minor significance, and appeared to have no consistent pattern across cultures. Its effects appeared to be largely culture-specific, and here only for the acts of incest, taking drugs, and homosexuality.

No other background factors were found to have a significant effect. These included specifically sex and social class as measured by occupation of household head.

Of special interest is the response variation to the act of incest, the so-called universal taboo. Religiosity had its most country-specific effects for this act, whereas the effects of education were clearly toward liberalization. On the other hand, age had a more conservative influence. Responses to the act of taking drugs were highly culture-specific with religiosity having a liberalizing effect in Iran and India, but a conservative effect in other countries. However, when linked with education, it was found consistently the well educated, non-religious in all countries were much more resistant to the control of taking drugs.

Our general conclusions are that the effects of background variables upon perceptions of deviance are minimal. We were unable to account for more than 45 percent of the variance in any of our dependent measures according to background factors, and even here, it was the country variable which accounted for 30 percent and more of that portion of variation accounted for, thus leaving only 10 percent and often much less of the variance to be accounted for by the other variables of religiosity, education, age, and urban/rural. Thus, although the analyses of variance do display these variables as having statistically significant effects, we should not lose sight of the fact that they are explaining little of the variation.

The conclusion, therefore, must be that although various social background variables are important determinants of differential perceptions of deviance, they are not all *that* important. Certainly, to suggest that there are hard and fast lines drawn between those who favor deviance control and those who do not according to sociological characteristics would be substantially to overstate the case. If conflict theory requires that there be a clear differentiation between social groups according to deviance control, then it is not adequately supported by the data. This applies especially to crimes *mala antiqua, mala in se*, and *mala prohibita*. It applies to every country sample studied.

nine

THE CRIMINAL LAW AND ITS SANCTIONS IN SIX CULTURES

INTRODUCTION

All criminal codes, whether written or unwritten, are highly specialized dicta, having developed an internal logic of their own, often over centuries of evolution. According to Sorokin's "ethico-juridical" theory (Sorokin, 1957), the normative content of the criminal law reflects the normative content of a culture, although the law may at times either lag or foreshadow changes in cultural patterns. However, it may be argued that many basic concepts of law, having their origins in early cultural history, but at the same time existing within a relatively autonomous linguistic framework (i.e. the accumulated body of argued cases) may develop according to their own logic, and therefore gaps may occur between some legal concepts or values and other normative components of culture.

The theory sometimes proposed in opposition to Sorokin is Becker's (See Cohen, 1966:33–36), which is basically a personalistic theory of history: that changes (in laws) are brought about by specific, acting individuals, whom Becker terms moral entrepreneurs. It is assumed by this view that the laws are not representative of the culture at large, but rather are a direct product of the campaigning of moral entrepreneurs and, in later formulations, of interest groups. However, as Cohen points out, the two approaches are not necessarily opposed, if one interprets the role of moral entrepreneurs as expressers or implementers of prevailing cultural mores.

But neo-Marxist theorists have not been satisfied with this interpretation. Nowadays it is often argued that Western criminal law does not represent the interests of the masses, but rather of the propertied, or more loosely, the "upper" classes (Quinney, 1974).[1] The "Carriers

---

[1] There are several variations on this position, each suffering from the same difficulty: the inability to settle upon a clear definition of "upper class." Quinney's work (1973) is

Case" is seized upon as the prime example of a criminal law catering to class or special interests. What is important is that although the law responds to changing social conditions, it does so on its own terms; i.e. by developing its own inner logic. While the structure of Western criminal law may easily be shown to be "class-based" in some areas (economic or white collar crime being a prime example), much of its logic and many of its concepts are not. The concept of intent, for example, cannot clearly be shown to be class-based in origin. In Western criminal law, concepts such as these have their origins deep in the roots of Judeo-Christian religion—perhaps before. They are retained and constantly refined in the face of an increasing secularization of Western criminal law.[2]

The sweep of Sorokin's work is so enormous (the comparative analysis of criminal codes from medieval times to the 20th century for five countries), that it is easy to relegate the effects of revolution to a minor position. Sorokin was able to show that the majority of laws were retained even after revolution; instead, basic changes in law came about very slowly: they were evolutionary.[3] This observation probably applies to all six of the countries in this study. Indonesia, India, Iran, and Yugoslavia especially have been occupied many times by foreign powers; Yugoslavia and the United States have undergone revolution; and Italy underwent a late unification in comparison to other countries, having had before that time a multifarious set of criminal codes in

---

especially remiss in this regard, in which he virtually defines anyone with an income of $16,000 or more to be "upper class." Dahrendorf (1969) and his criminological surrogate, Turk (1969), both manage to "go beyond" social class into an equally incomprehensible abstraction of "dominance" and "submission." The most realistic position appears to be one that recognizes that lines of conflict or confrontation shift according to the issue (Dahl, 1967), and that it is not classes but *interest groups* which effect immediate changes in laws. It is to be regretted that Quinney, having given much attention to interest groups in his early work, subsequently neglected the topic in his Marxist writings.

[2] Patrick Devlin (1968), among others, has made this observation. The works of the eminent legal theorist H. L. A. Hart (1963) are an excellent example of an attempt to secularize the criminal law. That the law is becoming more secularized and more concerned with materialistic problems supports Sorokin's contention that our culture has moved from an idealistic to a "super-sensate" culture.

[3] Sorokin's work laid the groundwork for a theory of culture that has since been applied (or assumed) by anthropologists and moral philosophers who have tried to investigate the question of cultural or ethical relativism. These works (e.g. Westermarck, 1906) have taken the formal written law as direct evidence of cultural form, or more precisely, "public opinion." Although most anthropologists have emphasized the diversity of criminal laws across cultures, a number have also re-emphasized the uniformity of certain basic laws such as murder with intent, incest, and rape (Kluckhon, 1955; Linton, 1952; Ginsberg, 1956). We shall take up the question of ethical relativism in much more detail in the final chapter. Of course, the identification of the common elements of criminal law is a strong preoccupation of comparative criminal law (Davis, 1969).

relation to its many autonomous states. Yet, as we will see, it is not so much the content of criminal law that has been substantially changed—more so its administration. In India, Indonesia, and Iran, criminal law administration had been early dominated by the Islamic religious courts. Later, colonial powers overlayed yet another administrative system. In Yugoslavia, although Soviet law dominated the Yugoslav criminal code, most of the basic crimes remained the same. Again, it was the criminal procedure and political reorganization of the courts that changed most radically in Yugoslavia, and this was repeated after the comminform conflict when Tito broke with the Soviets. In sum, the complexities of the criminal law are considerable in every country sampled. The structure of the law is interwoven with an internal logic of law, plus evolving historical, social, religious, and to a lesser extent, political conditions. The latter are more closely associated with changes in the administration of criminal law. What all of this means, then, is that to compare our necessarily very general act descriptions to the criminal law in each country is difficult. Because all of the codes have evolved in such a specialized way, relating our general act descriptions to them requires that one ignore many of the finer points of the particular codes. Quite often, because of the generality of the act descriptions, they might be covered by several different criminal laws.

Our aim here is to select from the criminal law in each country the relevant sections, especially punishments, in relation to our act descriptions. Additionally, since it is usual that the *practice* of criminal law may differ substantially from the criminal law as it is written, we shall try to observe any significant differences where applicable.

GENERAL BACKGROUND OF CRIMINAL LAW

India

The criminal law of India comprises mainly two statutes—the Indian Penal Code and the Code of Criminal Procedure. The Indian Penal Code was enacted in 1860, representing transplanted English jurisprudence. Prior to 1860, Islamic law was the basic law used in the administration of justice, having displaced the early provisions of Hindu law after the Moslem occupation. The code was revised in 1971, and further reforms were suggested by the Indian Law Commission, but these proposals are mostly unimplemented to date.

The Code of Criminal Procedure was enacted in 1898 and amended subsequently in 1923, 1955, and 1973. Some additional laws such as the Indian Opium Act were also passed which created crimes not covered by the Indian Penal Code.

Forms of punishments vary considerably. The death penalty is reserved for the most serious crimes. Imprisonment may be for life, a specified term, or an indeterminate term, "till the court rises." Two types of prison also exist: "rigorous" imprisonment (prison with hard labor), and "simple" imprisonment. Solitary confinement may also be imposed in addition to either of these.

Fines are also common sanctions which may be used alone or in addition to prison terms. If the offender defaults in payment of fines, he may be sentenced to imprisonment for an additional term according to the following scale: 2 months simple imprisonment for fines less than $50, 4 months for a fine of $50 to $100, and 6 months when the fine exceeds $100.

Finally, there are some mandatory minimum sentences prescribed by the Indian Penal Code for particular offenses. These are: a) waging war against the government, and murder (life imprisonment), b) murder by a person undergoing a life sentence (mandatory death penalty), c) robbery or dacoity, with attempt to cause death or grievous hurt and attempt to commit robbery or dacoity with a deadly weapon (7 years). Parliament and State Legislatures have recently tended to enact separate statutes providing mandatory minimums, where it has been felt that courts were not prepared to provide sentences of a sufficient deterrent effect. Examples of these statutes are the Prevention of Corruption Act, 1947, the Prevention of Food Adulteration Act, 1954; the Supression of Immoral Traffic in Women and Girls Act, 1956, and the Bombay Prohibition Act of 1949.

Indonesia

The origins of Indonesian Criminal Law are complex. Writing in 1948, E. Adamson Hoebel noted that there were basically four different systems of justice operating, often overlapping. These were:

1. "Government justice," administered by Europeans according to European Criminal Law, basically of Dutch origin.
2. "Native justice," where local tribunals rendered decisions "in the name of the king," based partly upon a mixture of European Criminal Law and local custom. Both these types of criminal

justice are formally organized around a set of criminal codes and court organization.

3. Village justice. Although in the early 1900s village justice was systematically being replaced by "native justive" due to the works of Von Vokenhoven and others, attempts were made to preserve village justice, and in 1935 a statute was enacted in which the higher officials of native justice were required to respect the decisions of judges in small autonomous communities. This had the effect of reviving village justice throughout many parts of Java. The law used at this level of justice is sometimes considered the "bottom level of adat law" or "customary law," terms which generally refer to unwritten laws and procedures which have roots in the cultural history of the local community, often appearing as ancient or mystical rites. No doubt they are related to various religious origins, but Hoebel formally separates the two spheres of law.

4. Religious justice, basically of Moslem structure and origin (although overlayed with various Hindu and Christian practices and concepts). In earlier times, provision was always made in the higher courts of Native Justice for a priestly adviser, and a Priest Court was also established as a parallel to the Native Superior Court. The power of these religious courts has always been a subject of controversy, so that their jurisdiction has tended to remain largely in the area of marriage and divorce, and not a great deal in criminal law.

In general, these four levels of law continue in Indonesia today. Modern arbitration councils in the city, and village councils in the rural areas continue to receive considerable recognition from the central government. Several attempts have been made in the past to codify or "unify" adat law, but these have failed largely because it has been argued that to unify adat law would be to destroy it, and since it represents such a deep part of Indonesian history, it would amount to an eradication of a rich aspect of Indonesian culture.

However, as far as can be ascertained, although the *substantive* criminal law of native justice is still adat law, the adat penalties are practically all gone, and have been replaced by those of the European criminal code. According to adat law, for example, there was no such thing as imprisonment. Most "punishments" were in the form of restitutions. Ter Haar (1948) reports a system, for example, in which an offense committed with the mouth required payment in chickens; offenses committed with the hand required payment with goats, with the whole body, buffaloes. Often, the payment was made by "jeruk"—offering a meal to the injured party and chiefs of the offended community. The ultimate sanction, if the individual did not perform these rites of restoration, was expulsion from the village.

Then, we may conclude that a dualism of substantive criminal law has existed for many decades since the Dutch colonial period. A European based code was first enacted in the Code of Civil and Criminal Procedure of 1848 and in the Criminal Code of 1866, intended for application to foreigners. A Criminal Code for Natives was enacted in 1872, and this was revised in 1918 with the provision for it to apply to all elements of the population (See: Engelbrecht, 1939:993f). This was the high point of attempts at unification of adat law. Attempts were also made to formalize an "intermediate law"—part adat and part European, but this was put aside and disparagingly termed "fantasy law." With the Japanese occupation, there was a return to dualism, and adat law was encouraged. Since independence, Indonesia has tried to enhance its adat law more fully, but at the same time has sought to unify the law. Court procedures have been standardized. A unified commercial law has recently been developed. Work goes on in an attempt to codify adat law.

It is clear, however, that as far as punishments are concerned, those of Western or European criminal law prevail: imprisonment and monetary fines. Thus, our use of imprisonment as the indicator of official sanction for crimes in Indonesia is probably reasonable.

Iran

Although Iran first adopted a constitution in 1906, its criminal law has early roots in Islamic law. The basic parameters of the Islamic law of crimes are as follows:

Lex Talionis: This "eye-for-eye," existed even before Islam. Mohammed the Prophet kept the principle, but modified it somewhat to allow the injured party to require restitution rather than a strictly "eye" for "eye" punishment. Thus, restitution in the form of goods or money would be handed to the injured party, or in the case that the victim was dead, to his relatives. *Lex talionis* was applied only to the common crimes of murder and aggravated assault.

Islamic Offenses: Basically four punishable offenses are clearly outlined in the Koran, and these are theft, adultery, unfounded accusation of adultery, and atheism. Another three crimes have been added by the

Mutjahids (religous jurists) as interpretations of certain passages of the Holy Book, or as interpretations of particular acts or pronouncements attributed to the Prophet. These crimes are homosexuality, adultery with a married woman, and drinking of alcoholic beverages.

Ta-Ziraat (Misdemeanors): Although superficially, such acts under this rubric were misdemeanors and therefore required only mild punishments, depending upon the social and political conditions of the times, this aspect of Islamic law could be heavily abused. According to this principle, *any act* not provided for under the above two headings could be punished in the light of Islamic rules and principles by means of a decision called *Fatra,* rendered by a Mutjahid. Since the Mutjahid was considered the supreme source of knowledge or interpreter of the Holy Scriptures, it was left to him freely to pronounce judgment on whatever action he deemed to be proscribed by the Koran. Discretion therefore was absolute, and severe punishments including the death penalty were frequently carried out.

This system of criminal law, basically unwritten and locating all power within the religious elites lasted well into the 20th century. Although the French Penal Code of 1810 was adopted almost wholesale in 1906, it has taken many years to overtake the religious courts. Now, there is a highly structured and complex judicial system, with Primary Courts in every district composed of a judge, a prosecutor, and an investigation officer. These courts deal with the bulk of criminal matters. The lower municipal courts are comprised usually of one judge to deal with minor offenses, with rights to give only 1–11 days imprisonment. In addition, there are a number of special courts to deal with criminal matters of government employees, and a few religious courts, mainly seated in Qum and Tehran. The jurisdiction of religious courts has been severely limited, however, since the Shah's policy of limiting the power of Mutjahids, especially by declaring Shiism (the lower order of Islamic religion) as the national religion.

In 1972, an attempt was made to revise the dominant French Code, and also to extend the jurisdiction of Houses of Equity and Arbitration Councils in an effort to relieve the burden of serious backlogs of the courts. (See : *Iran Almanac,* 1972:123). These courts are basically local councils comprised of elected officials. The House of Equity is a village or rural council and the arbitration council is an urban council. While education qualifications are not required of the elected officials of the House of Equity (an official may even be illiterate), those for the Arbitration Council must have a high school education and cannot be a government employee. However, a judge of the Ministry of Justice is attached to each of these councils.

Both of these councils deal mainly with petty and civil matters, although they concern themselves with misdemeanors where the sentence is up to two months imprisonment. The number of cases heard by these councils has increased rapidly from approximately 240 in 1964–1965; to 8213 in 1973–1974 (*Iran Almanac,* 1974).

By and large, however, apart from isolated revisions, the French Code remains basically the Iranian Criminal Code. The major revisions in recent years have been to abolish imprisonment of debtors (1973). Sanctions available are basically fines, prison, and prison with hard labor, although a move was made in 1974 to abolish the latter.

Italy

At the beginning of the 19th century, Italy was still divided into a myriad of small states. New penal codes, influenced by both the Napoleonic code of 1810, and by the principles of Beccaria, were enacted everywhere. There were, for example: the criminal code of the Dukedom of Parma in 1820; the criminal code of the States of the Church in 1832; the Tuscan criminal code of 1853.

After the unification of Italy in 1861, the Sardinian criminal code of 1859 gradually was extended to all of Italy. Eventually, the Italian legislature established a new penal code on 30 June 1889.

In 1919, a commission headed by Enrico Ferri was appointed to prepare a reform inspired by the new socio-criminological criteria. Guided by the postulates of the positive school, this commission finished its work in 1921, but its proposed code was never approved because of strong opposition.

With the rise of the Fascist regime in 1922, a new committee was appointed to prepare a definitive test that was enacted 19 October 1930. In 1931, a new criminal procedure code and prison rules and regulations were enacted. These codes are still in force in Italy today, with important modifications.

When the Fascist regime ended, Italy established a new constitution, in which there were various articles relating to the administration of criminal law. Article 27 was especially significant since it stated: that penal responsibility is personal; that the offender is not considered guilty until the definitive sentence; that the punishment may not consist of treatment contrary to the sense of humanity and that it must aim at the resocialization of the prisoner.

Various attempts have been made to enact an entirely new penal code: in 1948–1950, 1960, and 1968. All have been unsuccessful. Thus, the Fascist code is still the basis of Italian criminal law.

The code of 1930 can be considered as a clear compromise between two major schools of criminology: the classical and the positive schools. The present code has retained the principles of the classical school: punishment is based on the responsibility of the offender. But at the same time, the concept of "social dangerousness" has been introduced. Thus, there is in addition or alternatively to the classical "retributive punishment" (i.e. life sentence, imprisonment, fine, etc.), the possibility of "security measures" which are sentences (indeterminate) to various treatments or work house facilities depending upon the assessment (by the judge) of the degree of the offender's social dangerousness.

Perhaps the most unique feature of the Italian Penal Code and Procedure is the highly individualized system of identifying the penalty for each concrete case. The system works as follows: in the sentencing process, the judge starts by identifying the basic penalties to be applied within the minimum and maximum limitations established by the law in terms of prison time and/or money for each crime. In this operation the judge uses his discretion, but the law dictates precise criteria he must follow. These criteria (in Article 133 of the Italian Penal Code) must be used to weigh the gravity of the crime and the criminal "disposition" by means of an evaluation of the nature, type, means, time, place, and any other modality of the action; the extent of the harm and/or danger produced to the victim; and the degree of malicious intent concerned in the actual accomplishment of the act, but not concerning the consequences. The assessment of the criminal "disposition" of the offender should also result from an evaluation of the motive for the action and the character of the offender; the general conduct and life before the crime, and criminal and judicial records of the offender; his conduct both during and following the crime; and his individual, family, and social life conditions.

Once the judge has established what, in his opinion, is the appropriate basic penalty, he must calculate the effect of circumstances (both aggravating and mitigating). There are many types of circumstances, but for our purpose, it is sufficient to note that these circumstances fall into three main categories: common, generic, and special. When both aggravating and mitigating circumstances concur in the same case, the judge must follow one of two criteria: a prevalent judgment or an equivalent judgment. The former means that the judge decides that one type (aggravating or mitigating) prevails and therefore disregards the other, and the latter means that the judge decides that the two types of circumstances are equivalent and therefore takes neither into account. This choice is only allowed concerning common or generic circumstances, not where special circumstances exist; these must be considered separately. For each common or generic circumstance the judge adds (or subtracts) up to one third of the penalty, i.e. the basic penalty plus or minus amounts of circumstances already calculated. This means that in practice the judge can vary the penalty from one day or one lire up to one third of the basic calculation. As far as specific circumstances are concerned, the judge fixes the extra, or subtractable amount case by case; sometimes certain specific aggravating circumstances carry different autonomous minimum and maximum limitations of the basic penalty. When specific circumstances concur with common or generic circumstances, the latter two are calculated after the former have been accounted for. In Italian judicial practice it is quite exceptional for a crime to have no circumstances to be considered.

The judicial calculation of the final penalty with aggravating circumstances can be: triple the maximum limit established by law for the legal pattern of crime concerned, if "common" or "generic" circumstances; or triple the maximum limit established by law for the legal pattern of crime concerned plus the addition of that for the aggravating circumstances (special). However, there are some definite limits which the judge must always respect, outlined in Article 66 in the Italian Penal Code.

Regarding mitigating circumstances the final penalty can be: one quarter of the minimum limit established by law for the legal pattern of crime concerned, if "common" or "generic" circumstances; or one quarter of the minimum limit established by law for the legal pattern of crime concerned minus that for the special mitigating circumstances. Here, too, there are limits that the judge must respect.

The process described above applies both to crimes (*delitti*) and "*contravvenzioni*" (misdemeanors), the difference being that for crimes the detention is known as "*reclusione*" and the fine as "*multa*" whereas for "*contravvenzioni*" the detention is called "*arresto*" and the fine "*amenda.*" This distinction, however, is more theoretical than practical.

221

To complete the description of the Italian system, one sees that in some cases security measures are applied either instead of or in addition to the penalty. If the offender is judged to be mentally ill (*vizio totale di mente*) he may be committed to a criminal mental hospital if the crime he committed is of a certain gravity. If the offender has a minor mental illness, which does not affect his penal responsibility (*vizio partiale di mente*) the penalty will be diminished and in addition he may be committed to a criminal institution for mental care and custody. If the offender is mentally sound but is an habitual or professional criminal after the execution of the penalty, he may be committed to a criminal agricultural work institution or undergo a supervised period of liberty. Security measures are fixed by law as far as the minimum period is concerned. After this minimum period, a special judge reassesses the offender's personality to determine whether he is still socially dangerous. According to his findings, the offender may be released, or the security measure prolonged.

U.S.A.: New York

In contrast to other countries, American criminal law is not so much comprised of competing layers or systems of criminal justice, but rather represents a body of law, evolving from English Common Law. After the Revolution of 1776, the various states of the union sought to assert their independence. However, this independence was directed toward (or against) current or new English criminal law, rather than the older body of Common Law. There was, however, considerable confusion during that period, especially in New York State. Brown (1964) reports that in 1788 an Amendment to the Laws declared all British Statutes inoperable. Yet in 1821 the New York Constitution (Art. VIII, Sec. 13) stated that the common law would continue to be law "unless altered or repealed." Thus, "an undefineable, unknowable group of old laws somehow maintained a ghostly presence." (Friedman, 1973:97).

However, as societal and economic conditions changed in the 19th century, so did the consumer need for law. Friedman (1973) argues that this was the legislative era—an era when many new laws were passed to meet the needs of the masses of propertied middle and upper classes. While the law became increasingly secularized, or less interested directly in "moral" wrongs, it became more instrumentally concerned with the economic sphere, especially the protection of private property. There was a proliferation of statutory laws, and a proliferation of laws to protect the special interests of the industrialists.[4] But, there were many laws passed that concerned "sharp business practices," especially for consumer protection. Today many of these laws, of course, are not enforced.

Now each state has its own criminal code, having its own set of cases or "common law." The fact remains, however, in most states, early British Common Law can still be "received" into criminal cases if the case appears to warrant it, and most of the codes rest on the enormous proliferation of laws that occurred in the 19th century, many never repealed. Prior to that proliferation, judges were relatively free, by interpretation of the Common Law, to "create" new crimes. The frenzied legislation of the 1800s for a time took away that discretion. But, today, judges and prosecutors have at their disposal an enormous body of statutes and cases on which to draw. The discretion allowed them, therefore, is great. We shall see that this is most likely the unique feature about American law compared to other systems of criminal law reviewed here. American judges and prosecutors have an enormous range of alternatives and they do not shy away from using discretion individually. There are enormous variations in sentencing behavior not only from one jurisdiction to another, but from one judge to another (Gaylin, 1974; Frankel, 1973).

Yugoslavia

The Yugoslavian Penal Code should be viewed against the general history of Yugoslav Constitutional Law. When Tito took power in 1943, he had begun to establish the basic structure of a communist state. For the next 20 years this movement continued, with the enactment, based upon the model of Soviet Constitutional Law, of extremely detailed and comprehensive legislation. Thus, the law of Yugoslavia was highly centralized, even though the various "republics" within Yugoslavia were permitted to enact their own constitutions and other law. The fact was that the federal codes were so comprehensive as to make the enactment of separate republic laws unnecessary. This was especially the case with criminal law, which came under the type of federal law called "esclusive acts"—laws which could not be altered by the republics (Hondius, 1968:150).

---

[4]This is exemplified by the famous ruling that failed to hold companies responsible to lower employees for damages due to negligence of their officials: *Ryan v. New York Central Rr. Co.*

The battle between unification and diversity has been a constant one in Yugoslavian history. Thus, by 1963, a new constitution was enacted, explicitly recognizing the specific needs and rights of each republic of the Yugoslav Nation. Although the new Constitution still retained the three grades of law which originated from Soviet law—exclusive, basic, and general—major concessions were made to republic independence. The exceptions, however, were laws considered of outstanding importance to the country as a whole, especially in relation to action concerning individual vs. state rights, including criminal law. In addition to this highly centralized, federal supremacy of criminal law, the substance of the law was strongly overlayed with concern for economic development. Separate economic courts were established during the first 20 years of Soviet style government. However, the great changes after the comminform conflict also altered the court structure. Local government districts, which in point of fact had not been "local" at all, but rather outposts of the central government, were broken up, the districts were completely reapportioned, and the local community was reorganized as a unit, based upon a local referendum. Economic courts were replaced by general courts. Some of the excessive criminalization of "non-socialist" economic activity was relieved. The basic criminal law in operation, however, remains the Yugoslav Penal Code enacted in 1951.

The Code provides for two types of imprisonment. Simple imprisonment may be of the duration of three days to three years. "Severe confinement" refers to imprisonment of one to 15 years. Capital punishment may be substituted by severe confinement up to 20 years. Simple imprisonment is mostly of the minimal security, reformatory institution. Severe confinement is served under maximum security.

In principle, Yugoslav courts may pronounce only those sentences which are prescribed by the Penal Code. However, in certain specific situations, deviations from this rule are permitted. Thus, Article 42, Para. II of the Code states that "the Court may inflict a penalty below the prescribed limit on a milder type of penalty, if mitigating circumstances have been ascertained, indicating that a milder penalty may achieve the purpose of punishment." Further: "If a penalty of severe confinement or of imprisonment has been prescribed for a criminal act, and if the minimum limit has not been indicated, severe confinement may be substituted by imprisonment of a duration of at least 3 months" (Article 43, Para. II). Other sections of the Code provide for the discretionary substitution of imprisonment by a fine, or a fine by imprisonment (Article 59, Sec. II). The Code establishes the formula of 30 dinars ($2) as equivalent to one day imprisonment, up to a limit of 6 months.

Fines may also be inflicted not only as prescribed by law, but also in addition, " ... as a secondary penalty . . . for criminal acts motivated by cupidity." (Article 26, Para. II).

DIFFICULTIES OF RELATING LAW
TO GENERAL ACT DESCRIPTIONS

From this general survey of the criminal law and its sanctions, we have seen that in every system wide discretionary power resides with the judge. The kind of discretion and the level at which it may be exercised varies from country to country. All judges appear to have wide latitude in prescribing sentences. Sometimes this latitude is highly systematized, as in the Italian system, and other times it is so vague as to practically allow any judge complete discretion in sentencing, such as in New York. In other systems, the discretion lies in choosing one of several systems of law which may be applied to the offender—such as in Indonesia. In addition, the criminal law in the rapidly developing countries is in a state of flux, switching back and forth from centralized to localized jurisdictions as in Indonesia and Iran. In Iran the influence of early and pre-Islamic law remains in the administration of harsh punishments, but the organization of criminal justice has continued rapidly to divest itself of these religious roots. Yet, in spite of these complexities and changes, the influence of the Western system of criminal punishments is undeniable. All countries, regardless of the origin of their criminal laws have incorporated formal legal punishment in the form of fines, and most especially imprisonment as the major form of sanctions.

Prison, the comparatively young criminal sanction has become an almost universal penal sanction. It is for this reason that we will use prison as the major measure of what the written law in each country says about our nine acts, and hopefully also tempered with an understanding of what sanctions are applied in practice to cases similar to our act descriptions.   There are, however, some major difficulties in translating our general act descriptions into the relevant criminal law of each country. As we have already noted, the descriptions had to be general so as to be equally applicable to the wide range of criminal law categories of each country's code. The difficulties in this operation are possibly best summed up by those encountered in applying them to the

New York State Criminal Code. Although the problems confronted in other criminal codes are different in detail, the reader should obtain a clear idea of the general problems which apply to all countries from this analysis of just one country. They are:

The Problem of Jurisdiction: The United States has fifty individual state jurisdictions and a federal jurisdiction, as well as enumerable city and town codes. The first question, of course, is which one governs? The usual rule in the United States is that the law of the site where the act or crime occurs is the law that is followed. The problem is magnified because the United States has no national penal code. Each jurisdiction varies in what it first of all defines as a crime, in the sentences it provides both by statute and/or by practice, and finally, in the practical meaning of the sentences that are imposed.

The Problem of Sentence Parameters: Although we have used "maxima" and "minima" as parameters for comparison of criminal sanctions across countries, this is somewhat arbitrary, yet dictated because of the enormous discretion in sentencing allowed in each country. However, in New York, a "minimum" may refer to a wide range of potential sentences given to a judge by statutes that have never really been used or even considered by him. Sentences, as recorded in penal statutes, may range down to a meaningless "unconditional discharge" that is rarely used in any but the most trivial instances. On the other hand, some jurisdictions (e.g., California) have almost completely indeterminate sentences, with no stated minimum *ever* being applied (or even stated) by a judge in the majority of cases before him.

Other questions become important when one considers the various alternatives to a penal sentence that exist. For example, was the defendant or the "person" a drug addict? Was he insane at the time of the commission of the offense? Was he an alcoholic? Was he a juvenile? If the answer to one or more of these questions is in the affirmative, then there exists a whole new range of "sentencing" alternatives for the judge. Thus, for the purposes of our project, we assume that none of these circumstances obtains; further, that the "person" is male in all but the abortion act. To make comparisons between public perceptions of these act descriptions and legal perceptions, we must assume that all respondents made the same assumptions as the criminal law, or, if they did not, that their assumptions had no bearing on their responses.[5]

---

[5]A special study was conducted to test the hypothesis as to whether differential attributes of the actor affected perceptions of deviance. Although some effects were found, they were not found to be so substantial as to warrant changes in the act descriptions. See: Newman (1974).

Another question is the subject of extra-legal punishment or sanction. For example, although there may be statutory minima to an offense, charges are often dropped after arrest. Compassion is sometimes displayed by such a dropping of charges where it is felt that the arrest itself provided sufficient sanction; i.e., that the unfavorable publicity he received, or the restitution he made, or the shame he endured, served as a sufficient penalty.

Finally, in this area, are we only considering judicially-stated prison sentences? If so, we are being somewhat unrealistic since State Parole Board practice may vary in being less or more willing or reluctant to release a given "person." The question of stated sentence ignores reality in still another fashion in that "good time" in prisons is today a virtually mechanical process in several jurisdictions throughout the United States, habitually reducing sentences by anywhere from one-third to one-sixth automatically.

Sufficiency of the Act Descriptions: Many problems arise here. Were there aggravating or mitigating circumstances? What were the ages, sex, social, and economic conditions of the actors?[6] In terms of the law, almost an infinite variety of circumstances surrounding the acts or actors can be imagined. This does not mean that the descriptions are meaningless. Since we have obtained coherent responses from our samples, we know that the descriptions represent images of deviance, of "ideal type crimes" in their own right. The application of criminal law to the act descriptions is, of course, difficult just as it is to real life offenses. On the other hand, ordinary people are mostly unaware of the enormous variety of circumstances that the criminal law takes into account when passing sentence. Therefore, a rough approximation is defensible.

---

[6]To provide the flavor of the problems confronted in translating the descriptions into criminal law, some of the specific problems with each act were: *Robbery:* Although the $50 was taken forcefully, was it money which the taking "person" had good reason to believe rightfully belonged to him? How serious was the injury? How serious was the hospitalization? Was it prolonged? Were the injuries extensive? Was a weapon used? Was an accomplice involved? Was the forcible theft committed by a starving man in a Jean Valjean situation? *Incest:* Of what specific variety were the "sexual relationships" encompassed by this question, for the peanlty for various sorts varies in different jurisdictions. *Appropriation:* Was the "person" a government employee? How extensive was the theft? Did it involve a large or a small amount of funds? *Factory Pollution:* How "poisonous" are these gases? Are people actually being killed? Just what is the authority or the degree of responsibility of the factory director? *Homosexuality:* Is each "person" an adult? Even though the relations were in private, were the activities filmed for profit? Was the "consent" freely given or possibly one obtained under the influence of drugs? *Taking Heroin:* Does "takes" mean the same thing as "injects" or perhaps "uses"? Or does it mean "possess"? There are different penalties for each of

227

The Problem of Volition: The element of intent or *mens rea* is not touched on at all. In general, American law provides that an intentional act is a more serious event than an accidental one. This rule applies in different degrees to all the criminal codes of our six countries, and probably most intensely to the Italian Penal Code. However, some research has found that intention does not affect respondent's perceptions of the seriousness of crimes (Riedel, 1972).

We see from this list of problems that we can only hope to make very general approximations of the written law of criminal sanctions regarding each act in each country. In addition, since prison appeared to be the only universal and easily quantifiable sanction, we have chosen this as the focus for comparing public perceptions of deviance with legal perceptions. This is a summary of the criminal sanctions pertaining to each act in each country.

ESTIMATING OFFICIAL PRISON TERM

By "Official Prison Term" is meant an estimate based on the following criteria, when such information was available from either each country's criminal codes, sentencing practices, or prison statistics.

1. The minimum prison term if prescribed by law.
2. The conversion of fines to their equivalent in prison term if the applicable criminal code provided such a formula.
3. If the above were not available, an estimate of the sentence usually handed down by the judge. This was based upon the advice or assessment of a legal expert in each country.

---

these. And how *much* heroin is involved? *Abortion:* Was the pregnant woman's physical condition such as to make her unlikely to survive childbirth? *Not Helping:* Was there any relationship between the two people or were they strangers? Was the "person" someone who had a special expertise in terms of rescue effort? Was the "person" a lifeguard or someone with a legal responsibility to effect such a rescue? *Public Protest:* Just what degree of participation is involved? Would respondents give the same answers depending on what the "government" policy in question was? (For example, if the policy being protested is war in Vietnam, would respondents feel the same as if the policy being protested were government enforced integration being protested by a Klu Klux Klan member?) Is "public place," a street where traffic is disrupted or pedestrian flow is halted? The word "violence" obviously has many connotations to different people: What meaning is meant here? Specific exceptions abound even if violence does not result: for example, a person *would* be culpable if he advocated the violent overthrow of the entire governmental system.

Lest it appear that these problems are insuperable, one should note that the application of criminal law even to a real life crime is an extremely complex task. Usually, such offenses are "overcharged."

4. If none of the above were available, one-third of the maximum prison term provided by the relevant criminal code. This proportion is based upon reports from the legal experts of the six countries that generally judges tend to hand down the minimum sentences allowed by law; and where no minima are prescribed, the sentences usually given approximate one-fourth to one-third of the maximum allowed by law.

The results of this procedure are summarized in Table 28, along with the mean prison terms recommended by the public. The details of criminal sanctions applicable to each act now follow.

Robbery

India: This act clearly comes under the definition of the offense of robbery contained in Section 390 of the Indian Penal Code and is punishable by rigorous imprisonment for a term that may extend to ten years and a fine. If the robbery was committed on the highway between sunset and sunrise, the imprisonment may be extended to 14 years. If a person in committing or attempting to commit robbery voluntarily causes hurt, then the maximum punishment is enhanced to imprisonment for life or rigorous imprisonment for a term of up to ten years and a fine, (Section 394). Since the Indian Penal Code does not prescribe a minimum, we have entered 30 months into Table 28, roughly equivalent to the average time served for robbery (See: Newman, 1976a).

Indonesia: Under Article 365, Section 4 of the Indonesian Penal Code, the maximum penalty foreseen for such an offense is from 20 years to life imprisonment and death, depending on how seriously the victim is injured.

Iran: The Iranian Penal Code provides for a minimum of 11 days imprisonment to a maximum of one year.[7] Had the victim not been hospitalized according to this act description, the penalty would have been much less. One month has been entered in Table 28.

Italy: In the Italian Penal Code this description is covered by three alternative legal definitions depending upon the circumstances of the action.

The first is found in Article 625, No. 4, which concerns aggravated

---

[7]This sanction appears very puzzling in the light of the popular belief that extremely serious punishments are meted out to offenders in Moslem countries. The legal expert has assured us that this estimate is indeed accurate.

TABLE 28
Official and Recommended* Prison Terms for Six Countries

	INDIA PRISON TERM		INDONESIA PRISON TERM		IRAN PRISON TERM	
	RECOM-MENDED	OFFICIAL	RECOM-MENDED	OFFICIAL	RECOM-MENDED	OFFICIAL
Robbery	6.7	30.0	8.0	240.0	7.9	1.0
Incest	13.2	0.0	10.6	21.0	12.8	120.0
Appropriation	11.4	120.0 (life)	17.8	240.0	8.9 (bribery)	24.0
Homosexuality	1.9	30.0	1.7	0.0	10.3	36.0
Abortion	0.6	12.0	6.1	16.5	6.7	12.0
Taking drugs	1.0	9.0	1.7	1.0	1.6	6.0
Factory pollution	4.5	6.0	2.8	1.0	3.6	0.0
Public protest	0.2	6.0	0.6	21.0	3.0	0.0
Not helping	0.3	0.0	1.0	7.5	3.2	0.0

TABLE 28 (*cont'd*)

| | ITALY PRISON TERM | | U.S.A. PRISON TERM | | YUGOSLAVIA PRISON TERM | |
	RECOM-MENDED	OFFICIAL	RECOM-MENDED	OFFICIAL	RECOM-MENDED	OFFICIAL
Robbery	65.3	37.3	32.1	18.0	34.0	60.0
Incest	50.6	12.0	9.6	0.0	31.3	10.0
Appropriation	68.9	36.0	31.3	0.0	47.3	12.0
Homosexuality	14.5	0.0	0.5	0.0	5.6	2.5
Abortion	12.7	12.0	0.2	0.0	2.1	0.0
Taking drugs	6.4	38.0	4.4	3.0	5.9	0.0
Factory pollution	13.2	1.0	9.0	0.0	6.4	0.0
Public protest	2.4	1.0	0.0	0.0	5.8	0.0
Not helping	29.7	1.0	3.3	0.0	4.6	1.0

*Recommended prison term is computed as the mean months of prison, in which all respondents who did not choose prison are entered as zeros, and in which all prison terms above 20 years (or life) are entered as 20 years to avoid inflation of the mean by extreme values.

231

theft. This covers the case in which the victim has the money in his hands or on his person in such a way that it can be snatched by violence exercised directly on the money. The injury must be an indirect consequence, although voluntary. The penalty is one to six years imprisonment and $6 to $660 fine.

The second is in Article 628. This covers the case in which the money is obtained by direct violence of the person producing injury, and in this case the punishment is three to 10 years imprisonment and a fine of $330 to $1,320.

The third is in Article 629. This covers the case in which direct violence is exercised on the person in order that the money is handed over by the victim. Here the penalty is three to 10 years imprisonment and a fine of $330 to $1,320.

In all three cases the offender is sentenced to an additional term according to the quantity of physical injury produced and according to the time the victim takes to recover (Article 582). Assuming that the produced injury is minor, the additional penalty is three months to three years.

The description used in the questionnaire is covered more closely either by the second or third conditions. Thus, the official prison term is computed to 36 months plus one month and 10 days (200,000 Lire ($330) converted to its prison equivalent).

New York: Assuming that there was no weapon used, no accomplice, and the injury was not serious, the theoretical maximum is 15 years in prison plus $100 fine, and the minimum could be a conditional discharge. The latter assumes, of course, that this is a first offender. However, in practice, first offenders for this offense usually receive an "indeterminate" sentence of one to five years, of which they usually serve approximately one and one-half years. We have entered 18 months in Table 28.

Yugoslavia: Article 253/I of the Penal Code reads: "If in the course of armed robbery or brigandage with premeditation, a person is severely injured or, if the brigandage is committed by a group or band, the perpetrator will be sentenced to at least five years of severe punishment." The act described therefore is "a grave case of armed robbery and brigandage." Although the legislature did not describe a maximum, the generally accepted limit is 15 years of severe confinement. A perusal of prison and court records of 1968–1970 revealed that the usual sentence handed down, and the time served was roughly five years (See: Newman, 1976f). Thus, 60 months has been entered into Table 28.

Incest

India: Incest *qua* incest is not punishable under the Indian Penal Code. Hence, the act described would only be an offense if the facts relating to its commission constituted the offenses either of rape or adultery. If sexual relations were had against the will of the daughter or without her consent, then it would amount to rape under Section 375 of the Indian Penal Code, punishable with life imprisonment or with imprisonment of either type (simple or rigorous) for a term of up to 10 years and a fine.

If the daughter in the act described were a married woman, then the act would amount to the offense of adultery in the absence of the consent or connivance of the daughter's husband. Section 497 of the Indian Penal Code defines the offense of adultery and limits it only to instances of a man having sexual intercourse with the wife of another. Adultery is punishable by imprisonment of either type for a term up to five years or by a fine or by both fine and imprisonment.

Indonesia: This act fits the description in Article 294 of the Indonesian Penal Code and the maximum penalty is seven years imprisonment. This article can be applied also to "incestual" relationships between civil servants and their subordinates, and similarly to doctors, teachers, warders, et al. who may perform the act with persons under their supervision. As no minimum is prescribed by the Code, 21 months has been entered into Table 28, which is a quarter of the maximum.

Iran: A minimum of 10 years and a maximum of 15 years is prescribed for incest. However, a "grandfather clause" stating that this act is a crime only if the victim chooses to complain, results in practice that it is rarely prosecuted.

Italy: The description of this act fits two of the provisions included in Article 564 of the Italian Penal Code. In both provisions the deed is punishable only on condition that a public scandal results from the action, otherwise it does not constitute a crime.

The first provision concerns one occasion or more, but not habitual sexual intercourse, and the penalty for this is one to five years imprisonment. The second provision is concerned with habitual sexual intercourse and in this case the penalty is from two to eight years imprisonment. An official prison term of 12 months has been inserted in Table 28.

New York: The maximum penalty for this act is four years in prison, and the minimum an unconditional discharge. The act is, in practice rarely, if ever, prosecuted, and if it were, the penalty in practice would probably be probation of five years. There would be a strong possibility that the court would assume a "mental illness background" on the part of the offender. We have entered zero into Table 28.

Yugoslavia: This act is incriminated by Article 198 of the Yugoslavian Penal Code which reads: "A person committing incest with next-of-kin near in blood or with brother or sister, will be sentenced to imprisonment." Neither the lower nor the upper limit of the penalty has been explicitly prescribed by the legislature. However, according to general rules, it may be considered that the penalty foreseen for this offense varies from three days to three years of imprisonment, where Article 30 of the Penal Code allows for only a general maximum penalty of three years of imprisonment. Perusal of prison records covering 1968–1970, suggested that the average term handed down was 10 months, and we have entered this number into Table 28.

Appropriation

India: This act is punishable under Section 403 of the Indian Penal Code which makes it an offense of criminal misappropriation of property to dishonestly misappropriate or convert to one's own use movable property. Punishment for this offense is imprisonment of either type for a term of up to two years or fine or both. It is immaterial whether the property misappropriated is government property or that of a private individual.

More severe penalties for misappropriation of property are provided by other Sections of the Indian Penal Code depending on the circumstances surrounding the misappropriation. Thus, if the property misappropriated were in the trust of the offender, then it constitutes the offense of criminal breach of trust under Section 405 of the Indian Penal Code and the punishment can be imprisonment for a term extending to three years or fine or both. Aggravated forms of the offense of criminal breach of trust are also provided for by the Indian Penal Code as criminal breach of trust by a carrier of goods, a warehouse-keeper, a clerk or a servant is punishable with imprisonment for a term extending to seven years and also a fine; or criminal breach of trust by a public servant, banker, merchant, broker, attorney or agent, is an offense attracting the most severe punishment of imprisonment for life and fine.

234

Therefore, the Indian Penal Code defines a number of offenses involving misappropriation of property, offenses of varying degrees of seriousness. But, the seriousness of the offense is not dependent on the nature or character of the property misappropriated, but rather on the circumstances of the misappropriation and on the category of person committing the misappropriation.

Indonesia: This act conforms to the description in Article 1, Section (1) of the Special Law on the Abolition of Corruption (Act No. 3, 1971, *State Gazette,* 1971, no. 19) which stated that: "It shall be unlawful for any person knowingly or intentionally to acquire or obtain possession directly or indirectly of public funds for his or other person's benefit." The penalty for this offense is from 20 years to life imprisonment and fine of $7,500, 20 years being the minimum for this offense.

Iran: The act of bribery was substituted for appropriation in Iran. Bribery, like opium smoking, cannot be considered as an exactly deviant behavior in Iran—not only because of its prevalence, but because of its historical roots in the society. Before there was a strong centralized government in Iran, people who supposedly worked for the government, actually received their remuneration from the citizens for whom they did certain services. Governors who were sent to the provinces bid for their position and when they got it, they tried to get as much money out of the poor people as they could. This was done mostly through local people who acted on their behalf in collecting taxes and other undefined duties. In the capital too, government employees have always been miserably underpaid, and the recourse to bribery has always been an accepted method to supplement the meagre government salary. The Iranian Penal Code provides for a maximum of five years imprisonment and a minimum of two years plus the return of the bribe. Twenty-four months has therefore been entered into Table 28.

Italy: This act conforms to the description in Article 314 of the Italian Penal Code where the assumption is that the person taking personal advantage of public money has this money in his possession because of his position as a civil servant. The penalty is three to 10 years imprisonment and $60 fine. A legal disqualification also follows consisting of forfeiture of any position of public responsibility. Thirty-six months have been entered in Table 29.

New York: According to the New York Criminal Code, this act presents particular difficulties since the punishment not only varies according to the amount taken, but also as to whether the offender was a government employee. Assuming that the actor was a government employee, the punishment is as follows:

Less than $250:	maximum—1 year plus up to $500 fine minimum—unconditional discharge
$250 to $1,500:	maximum—4 years plus up to $3,000 fine minimum—unconditional discharge
More than 1,500:	maximum—7 years plus up to double amount taken minimum—unconditional discharge

It will be noted that the minimum in all cases is an unconditional discharge. In general, the practice for a minor offense is to give a conditional discharge. For a major offense, the practice is usually restitution plus a fine which may be roughly $10 to $1,500 for a first offender. Since prison in practice is rarely used for these offenders, it would seem reasonable to enter a zero as the official prison term.

Yugoslavia: This is a criminal act of misappropriation under Article 322 of the Yugoslavian Penal Code. Since this criminal act is committed frequently and has various aspects, the legislature has foreseen several alternatives of incrimination, proceeding from the simplest to graver forms and increasing at the same time the penalty for the latter. Thus, the legislature has prescribed a maximum penalty of five years of severe confinement for graver offenses which result in damage of $625 or more as outlined in Para. II of the same article.

There are two more aspects of this offense, graver than the above mentioned, incriminated in Article 255 of the Yugoslavian Penal Code. One of them applies when the value of property or money appropriated amounts to $1875, in which case the maximum penalty prescribed is 15 years of severe confinement. The other aspect applies "when the offense causes particularly grave consequences or when it is committed under particularly aggravating circumstances," in which case the court may inflict a penalty of 20 years.

In the latter case the Yugoslav penal legislation has prescribed a penalty of severe confinement from one to 15 years, except when capital punishment is substituted by a temporary penalty, in which case a penalty of severe confinement is pronounced for a duration of 20 years. Exceptionally, the criminal act of plunder under Article 255, Para. II which relates also to the above, foresees the possibility of inflicting a penalty of 20 years of severe confinement. This shows the importance attached by the legislature to this gravest aspect of appropriation of public property. A minimum of 12 months is mentioned here, and we have entered this into Table 28.

A mixture of severe confinement and imprisonment was handed down by the Yugoslav Courts during the period 1968–70. Of 4,726 persons convicted for this offense over the 1968–70 period, approximately three-quarters were sentenced to imprisonment and a quarter to severe confinement. The average sentence for simple imprisonment was two years, and for severe imprisonment, six months. It may be seen that the average of these two estimates is 15 months, close to the legal minimum used as our official estimate.

Homosexuality

India: This act is covered by Section 377 of the Indian Penal Code that states that whoever voluntarily has carnal intercourse against the order of nature with any man, woman, or animal, shall be punished with imprisonment for life, or with imprisonment of either type for a term of up to 10 years, also liable to fine. The case law on this Section has helped clarify its scope. The Section does not punish *all* homosexual acts. It applies only to acts performed by a male and not to lesbian acts. (*Khandu,* 1924, 26 Cr.L.J. 945). So far as males are concerned, it covers not only acts of sodomy and bestiality, but also oral intercourse. (*Khandu,* Cr.L.J. 1096; *Jacob's Case,* 1870; Russ. and Ry. 331).

The framers of the Indian Penal Code were clearly of the view that male homosexuality was a very serious criminal offense. Lord Macauley's comments on draft section 377 of the Indian Penal Code are illuminating: "It is desirable that as little as possible be said. . . . we are unwilling to insert either in the text or in the notes anything which could give rise to public discussion of this revolting subject." (Note M. to the Indian Penal Code, 1837). Since Macauley's days, however, the attitude of Indian society towards homosexuality has undergone marked change.

The courts have shown a marked reluctance to impose the maximum penalty prescribed by Section 377. Recently the Supreme Court of India heralded change when it reduced the sentence of an individual convicted under the section to the period of imprisonment already undergone by him during the appellate process and ordered the appellant to be released. The Court felt that such punishment was sufficient since the accused, being a highly educated and cultured individual, had suffered loss of service and other serious consequences to his career so the Court favored leniency. (*Chitaranjan Dass v. State of U.P.,* A.I.R.

1974, 2452). This Supreme Court judgment indicates an attitude toward the offense radically different from that of Lord Macauley, the draftsman of the Code.

Indonesia: Homosexual intercourse between two adult persons in private is not a crime in itself. It becomes a criminal act under Article 292 of the Indonesian Penal Code when an adult commits it with an adolescent or in public, and the maximum penalty for this action is five years imprisonment. Since we have assumed that our act description is of homosexuality between adults in private, a zero has been entered into Table 28.

Iran: A minimum of three years and a maximum of 10 years is prescribed for homosexuality. However, as for the act of incest, a "grandfather clause" in the Iranian Penal Code states that this act is a crime only if the victim chooses to complain.

Italy: A homosexual relationship is not a crime in itself. Nevertheless, it becomes a crime against morals when committed in public, as does any sexual intercourse. Since the description in this study specifies that the intercourse took place in private, no punishment is applicable.

New York: The theoretical maximum is three months prison plus $500 fine. The minimum is an unconditional discharge, probation, or up to $500 fine. In practice, this law is never enforced, and so we have entered a zero in Table 28.

Yugoslavia: Homosexual intercourse is incriminated by Para. II of Article 186 of the Penal Code which reads: "The perpetrator of non-natural lechery among males will be sentenced to imprisonment for up to one year." Lesbian intercourse is not incriminated by Yugoslav penal legislation. Therefore, the deed described in the project is punishable provided that males are involved, in which case the maximum penalty is one year of imprisonment.

Court statistics of 1968–69 suggested that the average sentence was 2.5 months, so in the absence of a legal minimum, this amount has been entered into Table 28.

Abortion

India: Section 312 of the Indian Penal Code provides that whoever voluntarily causes a pregnant woman to miscarry shall be punished by imprisonment of either type (simple or severe) for a term of up to three years or with fine or with both. The punishment may be enhanced and extended to seven years imprisonment "if the woman be quick with child." Quickening is the name applied to the sensations experienced by a woman about the fourth or fifth month of pregnancy—the sensations being ascribed to the first perception of the movements of the fetus. Under the penal provision mentioned above the person causing the miscarriage will be punishable for the offense and the woman may be punished as an abetter. However, the penal law does provide an exemption in that there shall be no offense committed if the miscarriage be caused in good faith for the purpose of saving the life of the woman.

In 1971 Indian Parliament enacted the Medical Termination of Pregnancy Act with a view to liberalizing abortions. Any abortion performed in accordance with the conditions laid down in Section 3 of this Act shall not attract the above mentioned provisions of the Indian Penal Code and therefore shall not be an offense. The conditions prescribed by Section 3 are as follows:

1. The pregnancy must be terminated by a registered medical practitioner.
2. Where the length of the pregnancy does not exceed 12 weeks such medical practitioner must be of the opinion formed of good faith that (a) the continuance of the pregnancy would involve a risk to the life of the pregnant woman or of grave injury to her physical or mental health, or (b) there is a substantial risk that if the child were born, it would suffer from such physical or mental abnormalities as to be seriously handicapped. Where the pregnancy was caused by rape, the continuance of such pregnancy will be presumed to constitute a grave injury to the mental health of the woman and such presumption will also apply to any pregnancy which occurred as a result of failure of any contraceptive device or method employed by a married woman or her husband.
3. Where the length of the pregnancy exceeds 12 weeks, but is less than 20 weeks, two registered medical practitioners must fulfill the condition prescribed in Para. 2 above.
4. No pregnancy shall be terminated except with the consent of the pregnant woman and if the woman has not attained the age of 18 years or is a lunatic, the consent in writing of her guardian is necessary.
5. The termination of pregnancy must take place either in a hospital established or maintained by Government or in a place approved for this purpose by the Government.

An abortion that was performed in compliance with these conditions will not constitute an offense under Indian penal law. All other abortions would be punishable as an offense under Section 312 of the Indian Penal Code as mentioned earlier.

It may also be mentioned that Section 313 of the Indian Penal Code makes it a very serious offense to cause miscarriage in a pregnant woman without that woman's consent and provides a maximum punishment for this offense of imprisonment for life.

Indonesia: This description fits that of Article 348, Para. 1 of the Indonesian Penal Code. The maximum penalty is five and one-half years imprisonment. If the end result of this act is death to the woman, the maximum penalty will be seven years imprisonment. One quarter of the maximum has been entered into Table 28.

Iran: According to Article 182 of the Iranian Criminal Code, if a woman "knowingly and without permission of a doctor" commits abortion, she is liable to one to three years in prison. We have, therefore, entered 12 months into Table 28.

Italy: This act fits the description in Article 547 of the Italian Penal Code and the penalty is from one to four years imprisonment. Twelve months has been entered into Table 28.

New York: This act was recently decriminalized in New York State. There is no punishment for this act.

Yugoslavia: Abortion is not a crime in Yugoslavia.

Taking Drugs

India: This act is not covered by the Indian Penal Code, but instead is covered by the "prohibition" laws of the various states in India. The provisions of the Bombay Prohibition Act, 1949 are typical of state legislation on this subject. Section 66(1)(b) of the said Act makes consumption, use, or even possession of gange or any drug produced from the *hemp* plant an offense punishable as follows:

1. For a first offense, imprisonment for a term of not less than three months and not more than six months *and* a fine of not less than $50 and not more than $100.
2. For a second offense, imprisonment for a term of not less than six months and not more than two years *and* a fine of not less than $100 and not more than $200.
3. For third and subsequent offenses, imprisonment for a term not less than nine months and not more than two years *and* a fine of not less than $100 and not more than $200.

The Court has discretion to impose a lower sentence than the minimum (either by way of imprisonment or fine) but only if there are "special and adequate reasons" for doing so and such reasons must be stated in the judgment of the Court.

Indonesia: According to Article 12 of the Narcotics Ordinance (*State Gazette,* 1927, No. 278), all persons are prohibited to own and or use narcotic drugs, except doctors and dentists in their capacity to cure their patients. The violator of this Article can be sentenced for up to three months in jail or a fine of $4 (Article 25, Section 3, Narcotics Ordinance 1927, No. 278). The Ordinance did not make distinction between soft drugs or hard drugs and there is no distinction between the users and the peddlars, traffickers, et al. In daily practice, the law enforcement officer usually does not make a case out for the user. An important aim is to rehabilitate the offender to restore him mentally and physically from the effects of his addiction.

Iran: Opium smoking was a common social passtime for very many Iranians before 1955, and did not involve any sense of shame. On the contrary, when people visited each other, it was usually expected of them to offer opium to the guest. After opium was banned, heroin became a serious problem, although there are no reliable statistics as to the number of addicts. Very serious penalties have been provided by the law for people who commit certain types of activities related to the importation and sale of heroin and opium. The death penalty is imposed in certain cases and more than 30 people have been already executed since a new law was passed in 1969. Taking opium is seen as a less serious crime than taking heroin. The minimum punishment for the former is six months imprisonment, although addicts may register at a special office to obtain treatment and thereby avoid punishment. The standard penalty for taking heroin is three years imprisonment, although there is no written minimum.

Italy: This act is not formally a crime under Italian law. Article 6 (October 22, 1951, No. 1041) of the law at present in force on drug control provides a number of provisions regarding punishable conduct relating to drugs of which the most salient is expressed as ". . . whoever is in possession of *(detiene)* . . . drugs." It is with reference to this passage that the prevailing Italian sentencing practice punishes people for taking drugs: not for actually taking them, but on the assumption that a drug to be taken must first be in the possession of the taker. Whatever the drug, in this case, the penalty is three to eight years imprisonment, and a fine of $500 to $6,600. We have, therefore, entered 38 months as the official prison term in Table 28.

New York: The penalty varies with the amount possessed. (The law refers to *possession* rather than "taking.") For less than 1/8 of an ounce, the maximum is one year, and the minimum, an unconditional discharge. There is then a gradation of penalties according to increasing amounts to the level of two ounces which receives a maximum of life and a minimum of 15 years imprisonment. Usually such persons would have previous arrests and be recidivists. On these assumptions, if we take the minimum amount of 1/8 ounce, the common practice may roughly be estimated at three months.

Yugoslavia: At the time of the study, taking drugs was not a criminal offense in Yugoslavia, although there were moves to make it so.

Factory Pollution

India: Environmental law is in its nascent stage in India. There have been no recent legislative measures dealing with air pollution and existing provisions of law on the subject are hopelessly dated. A lot of debate has gone into the question of water pollution, and the Water (Prevention and Control of) Pollution Act of 1974 represents the outcome of such debate and also is perhaps typical of the present Indian approach to the problem—an approach that seems to view law's role in environmental protection as providing the basis for cooperation rather than coercion. The approach of the Act is to set up Central and State Boards for Prevention and Control of Water Pollution. Such Boards are set up mainly to cooperate, coordinate and recommend measures. Section 24 of the Act prohibits the use of streams or wells for disposal of polluting matter, but the Act contains no penal provision for violators of this prohibition.

So far as air pollution is concerned, the main penal provisions are to be found in the Indian Penal Code. Section 278 is the pertinent provision and reads, "Whoever voluntarily vitiates the atmosphere in any place so as to make it noxious to the health of persons in general dwellings or carrying on business in the neighborhood or passing along a public way, shall be punished with fine which may extend to ($50)." Depending on the seriousness of the pollution, Section 284 of the Indian Penal Code may be applied. Section 284 punishes negligent acts or omissions with respect to poisonous substances which endanger human life or are likely to cause hurt or injury to any person, with imprisonment of either description for a term which may extend to six months or with fine which may extend to $100 or with both. Cases of factory pollution may also constitute the offense of public nuisance as defined by Section 268 of the Indian Penal Code. The offense of public nuisance is non-cognizable, bailable, and non-compoundable and the punishment prescribed is a fine extending to $20.

Invoking the public nuisance Section has one advantage in that provision is made for enhanced punishment in the event of continuance or recurrence of the public nuisance after an injunction to discontinue. For continued public nuisance the punishment is simple imprisonment for a term up to six months or fine or both.

The Factories Act of 1948 also contains provisions regarding industrial pollution but the Act is mainly concerned with the safety and health of individuals working in a factory and therefore the obligations under that Act are with a view to preventing the workers employed from inhaling "dangerous fumes." The Act compels effective measures to prevent the accumulation of fumes in any work room, but does not deal with questions of general air pollution. However, various Municipal Corporations in towns and cities in India are empowered to deal with the problem of air pollution. Thus, for example, Section 391 of the Bombay Municipal Corporation Act of 1888 prohibits the use of any furnace which does not, as far as practicable, consume its own smoke. The penalty for infringement of this provision is a fine of $10 on a first conviction and double the earlier punishment for subsequent conviction. The liability, so far as Section 391 is concerned is both of the owner and of the occupier and such liability is both joint and several.

Indonesia: This act conforms to the description in Article 1, Section 1, Para. XX of the 1926 Ordinance, No. 226. According to Article 15 of this Ordinance the maximum penalty is two months detention or a fine of up to $20. The crime is considered a misdemeanor.

Iran: Factory air pollution is not a crime in Iran.

Italy: This act conforms to the description in one of the hypotheses of Article 674 of the Italian Penal Code. The penalty is five days to one month detention or alternatively $1.50 to $130 fine. The omission is considered a *contravvenzione* and the punishment in theory is different from that foreseen for a crime. The official term of 1.0 month has therefore been entered.

New York: One must here assume violation of an injunction. In this case, the maximum is one year in prison, the minimum a suspended sentence. The practice is a suspended sentence.

Yugoslavia: At the time of the study, factory pollution was not a crime in Yugoslavia.

Public Protest

India: This act could possibly fall within the definition of the offense of being a member of an unlawful assembly depending upon the nature of the protest. Section 141 of the Indian Penal Code defines an unlawful assembly as an assembly of five or more persons if the common object of the persons comprising that assembly is:

1. To overawe by criminal force or show of criminal force the Central or any State Government, Parliament, the Legislature of any State, or any public servant in the exercise of the lawful power of such public servant.
2. To resist the execution of any law or legal process.
3. To commit any mischief or criminal trespass or other offense.
4. By means of criminal force or show of criminal force to compel any person to do what he is not legally bound to do or to omit to do what he is legally entitled to do.

Whoever is a member of an unlawful assembly shall be punished with imprisonment of either type for a term up to six months or with fine or both.

Depending upon the facts relating to the non-authorized nature of the meeting, the act may fall within the definitions of criminal conspiracy. If lack of authorization involves breach of any provision of penal law then participating in the protest meeting might constitute sufficient basis for a conviction under Section 120A of the Indian Penal Code which defines criminal conspiracy as: when two or more persons agree to do or cause to be done an illegal act or an act which is not illegal by illegal means, such an agreement is designated a criminal conspiracy. It is immaterial whether the illegal act is the ultimate object of such agreement or is merely incidental to that object. Whoever is a party to a criminal conspiracy to commit an offense punishable with death, imprisonment for life, or rigorous imprisonment for a term of two years or more shall be punished in the same manner as if he had committed such offense. Where the conspiracy is to commit any offense other than those mentioned above, the punishment is imprisonment of either description for a term not exceeding six months or fine or both.

Indonesia: This act conforms to the description of Article 154 of the Indonesian Penal Code and is punishable by a fine of $10. The maximum penalty is seven years imprisonment.

Iran: Political activities, except within an ideological framework and in a form provided by the Government, are banned in Iran. However, the ban is not formal, but sensed and learned through the use of different symbols and critical reactions against those who do criticize. Thus, we are forced to enter "zero" into Table 28 as the official prison term, although it is apparent that in practice such behavior may be sanctioned severely.

Italy: This action conforms to the description in Article 654 of the Italian Penal Code. The penalty is five days to one year detention, the action being considered a *contravvenzione*.

New York: There is no punishment for this act, assuming that the person does not advocate the violent overthrow of the entire government system. A zero has been entered into Table 28.

Yugoslavia: The act is officially not a crime.

Not Helping

India: This act is not an offense under Indian law. An omission is illegal only if such omission is a breach of some direction of law. Deliberate failure to rescue one who is in danger is not an offense under the Indian Penal Code (unlike the French Penal Code, Art. 63). The rationale for this was stated by Lord Macauley, one of the main draftsmen of the Indian Penal Code:

It is indeed most highly desirable that men should not merely abstain from doing harm to their neighbors but should render active services to their neighbors. In general, however, the penal law must content itself with keeping men from doing positive harm and must leave to public opinion, and to the teachers of morality and religion, the office of furnishing men with motives for doing positive good. (Macauley and other Indian Law Commissioners, *Note M,* pp. 53–56, 1837).

Indonesia: This act conforms to the description of Article 304 of the Indonesian Penal Code and the maximum penalty is two years and six months imprisonment or fine up to $12.

Iran: This act is not punished by the Iranian Penal Code.

Italy: This description fits that of the second paragraph of Article 593 of the Italian Penal Code. If the end result is not harm to the person or death, then the penalty is imprisonment from 15 days to three months or a fine of maximum $200. If the end result is physical or mental harm, then the above mentioned amounts are increased by up to one third and if the end result is death, the minimum and maximum penalties are doubled. We have, therefore, entered an official prison term of five months.

New York: Assuming no relationship between the two, there is no duty between strangers, and therefore no punishment.

Yugoslavia: Although it is not completely clear, this act is probably covered by Article 147 of the Penal Code. "A person not offering aid to another person in direct danger of death, although able to do so without exposing himself or another person to peril, will be sentenced to imprisonment up to one year." As may be seen, in order to relate to the present description, the danger menacing another person should be of a high degree, i.e. it should expose somebody to peril of death. If it is assumed that these factors are present in the offense described, the maximum penalty is one year of imprisonment. Perusal of court records for the 1968–70 period revealed an average sentence of one month, and this amount has been entered into Table 28.

"GAPS" BETWEEN LAW AND OPINION

Before we are able to discuss the "gaps" which may exist between law and opinion, an extremely important consideration must be borne in mind. The "gaps" are *relative* to the estimated official minimum prison term for each act in each country. Some gaps will appear very large, especially when the official minimum term is computed to "life," since it would appear from the data, that as a general rule, the mean prison term recommended by our samples is not likely to rise above five to six years, regardless of the act, or the country.

A number of fascinating interpretations may now be made from Table 28.

The two most economically developed countries of U.S. and Yugoslavia consistently recommended prison terms beyond the official minima. It is quite apparent, however, that with the exception of the act of robbery for the U.S., the official terms are generally much lower than those for all other countries. We should be careful to understand therefore, that this data does not mean that the Americans and Yugoslavians are "more punitive"—indeed, we have not found this to be the case using our other measures. What it does mean, however, is that for a number of acts, the official prison term is lower than that displayed by our other samples. This applies most clearly to the acts of robbery, incest, appropriation, and factory pollution in New York, and to the acts of incest, appropriation, and public protest in Yugoslavia.

246

The most striking cases were those of robbery and appropriation in New York where respondents recommended almost double the official minimum. And in Yugoslavia, respondents recommended prison terms three and four times greater than the official minimums for the acts of incest and appropriation of social funds. Yet, Yugoslavians recommended only half the official minimum for robbery. The differing effects of political and cultural conditions can clearly be seen here. New Yorkers fear violent crime, and the courts are often considered "too lenient." On the other hand, the appropriation of social funds is akin to a serious political crime in Yugoslavia.

In contrast, the less developed countries of India and Indonesia overwhelmingly recommended prison terms far less than the official minimum. In some instances, this may be explained by the relatively high official minimums in some countries compared to New York and Yugoslavia (e.g., life for robbery and appropriation in Indonesia). Certainly there are far less "zeros" entered as official minima for these two countries in comparison to the U.S. and Yugoslavia. Nevertheless, the amounts by which the respondents favored less prison terms are impressive: the Indian respondents recommended terms for robbery, appropriation, and homosexuality, more than 70 percent less than the official minima, and substantial, though somewhat less reductions for incest, abortion, taking drugs, and public protest. The Indonesians similarly favored drastically reduced terms for robbery, appropriation and public protest, and somewhat less terms for not helping and incest.

The transitional country was that of Iran, in which clearly less terms were favored for the acts of incest and homosexuality, and to a slightly lesser extent, bribery. On the other hand, the Iranians favored a term slightly longer than the official minimum for robbery. Differences from the law for other acts were not substantial.

The final and most interesting observation is that the Sardinian sample favored terms in excess of the official minima to the same, overwhelming extent as did the U.S. and Yugoslavian samples. This is especially significant since the official minima for Italy are roughly similar to those of U.S. and Yugoslavia—i.e., they are comparatively low (with the exception of taking drugs). For the acts of robbery, incest, appropriation, and not helping, prison terms of more than double the official minima were recommended. Higher terms, though less substantial, were recommended for homosexuality and factory pollution.

Since taking drugs is not a deeply held "right" or even practice in the Sardinian subculture of violence, this response is difficult to understand, except to suggest that perhaps respondents saw fit to abide by any value position which opposed government practice. Yet, if this were the case, similarly low terms would have been recommended for robbery, appropriation, and incest. We will delve further into this interesting puzzle in the following chapter. It may be that rural samples are generally higher "prisonizers" than urban samples.

CONCLUSIONS

One is tempted to conclude that our data suggest a cyclical movement of opinion and law. The industrialized countries of U.S. and Yugoslavia have more rapidly liberalized their criminal law than the less industrialized countries. Yet, it would seem that for these two countries, the liberalization may have gone too far, and that the public opinion now suggests that official prison minima should be increased. However, this conclusion is reached mindful of the fact that we have used official *minima* as our standard. Had we used *maxima,* the recommended terms would have been one-half to two-thirds less than the official terms for most acts. It is clear therefore, that the criminal law retains a prisonable power far beyond that envisioned by the man in the street.

The developing countries (India and Indonesia), on the other hand, display the earlier pattern of the law-opinion relationship. Law lags behind a liberalizing opinion, and in some cases quite a large gap exists. Iran represents the transitional case: liberalizing opinion is contrasted to law on sexual behavior that is traditionally the realm of the church, but opinion continues to favor the law as it stands on robbery and most other acts.

ten

SUBCULTURAL PERCEPTIONS
OF DEVIANCE

We will consider in this chapter differential perceptions of deviance in two kinds of subcultures: rural subcultures in India, Indonesia, Iran, and Yugoslavia and the subculture of violence in Sardinia.

RURAL SUBCULTURES

In Chapter 8, we attempted to assess the comparative importance of a number of sociological background variables in affecting perceptions of deviance. We treated every variable as having equal status both theoretically and methodologically. However, it is apparent that while this approach was useful in uncovering the comparative effects of variables, it ignored the fact that we had specifically sampled according to an urban/rural breakdown. Although some quota sampling was used in one country to ensure sufficient numbers for comparison of education, age, etc., the major sampling design called for a clear division between rural and urban respondents. While we were interested in looking at urban/rural differences in the light of various theories of social development, we were keen to establish an *a priori* case for a sampling of "subculture" within a major culture. This idea rests upon a particular theory of social development and political structure: that urban life dominates the politics of a nation and so becomes the major culture, leaving rural life as a subculture. The validity of this assumption will vary from country to country. If a country is largely agrarian according to population distribution (e.g., India or Indonesia) the extent to which the rural is a subculture, and the urban the "dominant" culture may be questioned. The answer to this problem has been confused by the one-sided definition of subcultures assumed by almost all sociologists in criminology, which has been to compare subcultures to cultures only in terms of value structures and patterns, rather than in terms of political power.[1] This one-sided preoccupation had led to misleading and often empty or static definitions of subculture.

Gordon (1964:39) defines a subculture in the broadest terms as containing ". . . both sexes, all ages, family groups, and which parallels the larger society in that it provides for a network of groups and institutions extending throughout the individual's life cycle." If one pictures the dominant culture as an orange, the subculture is seen as a segment of that orange. Yet, if it parallels the larger society, what is it that makes it different? Three kinds of answers have been given by sociologists.

First, a subculture is seen as existing more or less outside of the main stream of culture. In varying forms, this view is propounded by Miller (1958), Maurer (1955),[2] and Shibutani (1955). Shibutani explains this approach: ". . . people in different social classes differ in modes of life and outlook, not because of anything inherent in economic position, but because similarity of occupation and limitations set by income level dispose them to certain restricted communication channels."

The second approach is to conceptualize the dominant culture as merely the sum of all the subcultures. Some consider this position to be an extreme in pluralism, seeing culture as merely a hodge-podge of subcultures (Arnold, 1970:83). But the approach may range from the pluralism of Lasswell[3] (1965) to various conflict theories that picture society as a conglomeration of constantly warring factions: the Hobbesian paradigm applied to groups.[4]

---

[1]Of course, there are exceptions. Roszak's *The Making of a Counter Culture* (1969) does recognize this aspect. However, the most powerful work which spells out the political and psychological attributes of subcultures is Fanon's *Wretched of the Earth* (1968). The subculture (i.e. natives under colonial rule) is severed from the political and economic process of the dominant culture, yet Fanon shows that there is a deep interpenetration of psychological dependency between the two cultures. It is also true that Miller (1958) sees the dominant culture in terms of dominant political power rather than in terms of a broad consensus of values, but his analysis of the lower class subculture is basically in terms of values and life styles.

[2]Researchers such as Maurer who make detailed studies of deviant groups emphasize this view since it allows them to draw distinct lines between culture and subculture, so that they can treat the latter as an entity in its own right.

[3]". . . those variant cultural beliefs and behaviors from which the generalization of national character is drawn." (1968:211.)

[4]"Conflict theorists" may easily be categorized into this approach, (e.g. Turk, Taylor, et al.). If there is no consensus, it follows that there can be no dominant cultural themes or values, if "dominant" is defined in terms of the majority of the people acquiescing to particular values. For the conflict theorist, the only other way there can be a "dominant" culture is if one defines "dominant" in terms of raw political power. In this case, the term "subculture" may refer to a political elite. Yet this would surely be violating the meaning of the word, since "sub" means "under." Thus, the "subculture" may be defined as the mass of those subordinated to the "supra culture" of political elite. Again, this definition doesn't seem to fit, since it is difficult to conceive of a mass, or a majority, as being less than a minority except under tyranny.

A third approach argues that there is a mixing between or among the parent and subcultures. Here, the argument is that there is a continuum along which the values of society are located, from those enjoying high consensus to those affirmed by only small numbers. The dominant culture is therefore the lowest common denominator of all the values existing in society. As Etzioni states: "America is not a 'society' in Tonnies sense or a 'melting pot,' it is where all integrated groups accept *some* values, the universal values of American society, but at the same time hold their particularistic tradition and values" (1959:260). Although there has been much argument as to whether there is a set of identifiable values typical of the dominant American culture, a number of empirical studies have demonstrated a consensus about a number of core values (Williams, 1963; Cuber and Pell, 1941; Rokeach, 1968; Rettig and Pasamanick, 1959; Dahl, 1967; Gruen, 1966).[5]

DIMENSIONS OF SUBCULTURE

It must now be apparent that there are a number of dimensions according to which subcultures may be defined. These may be roughly identified as the political-economic (e.g., Lewis, 1966; and the various Marxist theories), the socio-cultural (e.g., those emphasizing differing value structures and life styles), and the ecological (those emphasizing geographical or regional variations in physical conditions; e.g., Blauner, 1970; Gastil, 1971; Hackney, 1969; Loftin and Hill, 1974).

From what we know of the socio-economic conditions of each country, we can make a good argument for the differentiation of rural from urban according to these three criteria, with some specific exceptions for particular countries. In all countries sampled, except the U.S. (which we will exclude from analysis) it is reasonably certain that the rural 1) are economically less well off than the urban; 2) have different life styles and patterns of behavior because of the different occupational and physical conditions in which they live; 3) are physically separated from the urban centers; and 4) are certainly politically less

---

[5]There are many variations on this theme, particularly in relation to theories of crime and delinquency. See, for example, Rodman (1963) on the "lower class value stretch," Cohen (1955) on reaction formation as a response of lower class individuals to middle class values, and Cloward and Ohlin (1960). All these theories assume an individual oriented both to the parent culture and to the subculture.

powerful than the urban population.[6] Thus, very roughly according to the three dimensions of subculture we may make a reasonable argument that the rural samples of India, Indonesia, Iran, and Yugoslavia represent definable rural subcultures.

A fact not clearly established, however, and indeed over which there is much argument in some countries (e.g. India, see: Gore, 1968), is whether there are marked differences in values between rural and urban groups. Although this study did not measure values *per se,* it has measured perceptions of deviance according to a number of dimensions that are related to values, or at least from which values may be inferred.

It is possible now to add a further deviance-related dimension, which we may loosely term "resistance potential." Thorsten Sellin (1938) coined this term to refer to a somewhat wide variety of factors, at different levels of analysis. He used it sociologically to refer to conflict between legal and cultural norms; psychologically to refer to conflict experienced by individuals when required to abide by conflicting normative demands; and social-psychologically to refer to group conflict where a subculture establishes its own norms either in contradiction or in separation from prevailing legal norms. The essence of the notion is that of conflict, both personal and social, which leads to a potentiality to resist laws or norms. Applied to our present study, we are able to develop three rough measures of this concept: 1) We may measure the gaps between law and opinion, which are set out in elementary form in Table 28. Here, we are taking law as equivalent to the "legal norms" and opinion as indicative of the "cultural norms." 2) We may look at the extent of conflict, if any, between urban groups (representative of the dominant culture) and the rural groups (the subculture), as measured by our questionnaire on perceptions of deviance. 3) We may also develop a combined measure by comparing rural/urban differences according to the measured gaps between law and opinion.

The following hypotheses may be advanced: according to various theories of subculture, we should expect that rural groups will display a higher conflict with the law (i.e. gaps between opinion and law) than will urban groups; and according to popular theories of social development, the rural group will display more conservative perceptions

---

[6]Once again, care should be taken in using the word subculture too broadly. It is apparent from our data and other information on Indonesia, for example, that Djakarta is "stacked" full of very conservative politically powerful government bureaucrats who dominate the political scene. Yet, the country's economy is largely agrarian, and the bulk of the people are engaged in rural occupations.

of deviance than the urban. This prediction should apply especially to the more value-related measures such as the seriousness scale.

Conflict with the Law

In an effort to develop a measure of "resistance potential" or conflict between opinion and law, the data on official and recommended prison terms as presented in Table 28 were used as a base. The differences between these two measures for each individual were treated as raw scores and then converted to z scores. Thus, we had a standardized measure of the "gap" that existed between each individual's opinion on the appropriate prison term and that theoretically provided by the law. Using the same procedure as outlined in Chapter 8, a multiple regression analysis was run using our new scale (the "conflict scale") as the dependent variable, with a saturated model of the independent variables of country effect coded (India, Indonesia, Iran, U.S., Yugoslavia) and the urban/rural factor. None of the results of this analysis were of significance. The only acts for which a significant multiple R was obtained were abortion ($F=6.06857$) and homosexuality ($F=2.90474$), but even here only two percent and one percent respectively of the variation was explained. Therefore, no evidence was found for the hypothesis that a greater conflict between opinion and law exists for rural groups as against urban groups, nor were there any significant cross-cultural variations.

Perceptions of Deviance

We saw in Chapter 8 that the urban/rural factor significantly affected perceptions of deviance for the acts of homosexuality, abortion, and public protest according to the NRS, and for the combined scale of the DCS. We may now look more closely at these findings in relation to particular countries. Since a case cannot be made out sufficiently strongly for the U.S. rural as representative of a rural subculture, it is excluded from the analysis. Similarly, the Sardinian sample is excluded because it is a special sample from a subculture of violence which will be discussed separately below.

INDIA

Abortion: The rural more often considered that this act should be prohibited by the law, and this was closely related to knowledge of the law, where a higher proportion of the urban thought that the act was not against the law. Fifty-six point three percent of the urban would report this act to no one, compared to only 28 percent of the rural who were more likely to report the act to agents outside the family. Yet, there were no differences in assessment of seriousness.

Homosexuality: No differences were found, as can be seen in Chart 17.

Protest: Fifty-one percent of the rural thought this act should be prohibited by the law compared to 28.9 percent of the rural, and in similar proportions, the rural believed that the act was in fact against the law, and that the government was active in stopping the behavior. A striking difference occurred in choice of control agent, where 65.6 percent of the urban would report the act to no one, compared to only 34.3 percent of the rural, who were more likely to report to the police or the actor's work superior. Both groups equally saw the act as not serious.

DCS: Using the combined scale, we are able to assess the interaction effects of urban/rural with other background factors. While F was not significant for the main effects of the urban/rural factor, its interaction with other factors is of interest, which can be seen clearly from Table 29. Whereas there are no noticeable effects according to urban/education background, there is a very steady drop in deviance control for the less educated rural. This would appear to be a "deviant" group, since other types of rural respondents strongly favored deviance control. The upper class rural, for example, favored control of deviance considerably more than the lower class rural, yet in contrast it is the lower class urban who more strongly favor control. And although the N is very small, the suggestion is that the lower class non-religious was much more tolerant of deviance.

We should note that these differences are not highly statistically significant, and that in the analysis of differences on individual items of the questionnaire, no differences were found in assessment of seriousness. Since "seriousness" is probably the closest measure we have of a measure of values, we may conclude that previous research in India which has not found differential value structure between urban and rural groups is supported. On the other hand, there were clear differences in preference for control agent with the rural displaying generally much more conservative responses than the urban who favored less formal control. The composite measure (DCS) which, it will be remembered, includes all acts except robbery, did not reveal any striking main effects of urban/rural background. However, it was apparent that the most "liberal" group was comprised of a small number of non-

TABLE 29
**Mean DCS Scores for India According to Background Factors of
Urban/Rural, by Education, Religiosity and Social Class**

	URBAN	RURAL	COMBINED	F**
EDUCATION				
Illiterate/elementary	7.40	5.90	6.65	
	N=20	N=20	N=40	
Secondary	7.78	7.53	7.69	
	N=97	N=58	N=155	
Higher	8.03	8.00	8.03	.8964
	N=272	N=25	N=297	NS
SOCIAL CLASS*				
"Upper"	7.42	9.24	7.76	
	N=211	N=42	N=253	
"Lower"	9.26	6.24	8.33	.9842
	N=113	N=50	N=163	NS
RELIGIOSITY				
Religious	7.96	7.44	7.86	
	N=357	N=109	N=467	
Not religious	7.67	3.0	7.35	.2128
	N=36	N=2	N=37	NS
COMBINED	7.94	7.30		1.9936
	N=393	N=112		N.S.

*"upper class" = self-employed business, civil servant, professional managerial
"lower class" = self-employed rural, laborers and blue collar workers, unemployed.
**F refers to one-way test of the combined categories.

religious, poorly educated rural respondents, along with the well-educated urban. Those favoring most control were the poorly educated urban along with the well-educated rural.[7]

INDONESIA

Abortion: The only dimension along which the rural differed significantly from the urban was in choice of control agent. The rural respondents preferred control at the village level, particularly by the village chief and/or council, whereas the urban preferred governmental

---

[7]However, for India it was found that age was the most significant discriminating factor. This is a finding one would expect in a country undergoing modernization. It is displayed in Chart 14 in Chapter 8, where it may be seen that none of the background factors, significant for other countries, was significant for India. F applied to an age breakdown of Mean DCS scores was 2.6257, significant at .05 level—the only factor to show overall significance for India.

or police control. Only 15.6 percent of the rural chose "police" to control this act compared to 34.6 percent of the urban.

Homosexuality: A slight tendency was found for the rural to favor less formal control of this act. Fourteen point seven percent chose police compared to 23.1 percent of the urban. Consistently, 32.1 percent of the rural rated the act as very serious compared to 50.4 percent of the urban.[8]

Public Protest: Again, the urban defined this act as criminal more often than the rural, with 53.3 percent choosing police compared to 36.2 percent of the rural. A difference was also found for the seriousness ratings, with 19.1 percent of the rural rating the act as "not serious" compared to 5.8 percent of the urban.

DCS: We can see from Table 30, that in contrast to India, the DCS produced quite strong differences according to a number of background factors. The urban/rural factor was highly significant, and interacted with education and age. For the urban respondents age was positively related to deviance control. However, within the rural sample this relationship is not apparent. Instead, the older rural were the most tolerant, followed by the younger. It was the middle aged rural who most favored deviance control. Education was clearly positively related to deviance control within the rural group, and also within the urban group, provided one excluded the illiterate respondents. This group may be identified as a somewhat "deviant" group since it was highly in favor of deviance control as are the well educated. Perhaps one may speculate that a little education has a highly liberalizing effect, but that "too much" brings about conservatism.

In summary, we can conclude that the hypothesis of a difference in value structure between rural and urban groups was supported. However, the popular belief that the rural are less tolerant of deviance than the urban is not supported. In fact the reverse is true for Indonesia because of the existence of an entrenched bourgeoisie residing specifically in Djakarta, working mainly in government bureaucracies.

IRAN

Abortion: A slightly higher proportion of the rural thought this act should be prohibited by the law and said that it was. However, this

---

[8]The data analysis at this level for seriousness was conducted by dividing the seriousness scale into three categories: not serious, 0–3; serious, 4–8; and very serious, 9–11. Chi square was used as the test of significance, focusing on each end of the scales. In this way, it was possible to minimize the effects of the heavily skewed distributions of responses.

TABLE 30
Mean DCS Scores for Indonesia According to Urban/Rural by Age and Education

	URBAN	RURAL	COMBINED	F*
AGE				
Young	12.40	9.20	11.57	
	N=146	N=51	N=197	
Middle-aged	13.25	10.16	12.41	.5683
	N=193	N=73	N=266	NS
Old	16.62	7.44	12.65	
	N=21	N=16	N=37	
EDUCATION				
Illiterate	14.14	5.83	8.16	
	N=7	N=18	N=25	
Elementary	11.90	7.52	10.56	4.432
	N=95	N=42	N=137	p<.01
Secondary	13.53	10.87	12.91	
	N=199	N=61	N=260	
Higher	13.74	12.95	13.54	
	N=57	N=19	N=76	
COMBINED	13.11	9.50		16.9912
	N=360	N=140		p<.001

*F refers to one-way test of the combined categories.

difference increased dramatically in perception of government activity, with twenty percent of the urban seeing the government as active compared to 96.2 percent of the rural. Similarly, only 18.7 percent of the urban would report this act to the police, compared to 73.1 percent of the rural. This difference was also repeated for assessment of seriousness.

Homosexuality: Slightly less urban respondents believed that this act was prohibited by the law. The difference between the two groups was striking in response to all other questions. Only 17.5 percent of the urban saw the government as active compared to 97.8 percent of the rural, and 63.9 percent of the urban saw the act as very serious compared to 98.4 percent of the rural.

Public Protest: Only 64.8 percent of the urban thought that this act should be prohibited by the law, as against 97.3 percent of the rural. Slightly less urban respondents reported that this act was prohibited (72.4 percent as against 97.3 percent). Consistently, 69.9 percent of the urban saw the government as active as against 96.2 percent of the rural, and 41.8 percent of the urban rated the act as very serious compared to

TABLE 31
*Mean DCS Scores for Iran According to Urban/
Rural Respondents by Education*

	URBAN	RURAL	COMBINED	F*
EDUCATION				
Illiterate	19.74	28.46	26.77	
	N=27	N=112	N=139	
Elementary	17.65	26.36	22.04	
	N=57	N=58	N=115	
Secondary	16.55	25.82	18.25	
	N=49	N=11	N=60	
				75.949
Higher	13.04	13.04	13.04	p<.001
	N=151	N=152	N=152	
COMBINED	15.21	27.55		286,7582
	N=284	N=182		p<.001

*F refers to one-way test of combined categories.

96.8 percent of the rural. Unexpectedly, there was no difference in choice of control agent.

DCS: We can see from Chart 14 in Chapter 8 that the effects of the urban/rural factor were the most striking for this country. Indeed, the urban/rural factor was a significant discriminator for all acts in Iran and on almost all items of the questionnaire. The only item on which the difference was slightly less, but still highly significant was on the seriousness scale. In addition, there were no strong interaction effects with other background variables, although it can be seen from Table 31 that for the higher educated, the urban/rural differences disappeared. The popular theory of a differentiation between urban and rural, with the rural pictured as much more conservative is well supported by the Iranian data.

YUGOSLAVIA

Abortion: The urban respondents saw the government as more active in stopping this act, but the rural respondents favored all forms of control of abortion than did the urban. Of the rural group, only 44.8 percent defined the act as non-deviant, compared to 83.5 percent of the urban, and 19.5 percent chose police compared to only 2.6 percent of the urban. Similarly, 30.5 percent of the rural saw the act as very serious as against only 6.8 percent of the urban.

Homosexuality: Thirty-nine point nine percent of the urban saw the government as *not* active compared to only 9.6 percent of the rural. The rural strongly defined homosexuality as criminal, with 61 percent choosing police, as against 31.9 percent of the urban. Similarly, 52.6 percent of the rural saw it as very serious as against only 34.9 percent of the urban.

Public Protest: Ninety-eight percent of the rural thought that the government was active as against 86.1 percent of the urban. However, 57 percent of the rural respondents defined the act as criminal as against 33.8 percent of the urban. In similar proportions, the rural rated the act as more serious.

DCS: With the exception of only the two acts of appropriation of social funds and incest, the rural group displayed the classic conservative pattern of responses: they saw the government as playing an active role in controlling deviant behavior; they generally defined acts more as deviant; and they rated them more seriously. The urban/rural was by far the most significant discriminator according to the DCS, as can be seen in Table 32, with the rural group displaying much greater preference for deviance control than the urban. When considered in relation to other independent variables, this difference was sometimes lessened, sometimes accentuated as can be seen in Table 32. There we see that the difference between urban and rural within a poorly educated sample is considerably diminished. On the other hand, the gap between urban and rural is strikingly accentuated when considered within the better educated samples. We may conclude that a large portion of the difference between urban and rural deviance control may be accounted for by the differences in education between the two groups. This interaction effect is repeated when we consider urban/rural differences in terms of social class, using occupational categories. When considered in relation to self-reported religiosity, we find that for the religious groups, the differences between urban and rural disappear. Only for the non-religious do these differences remain. Religion in this setting may be seen very much as a "class leveller" in terms of deviance control, and, it would seem that the tendency was to level the rural deviance controllers downward. Age was also an interesting interacting factor, where it is apparent that within the urban group, increasing age is concommitant with increasing deviance control, although the general level of deviance control still remains lower than the rural, even for the older groups. However, among the rural, it can be seen that it is the younger who favor controlling deviance more than the older. This is a surprising finding in the light of the usual theory

TABLE 32
Mean DCS Scores for Yugoslavia According to Urban/Rural Background by Age, Education, Social Class and Religiosity

	URBAN	RURAL	COMBINED	F*
EDUCATION				
Illiterate	12.84	10.87	11.97	
	N=17	N=15	N=34	
Elementary	15.04	19.07	15.09	
	N=122	N=43	N=165	11.1290
				p<.001
Secondary	12.34	18.95	13.6	
	N=161	N=38	N=199	
Higher	9.79	20.00	10.63	
	N=77	N=7	N=84	
SOCIAL CLASS				
"Upper"	12.05	20.61	13.17	
	N=153	N=23	NH176	
				2.3033
"Lower"	13.35	17.08	14.28	NS
	N=217	N=72	N=289	
RELIGIOSITY				
Religious	13.16	15.00	13.54	
	N=110	N=29	N=139	
				.6291
Not religious	12.71	19.58	14.08	
	N=270	N=67	N=337	NS
AGE				
Young	10.10	20.27	12.02	
	N=95	N=22	N=117	
Middle-aged	13.34	18.39	14.53	4.5202
	N=175	N=54	N=22	.05>p>.01
Old	14.23	14.59	14.28	
	N=114	N=22	N=136	
COMBINED	12.80	17.96		37.2012
	N=384	N=98		p<.001

*F refers to one-way test of combined categories.

concerning the strong traditional values held in rural areas, which are usually imputed to the older residents. It would be interesting to follow up these findings, especially as it is apparent that the Yugoslav programs of development and change have been largely unsuccessful in transforming the structure of rural life.

CONCLUSIONS AND SUMMARY

The hypothesis of subcultural differentiation in conflict between law and opinion as measured by a law/opinion conflict scale was not supported in any instance. Substantial differences in perceptions of deviance between the urban and rural groups were found for Iran, Indonesia, and Yugoslavia. For Iran and Yugoslavia, the direction of the difference was that predicted by the popular theories of modernization: that liberalization occurs mainly in the cities and the rural areas lag conservatively behind. The striking contrast to this finding was the difference in the opposite direction found in Indonesia. However, detailed analysis of those particular acts that displayed urban/rural differences showed that the major dimension of differentiation was related to the choice of control agent, or definition of the act, whereas the measure of seriousness more often did not display differences between the rural and urban groups. Taking seriousness as a value-related measure, and choice of control agent as our politically related measure, we might conclude that the theories arguing for differentiation in values between subculture and culture, have received less support than those which emphasize the political variable as the most important.[9]

Finally, the precept of Marxist-based conflict theory, which assumes a hard and fast division between basically two classes in society, was supported in only one country, Iran. We draw this conclusion on the observation that for this country there was extremely little interaction between the urban/rural factor and other independent variables, and this applied for all acts surveyed. Thus, in contrast to other countries, the lines did not shift according to the issue involved. The explanation for this finding may be found in the historical conditions of Iran where for centuries there has existed a strong antithesis between urban and rural, with constant or periodic uprisings resulting in periodic redistribution of rural landholdings.

---

[9]An additional speculative note concerning neo-Marxist theory is of interest. Most successful Marxist-based revolutions have been brought about through the organization of agrarian uprising, even though Marx's later writings were predominantly preoccupied with (unquestioningly accepting) the urban industrial scene. It has been argued that the Marxist revolution in China was an agrarian revolution, and certainly Che Guevarra's theory of revolution was based on the assumption of a sympathetic attitude from the peasants. (See: Mills, 1962:454–467.) Should this be the case, one could infer from our data that the situation in Indonesia is ripe for revolution, since the rural have displayed considerably more liberal perceptions than the urban.

THE SUBCULTURE OF VIOLENCE

If the definition of "subculture" is difficult, the definition of a "subculture of violence" is next to impossible! Wolfgang and Ferracuti (1967) who first developed the thesis, never settled upon a single, precise definition, but rather settled on a list of seven general postulates, which recognized two of the three basic dimensions for defining a subculture mentioned above, but strangely left out the ecological dimension. Subsequent research has been severely limited by the failure to specify clearly, or perhaps more precisely, to *agree* on the basic dimensions of the subculture of violence.

The major hypothesis of the subculture of violence that we may test with the data at hand is that persons from a subculture of violence will display different values toward crime and deviance than those who are not from a subculture of violence.[10]

Two previous studies have attempted to test this hypothesis, and both have failed to produce significant findings. Using questionnaires, Ball-Rokeach (1973) found that samples of offenders with records of violence displayed no difference in values related to violence as compared to non-offenders. One may argue, however, that this test of the subculture of violence hypothesis is too specific an interpretation of the thesis because it views the idea of a subculture of violence as a causal-reductionist theory to explain individual acts of violence rather than as a general explanatory theory, which characterizes conditions under which more violence may occur.[11] This confusion may be partly attributed to the fact that the subculture of violence thesis has usually been advanced as an "interdisciplinary" theory. But "interdisciplinarity" does not mean to ignore the fundamental distinction made by Durk-

---

[10]One may note that although a chapter in Wolfgang and Ferracuti's *Subculture of Violence* was devoted to the methodology of measuring values with a view to measuring differences between the subculture of violence and the parent culture, their subsequent research did not take this direction. Instead, a series of studies were conducted in an attempt to demonstrate postulated psychological differences between offenders from a subculture of violence and offenders from the parent culture. See, e.g., Ferracuti, et al. (1970); Ferracuti and Wolfgang (1973). The results of these studies were only mildly supportive of the thesis.

[11]That is, one cannot assume a one-to-one relationship between individual behavior and social causation. To try to test hypotheses of social causation by studying the individual products of the process is like trying to study the hypothesis that sneezes are caused by a virus, studying only the sneezes.

heim that social facts are of a different order from individual or psychological facts. Thus, the proper test of the subculture theory of violence as a *sociological* construct is to compare the values of the whole subculture (which includes offenders and non-offenders) with the values of the comparison culture. A further criticism of the Ball-Rokeach study is that its experimental group did not represent a subculture of violence at all, but rather a statistical collection of persons who had committed crimes (i.e., their sample of incarcerated males). Furthermore, the "groups" of lower class individuals or violent persons, according to self report which Ball-Rokeach extracted from a national sample, do not constitute subcultures, if one argues that a central feature of a subculture is the geographical and social proximity of the individuals to each other.

A similar study was conducted by Erlanger (1974) who postulated that violent values should be positively correlated to self-perceptions of "happiness" in the subculture of violence. Instead, the correlation was −0.33 for the black lower class. But, again we are faced with the simplistic translation of the definition of subculture of violence into race, social class, or a combination of both. Indeed, Curtis (1975) developed a whole thesis on this assumption.

There are two additional shortcomings with both these studies, and these may be highlighted by a brief recapitulation of the subculture of violence that has been the subject of detailed study in Sardinia. There are a number of significant attributes of that subculture of violence that are completely overlooked when the thesis is applied to American conditions:

1. The geography of the area is such as physically to cut off the subculture from the parent culture. Although this is not such a great factor today, historically this has been of great importance.
2. The people since the beginning of history have had a reputation of aggressiveness. There is substantial socio-historical evidence that the subculture *is* violent.
3. The very detailed study by Pigliaru (1970) has clearly demonstrated that there is a highly organized informal system of social control, complete with its own "laws," specifically to deal with crimes, especially violent crimes.
4. Related to the above, the people display a close-mouthed attitude to outsiders, adhering to the code of silence *(omerta),* showing distrust to formal arms of government.

263

Thus, if one wished to test the subculture of violence hypothesis in American conditions, the first test would be to *find* a subculture that adhered to the above criteria. Only then would it make sense to take the next step to compare the values of that subculture of violence with those of the parent culture.[12]

The second major difficulty with those studies is that they do not really give violence itself, as an independent variable, "a fair chance." Social class and race are assumed in advance to be central dimensions of the subculture of violence. Yet, if a subculture of violence, defined in terms of lower class and black, is compared to the present culture, it is difficult to see whether the difference, or lack thereof, is due to the assumed violence or to the factors of race and class, which are clearly not controlled.

With our data, we are able to get around these problems to some degree. First, our sample is taken from a subculture of violence which we are able to claim, on the basis of considerable previous research, clearly fits all the dimensions of subculture, and *really is* a subculture of violence. Second, we will compare this subculture to another subculture similar in background in that it is rural and poor. The comparison sample we will use here is that of the rural Yugoslavians. Although there are obviously cultural differences between Yugoslavians and Italians which we cannot control with this design, nevertheless, since we have found that rural groups (with the exception of the Indonesians)[13] are essentially similar in their conservative reactions to deviance, it seems reasonable to propose that any *substantial* differences between the two samples may be attributed to unique perceptions of deviance displayed by the Sardinians. The level for statistical significance has therefore been set at .001 instead of the conventional .05.[14]

Another factor in our favor is that our data provides us with measures not only of value-related attributes (e.g., seriousness) but also perceptions of social control agents, a dimension of central significance attended to by previous researchers on the subculture of violence in Sardinia, but rarely considered by American researchers.

---

[12]One suspects that the attributes described here would fit more likely certain subcultures in the wilds of the Ozarks, rather than to apply wholesale to poor blacks. It is of interest that Wolfgang and Ferracuti are ambivalent about the ecological hypothesis. At one point, they review research and conclude that residential area is not a causal factor in violent crime: "Among persons from . . . an ecological residence characterized by poverty, general physical deterioration, transiency, and density, very few persons commit homicide or other aggressive crimes." (1967:67). But this observation must be taken to apply only to American research, since in all the instances in which the authors affirm that the ecological hypothesis is in some way causally related are

The Data

CONFLICT SCALE

T-tests were computed to compare the mean conflict scale scores of each sample. No differences significant at .001 level were found. The most significant difference was that of public protest with t of −2.15 (p=.033), with Yugoslavia displaying the higher conflict score, contrary to the predicted direction.

DIFFERENCES IN VALUES

As a test of the differential values hypothesis, we may use the seriousness scale and the NR scale as rough measures of value-related responses. As we have seen in Chapter 7, there was quite a close similarity in basic structure of deviance perception in terms of the grouping of the acts by factor analysis between Yugoslavia and Italy. T-test applied to the differences between the means of NRS and seriousness produced differences significant at .001 level or better for the acts of robbery and public protest on both scales, for the acts of not helping and abortion on the seriousness scale, and drugs, incest, and homosexuality for the NRS. The *direction* of these differences is particularly fascinating.

The subculture of violence hypothesis of value differentiation would predict that robbery would be seen as much less serious by the Sardinians than by the rural Yugoslavs. In fact, the direction of the difference was the opposite—an explanation of this finding shortly. In regard to protest, one would predict a more tolerant attitude toward their

---

when they discuss the Sardinian or Colombian subcultures of violence. In addition, they base their main policy prescriptions upon ecological premises (i.e. the "dispersal" of subcultures).

[13]It may be noted that the "rural" or upstate New Yorkers were generally more conservative in their reactions. The reasons for this are obviously quite different to the similar results found for India, Iran, and Yugoslavia.

[14]A matrix of Spearman's Rank Order Corrections was set up, using the order in which the acts were ranked within each country rural sample according to their Norm Resistance. The correlations ranged from .22 between the U.S. rural and Iranian rural, to a high of .88 between the Indian and Sardinian samples. The next highest correlation of .77 was between Sardinian and Yugoslav rural, which suggests that our choice of the Yugoslav rural sample as being the most similar to the Sardinian is a reasonable one.

behavior by the Sardinians, since we know that there is a tradition of antipathy toward government. Although this has not been discussed in any of the latest literature on subculture of violence, it would appear to be a most important dimension. The mean seriousness on public protest for the Sardinians was a meagre 2.62, compared to the Yugoslavs' of 8.58. This was by far the greatest difference found. The Sardinians were also far less resisting on the NR scale than the Yugoslavs for this act.

The Sardinians also rated not helping and abortion significantly as more serious than did the Yugoslavs. However, for the acts of drugs, incest and homosexuality, they displayed more tolerant attitudes.

ANTIPATHY TOWARDS EXTERNAL CONTROL

We have already seen evidence for this view from the response to the protest item. Our question on choice of control agent can further investigate this area, since we would expect extensive differences in response, if our hypothesis concerning the antipathy by the subculture of violence toward government is born out. Table 33 shows that the dominant control agents to which Sardinian respondents would report deviant behavior were limited to police or judiciary and family. Other possible control agents such as priest, union official, employer, doctor, social worker, mayor were rarely chosen. The police were never chosen by more than sixty-eight percent of the Sardinians for any act. Indeed, only fifty percent of the Sardinians selected police for robbery, an act which one would expect clearly to be categorized as criminal (and was by all other national samples studied), especially since the respondents have rated the act as very serious. The impression gained from the data is a pattern of deviance control strongly dominated by the family system.

It is usually argued that rural communities are more strongly dominated by the family system. Assuming this hypothesis, we would have expected our Yugoslav rural sample to show response patterns similar to those of the Sardinians, assuming an hypothesis of no subculture of violence. On the contrary, the dominant control agent chosen by the rural Yugoslavs was the police, and government officials were almost equally popular. In no case did the percentage of those choosing "family" as control agent exceed twelve percent. Other findings also indicate the strong resistance of respondents from the violence subculture to formal means of social control, compared to the nonviolent subculture in Yugoslavia. The proportions of Sardinians choosing "no one" were more than double the rural Yugoslavs for all acts except those of factory pollution and taking drugs. Forty-one percent of the Sardinians would tell no one of robbery, compared to only 4.1 percent of the Yugoslavs. Seventy-seven percent would tell no one of public protest compared to seventeen percent of the comparison group. Overall, the Sardinians clearly chose the police less often. Although choices of doctor or social worker were very low for both samples, the choice of these agents by the Yugoslavians is definitely less frequent. The high proportion of Yugoslavs choosing the doctor for abortion probably shows that country's liberal attitude, since abortion is legal in Yugoslavia.

It seems reasonable to conclude from this data, since the differences between the two groups are so striking, that a distrust or antithetical attitude toward the formal means of deviance control is more typical of a subculture of violence than it is of a non-violent subculture of similar attributes. A final piece of evidence supports this conclusion. We have seen that even though the Sardinians rated robbery as very serious, yet forty-one percent would tell no one of the crime. And when it came to recommending sanctions, we can see from Table 28 that they favored extremely severe prison terms. Our interpretation may be that the Sardinians *evaluate* robbery as serious in similar degree to other countries sampled, and therefore favor the available penal sanctions. What they do *not* approve of is the process by which these sanctions are attached to the offenders. This interpretation suggests that it is important, when defining the dimension of a subculture of violence to draw a clear distinction between values relating to violence itself, and values relating to the social system which deals with that violence. Previous research has concentrated solely on the former.

PERCEPTIONS OF DEVIANCE WITHIN THE SUBCULTURE OF VIOLENCE

The acts of cattle stealing and kidnapping were added to our questionnaire in Sardinia, because these two acts are very specific to the cultural context, typical of the patterning of Sardinian criminality (Camba, et al., 1970). These crimes showed such an upsurge during the 1960s that a special commission was set up by the Italian Parliament to investigate the phenomenon of banditry. But, of more importance, these acts, according to the *Barbaracino Code,* are considered "crimes" with which the State has no right to interfere. The Code requires that these acts be regulated "in private" by members of the

TABLE 33
Comparison of Subcultures
Definition of the Act: "To Whom Would You Report This Act?"
(Sardinia N-200, Yugoslavia N-85)

ACT	NO ONE		FAMILY ONLY		DOCTOR, SOCIAL WORKER, PSYCHIATRIST, ETC.	
	SARDINIA	YUGOSLAVIA	SARDINIA	YUGOSLAVIA	SARDINIA	YUGOSLAVIA
Robbery	41.0	4.1	3.5	1.0	.5	0.0
Incest	23.5	9.2	18.0	11.2	6.5	4.6
Appropriation	20.0	11.7	1.5	0.0	0.0	0.0
Homosexuality	49.0	17.1	19.0	4.9	4.0	6.1
Abortion	73.5	44.8	12.0	6.9	1.0	20.7
Taking drugs	29.0	7.2	37.0	9.6	7.5	14.5
Factory pollution	15.0	15.1	12.5	0.0	2.5	5.4
Public protest	77.0	31.2	17.0	2.2	0.0	0.0
Not helping	18.5	16.3	24.5	9.8	0.0	3.3
Kidnapping**	37.0	NA	0.5	NA	0.0	NA
Cattle stealing**	50.5	NA	4.5	NA	0.0	NA

TABLE 33 *(cont'd)*

ACT	GOVERNMENT OFFICIAL			POLICE		
	SARDINIA	YUGOSLAVIA		SARDINIA	YUGOSLAVIA	
Robbery	0.0	5.2		50.0	89.7	
Incest	0.5	5.7		39.5	69.0	
Appropriation	2.0	30.9		68.0	57.4	
Homosexuality	0.5	11.0		18.5	61.0	
Abortion	0.0	8.0		10.0	19.5	
Taking drugs	0.0	4.8		19.0	63.9	
Factory pollution	19.5	7.8		45.0	31.5	
Public protest	0.0	9.7		5.0	57.0	
Not helping	0.0	7.6		44.5	63.0	
Kidnapping	0.0	NA		59.0	NA	
Cattle stealing	0.5	NA		39.0	NA	

*Only those control agents chosen in any significant proportion have been included. Percentages do not add up to 100% because the "other" category has been excluded.
**Question not asked in Yugoslavia.

269

community. They are usually considered to represent the most striking aspects of the discrepancy between the law of the State and the culture of the island. But we should note here that this discrepancy is not so much in terms of whether the acts should be punished, or how severely (although the *Barbaracino Code* is probably more severe) but rather, as to who has the right to punish. Thus, we again note that values concerning the behavior itself may not be especially different in this subculture. But values concerning who should deal with it should be very different.

Pigliaru (1970) has made an extensive study of the *Barbaracino Code* and has attempted to translate it into the equivalent of a written criminal code. In regard to cattle stealing, he notes that the theft of a goat is not an "offense" unless the goat's milk is used by the family or there is a clear intent to "offend" or spite the victim. Such an offense *must* be avenged by an act more offensive. The code requires that this act also be avenged, so that the reciprocal offenses may spiral into murder. And, death, as an offense or as revenge constitutes a new offense, punishable by death: there is no "statute of limitations."

The reactions given by our respondents to kidnapping and cattle stealing give evidence that these norms are still internalized in the Sardinian inhabitants and that they are still actual and applied. Although they rated both acts as very serious and they favored heavy forms of official punishment for them, only fifty-nine percent of our respondents would report kidnapping to the police and only thirty-nine percent would report cattle stealing. If these data are combined with the consideration that thirty-seven percent for kidnapping and 50.5 percent for cattle stealing *would not report these acts to anyone*, the picture that emerges shows in this area the law of silence is still valid *("legge dell'omerta")* and that the mistrust in law enforcement agencies is great. Also, since they rated the acts as very serious, on a par with the most serious of crimes, it must be concluded that members of a subculture of violence do *not* necessarily display positive attitudes toward violent and/or serious criminal behavior.

SOCIOLOGICAL CORRELATES OF
DEVIANCE PERCEPTION

ROBBERY, CATTLE STEALING AND KIDNAPPING. Differential responses to these three acts were virtually identical. A clear difference in perceptions of these acts was found according to education, age, and religiosity. The effects of education and age were particularly interesting. Only 64.5 percent of the younger group assessed robbery as very serious compared to eighty-eight percent of the oldest group. The less educated were considerably less likely to define the act as criminal (forty-five percent of the illiterate chose police compared to 73.9 percent of the well educated and 57.1 percent of these with elementary education). Contrary to what might be supposed to be the usual situation in a "modern" society, it would appear that the *older less educated* respondents were those who had least faith in the established agencies of control (the police) concerning robbery, since significantly less of them were prepared even to define the act as criminal. Yet it is apparent that this very group viewed the act as very serious and desired severe punishment for the actor. These findings are, of course, consistent with the subculture of violence, as we have described it, which rests on deep customs of antipathy to external control. The young, one might argue, have not yet been socialized into the ways of the *Barbaracino Code*. However, the effects of religiosity were also interesting. Thirty-six point one percent of the non-religious group defined this act as criminal compared to 54.8 percent of the religious and 61.9 percent of the very religious. Further, the non-religious saw the act as less serious with fifty percent rating it as very serious compared to eighty-five percent of the religious groups. This data would suggest that religiosity may be a factor that works against adherence to the *Barbaracino Code*.

APPROPRIATION AND FACTORY POLLUTION. Tabular analysis of these acts revealed a similar pattern of differentiation. We shall use the data from the act of appropriation as our example. Age and religiosity were the significant factors affecting perceptions of these acts. With regard to appropriation, the older group saw the government as more active than the younger group, with 53.3 percent perceiving the government as active, as against only 30.7 percent of the younger group. Although the youngest group perceived the government as less active in stopping this act, they were nevertheless much more prepared to report the behavior to a government official than were the older groups (44.8 percent compared to 69.1 percent and 62.5 percent). Similarly, only 8.6 percent of the younger group defined the act as non-deviant as against thirty-five percent of the oldest group. Consistent with these findings, the 16–30 year group assessed this act as more serious than the older groups, with 72.4 percent of the 16–30 group assessing the act as very serious as against 64.6 percent for the other two groups.

The non-religious significantly saw the government as not active in comparison to the religious groups. However, the *non-religious* this time clearly defined appropriation as criminal with 86.1 percent choosing police, as against 72.7 percent of the religious and 63.2 percent of the very religious. Also in the ratings of seriousness 57.2 percent of the very religious assessed the act as very serious, as did 65.3 percent of the religious, and 84.3 percent of the non-religious.

We can see here a clear shift in perceptions of this act. The non-religious younger respondents tended to respond more harshly to appropriation, in contrast to their response to the traditional crimes of robbery, kidnapping, and cattle stealing. It would seem that those more likely to be "closer" or "involved" in such acts (i.e., the older educated persons) were less likely to criminalize this act.

The reversal in the effects of religiosity is a fascinating finding. One is tempted to interpret it as typical of the "other worldly" orientation of the Catholic religion. Given what we know of this subculture, however, it is more likely indicative of the closer affinity of Church and State in Italy, so that those who are more religious are likely to be less antagonistic to controls of the State.

INCEST. This "traditional" act of deviance produced the classic differentiation in responses that one would expect from a rural subculture. The less educated, older and religious respondents clearly saw this act as more serious, more deviant, more criminal, and deserving of more punishment than did their opposite groups, which again is consistent with the attributes of the subculture of violence as outlined above. Tabular analysis revealed striking differences in perception of government activity according to age, with the younger, once again, seeing the government as inactive (54.3 percent as against 15.6 percent of the oldest group). Several differences were found for the definition of this act. The younger were more likely to define the act as non-deviant, or to keep it within the family, and the older, though they favored keeping the act secret, also preferred in comparison to the younger to define it as criminal. The younger group assessed this act as less serious than the older groups. One hundred percent of the 51 and over group assessed the act as very serious, as against 76.3 percent for the youngest group. Treatment model responses were chosen by the younger group significantly more often than the older groups. Forty point nine percent of the younger group chose treatment as against twenty percent of the over 51 group.

The less educated saw the government as more active in stopping incest. Seventy point two percent of this group saw the government as either active or very active in stopping incest, as against 45.4 percent of the well educated, and 52.3 percent of those with elementary education. Only 20.6 percent of the less educated defined the act as non-deviant as against 43.5 percent of the well educated. Conversely, 26.1 percent of the latter group defined the act as criminal, as against 47.6 percent of the poorly educated group. Marked differences occurred in choice of disposition. Sixty point eight percent of the well educated group chose treatment or "lenient" responses, as against only 28.2 percent of the poorly educated and 40.8 percent of those with elementary education. Both the uneducated and those with elementary education chose prison as the main disposition (46.6 percent and 47.7 percent respectively) in contrast to the well educated group (26.1 percent).

The non-religious were clearly less impressed by the activity of the government in stopping this behavior, with 64.7 percent rating the government as non-active compared to 33.6 percent of the religious and 14.3 percent of the very religious.

TAKING DRUGS AND HOMOSEXUALITY. The effects of background variables were basically similar to those for incest.

ABORTION. Responses to this act produced an unexpected finding: there were very few significant differences according to background factors, and this included a lack of any substantial difference between the religious and non-religious. This is quite surprising when one considers the substantial effects religiosity has had on all other acts. It would seem that abortion is not the subject of factional controversy as it is in other countries, especially the U.S. In addition, since the perceptions of this act are relatively tolerant, the presumed power of the Catholic Church over such an important moral issue would appear somewhat thin. The results of the recent referendum on divorce in Italy support the validity of these findings.

NOT HELPING. No differences were found.

PUBLIC PROTEST. Our earlier speculation concerning the role of religiosity is born out in the analysis of this act. We find that, in contrast to other acts, only 15.8 percent of the non-religious saw the government as not active, compared to thirty-five percent of the religious groups. Indeed, 36.8 percent of the non-religious thought the government was very active. Consistently, 92.1 percent of the non-religious defined the act as non-deviant compared to seventy-five percent of the religious groups, and a similar pattern of differences was found in the seriousness rating, where non-religious clearly rated the act as less serious than the religious. It is clear that the pattern of responses here is similar to that for the traditional crimes. The same applies to the age variable.

Twenty-four percent of the youngest group saw the government as not active, as against forty percent of the oldest group. Also, as age increased, so did assessment of the seriousness of this act. Sixty-three point one percent of the youngest group assessed protest as not serious, compared to 54.8 percent of the middle aged group, and 46.6 percent of the older group. We found no differences according to education.

Before we draw our general conclusions from this detailed tabular analysis of individual acts, it is necessary to assess the general comparative importance of each variable. Thus, a series of analyses of variance were run, using the DCS. No significant differences were found for sex, "social class," education, or age. The only variable to produce a significant F by analysis of variance was religiosity, as seen in Table 34. There were, however, some interesting interactions between other variables and religiosity. But these results may be questioned because of the very small N in some cells. Some of the interactions are sufficiently great to warrant consideration. The very religious young of our sample were strong controllers as were our old nonreligious. A quite symmetrical relationship is displayed in those results.

As far as education is concerned, Table 34 shows that the generally controlling effects of religiosity were diminished when we considered only illiterate respondents, but highly accentuated for those with elementary education and secondary education.

SUMMARY

In comparison to the analysis of the comparative effects of background variables for other country samples, the effects in Sardinia appear to have been far less. We should expect this, since we have noted that the subculture of violence is an isolated, very homogeneous group. However, we may conclude from our tabular analysis that the older, less educated, religious person is more likely to favor the control of deviance than any other type of respondent. Substantial differences ac-

TABLE 34
Mean DCS Scores for Religious and Non-Religious
by Age and Education for Sardinia

	RELIGIOUS	NOT RELIGIOUS	COMBINED	F*
AGE				
Young	10.58	7.42	9.50	
	N=50	N=25	N=76	
				1.5508
Middle-aged	10.14	11.75	11.20	NS
	N=65	N=8	N=73	
Old	10.76	15.00	11.04	
	N=42	N=3	N=45	
EDUCATION				
Illiterate	10.89	10.25	10.81	
	N=115	N=16	N=131	
Elementary/secondary	10.67	8.65	9.89	
	N=27	N=17	N=44	.8178
				NS
Higher	10.06	6.20	9.22	
	N=18	N=5	N=23	
COMBINED	10.76	9.00		2.4823
	N=160	N=38		p<.05

*F refers to one-way test of combined categories.

cording to types of acts were observed. It was apparent, for example, that for the traditional crimes of robbery and kidnapping, the older non-religious respondents were clearly less likely to report such acts to the police. This suggests that the subcultural ethos of violence holds sway much more with older persons, but has not, as yet, overtaken the young.

On the other hand, we saw how the younger persons were much more controlling than older respondents when it came to perceptions of acts to do with government inaction or money crimes (i.e., appropriation of government funds, environmental pollution).

Predictably, "traditionally deviant" acts such as homosexuality, taking drugs, and incest, were most highly punished by the older religious groups, and least punished by the better educated, younger non-religious person. A small group of young, educated but very religious respondents was also found which strongly favored the control of deviance.

Finally, a striking finding was that there was basically no difference in responses to perceptions of abortion—not even according to religiosity. The overwhelming response of all groups was that it should not be criminalized.

Public protest, it will be noted, was the only act clearly seen as non-deviant, and this perception held across all classes and subgroups.

eleven

CONCLUSIONS: TOWARDS UNITY...AND DIVERSITY

THE STATUS OF CULTURAL RELATIVISM

Since Benedict's famous pronouncement that all cultures are "equally valid" (Benedict, 1934:278), much has been written for and against cultural relativism. Most of the issues have become reasonably clear cut, few resolved. Some have objected that cultural relativism does not mean that all cultures are equally valid (Herskovits, 1972), but rather that cultural relativism is a kind of ethico-scientific doctrine that encourages "respect" for other cultures. In other words, to use Herskovits' phraseology, there is "tough minded" and "tender-minded" cultural relativism. With the exception of Benedict's more extreme statements, most writers have concluded that there *is* some invariance of values across cultures, but at the same time that there is also a great diversity of values across cultures. What they have not been able to agree on is the emphasis or direction that research should take. For example, Asch (1952), Linton (1952), Firth (1951), and Ginsberg (1956) have complained that too little attention has been given to the universal aspects of human behavior.[1] On the other hand,

---

[1] It is of interest to note that the sentiment underlying this issue, having remained pretty much dormant in social psychology since these statements of the 1950s has been regenerated in a new and more sophisticated form by Donald Campbell in his Presidential address to the American Psychological Association where he draws attention to the importance of moral absolutes in all cultures (Campbell, 1975). This is a particularly interesting position. Social scientists over the last decades have increasingly espoused a relativistic ethic. It was assumed that a cultural relativist could accept no absolutist ethic. Now it is suggested that, even though values may be ostensibly culturally relative, it may be necessary ("for the good of society," which means for Campbell an evolutionary ethic), that one accept certain central values of one's own culture *as if* they were absolutes. The search for, or need for some kind of universal schema is also attested to by the attendance of a number of illustrious scientists (both from the social and hard sciences) at the annual Sun Moon symposia which have the stated aim of reducing the world, including science, to a set of universal values. See: *Science and Universal Values,* Report of the Sun Moon Symposium, 1974.

Herskovits cautiously advocates the study of diversity (Herskovits, 1972). So also did Durkheim (1933):

> The method of finding the permanent and pervasive element in crime is surely not by enumerating the acts that at all times and in every place have been termed crimes . . . for they are the smallest minority . . . such a method would give us a very mistaken notion, since it would apply only to exceptions.

Do our data shed light on this controversy? Indeed, they do. Without exception, all studies cited either for or against the position of cultural relativism in relation to moral values have been anthropological or historical studies that have assumed because formal rules (in the form of written or unwritten law) could be identified in various cultures, that this was evidence sufficient for the approval or disapproval of particular kinds of conduct. Without exception, all such studies (especially that of Westermarck (1906), and others drawing upon the secondary data of the Human Relations Area Files) have assumed a one-to-one relationship between a formal rule and public acquiescence. While this assumption might more easily be defended in regard to a primitive society, it certainly cannot be assumed in regard to a complex society. We have seen throughout this book that there are different levels of social control perceived by the public at large. We have seen that the meaning of "approval" is highly variable depending on the structure of society's control mechanism and on the methods used to measure the public's perceptions of the behavior to be controlled.

These observations suggest that the data from our study should provide us with novel insights into the problems previously examined by the cultural or ethical relativists. But, it is obvious that there are serious problems with the definition of the word relativism. It will be useful to run through a number of different types of relativism, noting the most common controversies surrounding each, and afterwards to consider their relevance to this study.

Descriptive Relativism

This type of relativism is that which is most commonly equated with cultural relativism. It has two major dimensions: space and time. The massive study by Westermarck (1906) described the very wide differences in moral practices and values across many diverse cultures. On the basis of his observations of these differences, he concluded that morals were relative to the particular society or culture. Although he used some historical material, Westermarck's work was basically concerned with the spatial dimension, comparing values of cultures that had ostensibly vastly different origins. The time dimension has been considered, again in a massive work by Lecky (1887). However, although recognizing the interpretation of moral values and their priorities as relative to the particular historical period, Lecky considered that the *essential* nature of values was that they changed only slowly. This leads us to the major argument against descriptive relativism. It may be insisted that divergent practices are merely exterior adaptations of the same higher order values. Asch (1952) and Ginsberg (1956), among others, have argued that one cannot infer simply from the observation of divergent practices in different cultures that these differences represent different underlying values.[2] And also that the reverse must hold: that one cannot assume, upon the observation of *similar* practices, that they represent the same underlying values. They may represent different values.

Another interpretation is that descriptive differences may be taken as valid, but it may be argued that the differences are products of different stages of the same evolutionary morality. On a general scale, this may suggest that "primitive cultures" are at an early stage of moral development, and that as they develop, so also will their morality. The implication, however, is that all societies are progressing according to some kind of universal evolutionary order. This may take either a religious or Darwinian form (Flew, 1967), or may simply be an argument that every culture "learns by its mistakes," otherwise history would indeed repeat itself (McIntyre, 1971:3).[3] It also assumes that morality is inextricably a part of social life (McIntyre, 1971). Thus, arguments against these relativistic views have tried to put forward

---

[2]Thus, the divergent examples of senilicide used by Turk (1969) to which we referred in Chapter 5, may easily be reduced to moral values of laudable intent: i.e., the preservation of society.

[3]A fine distinction may be drawn between a cyclical view of the history of morals, compared to an evolutionary view. The evolutionary model is clearly non-relativistic, since the universal laws of evolution are held to apply—thus, ethics are a product of a virtually absolute moral order. The cyclical view is only anti-relativistic if one assumes that the "return to go" is the absolute: that is, zero. From this view, one is necessarily led into pronouncements regarding the zero level—that is, the nature of primitive man (or, vice-versa, but presumably the same thing: the primitive nature of man), and the nature of primitive society (or, synonymously, the primitive nature of society). A strict relativist would even have to deny any basic human nature, since it implies a universality. In this case, the cyclical view must become *circular*, since there can be no beginning; there is nowhere to return to, nowhere to go. But, provided it accepts certain basic assumptions about a starting point, the cyclical view is not necessarily relativistic. It may work against "progress" or evolution. But it does not automatically require that basic universals be discarded.

what they regard to be the essential and universal elements of all societies (e.g., Firth, 1951; Linton, 1952).

Individual Relativism

This form of ethical relativism is that which argues that the only forms of morality, or "right" are what a person considers is "right for himself." It is argued that provided a person believes his own action to be right, it is right, regardless of other criteria. Most modern moral philosophers, especially the British, have strongly rejected this argument (e.g. McIntyre, 1971; Hare, 1952). It is represented in its most extreme form in Sartre's early existential philosophy, where it was argued that the only valid values were those which the individual created for himself.[4]

Other variations of this view are those in which all moral statements are reduced to particular kinds of individualistic psychology. Thus, "this is wrong," is translated as "I feel that this is wrong." Rationality, in this case, is given an inferior role. Morality becomes rather an expression of individual desires, or depending on one's brand of psychology, a function of stimulus-response mechanisms.[5] But the distinction should be made that S-R theories reduce moral behavior to a

---

[4]In his existential philosophy, Sartre (1969) refused to recognize the basic distinctions made by all modern English moral philosophers between "is" and "ought." Satre reduced all is statements to ought, or, more precisely to acting statements. In their zealous attempts to reject naturalism most of the leading English moral philosophers (e.g., Bradley, Moore) had established what appeared to be an irreconcilable split between fact and value, is and ought. This is because they were concerned abstractly with "the good," or "the right." Sartre (1969), while rejecting naturalism, nevertheless managed to present essence ("is") as necessarily created by existence ("acting," "doing"). Only by spontaneously acting, selecting one's own choices, does one create values and thus the oughtness of action. Is and ought are reduced to the common denominator of existential action. The approach introduces an individual relativism of the extreme, and it flies in the face of the English moral philosophers of the beginning of this century who were preoccupied with establishing what was the "good" and who assumed that moral choices were made upon the basis of some abstract, guiding principle (e.g., "duty.") Although the English philosophers have strongly criticized Sartre for his often incomprehensible jargon, Warnock (1968) does give him his "due," mainly for shifting attention away from an abstract notion of "good" onto how moral decisions are made. The distinction between fact and value made by anti-naturalists from various disciplines is crucial to an understanding of cultural relativism, since much of the diversity in cultures is often explained away by pointing to diversity in *facts* rather than values (Ginsberg, 1956).
[5]Asch (1952) strongly criticizes the S-R theorists as having eradicated the rational meaning of values as such. Skinner, of course, is now the prime target for such attacks, especially for his Utopian novel *Walden II* and his *Beyond Freedom and Dignity* (1953). Many of the critics of cultural relativism and relativism in general base their criticisms on the charge that relativists deny the role of rationality, thinking, and making of choices by individuals, which they consider to be central to any moral thinking. The

series of behaviors that have no moral, "rational," or even emotive base. Rather, they are governed by the scientific laws of the relationships between stimulus and response. The relativism involved here is often a relativism to the Other's action, since Others are most often the source of stimuli. This may be identified as another type of relativism, situational relativism, which we will discuss next. The existential relativism of Sartre is quite different. What is moral is held to be relative to each individual; there can be no general moral principle, only a "right" for each individual. Yet this position becomes dangerously close to the establishment of the individual as absolute, a position which some later existential writers adopted (e.g. Camus). Sartre was at pains not to take this position, as his later Marxist writings testify.

Situational Relativism

Situational relativism is perhaps the most popular form of relativism currently in vogue in sociology and social psychology. A great deal of emphasis has been placed in social psychology during the 1970s on the situational determinants of behavior. Values, it is argued, can only be understood in relation to the situations in which they gain expression. And since situations are infinitely variable, this is a value relativism of an extreme form. This conclusion is a fascinating contrast to the arguments of Asch in the 1950s, who insisted that only by a detailed analysis of the situational aspects of moral behaviors in contrasting cultures would it be possible to arrive at the underlying *invariant* values across divergent cultures. Asch's argument was that it was only the situations that were different, but the underlying values were the same.

The early premises of the "labelling" or symbolic interactionist schools in sociology were concerned to negate that view. Even though much of the early interactionist theorists began with the basic premise of Cooley (the "looking-glass self") they disregarded the fundamental, universal values put forward by Cooley such as sympathy, love, jealousy, respect (Kluckhohn, 1955).

George Mead's translation of Cooley's interactionist theory changed

---

work of Ayn Rand is an excellent example of such a view (e.g., *Atlas Shrugged*). We have seen, however, that there are types of relativism such as that of Sartre's that emphasize the acting, choosing side of man's behavior. This contradiction can be resolved if one takes the view, as does Rand, that we are not speaking here of relativism at all, but rather of an absolutist ethic, in which the individual is taken as the absolute standard. There is much to be said for the applicability of this view to Sartre's early work.

all this, especially with his well-argued thesis that the mind exists outside the body (Mead, 1934). While we have seen that the various forms of individualistic relativism were close to an absolutist individualism, this cannot be the case with symbolic interactionism, since the locus or point of comparison can never be one individual to himself, but only an individual in relation to another or others, and in addition modified by the situational context (e.g., the number present, proximity to each other, etc.). Thus, all action is morally unique, because it can only be understood (evaluated) in relation to others and situations, all of which vary and constantly change to an infinite degree. In this case, there can, therefore, be no moral principles, no norms or guides to action, excepting what is discovered during the course of interaction ("constitutive rules"). This is a radical relativism in which moral evaluation is impossible. Although it is not true that all forms of relativism preclude ethical statements, it is this form of ethical relativism that makes it contradictory for its exponent to utter ethical statements (see Brandt, 1959:277).[6]

Normative Relativism

This is by far the most complex and confused type of relativism. Sometimes termed "sociological relativism," it is most clearly defined by Ginsberg (1956:27) as a theory in which ". . . morals are tied to the group, so that different groups have different moralities, and there is no common standard by which they may be judged." There is a direct link between this view and political theory. The purely relativistic view is that there are different groups in society, each with its own standards of right and wrong—each as valid as the other. This is, perhaps, the theoretical principle underlying the civil rights movement in the U.S. It is, however, neither realistic, nor does it seem to make common sense—that all groups in a society have equally valid moral standards.

---

[6]The relativism underlying labelling theory, though recognized as a difficulty, has been dismissed all too lightly by sociologists (e.g., Gibbs, 1966; Schur, 1971). It is most strange that labelling theorists have rarely claimed to be value free in their research (indeed they have prided themselves as "reformers" and often crusaders), yet if ever the term could be applied to a school of thought it is to the symbolic interactionists who have, in point of fact, atomized the concept of value. There is nothing in their theoretical premises that dictates "whose side they should be on," yet they have consistently defended the "defined" against the "definer." This has to be a purely arbitrary position, since as we have seen, the form of radical relativism subscribed to by interactionists precludes any evaluation of action, according to moral principle. This is one of the points made by Gouldner (1968). I have also tried to reshape interactionist theory so that it is not open to these charges (See Newman, 1975).

Would a commune of cannibals living in the wilds of Montana be considered as having equally valid moral values as a group of Quakers in Philadelphia? And besides, what does one define as a group? Do homosexuals form a group? Housewives? To say nothing of the popular, yet more difficult to define category of social class. Are values *relative* to social classes, and may one, true to relativism, argue that all social classes are "equally valid?"

A further alternative is to define "group" as equivalent to "society" and to argue that a normative consensus exists about certain central moral values of society. Such a view was put forward by Durkheim (1951) and later by Merton (1967).[7] Again, there is only a very fine distinction between this view advanced as an absolutist ethic as against a relativistic ethic. As an absolutist ethic, the consensus of the group is seen as the supreme authority or standard of morality. It can be seen that this position is essentially the same as one that ascribes the supreme standard of moral authority to God or religious leaders. Thus, whatever the group approves is automatically "right" regardless of time or place. We must be clear here that we are speaking of a universal consensus within a society, on the assumption that there are no other conflicting or competing groups. Clearly, this can never be the case. There *are* diverse and different societies on this planet. Furthermore, each and every society evolves and changes, so that what the public thought was "right" in the 16th century may no longer be considered as "right" in the 20th century. As Sumner puts it, "For the people of a time and place, their own mores are always good, or rather . . . In them there can be no question of the goodness or badness of their mores . . ." (Sumner, 1934:58). But, if it can be shown that certain values have *always* been promoted (e.g., the disapproval of robbery, murder), then this view is not relativistic. Brandt (1959:59) unfairly chooses examples of laws that change and vary considerably (divorce laws) in his criticisms of Sumner. If it can be shown that some mores *do not* change over time or space, or if they do, only very, very slowly, it may be argued that the burden of proof is on the relativistic interpre-

---

[7]As Ginsberg (1956) has shown, this view lends itself to a totalitarian doctrine, in that if one argues that morality has its origins in the needs of the group (society) it follows that the individual needs must be subjected to the group needs. Thus, both Durkheim and Merton eventually placed emphasis on individual reaction against the society. Durkheim reinstated the notion of choice or voluntariness on the part of individuals to obey, and Merton emphasized the reactive nature of adaptations to societal norms and especially emphasized the role of the non-conformist, who Merton went to great pains to contrast as the rational thinker as against the then psychoanalytical stereotype of the "different" person as necessarily mentally ill.

tation of normative ethics. We cannot assert that public opinion is always, or even mostly, right. But we can say that, about particular classes of acts (e.g., traditional crimes) the chances are that the public is right, and the individual if he pits himself against the public, is wrong.

Normative relativism ascribes to all groups equal validity in the rightness of their moral evaluations. We have seen, however, that we are unable to make any sense of this position unless we ascribe to one or several of the groups moral authority that the others do not have. But if we do this, we have broken the premise of relativism. Durkheim saw this difficulty and attempted to derive the justification for ethical principles from a scientific analysis of the basic needs of society. Various anthropologists have also tried to justify, or reduce ethical principles to what they argue are the universal basic *human* needs, as well as universal basic needs of any society (Firth, 1951; Linton, 1952; Aberle, 1950). They argue that all societies everywhere have a social order which regulates its members and is backed up by a moral demand system.[8] Moral evaluation is derived from a comparison of the individual's action to the social institutions of society which are taken to represent a moral society. Again, it is clear that although this position may be valid much of the time, we are also well aware that any society *qua* society is not necessarily moral.

THE FINDINGS AND THEIR SIGNIFICANCE FOR CULTURAL RELATIVISM

Cross-Cultural Specificity of Act Descriptions

Although we have commented on the generality of the act descriptions presented to the respondents, in comparison to the evidence referred to by cultural relativists, these acts have been quite specific.

---

[8]It may be seen that this approach faces us directly into the chicken-and-egg-problem of political theory. Marxists would argue that although humans may have the same basic needs, the crucial element in the development of social institutions has been the fact of scarce resources. The moral demand system of a society is seen by Marxists as buttressing social institutions that are only necessary to a society which has developed a structure based on private property and the exploitation of labor. Although it is not altogether clear, it seems that Marx and Engels view the early competition of scarce resources in relation to basic human needs as having set the early historical conditions for the development of capitalistic economy (See: Marx and Engels, 1970). Thus, if one chooses a different paradigm for an assessment of the basic needs of a society, then one is bound to differ from these anthropologists.

Comparatively speaking, they mean the same thing to each person in each culture. An abortion is an abortion, after all. The same may be said for all other acts. In this sense they are quite specific, their circumstances and surrounding situational aspects either self-defined, (i.e., in terms of it being an interview situation for *all* respondents), or pre-defined by us in the act description. The abortion was specified as two months; homosexuality was specified as consenting and in private; the amount of harm done to the victim was specified in the act of robbery. Although the descriptions often appeared vague when we tried to interpret their relationship to the law, as act descriptions in themselves, they are much more specific than other anthropological evidence taken from studies that have often relied upon secondary data collected for other purposes. The criticism levelled at such studies by Asch and others, that the situational elements are not accounted for, is not so serious for this study. We can be more certain of accepting any diversity or universality at face value. We have noted many sources of error, and to be sure, our methodology is far from perfect. But, the specificity of the data is considerably better than has previously been available.

Act Differentiation

The most serious charge against the illuminating work of the moral philosophers and some criminologists and sociologists (who adhere to a relativistic ethic), is in their failure to recognize that there may be different orders of moral action. The tendency has been to snap examples out of the air, preferably those which would easily support one's case. But, we have seen in this book that not only is it possible to develop a general classification of deviant behaviors on the basis of a formal theoretical analysis undertaken in the second chapter, but by and large, the respondents in all cultures tended to classify the acts into similar groupings. This in itself is strong evidence to suggest that different categories of moral action may warrant different kinds of analysis, and that one grand system of moral philosophy is not sufficient to apply to every category of action.

Looking more closely at the data, we draw out some of these possibilities. For traditional crimes, a high degree of consensus was found for their disapproval, and this certainly applied across all countries. One might argue that these crimes have *always* been disapproved of. They are therefore not relative to particular periods or places, but are standards; one hesitates to say it, but they are, functionally speaking, *absolute* standards.[9]

We also found characteristic response patterns to "traditionally deviant" acts of homosexuality, abortion, and taking drugs. These acts were, furthermore, consistently grouped together as similar by respondents in all cultures. The typical pattern of response was in the form of a U shaped curve, suggestive of considerable factional conflict. They were also those acts for which sociological background factors were able to explain significant portions of the variation (though never more than fifty percent). These three acts have been the traditional sources of conflict and loud moral debate for many centuries in Western society and to some extent in other Eastern or Middle Eastern societies. The principles of normative relativism may more easily apply to this class of acts, which appears to be susceptible to the campaigning of interest groups and where persons' moral evaluations of them are strongly affected by the norms of particular societal groups or cultures. We should note, however, that even in this case, at least half (usually more) of the variation in perception of this class of acts was unexplained by variables external to the individual. By inference, we may conclude that even for those acts most susceptible to a normative ethic, still factors *within* individuals were more likely to explain variation in perceptions of this class of acts.

This conclusion gains much more support from the findings for the *mala ambigua* act of not helping. We saw that this act elicited probably the widest variation (as measured by the variance) in responses in all country samples. Yet, when it came to assess the effects of background factors, none was found significant. We find, again, a class of moral behavior which should be analyzed in a different way than other classes of moral behavior—yet ambiguous or moral dilemma situations are often the favorite examples of moral philosophers. No consistent group patterns of response were found across all cultures, or even within cultures. It was as if each individual had made up his mind according to his own beliefs, without reference to any external criteria. The principles of individualistic relativism may more easily be applied to this class of action.

---

[9]The extreme Marxist theorists in criminology insist that all crime (including traditional crimes) is *political* and only political. But even if one were to accept this charge, it does not alter the fact that regardless of the political structure of any society in any period, these crimes have always been crimes with public disapproval. Political fortunes and structures may change, but it takes a revolution of fantastic proportions to wipe out the work of eons of culture. Of revolutionaries, it is only Mao who has understood this point.

Consensus and Dissensus

The consensus-dissensus debate is germaine to the problems of normative relativism. But, before we can settle the dispute about consensus or dissensus and deviance, it is necessary to be clear about what we mean by the terms. There are three crucial points around which any analysis must turn. First, what kinds of response are used as indicators of consensus or dissensus? Second, what kinds of deviance are involved? And third, what proportion of the total is enough for consensus?

By the first point, we mean how shall we measure the responses? We have seen that, depending on the questions asked, or the level of measurement involved, we can almost engineer the degree of consensus we want. At the level of opinion, for example, there was unanimous agreement that robbery should be prohibited by the law. But unanimity was not so clear when we asked other questions to do with who should control the behavior or what prison terms were recommended.

Secondly, we have seen that it is simplistic to speak of "consensus" as though it were an all-embracing phenomenon that applied to every aspect of deviance. It is clear that it is more applicable to traditional crime than it is to traditional deviance.

Finally, we must ask, what proportion of the total constitutes consensus? And, further, are particular social groupings required to formulate a dissensus? For example, one can conceive of a situation in which, say, eighty-five percent of the public approves of the legalization of abortion. One could say that this represents a consensus *among the eighty-five percent*. But, dissensus may also exist, if the remaining fifteen percent are a highly organized and vociferous group. Semantic difficulties immediately arise, since one would have to argue that there was also a consensus among the dissenters! For this reason, it seems necessary to distinguish among consensus, dissensus, conflict, and, a term I am forced to invent, asensus. In relation to the data presented in this book, these terms may be defined and described.

CONSENSUS. At the level of opinion, there was unanimous agreement across all cultures that robbery and incest should be prohibited by the law. In addition, taking a rank ordering within each country, robbery was invariably rated as the most serious and the most necessary to be controlled of all acts. Where small proportions did not agree, evidence from other questions did not suggest that they were a highly organized minority (the exception was the subculture of violence in Sardinia). This represents the ideal case for consensus both within and across cultures.

DISSENSUS. We saw that "white collar" crimes of appropriation and factory pollution elicited responses that rose gradually toward the very serious end of the seriousness scale, generally displaying this pattern on all other scales, including the composite scales. The conclusion here is that although there is a fair amount of consensus concerning the criminality and extent to which these acts should be formally controlled and sanctioned, the *intensity* or degree of feeling is not as great as for the consensus displayed for traditional crimes, nor was there any identifiable serious opposition. Dissensus, therefore, may be defined as a "soft" or "weak" consensus.

CONFLICT. Coser defines social conflict as ". . . a struggle over values and claims to scarce status, power and resources in which the aims of the opponents are to neutralize, injure or eliminate their rivals" (Coser, 1956:7). The acts typified by conflict in this book are those that elicited often incredible splits in response. The act of public protest often elicited response distributions in the form of a U shaped curve, suggesting simultaneously strong opposition to, and strong approval of, the behavior. Similarly, other acts of deviance such as drugs, homosexuality, or abortion were often defined as non-deviant by a sizeable proportion of a country sample, and at the same time, defined as criminal by an equally large proportion. This was not a consistent response for each of these acts in all countries, but the pattern occurred in every country, depending on the act concerned. Is this sufficient evidence to warrant the term conflict? Not yet, if in Coser's words, conflict requires the recognition of rivals. It is necessary to identify the *groups* or factions of those who disagree. As we have shown, contrary to the claims of conflict theorists, social class was not found to be the key to these factional groups. Rather, in all countries, strength of religious belief, urban/rural background, and to some extent amount of education were found to be the crucial variables which identified these factions. But, one could not go so far as to say that even these factors identified stable and enduring factions or classes of people in all countries. It was apparent that generally, the factional divisions were not hard and fast, but shifted with the particular act in question. Only in Iran did there appear to be a hard, clear division between urban and rural.

ASENSUS. We have seen the act of not helping as a *mala ambigua*. The distribution of responses to this act is generally a straight line, typifying total disagreement. In addition, we found no significant factional groupings according to any background variables. This is a situation in which every individual truly "makes up his own mind," where in society there is no consensus, dissensus, or conflict. It is a situation of *asensus,* a kind of normlessness that applies to specific kinds of acts, mainly those of moral dilemma or ambiguous moral situations.[10] It is this category of action that we would expect the interactionists to find themselves at home, since, if there are no normative guides to action for this category of behavior, we would expect constitutive rules of behavior to be discovered or established during on-going interaction.[11]

MODERNIZATION AND DEVELOPMENT

The most economically developed countries have the most liberal laws and liberal public opinion on deviance. In addition, it appears that the more totalitarian and the less developed, the more repressive were both public opinion and the law. We found, however, that in the U.S., the most economically developed country, the law on traditional crimes was much more liberal in its sanctions than the public would like. Public opinion, having gone through a very liberal stage, appears

---

[10]We should of course, be careful to distinguish this "normlessness" from anomie that refers to a *general state* of normlessness in society. Again, we can agree with the critics of Merton (e.g. Lemert, 1972) that there are many situations in which there are no normative demands as to how one should act. However, our data suggest that this criticism applies only to a specific category of action, and certainly not to all, or even the majority of moral behavior. Both Merton and the interactionists are probably correct—within a limited framework in regard to specific categories of moral behavior.

[11]It is of interest to note that moral philosophers have been preoccupied with the concept of *duty* as an explanatory variable to justify moral action. Similarly, Merton and Parsons have used the concept of role and role relationship in an attempt to weld individual behavior into the normative framework of society. Both the concept of role and duty are heavily imbued with moral obligation, as Downie (1971) argues. They are also used by moral philosophers especially in an attempt to solve their ever popular moral dilemmas. The fact is, however, that men do not face moral dilemmas everyday of the proportions presented by philosophers. In addition, Merton especially was aware of the difficulties in maintaining on-going interaction, and invoked the concept of role as an explanatory variable to hook the individual into the interactive setting. Roles and duties are seen as facilitators of interaction: they are not guiding moral principles, but rather habitual forms of behavior. They are concepts invoked to deal with situations that are *normless,* yet situations that appear to be conducted in a patterned way. What we must realize now is that these concepts may be applicable only to particular forms of categories of behaviors and situations, not to *all* behaviors or *all* situations as has hitherto been assumed.

to have swung back, calling for stricter penal sanctions. In areas of deviance, opinion appeared to be pretty much equally liberal to the law.

For less developed countries, the story is the opposite. The law lagged way behind strong liberalizing public opinion in regard to almost all acts surveyed.

In terms of the sophistication in perception of deviant behavior, the less-developed countries appeared to discriminate among or classify the acts into categories to a lesser degree than the more developed countries. This finding lends support to the evolutionary view of ethics, if one accepts the proposition that the ability to assess acts in other terms than black and white is a higher level of moral evaluation.[12]

Finally, contrary to predictions made according to various political and culture-conflict theories, we were unable to find any instances where gaps between public opinion and the law were severe for any particular sub-group of society—except as we had expected, for the subculture of violence in Sardinia.

We may make some speculations about the criminal law upon the basis of these findings. It would seem that the law, while it responds to social conditions of the times, nevertheless remains as a relatively stable cultural phenomenon, around which public opinion wavers to an often startling degree. If this is the case, it is a small wonder that the law, next to the military, has traditionally been seen by political theorists to represent the backbone of a society's social order. It also provides considerable justification for the view that the law should to some extent remain insulated from public opinion.

---

[12]The evidence for an evolutionary ethic is quite considerable. Several attempts have been made to derive ethical principles directly from Darwinian evolution. See, for example, Flew (1967), now revived in a popular form in sociobiology by Wilson (1975). See also Campbell (1975, 1965) for a review of the literature. Other arguments for an evolutionary ethic have been suggested by Kohlberg and Turiel, 1972) and Tapp (1970) who have derived a theory of moral development closely wedded to the Piagetian model of cognitive development. These cross-cultural studies have suggested that different cultures are at different stages of moral development, according to a universal scale. There are many philosophers and social scientists, of course, who insist that we have made no progress whatever in our moral ideas. MacIntyre (1971) forcefully demolishes this view with his succinct *History of Ethics*. This is not to say that we are necessarily going in the "right direction." But MacIntyre presents clear evidence that our understanding of moral ideas has developed through many important phases and insights. We have learned by our mistakes, argues MacIntyre. However, since technological and other aspects of society are also developing, often at an extremely rapid pace, it is difficult for ethics to keep in step. Additionally, MacIntyre argues that ethical principles are inextricably part of our social fabric. Therefore, the evolution of change in other aspects of society will necessarily affect the direction of change in ethical ideas. This suggests that ethical principles can be derived from society, but that society cannot be derived from ethical principles.

Further evidence for the effects of modernization and development was investigated in the analysis of urban/rural differences. Current research on the modernization process has shown the relationship between urbanization and modernization to be only a tenuous one (Eisenstadt, 1973:100). That developing or traditional societies generally display marked differences between urban and rural attitudes is no longer so clear, nor is the direction of the difference invariant. Previous research had suggested that we would find no urban/rural difference in India; this was supported. Only in Iran did the rural display much more conservative attitudes to deviance than the urban. This urban/rural difference was also found for Yugoslavia, but this country would not be classified as "developing." A difference in the opposite direction was found for Indonesia, which was explained by the special make-up of the urban sample from Djakarta. The effects of modernization upon developing countries are probably culture-specific.

It is probable that some universalization of norms has also occurred. The act of pollution may be considered as a deviant act arising specifically from the problems created by industrialization. Although respondents from the most industrialized countries favored police or government control of pollution more than other countries, it is nevertheless apparent from Chapter 6 that there was a quite consistent criminalization of factory pollution across all countries. It seems reasonable to conclude that some universalization of norms has occurred. The case of taking drugs may be another example, but more complex. Taking drugs has traditionally been seen in the U.S. as a seriously deviant act, and the U.S. has from time to time tried to influence other countries not to cultivate opium. Iran and Indonesia both agreed to limit cultivation, and indeed in Iran, severe penalties for smoking opium or taking heroin were introduced. These laws were introduced in the face of cultural mores and folkways that permitted the social use of opium. Thus, the high criminalization of drugs shown by both Indonesians and Iranians suggests that the people are becoming "modernized" to the Western point of view. They have not reached the point where they will view taking drugs as an illness, although one may speculate that the Iranians are moving in this direction.

Perhaps the most fascinating act in relation to the process of modernization is that of incest, the responses to which were certainly quite unexpected. The idea of incest as the universal taboo has been shown to be an oversimplification. Its criminalization was by no means universal, and in fact almost one quarter of the New York and Sardinian respondents saw it as not deviant at all. One is tempted to interpret this as evidence that the modernization process breaks down even the most entrenched of traditional values. However, the proportions are so great here, that one is tempted to ask whether in fact incest has ever been a "universal taboo" as far as ordinary people are concerned. In addition, Iran and Yugoslavia were the high criminalizers for both incest and homosexuality. One might conclude that sexual mores are not directly related either to economic development, political structure, or dominant religion of a society since the samples from these two countries differed considerably according to these factors.

CRIMINALIZATION AND DECRIMINALIZATION: A QUESTION OF ATTITUDES, BEHAVIOR AND POLICY

A number of writers have suggested that the criminal law has "over-reached" itself and that many borderline deviant acts should not be subject to the control of the criminal law (e.g. Morris and Hawkins, 1972). Among the several arguments used in support of this view is the one that many of these laws do not have the support of public opinion, so that to enforce them is disruptive of society, undermining the moral status of the traditional core of criminal law. Opponents of this view argue that to decriminalize any law would seriously weaken the "moral fibre" of society, resulting in a disintegration of social life (Devlin, 1968). Devlin, of course, does not accept that deviant acts (e.g., homosexuality, taking drugs) are "borderline" to the criminal law—rather they are central to the morality of society. The data presented in our study raise some fascinating questions in this regard. We must be careful how we interpret the responses to questions in the light of preferred decriminalization. For example, to advocate decriminalization does not imply that the behavior should not be controlled by some other agency of social control in society.

The New York and Yugoslavian respondents, for example, tended either to criminalize an act or to see it as non-deviant, making little use of "intermediate" control institutions of the family. And, of course, village control of the kind available in South East Asian and Muslim countries is not available to them. Thus, to decriminalize particular acts in Yugoslavia and New York would mean the actual lifting of all controls. In contrast, in the more traditional societies, the family and village level of control were still heavily referred to, so that to decriminalize many acts would not necessarily mean that the social control of these acts would also be removed. One might predict, therefore, that decriminalization in traditional societies should be possible with less social upheaval than decriminalization in developed societies. This hypothesis might be taken further to speculate that to criminalize behavior in traditional societies (as often happens in colonization) may be more difficult to achieve because it undermines the traditional village and family modes of social control. The other branch of the hypothesis is a provocative one: that it may be easier to criminalize behavior in developed societies, than to decriminalize.

But there are important assumptions involved in the development of these hypotheses.

The first assumes that there is a relationship between attitudes, opinions (or a person's responses to a questionnaire), and actual behavior. There is much controversy about this, although probably the research claiming that attitudes are unrelated to behavior has been overly stated. Kelman (1974) has pointed out that most of the research that has displayed a lack of relationship between attitudes and behavior has been conducted within the highly confined conditions of the laboratory.[13] Very few have been conducted under social survey conditions which is where, after all, attitudes are important. Indeed, the success of much marketing research depends on the ability to predict individuals' behavior from their answers to questionnaires. Nowhere is this clearer than in opinion polling in regard to elections. The notorious errors in prediction of elections by pollsters are always used, but as is clear from Bogart's brief outline of political opinion polling in America, the successes far outweigh the failures (Bogart, 1972).

As Fishbein (1973) and others have found, there are, of course, many other factors that determine behavior besides attitudes, so that one should not expect it to be easy to demonstrate clear and consistent relationships between attitudes and behavior. But even if it is found that there is a limited or even no relationship between attitudes and behavior, Kelman emphasizes that this does not mean the concept is bankrupt. The division between "inner" and "outer" behavior is after all a somewhat arbitrary one as interactionists since Mead have taught us. One may argue that attitudes and opinions *are* behaviors and are deserving in themselves of study. This would seem to be especially the case in regard to the kinds of moral behavior that we have seen are ambiguous, which depend in large part on individualistic factors.

---

[13]Kelman also points out that the famous study by LaPiere (1934), so often quoted as the first clear demonstration of the lack of relationship between attitudes and behavior, was not a study of attitudes at all, but a request from managements for a statement of *policy*. One could recount many examples of successful predictions of behavior from marketing research polls.

But, one may also argue in the present case, that obtaining opinions in answers to questionnaires is more similar to the real life behavior of *voting,* rather than to whether the person actually leads his life according to the attitudes he expresses about deviance. For example, suppose one investigates opinions on adultery. One could more safely infer voting behavior concerning some change in adultery laws, than one could predict whether or not a person would (or does) engage in adultery commensurate with the opinions he expresses. A case can be made, therefore, that a survey of this kind may be extremely useful for political or legislative guidance, in an effort to gauge public opinion. As Bogart points out, most leading political figures in the U.S. regularly employ polls as a guide to the kinds of issues to speak about or to avoid.

On face value, it seems as though, in a democracy, that almost by definition the regular polling of the public should be an integral part of the political process. There are, however, two serious difficulties with this—one political, the other related to one's theory of the role of the criminal law in society.

First, it may be argued (and Bogart gives many examples) that the polls may be used (either intentionally or unintentionally) by political candidates or interest groups to *create* a climate of opinion, a kind of snowballing effect. In this sense, polls, instead of becoming the reflectors of public opinion, become also the instigators of opinion. Second, it has been a common view of criminal lawyers and jurists that the insularity of the criminal law from public opinion is an important virtue. Montero's aim, after all, was to prevent the public from wreaking uncontrolled havock upon hapless criminals. As we saw earlier, one of the conclusions drawn from this study was that criminal law appears as a stable influence in societies, around which public opinion wavers considerably. The criminal law behaves according to its own logic. It responds to changing social conditions, but it does so slowly—on its own terms.

Surveys such as those described here may be of use in deciding on issues of criminalization or decriminalization depending upon one's view of the role of criminal law in society, and on one's view of the role of the democratic process as a political structure sensitive to the opinion of the masses.[14]

On the basis of our study, if one were to recommend any changes in

---

[14]Bogart (1972) argues that a most positive feature of national opinion polls is that they direct attention to the opinions of the masses, which are sometimes overridden by the louder cries of well organized minority interest groups.

the criminal law concerning any of the acts, this is what one could recommend:[15]

India: Large gaps were found between law and opinion for the acts of taking drugs, abortion, homosexuality, and public protest. From data in Table 28, prison terms for all these acts could be reduced to a nominal one month. Complete decriminalization would not be recommended since there were large majorities who favored the nominal legal prohibition of all these acts except public protest. In the latter case, complete decriminalization could be considered.[16]

Indonesia: Large gaps were found between law and opinion for the acts of public protest, robbery, appropriation, and not helping. The minimum term for robbery could safely be reduced from 20 years to 24 months; for appropriation from 20 years to 48 months; public protest should be completely decriminalized; and not helping could be reduced to a nominal one month but not completely decriminalized since a sizeable proportion did favor its punishment.

Iran: Although there were apparently large gaps between opinion and law as displayed in Table 28, we must remember that there was also high resistance to the criminalization of these acts. Since neither of these acts is formally criminalized by the criminal law, no change in the law seems warranted. The gap here is one concerning the public perceptions of the *informal* criminalization of these acts. Prison terms could be decreased for the following: for homosexuality, from 3 years to 10 months; for incest from 10 years to 1 year; taking drugs could be decriminalized completely; for abortion from 12 to six months. The minimum prison term for robbery could be *increased* by six months.

---

[15]This is admittedly a rash exercise, but one too tempting to resist. This survey has been a simple "one-shot" affair. Professional pollsters have a store of questions that have been well tried over the years, and they are able to do a series of surveys over long or short periods of time. In this way, they are able considerably to buttress the validity and reliability of their findings. The recommendations are made as an exercise to demonstrate the possibilities of these kinds of surveys to legislative and policy aspects of the criminal law. One should also note, that there are two ways to reduce the gaps between opinion and law: one may change the law or one may change public opinion.

[16]Since this survey was conducted, India has indeed done the opposite to these recommendations. Public protest has been severely repressed, and taking drugs along with alcohol outlawed on a national basis. We should predict that very large gaps between opinion and law may be productive of underlying severe social conflict. We have tended to abide by the view that the law should remain a stable influence. In this way, it provides an "anchor" for public opinion. This view suggests that legislative changes (whether criminalizing or decriminalizing) should be minimal. That is, opinion and law should be allowed to be mutually self-regulating. However, in the case of India, where drastic changes in the law have increased the gap between the public and the law, we may expect considerable social conflict to develop—especially over public protest, an act that we have seen to be repeatedly a form of deviance that elicits highly factional public response patterns.

Italy (Sardinia): Minimum prison terms could be increased for the following acts: not helping, an increase to 2 years; for homosexuality and factory pollution, to one year. The prison term for taking drugs could be decreased to six months, and public protest could be completely decriminalized.

U.S.A. (New York State): Increased penalties for the following acts could be introduced: for robbery a minimum of four years (possibly more); for factory pollution and incest, an increase of six to twelve months; for not helping, the introduction of a three to six month sentence. *No change* in the law should be attempted for the acts of abortion, homosexuality, taking drugs or public protest because of the factional response distributions to these acts. This would mean that severe enforcement of the law on homosexuality or public protest would be inadvisable.

Yugoslavia: The greatest gaps between law and opinion occurred for the acts of public protest and not helping. Public opinion strongly favored an increased prison term for both these acts, but there was also strong norm resistance for these acts. Therefore, no change is recommended, since one would expect to arouse considerable social conflict. A particularly interesting observation in Yugoslavia is that over three quarters of the respondents thought that at least seven out of the nine acts should be prohibited by the law. However, we found the same respondents, if asked to recommend a judicial sentence, would not recommend punishment. This occurred most pointedly for incest and taking drugs. We interpret this to mean that respondents view the symbolic role of the criminal law (See, e.g. Edelman, 1964) as extremely important. It may be simply by having acts prohibited by the law, regardless of whether they are eventually enforced or punished, is a sufficient source of social control.

SUMMARY AND CONCLUSIONS

There are different classes of moral and deviant action. At present, there is insufficient research to suggest whether these classes may be seen in a hierarchical order, or whether they are classes as different as apples and oranges, or both. However, it appears that economically well-developed countries discriminate more clearly among classes of deviant behavior than do less developed countries. This evidence may be taken to be roughly indicative of an evolutionary ethic. Conflict and consensus models each apply to different classes of action.

There is a consistency across cultures in their disapprobation of traditional crimes, a consistency of such strength as to warrant the treatment of these acts or prescriptions as universals, or functionally absolute values. Therefore, the blind acceptance of relativism in any of its forms by social scientists must be thoroughly reassessed.

While there appears to be a basic invariance in the structure of deviance perception across cultures, and in the classifications of deviant action, there is also a very broad diversity in particular aspects of perception. This applies especially to respondents' preferences for the types of social control. Such diversity may be seen as clearly explained by the facts of the particular culture. In other words, the means of deviance control preferred by the respondents are relative to the structure and organization of the society in which he lives. This factual relativism should not be confused with cultural or any kind of moral relativism. It is a relativism in the sense that an igloo is relative to an eskimo, but not to an aborigine in the Australian desert. It is nonsensical in this situation to compare an igloo to a bark hut to decide which is "more valid."

The role of the criminal law appears to be one of a stable cultural influence which acts as an anchor to an ever-swaying public opinion. Changes in the criminal law should therefore be made only under extreme circumstances.

Since the role of sociological background factors has been found to be minimal for a number of acts even where there was nevertheless wide variation in responses, it would seem that the role of individual choice, or at least some kind of idiosyncratic psychological process is central to the evaluation of deviant behavior. Since those acts which were most strongly affected by sociological factors were those which are most often the subject of public debate and the campaigning of interest groups, it would appear that individualistic processes of moral evaluation may be subject to external manipulation.[17]

A final caveat: this has been a one time cross-sectional study. The results should not be taken as representing enduring cultural traits. But

---

[17]The most cynical interpretation of the "unexplained" portion of the variance is that it represents random responses from respondents who have never before thought of the issues raised by our questionnaire. If this is true, then of course, the whole basis of survey research is destroyed, since it fails to separate its measuring instrument from the phenomena it measures—one of the oldest problems of science.

they are, to a limited degree, representative of six vastly different cultures. Even when there is a close similarity between two countries according to one dimension (e.g., India and the U.S. on educational level), the cultural backgrounds of all the samples are surely different.

Throughout the book, I have not emphasized the obvious diversity in deviance perception among the six cultures because I did not want to lose sight of the *possibility* of universals. Seen in this light, the results, and inferences I have drawn from those results, should be taken as suggestive and perhaps even as provocative. They are sufficient to warrant reopening the case, but not sufficent to close it.

References

Aberle, D. F., "The Functional Prerequisites of a Society," *Ethics,* 1960, *60,* 100–111.

Adorno, T. W.; Frenkel-Brunswick, E.; Levinson, D. J.; and Sanford, R. N., *The Authoritarian Personality,* New York: Harper and Row, 1950.

The Age (Melbourne), March 27, 1971.

Akman, D. D., and Normandeau, A., "Towards the Measurement of Criminality in Canada: A Replication Study," *Acta Criminologica,* 1968, *1,* 137–254.

Allport, F. H., *Theories of Perception and the Concept of Structure,* New York: Wiley, 1955.

Allport, G. W., "Attitudes," in C. Murchison (ed.), *Handbook of Social Psychology,* Worchester, Mass.: Clark University Press, 1935.

———, *The Nature of Prejudice,* Cambridge, Mass.: Addison-Wesley, 1954.

———, and Pettigrew, T. F., "The Trapezoidal Illusion among Zulus," *Journal of Abnormal and Social Psychology,* 1957, *55,* 104–113.

Almond, G., and Verba, S., *The Civic Culture: Political Attitudes and Democracy in Five Nations,* Princeton, N.J.: Princeton University Press, 1963.

American Institute of Public Opinion, Studies nos. 704, 709, 1965; no. 774, 1969; no. 856, 1972; no. 862, 1922.

Anderson, L. R., and Fishbein, M., "Prediction of Attitude from the Number, Strength, and Evaluative Aspect of Beliefs about the Attitude Object: A Comparison of Summation and Congruity Theories," *Journal of Personality and Social Psychology,* 1965, *3,* 437–443.

Arnold, D. (ed.), *The Sociology of Subcultures,* Berkeley, Calif.: The Glendessary Press, 1970.

Asch, S. E., *Social Psychology,* Englewood Cliffs, N.J.: Prentice-Hall, 1952.

Aubert, V. (ed.), *Sociology of Law,* London: Penguin, 1970.

Bagby, J. W., "Dominance in Binocular Rivalry in Mexico and the United States," *Journal of Abnormal and Social Psychology,* 1957, *54,* 331–334.

Ballard, L. V., *Social Institutions,* New York: Appleton Century, 1936.

Ball-Rokeach, S., "Values and Violence: A Test of the Subculture of Violence Thesis," *American Sociological Review,* 1973, *38,* 736–749.

Banks, A. S., and Textor, R. B., *A Cross Polity Survey,* Cambridge, Mass.: Massachusetts Institute of Technology Press, 1963.

Barton, A. H., Denitch, B., and Kadushin, C. (eds.), *Opinion-Making Elites in Yugoslavia,* New York: Praeger, 1973.

Basham, A. L., *The Wonder That Was India,* London: Sidgwick and Jackson, 1954.

Beccaria, C. B., *On Crimes and Punishments* (trans. H. Paolucci, 1963) Indianapolis, Ind.: Bobbs-Merrill, 1968.

Becker, H., *Outsiders,* Glencoe, Ill.: The Free Press, 1964.

Bendix, Reinhard, "Concepts and Generalizations in Comparative Sociological Studies," *American Sociological Review,* 1963, *28,* 532–539.

Benedict, R., "Anthropology and the Abnormal," *Journal of General Psychology,* 1934, *10,* 59–82.

————, *Patterns of Culture,* New York: Penguin, 1934.

Bentz, W. K., and Edgerton, J. W., "Consensus on Attitudes toward Mental Illness: Between Leaders and the General Public in a Rural Community," *Archives of General Psychology,* 1970, *22,* 468.

Beteille, A., *Caste, Class and Power,* Berkeley: University of California Press, 1965.

Bickman, L., and Green, S., "Is Revenge Sweet? The Effect of Attitude toward a Thief on Crime Reporting," *Criminal Justice and Behavior,* 1975, *2,* 2, 101–112.

Bill, J. A., *The Politics of Iran,* Columbus, Ohio: Charles Merrill, 1972.

Binder, L., *Iran,* Berkeley: University of California Press, 1962.

Blackwell, B., "The Literature of Delay in Seeking Medical Care for Chronic Illnesses," *Health Education Monographs,* 1963, *16,* 3–31.

Blauner, P., "Black Culture: Lower Class Results or Ethnic Creation?" in L. Rainwater (ed.), *Soul,* Chicago: Aldine, 1970.

Blom, R., "Continued Differentiation of Penal Demands and Expectations in Regard to Justice," Tampere, Finland: University of Tampere, 1968, *2.*

Blumenthal, M.; Kahn, R. L.; Andrews, F. M.; and Head, K. B., *Justifying Violence: Attitudes of American Men,* Ann Arbor, Mich.: Institute for Social Research, 1972.

Bogart, L., *Silent Politics,* New York: John Wiley and Sons, 1972.

Bord, E.; Richard, M.; and James, G. R., "Rejection of the Mentally Ill," *Social Problems,* 1971, *18,* 496.

Bose, A., *Studies in India's Urbanization 1901–1971,* New Delhi: Tata McGraw-Hill, 1973.

Bouchier, E. S., *Sardinia in Ancient Times,* New York: Longman Green,1917.

Boydell, C. L., and Grindstaff, C. F., "Public Attitudes toward Legal Sanction for Drug and Abortion Offenses," *Canadian Journal of Criminology and Corrections,* 1971, *13,* 3, 209–232.

————, and ————, "Public Opinion toward Legal Sanctions for Crimes of Violence," *Journal of Criminal Law and Criminology,* 1974, *65,* 1, 259–267.

Brandt, R. B., "Ethical Relativism," in P. Edwards (ed.), *The Encyclopaedia of Philosophy,* New York: Macmillan, 1967.

————, *Ethical Theory,* Englewood Cliffs, N.J.: Prentice-Hall, 1959.

Brehem, J., "A Dissonance Analysis of Attitude Discrepant Behavior," in C. Hovland and M. Rosenberg (eds.), *Attitude Organization and Change,* New Haven, Conn.: Yale University Press, 1960.

Brown, A., *Yugoslav Life and Landscape,* London: Elek Books, 1954.

Brown, E. G., *British Statutes in American Law 1776–1836,* Ann Arbor, Mich.: University of Michigan, 1964.

300

Brown, W. N., "The Content of Cultural Continuity in India," *Journal of Asian Studies,* 1961, *20,* 427–434.

Bruce, W., and Anderson, R., "On the Comparability of Meaningful Stimuli in Cross-Cultural Research," *Sociometry,* 1967, *30,* 124–136.

Calder, B. J., and Ross, M., *Attitudes and Behavior,* Norristown, N.J.: General Learning Press, 1973.

Camba, R.; Puggioni, G.; and Rudas, N., "Aspects of Rural Sardinian Criminality," in Ferracuti, Lazzari, and Wolfgang (eds.), *Violence in Sardinia,* Rome: Bulzoni, 1970.

Campbell, D. T., "On the Conflicts between Biological and Social Evolution and between Psychology and Moral Tradition," *American Psychologist,* 1975, *30,* 12, 1103–1126.

———, "Variation and Selective Retention in Socio-cultural Evolution, in H. R. Barringer, G. I. Blanksten, and R. W. Mack (eds.), *Social Change in Developing Areas,* Cambridge, Mass.: Schenkerman, 1965.

Cantril, H., *The Pattern of Human Concerns,* New Brunswick, N.J.: Rutgers University Press, 1965.

Chambliss, W. J., and Seidman, R. B., *Law, Order and Power,* Reading, Mass.: Addison-Wesley, 1971.

Chein, I., "Behavior Theory and the Behavior of Attitudes," *Psychological Reports,* 1948, *55,* 175–188.

Clinard, M. B., and Abbott, D. J., *Crime in Developing Countries,* New York: Wiley, 1973.

Cloward, R. A., and Ohlin, L. E., *Delinquency and Opportunity,* Glencoe, Ill.: The Free Press, 1960.

Cohen, A. K., *Delinquent Boys,* Glencoe, Ill.: The Free Press, 1955.

———, *Deviance and Control,* New Jersey: Prentice-Hall, 1966.

Converse, P. E., "New Dimensions of Meaning for Cross-Section Sample Surveys in Politics," *International Social Science Journal,* 1964, *16,* 20–34.

Coser, L., *The Functions of Social Conflict,* Glencoe, Ill.: The Free Press, 1956.

———, "Some Functions of Deviant Behavior and Normative Flexibility," *American Journal of Sociology,* 1962, *68,* 174ff.

Crane, R. I. (ed.), *Regions and Regionalism in South East Asia,* Durham, N.C.: Committee on South East Asian Studies, Duke University, 1966.

Crissman, P., "Temporal Change and Sexual Difference in Moral Judgment," *Journal of Social Psychology,* 1942, *16,* 29–38.

Crumpton, H. G., "What Mental Illness Labels Means to Schizophrenics," *Psychological Reports,* 1966, *19,* 927–933.

———; Weirstein, A. D.; Acker, C. W.; and Annis, A. P., "How Patients and Normals See the Mental Patient," *Journal of Clinical Psychology,* 1967, *23,* 46–49.

Cuber, J. F., and Pell, B., "A Method of Studying Moral Judgments Relating to the Family," *American Journal of Sociology,* 1941, *47,* 12–23.

Cumming, E., and Cumming J., *Closed Ranks: An Experiment in Mental Health Education,* Cambridge, Mass.: Harvard University Press, 1957.

Curtis, L. A., *Violence, Race and Culture,* Lexington, Mass.: Lexington Books, 1975.

Dahl, R. A., *Pluralist Democracy in the United States: Conflict and Consent,* New York: Rand McNally, 1967.

————, "Power," *Behavioral Science*, 1957, *2*, 3, 201–215.

Dahrendorf, R., "On the Origin of Inequality among Men," in A. Beteille (ed.), *Social Inequality*, London: Penguin, 1969.

Dator, J. A., "Measuring Attitudes across Cultures," in G. Schubert and D. Danelski, *Comparative Judicial Behavior*, London: Oxford University Press, 1969.

Davis, F., "Comparative Law Contributions to the International Legal Order: Common Core Research," *George Washington Law Review*, 1969, *37*, 615.

Davis, K., "Urbanization in India: Past and Future," in Turner (ed.), *India's Urban Future*, Berkeley: University of California Press, 1962.

Davis, R., "The Fitness of Names to Drawings in Tanganyika," *British Journal of Psychology*, 1961, *52*, 259–268.

Dawson, J. L. M., "Cultural and Physiological Influences upon Spatial-Perceptual Processes in West Africa—Part 1," *International Journal of Psychology*, 1967, *2*, 115–125.

DeFleur, M., and Westie, F., "Verbal Attitudes and Overt Acts," *American Sociological Review*, 1958, *23*, 667–673.

Dennis, W., "Goodenough Scores, Art Experience and Modernization," *Journal of Social Psychology*, 1966, *68*, 211–228.

Devlin, P., *The Enforcement of Morals*, Oxford, England: Oxford University Press, 1968.

Dickson, D. T., "Bureaucracy and Morality: An Organizational Perspective on a Moral Crusade," *Social Problems*, 1968, *16*, 143–156.

Dohrenwend, B. P., and Chin-Shong, E., "Social Status and Attitudes toward Psychological Disorder: The Problem of Tolerance of Deviance," *American Sociological Review*, 1967, *32*, 417–433.

Doob, L. W., "The Behavior of Attitudes," *Psychological Review*, 1947, *54*, 135–156.

Douglas, J. D. (ed.), *Deviance and Respectability*, New York: Basic Books, 1970.

Dow, T. E., "The Role of Identification in Conditioning Public Attitudes toward the Offender," *Journal of Criminal Law, Criminology and Police Science*, 1967, *58*, 75–79.

Downie, R. S., *Roles and Values: An Introduction to Social Ethics*, London: Methuen, 1971.

Duijker, H. C. J., "Comparative Research in Social Science with Special Reference to Attitude Research," *International Social Science Bulletin*, 1955, *7*, 7–13.

Durkheim, E., *The Division of Labour in Society*, trans. G. Simpson, New York: Macmillan, 1933.

————, *The Rules of Sociological Method*, trans. S. A. Solovay and John H. Mueller, Chicago: University of Chicago Press, 1938.

————, *Suicide*, Glencoe, Ill.: The Free Press, 1951.

Edelman, M., *The Symbolic Uses of Politics*, Urbana: University of Illinois Press, 1964.

Edgerton, R. B., *The Cloak of Competence: Stigma in the Lives of the Mentally Retarded*, Berkeley: University of California Press, 1967.

Ehrlich, H. J., *The Social Psychology of Prejudice*, New York: Wiley Interscience, 1973.

Eisenstadt, S. N., *Tradition, Change and Modernity*, New York: Wiley and Sons, 1973.

Ellis, D M.; Frost, J. A.; Syrett, H. C.; and Carman, H. J., *A History of New York State*, Ithaca, N.Y.: Cornell University Press, 1967.

Engelbrecht, W. A., *De Nederlandsch—Indische Wetboeken*, Leiden: Netherlands Indies Law Books, 1939.

English, P. W., *City and Village in Iran*, Milwaukee: University of Wisconsin Press, 1966.

Erikson, K., "Notes on the Sociology of Deviance," in H. S. Becker (ed.), "The Other Side—Perspectives on Deviance," *Social Problems*, 1962, *9*, 307–314.

———, *Wayward Puritans*, New York: John Wiley and Sons, 1966.

Erlanger, H. S., "The Empirical Status of the Subculture of Violence Thesis," *Social Problems*, 1974, *22*, 1, 280–291.

Etzioni, A., "The Ghetto—A Re-evaluation," *Social Forces*, 1959, *37*, 255–260.

Eysenck, H. J., *Crime and Personality*, Boston: Houghton Mifflin, 1964.

———, *The Psychology of Politics*, London: Routledge and Kegan Paul, 1954.

Fanon, F., *The Wretched of the Earth*, New York: Grove Press, 1968.

Feierabend, I. K.; Feierabend, R.; and Nesvold, B. A., "Social Change and Political Violence," in H. D. Graham and T. R. Gurr (eds.), *Violence in America*, Washington, D.C.: Government Printing Office, 1969.

Fernandez, D., *The Mother Sea*, trans. M. Callum, New York: Hill and Wang, 1967.

Ferracuti, F.; Lazzari, R.; and Wolfgang, M., *Violence in Sardinia*, Rome: Bulzoni, 1970.

Ferracuti, F., and Wolfgang, M., *Psychological Testing of the Subculture of Violence*, Rome: Bulzoni, 1973.

Firth, R., *Elements of Social Organization*, New York: Philosophical Library, 1951.

Fishbein, M., "A Consideration of Beliefs, and Their Role in Attitude Measurement," in M. Fishbein (ed.), *Attitude Theory and Measurement*, New York: Wiley, 1967, 257–266.

——— (ed.), *Attitude Theory and Measurement*, New York: Wiley, 1967.

———, "The Prediction of Behaviors from Attitudinal Variables," in C. D. Mortensen and K. K. Sereno (eds.), *Advances in Communication Research*, New York: Harper and Row, 1973.

———, and Ajzen, I., "Attitudes and Opinions," *Annual Review of Psychology*, 1972, *23*, 487–544.

Fisher, J., *Yugoslavia, a Multi-national State*, San Francisco: Chandler, 1966.

Flew, A. G. N., *Evolutionary Ethics*, New York: St. Martin's Press, 1967.

Foucault, M., *The Birth of the Clinic*, New York: Vintage, 1975.

———, *Madness and Civilization*, New York: Random House, New American Library, 1965.

Frank, G., *Psychiatric Diagnosis: A Review of Research*, New York: Pergamon Press, 1975.

Frankel, M., *Criminal Sentences: Law without Order*, New York: Hill and Wang, 1973.

Freeman, H. E., and Kassebaum, G. E., "Relationship of Education and

Knowledge to Opinions about Mental Illness," *Mental Hygiene*, 1960, *44*, 42.

———, and Simmons, O., "Feelings of Stigma among Relatives of Former Mental Patients," *Social Problems*, 1961, *8*, 312–321.

Freidson, E., *Patients' Views of Medical Practice*, New York: Russell Sage Foundation, 1961.

———, and Lorber, J. (eds.), *Medical Men and Their Work: A Sociological Reader*, New York: Aldine, 1971.

Frey, F. W., "Surveying Public Attitudes in Turkey," *Public Opinion Quarterly*, 1963, *27*, 3, 335–355.

Friedman, L., *A History of American Law*, New York: Simon and Schuster, 1973.

Fris, T., "On Attitudes towards Crime and the Criminal," *Nederlands Tijdschrift Voor Criminologie*, 1968, *6*, 254–259.

Frye, R. N., *Persia*, New York: Schocken, 1969.

Furstenberg, F. F., Jr., "Public Reaction to Crime in the Streets," *The American Scholar*, 1971, *40*, 4.

Garofalo, J., *Social Stratification and Victimization*, Ph.D. Dissertation, State University of New York at Albany, 1976.

Gastil, R. D., "Homicide and a Regional Culture of Violence," *American Sociological Review*, 1971, *36*, 412–427.

Gaylin, W., *Partial Justice: A Study of Bias in Sentencing*, New York: Knopf, 1974.

Geertz, C., *The Religion of Java*, Glencoe, Ill.: The Free Press, 1960.

Geertz, H., "Indonesian Cultures and Communities," in R. T. McVey (ed.), *Indonesia*, New Haven, Conn.: Hraf Press, 1963.

Genet, J., *The Balcony*, New York: Grove Press, 1966.

Gerth, H. H., and Mills, C. W., *From Max Weber*, New York: Oxford University Press, 1946.

Getzels, J. W., and Jackson, P. W., *Creativity and Intelligence*, New York: Wiley, 1962.

Ghirshman, R., *Iran*, Baltimore: Penguin, 1954.

Ghurye, G. S., *Caste, Class and Occupation*, Bombay: Popular Book Depot, 1961.

Gibbons, D. C., "Crime and Punishment: A Study in Social Attitudes," *Social Forces*, 1969, *47*, 4, 391–397.

Gibbs, J. P., "Conceptions of Deviant Behavior: Old and New," *Pacific Sociological Review*, 1966, *9*, 9–14.

Ginsberg, M., *Essays in Sociology and Social Philosophy: On the Diversity of Morals*, vol. I, London: Heinemann, 1956.

Goffin, Pierre, "A Sounding of Opinion," *Sociologie du Droit et de la Justice*, Proceeding of the Research Committee on the Sociology of Law, International Sociological Association, Brussels, Belgium, 1969.

Goffman, E., *Asylums*, New York: Doubleday-Anchor, 1961.

———, *Stigma: Notes on the Management of Spoiled Identity*, Englewood Cliffs, N.J.: Prentice-Hall, 1963.

Goodnow, J. J., "Cultural Variations in Cognitive Skills," in P. Williams (ed.), *Cross-Cultural Studies*, Baltimore: Penguin, 1970.

Gordon, M., *Assimilation in American Life: The Role of Race, Religion, and National Origins*, London: Oxford University Press, 1964.

Gore, M., *Urbanization and Family Change*, Bombay: Popular Pakistan, 1968.

Gouldner, A. W., "The Sociologist as Partisan: Sociology and the Welfare State," *American Sociologist*, 1968, *3*, 103–116.

Gove, W., "Individual Resources and Mental Hospitalization: A Comparison and Evaluation of the Societal Reaction and Psychiatric Perspectives," *American Sociological Review*, 1974, *39*, 86–100.

———, "Societal Reaction as an Explanation of Mental Illness: An Evaluation," *American Sociological Review*, 1970, *35*, 873–888.

Greenfield, P. M., "On Culture and Conservation," in J. S. Bruner, R. R. Olver and P. M. Greenfield (eds.), *Studies in Cognitive Growth*, New York: Wiley, 1966.

Gruen, W., "Composition and Some Correlates of American Core Culture," *Psychological Reports*, 1966, *18*, 483.

Guido, M., *Sardinia*, New York: Praeger, 1964.

Guilford, J. P., *Fundamental Statistics in Psychology and Education*, New York: McGraw-Hill, 1956.

Gurr, T. R., "A Causal Model of Civil Strife: A Comparative Study Using New Indices," *American Political Science Review*, 1968, *62*, 1104–1124.

Gusfield, Joseph, "On Legislating Morals: The Symbolic Process of Designating Deviance," *California Law Review*, 1968, *56*, 54.

Guskin, S., "The Influence of Labelling upon the Perception of Subnormality in Mentally Defective Children," *American Journal of Mental Deficiency*, 1962, *67*, 402–406.

Haar, Barend, *Adat Law in Indonesia*, trans. E. A. Hoebel and A. A. Schiller, New York: International Secretariat, Institute of Pacific Relations, 1948.

Hackler, J. C.; Ho, Kwai-Yiv; and Urquhart-Ross, C., "The Willingness to Intervene: Differing Community Characteristics," *Social Problems*, 1974, *21*, 3, 328–344.

Hackney, S., "Southern Violence," in H. Graham and T. Gurr (eds.), *Violence in America*, Task Force on Historical and Comparative Perspectives, National Commission on Causes and Prevention of Violence, Washington, D.C.: Government Printing Office, 1969.

Hakeem, M., "A Critique of the Psychiatric Approach to Crime and Correction," *Law and Contemporary Problems*, 1958, *32*, 4.

Hall, Jerome, *Theft, Law and Society*, Indianapolis, Ind.: Bobbs-Merrill, 1952.

Halpern, J. M., and Halpern, B. K., *A Serbian Village in Historical Perspective*, New York: Holt, Rinehart and Winston, 1972.

Hanna, W. J., and Hanna, J. L., "The Problem of Ethnicity and Factionalism in African Survey Research," *Public Opinion Quarterly*, 1966, *30*, 2, 290–294.

Hare, R. M., *The Language of Morals*, London: Oxford University Press, 1952.

Harnack, C., *Persian Lions, Persian Lambs*, New York: Holt, Rinehart and Winston, 1965.

Harris, L., and associates, "The Public Looks at Crime and Corrections,"

Report to the Joint Commission on Correctional Manpower and Training, 1967.

Hart, H. L. A., *Law, Liberty and Morality,* London: Oxford University Press, 1963.

Havelin, Arnold, "Political Attitudes towards Homosexuals and Homosexuality," *Tidss Krift for Sanfunnsforskning* (Norway), 1968, *9,* 1.

Heeren, H. J. (ed.). *The Urbanization of Djakarta,* Report on a research project sponsored by UNESCO carried out by the Institute of Economic and Social Research of the Djakarta School of Economics, 1955.

Herskovits, M., *Cultural Relativism: Perspective in Cultural Pluralism,* New York: Random House, 1972.

Hertzler, J. O., *Social Institutions,* New York: McGraw-Hill, 1929.

Hindelang, M. J., "Moral Evaluation of Illegal Behavior," *Social Problems,* 1973, *21,* 3, 370.

————, "Public Opinion Regarding Crime, Criminal Justice and Delinquency," *Journal for Research in Crime and Delinquency,* 1973, *11,* 2, 101–116.

Hirschi, T., *Causes of Delinquency,* Berkeley: University of California Press, 1969.

Hoebel, E. A., *The Law of Primitive Man,* Cambridge, Mass.: Harvard University Press, 1954.

Hogarth, J., *Sentencing as a Human Process,* Toronto: University of Toronto Press, 1971.

Hollingshead, A. B., and Redlich, F. C., *Social Class and Mental Illness,* New York: Wiley, 1958.

Hondius, F. W., *The Yugoslav Community of Nations,* The Hague: Mouton, 1968.

Hsu, M., "Cultural and Sexual Differences on the Judgment of Criminal Offenders: A Replication Study of the Measurement of Delinquency," *Journal of Criminal Law and Criminology,* 1973, *64,* 3, 348–353.

Hudson, B. B.; Barakat, M. K.; and La Forge, R., "Problems and Methods of Cross-Cultural Research," *Journal of Social Issues,* 1959, *15,* 5–19.

Hudson, W., "Pictorial Depth Perception in African groups," *Journal of Social Psychology,* 1960, *52,* 183–208.

Iran Almanac, Tehran: Ecko of Iran, 1972.

Jacobs, N., *The Sociology of Development: Iran as an Asian Case Study,* New York: Praeger, 1966.

Jacobson, E., "Methods Used in Producing Comparable Data in the OCSR Seven Nation Attitude Study," *Journal of Social Issues,* 1954, *10,* 40–51.

Jahoda, G., "Geometric Illusions and Environment: A Study in Ghana," *British Journal of Psychology,* 1966, *57,* 193–199.

Jay, R. R., *Religion and Politics in Rural Central Java,* Cultural Report Series no. 12, Southeast Asia Studies, New Haven, Conn.: Yale University, 1963.

Jones, E. L., "The Courtesy Bias in Southeast Asian Surveys," *International Social Science Journal,* 1963, *15,* 70–76.

Kaplan, B.; Reed, R. B.; and Richardson, W., "A Comparison of the Incidence of Hospitalized and Non-Hospitalized Cases of Psychosis in Two Communities," *American Sociological Review,* 1956, *21,* 472–479.

306

Karve, I., *Kinship Organization in India,* Bombay: Asia Publishing House, 1965.

Kaupen, W., "Public Opinion of the Law in a Democratic Society," in A. Podgorecki, W. Kaupen, J. Van Houtte, P. Vinke, and B. Kutchinsky (eds.), *Knowledge and Opinion about Law,* London: Martin Robertson, 1973.

Kaupen, W., and Werle, R., "Knowledge and Opinion of Law and Legal Institutions in Federal Republic of Germany," presented at the 7th World Congress of Sociology (3rd open meeting of Research Committee on Sociology of Law: Public Opinion about Law and Legal Reform), 1969.

Kelman, H. C., "Attitudes are Alive and Well and Gainfully Employed in the Sphere of Action," *American Psychologist,* 1974, *29,* 5, 310–324.

Kendall, R. E., "Psychiatric Diagnoses: A Study of How They Are Made," *British Journal of Psychiatry,* 1973, *122,* 437–445.

Kennedy, R., *Bibliography of Indonesian Peoples and Cultures,* ed. T. W. Maretzki and H. T. Fisher, revised ed., New Haven, Conn.: Human Relations Area Files, 1955.

Kerlinger, F. N., and Pedhazur, E. J., *Multiple Regression in Behavioral Research,* New York: Holt, Rinehart and Winston, 1973.

Kitsuse, J. I., "Societal Reaction to Deviant Behavior: Problems of Theory and Method," *Social Problems,* 1962, *9,* 247–256.

———, and Cicourel, A. V., "A Note on the Use of Official Statistics," *Social Problems,* 1963, *2,* 131–139.

Kittrie, N. N., *The Right to Be Different,* Baltimore: Johns Hopkins, 1971.

Klett, C. J., and Yaukey, D. W., "A Cross-Cultural Comparison of Judgments of Social Desirability," *The Journal of Social Psychology,* 1956, *49,* 19–26.

Kluckhohn, C., "Ethical Relativity," *Journal of Philosophy,* 1955, *52,* 663–677.

Kohlberg, L., and Turiel, E. (eds.), *Research in Moralization: The Cognitive Developmental Approach,* New York: Holt, Rinehart and Winston, 1972.

Kopf, D., *British Orientalism and the Bengal Renaissance,* Berkeley: University of California Press, 1969.

Kumar, R., "Rural Life in Western India on the Eve of the British Conquest," *The Indian and Economic Social History Review,* 1955, *2,* 3, 201–219.

Kutschinsky, B., "A New Series of Danish Investigations on Knowledge and Opinion about Law (KOL)," Appendix to Information Circular no. 4, Copenhagen: The International Research Committee on Knowledge and Opinion about Law, 1969.

———, "Law and Education: Some Aspects of Scandinavian Studies into the 'General' Sense of Justice," *Acta Sociologica,* 1966, *10,* 21–41.

———, "The Legal Consciousness: A Survey of Research on Knowledge and Opinion about Law," in A. Podgorecki et al., 1973.

———, *On the Construction of SKOL—A Simple Instrument to Be Used in Experimental or Comparative Studies of Knowledge and Opinion about Law,* a Preliminary Report, Copenhagen: Institute of Criminal Science, University of Copenhagen, 1970.

———, "Sex Crimes and Pornography in Copenhagen: A Survey of Attitudes," *Technical Report of The Commission on Obscenity and Pornography*, vol. VII, Washington, D.C.: Government Printing Office, 1970.

Laing, R. D., *Knots*, New York: Random House, 1972.

———, and Esterson, A., *Sanity, Madness and the Family*, Baltimore: Penguin, 1972.

LaPiere, R. T., *A Theory of Social Control*, New York: McGraw-Hill, 1954.

———, "Attitudes Versus Actions," *Social Forces*, 1934, *13*, 230–237.

———, *Sociology*, New York: McGraw-Hill, 1946.

Lasswell, T., *Class and Stratum*, Boston: Houghton Mifflin, 1965.

Lawrence, D. H., *Sea and Sardinia*, London: Penguin, 1923.

Lebar, F. M. (ed.), *Ethnic Groups of Insular South East Asia*, New Haven, Conn.: Human Relations Area Files, 1972.

Lecky, W. E. H., *History of European Morals*, 3rd ed. revised, New York: Appleton-Century, 1887. (First published 1869.)

Legge, J. D., *Indonesia*, Englewood Cliffs, N.J.: Prentice-Hall, 1965.

Lemert, E. M., *Human Deviance, Social Problems, and Social Control*, Englewood Cliffs, N.J.: Prentice-Hall, 1967; revised ed., 1972.

———, "Paranoia and the Dynamics of Exclusion," *Sociometry*, 1962, *25*, 2–20.

Lemkau, P. V., and Crocetti, G. M., "An Urban Population's Opinion and Knowledge about Mental Illness," *American Journal of Psychiatry*, 1962, *118*, 692–700.

Lerner, D., *The Passing of Traditional Society*, London: Collier-Macmillan, 1958.

Levine, D., "A Cross-National Study of Attitudes toward Mental Illness," Invited Paper at the colloquium on Social Psychology and Mental Health of the XVII International Congress of Applied Psychology, Liege, Belgium, July 1971.

Lewis, D., *La Vida: A Puerto Rican Family in the Culture of Poverty*, New York: Random House, 1966.

Lindesmith, A. R., *The Addict and the Law*, Bloomington: Indiana University Press, 1965.

Linsky, A. S., "Changing Public Views of Alcoholism," *Quarterly Journal of Studies on Alcohol*, 1970, *31*, 3.

Linton, R., "Universal Ethical Principles: An Anthropological View, in R. N. Anshen (ed.), *Moral Principles of Action*, New York: Harper, 1952.

Lippman, L., "Deviancy: A Different Look," *Mental Retardation*, 1970, *8*, 6–8.

Loftin, C., and Hill, R., "Regional Subculture and Homicide: An Examination of the Gastil-Hackney Thesis," *American Sociological Review*, 1974, *39*, 714–724.

Lombroso, C., *The Man of Genius*, London: W. Scott, 1896; New York: C. Scribner's Sons, 1891.

Lukic, R., "Yugoslav Social Structure and the Formation of Public Opinion," in Barton, Demitch, and Kadushin, 1973.

Macciotta, L., *La Sardegna e La Storia*, Cagliari: Fossataro, 1971.

MacIntyre, A., *A Short History of Ethics*, London: Routledge and Kegan Paul, 1971

Maclay, H., and Ware, E. E., "Cross-Cultural Use of the Sematic Differential," *Behavioral Science,* 1961, *6,* 185–190.

Makela, K., "Public Sense of Justice and Judicial Practice," *Acta Sociologica,* 1966, *10,* 42–67.

Malinowsky, B., *Crime and Custom in Savage Society,* Totowa, N.J.: Littlefield, Adams, 1964.

Mandelbaum, D. G., *Society in India,* Berkeley: University of California Press, 1970.

Manning, P. K., "On Deviance," *Contemporary Sociology,* 1973, *2,* 123–128.

Marsh, R., *Comparative Sociology,* New York: Harcourt, Brace and World, 1967.

Marx, K., and Engels, F., *The German Ideology,* ed. C. J. Arthur, New York: International, 1970.

Matejko, A., Book Review of *The Yugoslavian Village,* and *The Peasant Urbanites in Contemporary Sociology,* 1974, *3,* 2, 139–140.

Matza, D., *Delinquency and Drift,* New York: Wiley, 1968.

Mauer, D., *Whiz Mob,* Gainesville, Fla.: American Dialect Society, 1955.

McConell, J. P., and Martin, J. D., "Judicial Attitudes and Public Morals," *American Bar Association Journal,* 1969, *55,* 1129–1133.

Mead, G., *Mind, Self and Society,* Chicago: University of Chicago Press, 1934.

Mechanic, D., *Medical Sociology: A Selective View,* Glencoe, Ill.: The Free Press, 1968.

———, *Mental Illness and Social Policy,* Glencoe, Ill.: The Free Press, 1969.

———, "Some Factors in Identifying and Defining Mental Illness," *Mental Hygiene,* 1962, *46,* 66–74.

Meilof-Onk, S., *Opinions on Homosexuality: A Study on Image Formation and Attitudes in the Adult Dutch Population,* Amsterdam: Stichting tot Beuordering Sociaal Onderzoek Minderheder, 1969.

Merritt, R. L., and Rokkan, S., *Comparing Nations: The Use of Quantitative Data in Cross-National Research,* New Haven, Conn.: Yale University Press, 1966.

Merton, R. K., *Social Theory and Social Structure,* revised ed., New York: The Free Press, 1967.

Michael, D. N., "The Use of Culture Concepts in the Functional Analysis of Public Opinion," *International Journal of Opinion and Attitude Research,* 1951, *5,* 38–46.

Miller, J. B., *Psychoanalysis and Women,* Baltimore: Penguin, 1973.

Miller, W., "Lower Class Culture as a Generating Mileau of Gang Delinquency," *Journal of Social Issues,* 1958, *14,* 5–19.

Mills, C. W., *The Marxists,* New York: Dell, 1962.

Minuchin, S., *Families and Family Therapy,* Cambridge, Mass.: Harvard University Press, 1974.

Moore, F. W., "Sampling Utilized in 50 Cross-Cultural Studies," *Behavior Science Notes,* 1967, *2,* 261–273.

Morris, N., and Hawkins, G., *The Honest Politician's Guide to Crime Control,* Chicago: University of Chicago Press, 1972.

Mundy-Castle, A. C., "Pictorial Depth Perception in Ghanaian Children," *International Journal of Psychology,* 1966, *1,* 290–300.

Needham, R. A., *Structure and Sentiment: A Test Case of Social Anthropology,* Chicago: University of Chicago Press, 1969.

Newcomb, T., *A Dictionary of the Social Sciences,* London: 1964.

Newman, G. R., "Acts, Actors and Reactions to Deviance," *Sociology and Social Research,* 1974, *58,* 4, 434–440.

———, *Deviance and Removal,* Ph.D. Dissertation, Department of Sociology, University of Pennsylvania (Unpublished), 1972a.

———, "The Effects of Stereotypes on Perceptions of Deviance," *Australian New Zealand Journal of Criminology,* 1975b, *7,* 3, 135–144.

———, "Normality and Criminality Revisited: A View from the Sociology of Deviance," *British Journal of Criminology,* 1970, *10,* 64–73.

———, *Perceptions of Deviance in India,* Rome: United Nations Social Defense Research Institute (in Press), 1976a.

———, *Perceptions of Deviance in Indonesia,* Rome: United Nations Social Defense Research Institute (in Press), 1976b.

———, *Perceptions of Deviance in Iran,* Rome: United Nations Social Defense Research, 1976c.

———, *Perceptions of Deviance in New York,* Rome: United Nations Social Defense Research Institute (in Press), 1976d.

———, *Perceptions of Deviance in Sardinia,* Rome: United Nations Social Defense Research Institute (in Press), 1976e.

———, *Perceptions of Deviance in Yugoslavia,* Rome: United Nations Social Defense Research Institute (in Press), 1976f.

———, *Perceptions of Deviance: Suggestions for Cross-Cultural Research,* Rome: United Nations Social Defense Research Institute, S.P. no. 3, 1972b.

———, "A Theory of Deviance and Removal," *British Journal of Sociology,* 1975a, *26,* 2, 203–217.

———, Articolo, D., and Trilling, C., "Authoritarianism, Religiosity and Reactions to Deviance," *Journal of Criminal Justice,* 1974, *2,* 3, 249–259.

———, and Trilling, C., "Drugs and Deterrence in New York State," *New Society,* March 14, 1974, *27,* 633–635.

"The Public: A Hard Line," *Newsweek,* March 8, 1971.

Nie, N. H.; Hull, C. H.; Jenkins, J. G.; Steinbrenner, K.; and Bent, D. H., *Statistical Package for the Social Sciences,* 2nd ed., New York: McGraw-Hill, 1975.

Nietszche, F., *Beyond Good and Evil,* trans. W. Kaufman, New York: Vintage Books, 1966.

Nowak, S., "Correlational Approach to the Control of Meaning of Attitudinal Variables in Cross-Cultural Surveys," *Polish Sociological Bulletin,* 1962, 5–6.

Nunnally, J. C., Jr., *Popular Conceptions of Mental Health,* New York: Holt, Rinehart and Winston, 1961.

Olsen, M. E., "Multivariable Analysis of National Political Development," *American Sociological Review,* 1968, 699–712.

Osgood, C. E., "Cross-Cultural Comparability in Attitude Measurement Via Multilingual Semantic Differentials," in Steiner and Fishbein (eds.), 1965.

——, "The Cross-Cultural Generality of Visual-Verbal Synesthetic Tendencies," *Behavioral Science,* 1960, *5,* 146–169.

——, "On the Strategy of Cross-National Research into Subjective Culture," *Social Science Information,* 1967, *6,* 23–30.

Panunzio, C. M., *Major Social Institutions: An Introduction,* New York: Macmillan, 1939.

Parsons. T., *The Social System, Glencoe, Ill.: The Free Press, 1951.*

——, *Societies,* Englewood Cliffs, N.J.: Prentice-Hall, 1966.

——, "Some Theoretical Considerations Bearing on the Field of Medical Sociology," in T. Parsons, *Social Structure and Personality,* New York: The Free Press, 1965.

——, *The Structure of Social Action,* vols. I and II, New York: The Free Press, 1968.

Petrazycki, L., *Law and Morality,* trans. H. W. Babb, Cambridge, Mass.: Harvard University Press, 1955.

Pettigrew, T. F., "Intergroup Attitudes in South Africa and Southern United States," *Journal of Conflict Resolution,* 1958, *2,* 29–42.

Phillips, D. L., "Rejection: A Possible Consequence of Seeking Help for Mental Disorders, *American Sociological Review,* 1963, *28,* 963–972.

——, "Rejection of the Mentally Ill," *American Sociological Review,* 1964, *29,* 679–687.

Pigliaru, A., *Il Banditismo in Sardegna: La Vendetta Barbaricina,* Milan: Giuffre, 1970.

Podgorecki, A., *Law and Society,* London: Routledge and Kegan Paul, 1974.

——; Kaupen, W.; Van Houtte, J.; Vinke, P.; and Kutschinsky, B., *Knowledge and Opinion about Law,* London: Martin Robertson, 1973.

Posse-Brazdova, A., *Sardinian Sideshow,* London: E. P. Dutton, 1933.

Przeworski, A., and Teune, H., "Equivalence in Cross-National Research," *Public Opinion Quarterly,* 1966–1967, *30,* 4, 551–568.

Quinney, R., *Critique of Legal Order,* Boston: Little, Brown, 1973.

——, *The Social Reality of Crime,* Boston: Little, Brown, 1970.

Ramsey, C. E., and Collazo, J., "Some Problems of Cross-Cultural Measurement," *Rural Sociology,* 1960, *25,* 91–106.

Ranulf, S., *Moral Indignation and Middle Class Psychology: A Sociological Study,* Copenhagen: 1938.

Reich, W., *The Mass Psychology of Fascism,* trans. V. R. Carfagno, Wilhelm Reich Infant Trust Fund, 1971.

Reisner, R., and Semmel, H., "Abolishing the Insanity Defense: A Look at the Proposed Federal Criminal Code Reform Act in Light of Swedish Experience," *California Law Review,* 1974, *62,* 3, 774–776.

Rettig, S., and Pasamanick, B., "Changes in Moral Values among College Students: A Factorial Study," *American Sociological Review,* 1959, *24,* 856.

——, and ——, "Changes in Moral Values over Three Decades: 1929–1958," *Social Problems,* 1959, *6,* 320–328.

——, and ——, "Moral Value Structure and Social Class," *Sociometry,* 1961, *24,* 21–35.

Riedel, M., "The Perception of Crime: A Study of the Sellin-Wolfgang Seriousness Index," Paper presented at the Annual Meetings of the Inter-American Association of Criminology and the American Society of Criminology, Caracas, Venezuela, November 1972.

Robinson, J. P., "Public Reaction to Political Protest: Chicago 1968," *Public Opinion Quarterly,* 1970, *34,* 1, 1–9.

Rodman, H., "The Lower Class Value Stretch," *Social Forces,* 1963, *42,* 205.

Rokeach, M., *Beliefs, Attitudes and Values,* San Francisco: Josey-Bass, 1968.

Rokkan, S., "Party Preferences and Opinion Patterns in Western Europe: A Comparative Analysis," *International Social Science Bulletin,* 1955, *7,* 575–596.

———, "The Use of Sample Surveys in Comparative Research," *International Social Science Journal,* 1964, *16,* 7–18.

———, and Duijker, H. C. J., "Organizational Aspects of Cross-National Social Research," *Journal of Social Issues,* 1954, *10,* 4, 8–24.

Rommetneit, I. J., Notes on Standardization of Experimental Manipulations and Measurements in Cross-National Research, *Journal of Social Issues,* 1952, *10,* 4, 61–68.

Rose, A., and Prell, A., "Does the Punishment Fit the Crime?: A Study of Social Valuation," *American Journal of Sociology,* 1955, *65,* 247–259.

Rose, G. N. D., "Merits of an Index of Crime," in European Committee on Crime Problems, *The Index of Crime: Some Further Studies,* Strasbourg, France: The Council of Europe, 1970.

Rosenzweig, M. R., "Comparisons of Word Association Responses in English, French, German and Italian," *American Journal of Psychology,* 1961, *74,* 347–360.

Rossi, P. H.; Waite, E.; Bose, C. E.; and Berk, R. E., "The Seriousness of Crime: Normative Structure and Individual Differences," *American Sociological Review,* 1974, *39,* 2, 224–237.

Roszak, T., *The Making of a Counter Culture,* Garden City, N.Y.: Doubleday, 1969.

Roth, J., *Timetables: Structuring the Passage of Time in Hospital Treatment and Other Careers,* Indianapolis, Ind.: Bobbs-Merrill, 1963.

Rubington, E., and Weinberg, M., *Deviance: The Interactionist Perspective,* Toronto: Macmillan, 1968.

Sartre, J. P., *Being and Nothingness,* trans. H. E. Barnes, New York: Washington Square Press, 1969.

Schachter, S., "Interpretive and Methodological Problems of Replicated Research," *Journal of Social Issues,* 1954, *10,* 4, 52–60.

Scheff, T. S., "The Labelling Theory of Mental Illness," *American Sociological Review,* 1974, *39,* 3, 444–452.

———, *Mental Illness and Social Process,* New York: Harper and Row, 1967.

———, "Negotiating Reality: Notes on Power in the Assessment of Responsibility," *Social Problems,* 1968, *16,* 3–17.

———, "The Role of the Mentally Ill and the Dynamics of Mental Disorder," *Sociometry,* 1963, *26,* 436–453.

———, "The Societal Reaction to Deviance: Ascriptive Elements in the Psychiatric Screening of Mental Patients in a Midwestern State," *Social Problems,* 1964, *11,* 401–413.

Schur, E., *Crimes without Victims,* Englewood-Cliffs, N.J.: Prentice-Hall, 1965.

——, *Labelling Deviant Behavior,* New York: Harper and Row, 1971.

——, *Our Criminal Society,* Englewood Cliffs, N.J.: Prentice-Hall, 1969.

Scott, R. A., *The Making of Blind Men,* New York: Russell Sage Foundation, 1969.

Scott, W. A., "Attitude Movement," in G. Lindzey and E. Aronson (eds.), *The Handbook of Social Psychology,* vol. II, 2nd ed., 1968.

Segall, M. H.; Campbell, D. T.; and Herskovits, M. J., "Cultural Differences in the Perception of Geometric Illusions," *Science,* vol. CXXXIX, 769–771, 1963.

Sellin, T., *Culture Conflict and Crime,* New York: Social Science Research Council, 1938.

——, and Wolfgang, M. E., *The Measurement of Delinquency,* New York: Wiley and Sons, 1967.

Sherif, C. W., and Sherif, M. (eds.), *Attitude, Ego Involvement and Change,* New York: Wiley and Sons, 1967.

——, and ——, "The Own Categories Procedure in Attitude Research," in M. Fishbein (ed.), *Attitude Theory and Measurement,* New York: Wiley and Sons, 1967, 190–197.

Shibutani, T., "Reference Groups as Perspectives," *American Journal of Sociology,* 1955, *60,* 565–566.

Simic, A., *The Peasant Urbanites: The Study of Rural-Urban Mobility,* New York: Seminar Press, 1973.

Simmel, G., *The Sociology of Georg Simmel,* trans. K. Wolff, New York: The Free Press, 4th printing, 1959.

Simmons, J. L., *Deviants,* Berkeley, Calif.: The Glendessary Press, 1969.

Singh, K., *Train to Pakistan,* New York: Grove Press, 1956.

Singleton, F. B., *Yugoslavia: The Country and Its People,* London: Queen Anne Press, 1970.

Skinner, B. F., *Beyond Freedom and Dignity,* New York: Alfred Knopf, 1953.

Slesinger, Jonathan, A., *Milwaukee Study of Civil Disorder,* Madison: Survey Research Laboratory, University of Wisconsin, 1967.

——, "Study of Community Opinion Concerning Summer of 1967 Civil Disturbance in Milwaukee," Milwaukee Office of Applied Social Research and Institute of Human Relations, 1968.

Smigel, E. O., "Public Attitudes towards Stealing as Related to the Size of the Victim Organization," *American Sociological Review,* 1956, *21,* 3, 320–327.

Smith, D. H., and Inkeles, A., *The OM Scale: A Comparative Socio-Psychological Measure of Individual Modernity,* Abridged version of Paper presented to Section 61, "Modernization, Economy and Society," at American Sociological Association. Annual Meeting, August 31, 1966.

Socialist Federal Republic of Yugoslavia, Federal Institute of Statistics, Statisticki Godisnjak SFRJ, Beograd, 1974.

Solzhenitzyn, A. I., *Cancer Ward,* London: Penguin, 1968.

——, *The Gulag Archipelago,* New York: Harper and Row, 1973.

Sorokin, P. A., *Contemporary Sociological Theories,* New York: Harper and Brothers, 1928.

————, *Social and Cultural Dynamics,* vol. II, Boston: Porter Sargent, 1957.

Spaeth, J. L., "Public Reactions to College Student Protests," *Sociology of Education,* 1969, *42,* 2, 199–206.

Spear, P., *India,* Ann Arbor: University of Michigan Press, 1972.

Spence, K. W., "A Theory of Emotionally Based Drive and Its Relation to Performance in Simple Learning Situations," *American Psychologist,* 1958, *13,* 131–141.

Star, S., *The Public's Ideas about Mental Illness,* (mimeographed), National Opinion Research Center, University of Chicago, 1955.

Steiner, I. D., and Fishbein, M. (eds.), *Current Studies in Social Psychology,* New York: Holt, Rinehart and Winston, 1965.

Stycos, J. M., "Sample Surveys for Social Science in Underdeveloped Areas," in R. N. Adams and J. J. Preiss (eds.), *Human Organization Research,* Homewood, Ill.: The Dorsey Press, 1960.

Suchman, E. A., "The Comparative Method in Social Research," *Rural Sociology,* 1964, *29,* 123–137.

Sudnow, D., "Normal Crimes: Sociological Features of the Penal Code," *Social Problems,* 1965, *12,* 255–270.

Summers, M., *Malleus Maleficarum,* London: Hogarth Press, 1969.

Sumner, W. G., *Folkways, a Study of the Sociological Importance of Usages, Manners, Customs, Mores, and Morals,* Boston: Ginn, 1934.

————, and Keller, A. G., *The Science of Society,* vol. I, New Haven, Conn.: Yale University Press, 1927.

Szasz, Thomas, *The Myth of Mental Illness,* New York: Paul B. Hoeber, 1961.

Tapp, J. L., "A Child's Garden of Law and Order," *Psychology Today,* 1970, *12,* 29–62.

Taylor, I.; Walton, P.; and Young, J., *The New Criminology,* New York: Harper, 1974.

Tedeschi, J.; Schlenker, B.; and Bonoma, T., *Power and Conflict: An Approach to Experimental Social Psychology,* New York: Aldine-Atherton, 1973.

Ter Haar, B., *Adat Law in Indonesia,* ed. E. Adamson Hoebel and A. Arthur Schiller, New York: Institute of Pacific Relations, 1948.

Timasheff, N. S., *An Introduction to the Sociology of Law,* Cambridge, Mass.: Harvard University Committee on Research in the Social Sciences, 1939.

Time, June 6, 1969.

Triandis, H. C., and Triandis, L. M., "Social Distance among Greek and United States College Students," *Psychological Monographs,* 1962, *76,* 540.

Turk, A. T., *Criminality and Legal Order,* Chicago: Rand McNally, 1969.

Turner, R., *India's Urban Future,* Berkeley: University of California Press, 1962.

Tylor, E. B., "On a Method of Investigating the Development of Institutions Applied to Laws of Marriage and Descent," *Journal of the Anthropological Institute of Great Britain and Ireland,* 1889, *18,* 245–269.

————, *Primitive Culture,* 6th ed., London: J. Murray, 1920.

United Nations, *Demographic Year Book, 1973,* New York: Statistical Office of Department of Economic and Social Affairs, 336–356.

Van Houtte, J., and Vinke, P., "Attitudes Governing the Acceptance of Legislation among Various Social Groups," in A. Podgorecki et al., *Knowledge and Opinion about Law,* Bristol, England: Barleymar Press, 1973.

Velez-Diaz, A., and Megargee, E. I., "An Investigation of Differences in Value Judgments between Youthful Offenders and Non-Offenders in Puerto Rico, *Journal of Criminal Law, Criminology and Police Science,* 1970, *61,* 549–553.

Vernon, P. E., "Abilities and Educational Attainments in an East African Environment," *Journal of Special Education,* 1967, *1,* 335–345.

Walker, N., "Psychophysics and the Recording Angel," *British Journal of Criminology,* 1970, *11,* 191–194.

Walker, N., and Argyle, M., "Does the Law Affect Moral Judgments?" *British Journal of Criminology,* 1964, *4,* 6, 570–581.

Wanklin, J. M.; Fleming, D. F.; Buck, C. W.; and Hobbs, G. E., "Factors Influencing the Rate of First Admission to Mental Hospital," *Journal of Nervous and Mental Diseases,* 1955, *121,* 103–116.

Warne, O. H., *Your Guide to Sardinia,* London: Alvin Redman, 1965.

Warner, L., "Verbal Attitudes and Overt Behavior," *Social Forces,* 1967, *46,* 106–107.

Warnock, M., *Ethics since 1900,* New York: Oxford University Press, 1968.

Weber, M., "Objectivity in Social Science and Social Policy," in M. Weber, *The Methodology of Social Sciences,* trans. and ed. E. Shils and H. Finch, New York: The Free Press, 1949.

———, *The Protestant Ethic and the Spirit of Capitalism,* New York: Scribner, 1958.

———, *The Theory of Social and Economic Organization,* ed. T. Parsons, New York: The Free Press, 1966.

Wertheim, W. F., *Indonesian Society in Transition,* The Hague: W. van Hoeve, 1956.

Westermarck, E. A., *The Origin and Development of Moral Ideas,* New York: Macmillan, 1906.

Whiting, J., "The Cross-Cultural Method," in F. W. Moore (ed.), *Readings in Cross Cultural Methodology,* New Haven, Conn.: Hraf Press, 1961.

Wilber, D. N., *Contemporary Iran,* New York: Praeger, 1963.

Wilkins, L. T., *Social Deviance,* London: Tavistock, 1964.

Williams, R., Jr., *American Society,* New York: Knopf, 1963.

Wilson, E. O., *Sociobiology: A New Synthesis,* Cambridge, Mass.: Harvard University Press, 1975.

Wober, M., "Adapting Witkin's Field Independence Theory to Accommodate New Information from Africa," *British Journal of Psychology,* 1967, *58,* 29–38.

Wolfgang, M. E., and Ferracuti, F., *The Subculture of Violence,* London: Methuen, 1967.

Woodward, J. L., "Challenging Ideas on Mental Illness and Its Treatment," *American Sociological Review,* 1951, *16,* 443.

Wootton, Lady B., *Crime and the Criminal,* London: Stevens and Sons, 1963.

Wright, D., and Cox, E., "Religious Belief and Co-education in a Sample of 6th Form Boys and Girls," *British Journal of Social and Clinical Psychology,* 1967a, *6,* 23–31.

———, and ———, "A Study of the Relationship between Moral Judgment and Religious Belief in a Sample of English Adolescents, *Journal of Social Psychology,* 1967b, *72,* 135–144.

Zinkin, T., *Challenges in India,* London: Chatto and Windus, 1966.

Appendix

SAMPLE QUESTIONNAIRE
AND SCALE CONSTRUCTION

QUESTIONNAIRE

Act Descriptions

Robbery: A person forcefully takes $50 from another person who, as a result, is injured and has to be hospitalized.

Incest: A person has sexual relations with his adult daughter.

Not Helping: A person sees someone in a dangerous situation and does nothing.

Abortion: A woman who is two months pregnant seeks and obtains an abortion.

Factory Pollution: A factory director continues to permit his factory to release poisonous gases into the air.

Homosexuality: A person has homosexual relations in private with the consent of the partner.

Protest: A person participates in a protest meeting against government policy in a public place. No violence occurs.

Appropriation: A person puts government funds to his own use.

Taking Drugs: A person takes drugs (specified "heroin" in U.S., "soft" in Sardinia, "opium" in Iran, "gange" in India and Indonesia).

UNITED NATIONS SURVEY ON SOCIAL BEHAVIOR

The United Nations is conducting a cross-cultural study to investigate people's attitudes towards the way others behave. The project is being implemented in Italy, Yugoslavia, Iran, Indonesia and India. The American part of the project is being conducted by the School of Criminal Justice, State University of New York at Albany in collaboration with the United Nations Social Defense Research Institute, Rome, Italy.

We would greatly appreciate your cooperation in answering the questions which follow. *There are no right or wrong answers.* We are interested only in what *you* think.

QUESTION 1:

Do you think this act should be prohibited by the law?

    a. Yes

    b. No

    c. D.K.

QUESTION 2:

Is this act prohibited by the law?

    a. Yes

    b. No

    c. D.K.

QUESTION 3:

How active do you think the government is in trying to stop acts of this kind?

    a. Very active

    b. Active

    c. Not active

QUESTION 4:

To whom (if anyone) would you report this act? (Choose only the one you think is the most important.)

    a. No one

    b. Only the person's family

    c. The police

    d. Church, or religious leader

    e. To a civil servant, government inspector, or official

    f. To a doctor or psychiatrist

    g. To the person's teacher

    h. To a social worker

    i. To a trade union official

    j. To an official of a political party

    k. To his lawyer

    l. Other

QUESTION 5:

How serious do you think this act is? Use the ladder below to help you choose the corresponding number in the answer booklet. Choose a number at the left of the ladder if you think the act is not at all serious. Or choose a number anywhere in between, or one at the right if you think it is very serious. (*This ladder was vertical for all countries except the United States.*)

0	1	2	3	4	5	6	7	8	9	10	11

Not Serious   Very Serious

QUESTION 6:

What do you think should be done with a person who performs an act of this kind? (Choose only the one you consider most important.)

    a. Nothing at all should be done
    b. Probation
    c. Mental asylum
    d. Other treatment (specify)

    _____

    e. Fine (specify)

    _____

    f. Corporal punishment (specify)

    _____

    g. Give only a warning, but do nothing
    h. Other punishment (specify)

    _____

    i. Other

    _____

    j. Prison
       Years_____Months _____

319

QUESTIONNAIRE: BACKGROUND DATA

AREA	SUBJECT NUMBER	DATE	
1 2	3 4 5	6 7	8 9
		MONTH	YEAR

1. Address:_____
                  Town or City   County   State

2. Date of Birth: _____
                     Month   Year

3. Sex: Male_____Female_____

4. How many years in all have you attended school?
   _____years

5. What is or was the occupation of the male head of your household?
   _____

6. How religious are you? (Circle which one applies.)
   a. Very religious
   b. Religious
   c. Not religious

CONSTRUCTION OF THE NORM RESISTANCE SCALE (NRS)

The operational definition of Norm Resistance is a reaction to a description of behavior characterized by a) *a strong decriminalizing attitude,* b) *a preference for informal or no control of such behavior over other more formal social controls,* c) *an assessment of the act as not serious and,* d) *the preference for "nothing" or "only a warning" to be given to the actor over other possibly harsher and controlling dispositions.*

   a. *Strong Decriminalization:* Two response patterns have been used for this indicator:

     (i) Response that the act should not be prohibited by law (opinion) and the respondent's knowledge (whether "correct" or not) that it is against the law.   SCORE: 2 points

    (ii) Response that the act should not be prohibited by the law (opinion) and perception of the government as being active or very active in stopping the behavior described. SCORE: 2 points

b. *Control Agent:* Choice of "no one" or "family only" to the question: "To whom would you report this act?"

SCORE: "no one"-2 points

"family only" - 1 point

c. *Seriousness:* Using the category scale   SCORE: 0–2 - 2 points

3–5 - 1 point

d. *Disposition:* In answer to what should be done with the actor:

SCORE: "Nothing" - 2 points

"Warning" - 1 point

Maximum Possible Score for Each Act: 10 points

CONSTRUCTION OF THE DEVIANCE CONTROL SCALE (DCS)

The procedure for scoring of the scale was as follows:

a. *Criminalization*:

(i) Response that the act should be prohibited with knowledge (whether legally correct or not) that it is not prohibited. Only those acts are included which provided sufficient data for such scoring.

SCORE: 2 points each for acts of no help, abortion, factory pollution.

(ii) Response that the act should be prohibited with perception of the government as not active in stopping the act.

SCORE: 2 points each for the acts of no help, abortion, factory pollution, incest, robbery, homosexuality, protest, appropriation.

b. *Definition—Control Agent*:

(i) For the acts of factory pollution, no help, appropriation, incest.

SCORE: 3 points for "police," 2 points for "government official," 1 point for "doctor."

(ii) The acts of protest, homosexuality, and abortion (acts generally least controlled by the sample) are scored double on these items.

SCORE: 6 points for "police," 4 points for "government official," 2 points for "doctor."

c. *Seriousness*:
  (i) For appropriation, incest, no help.
                            SCORE: 1 point each for 9–11.
  (ii) For abortion, homosexuality, public protest.
                            SCORE: 2 points each for 9–11.
  d. *Disposition:* SCORE: One point if chose prison or mental asylum for pollution, incest, no help, abortion, homosexuality, or protest. This produced a full number of 30 items, with a maximum possible score of 67. The use of the categories of mental asylum or prison as indicators of deviance control, is somewhat arbitrary. However, removal from society has been argued to be a useful indicator of tolerance of deviance: See, Newman (1975).

Author Index

Abbott, D. J., 108
Aberle, D. F., 284
Acker, C. W., 37
Adorno, T. W., 32
Ajzen, I., 33
Akman, D. D., 47, 64
Allport, F., 28, 30
Allport, G. W., 28, 64n., 106n.
Almond, G., 57
Anderson, L. R., 28
Anderson, R., 57
Andrews, F. M., 42
Annis, A. P., 37
Argyle, M., 47, 57n., 166, 167
Arnold, D., 250
Articolo, D., 34n., 47, 50, 60
Asch, S. E., 277, 279, 280
Aubert, V., 117

Bagby, J. W., 106n., 107n.
Ballard, L. V., 22
Ball-Rokeach, S., 5, 262, 263
Banks, A. S., 70, 192n.
Barakat, M. K., 56, 68n.
Barton, A. H., 98
Basham, A. L., 79
Beccaria, C. B., 25, 219
Becker, H., 2, 4, 10, 114, 193, 212
Bendix, R., 68n.
Benedict, R., 56, 154n., 277
Bent, D. M., 193n.
Bentz, W. K., 38, 50
Berk, R. E., 47
Beteille, A., 80, 136n.
Bickman, L., 26n., 59n.
Bill, J. A., 86, 90, 91
Binder, L., 88, 92
Blackwell, B., 26n.
Blauner, P., 251
Blom, R., 51
Blumenthal, M., 42
Bogart, L., 19, 293, 294
Bonoma, T., 19n.
Bord, E., 41
Bose, A., 82, 83

Bose, C. E., 47
Bouchier, E. S., 104
Boydell, C. L., 49–50
Brandt, R. B., 154, 282, 283
Brehem, J., 29
Brown, A., 94, 95, 98
Brown, E. G., 222
Brown, W., 79
Bruce, W., 57
Buck, C. W., 22

Calder, B. J., 28, 29
Camba, R., 267
Campbell, D. T., 106n., 277n., 290n.
Cantril, H., 61–62, 70n., 71, 112n.
Carman, H. J., 101
Chambliss, W. J., 4
Chein, I., 30
Chin-Shong, E., 39, 41, 50
Cicourel, A. V., 10
Clinard, M. B., 108
Cloward, R. A., 251n.
Cohen, A. K., 212, 251n.
Collazo, J., 57, 68n., 106
Converse, P. E., 57, 107
Coser, L., 13, 288
Cox, E., 44
Crane, R. I., 81
Crissman, P., 45
Crocetti, G. M., 36
Crumpton, H. G., 37
Cuber, J. F., 251
Cumming, E., 22, 38, 39–40
Cumming, J., 22, 38, 39–40
Curtis, L. A. 263

Dahl, R. A., 5, 19n., 20n., 213n., 251
Dahrendorf, R., 213n.
Dator, J. A., 106n.
Davis, F., 213n.
Davis, K., 82
Davis, R., 106n., 107n.
Dawson, J. L. M., 106n.
DeFleur, M., 29
Denitch, B., 98

323

Subject Index

Abortion, 17
  Catholic Church and, 23, 273
  consensus and, 114
  decriminalization of, 1, 114, 137, 240
  definition of act, 133
  deviance perception and, 156–161,
    163,·166, 177, 182, 184–186, 189
    subcultural, 253–258, 273–274
  norm resistance to, 156, 157, 198,
    205–208, 210
  preferred societal sanction and, 141,
    142, 149
  prison term for, estimating, 238–240
  public attitudes toward, 44, 45, 114
Act descriptions
  construction of, 63–64
  cross-cultural specificity of, 284–285
  relating law to, 225–228
Act differentiation, 285–286
Act-extrinsic factor, 182, 184–185
Act-intrinsic factor, 180, 184–185
Activity
  deviance perception and, 168, 169,
    171, 175
  government, perceptions of, 151–153
Age
  and deviance control, 256, 257, 259,
    260, 275
  and deviance perception, 270, 271
  and norm resistance, 199–206,
    210–211
  sampling and, 108–109
Alcoholism, decriminalization and, 1
Appropriation, 17
  definition of act, 132
  deviance perception and, 124, 156,
    157, 160–164, 166, 271–272
  norm resistance to, 156, 157, 197, 198
  preferred societal sanction and, 141,
    142, 148
  prison term for, estimating, 234–237
Asensus, 289
Attitude(s), 28–35
  and behavior, 32–33, 293
  definitions of, 28, 31

organization of, 33–34
and personality, 32–33
public (*see* Public attitudes, areas of)
structural components of, 29–30
Attitudinal response, 30–33
Australia, deviance perception in 44–45
Authoritarian personality, 32

Back translation, 52–53
Barbaracino Code (Sardinia), 104–105,
  185, 267, 270, 271
Behavior
  attitude and, 32–33, 293
  criminal, public attitudes toward,
    41–51
Bourgeois criminal law, 6
Bribery, 17, 153, 160–162

Caste system (India), 79–84
Cattle stealing, 267, 269–272
Charisma, notion of, 19–20, 86
Communist countries
  criminal law in, 25
  deviance control in, 170, 192
Conflict scale, 265
Conflict theory, 4–6, 15, 16, 21, 51, 117,
  188, 211, 261, 288, 297
Consensus, 5–7, 15, 50, 113–122, 285–288,
  297
Criminal behavior, public attitudes
  toward, 41–51
Criminal law, 25, 166, 212–248
  and act descriptions, 225–228
  bourgeois, 6
  class-based, 16, 213
  in communist countries, 25
  cross-cultural study, 212–248
    See also specific countries
  Italian, 105, 219–222, 225, 228–233,
    235, 238, 240, 241, 243, 245–246
  knowledge of, 35, 148–151, 166–169,
    171, 175
  New York State, 222, 225–226,
    232–233, 235–236, 238, 240, 242,
    243, 245, 246

327

Governmental authority, resistance to, 156, 158
Gross National Product, deviance control and, 192

Homicide, 4, 103–104
Homosexuality, 17, 50
  consensus and, 114
  decriminalization of, 1, 114, 132–133
  definition of act, 132–133
  deviance perception and, 114, 120, 156–162, 166
    subcultural, 254, 256, 257, 259,273
  norm resistance to, 156, 157, 198, 204–206, 210–211
  preferred societal sanction and, 141, 142, 148
  prison term for, estimating, 237–238
  public attitudes toward, 44, 45, 114
Households (*see* Kinship patterns)

Incest, 4, 14, 17
  definition of act, 132
  deviance perception and, 120, 157, 158, 160–164, 177, 178, 184–186
    subcultural, 272–273
  norm resistance to, 157, 198–201, 210–211
  preferred societal sanction and, 141, 142, 147
  prison term for, estimating, 233–234
India, 79–85
  caste system, 79–84
  criminal law, 214–215, 229, 233–235, 237–245
  deviance perception, 156–161, 163–164, 168, 169, 171, 174–176, 178, 184
    subcultural, 253–255
  education, impact on deviance control, 194
  housing, 84–85
  kinship patterns, 81–83
  languages, 79, 81, 84
  literacy rates, 82, 83
  modernization, 185
  norm resistance, 156–158, 199, 200, 204, 205, 207, 211
  population growth, 82, 84
  religions, 79, 81, 185
  rural sample, 83–84
  urban/rural differences, 82–83
  urban/rural influence, 196
  urban sample, 84–85
Indignation
  moral (*see* Moral indignation)
  proactive, 184, 185
  reactive, 180–182, 185, 186
Individual pollution, 156

Individual relativism, 280–281
Indonesia, 71–78
  criminal law, 78, 215–217, 225, **229**, 233, 235, 240, 241, 243–245
  deviance perception, 156–165, 168, 170, 173–174, 177–179, 184
    subcultural, 255–257
  education, impact on deviance control, 194, 196
  ethnic differences, 71, 73, 78
  Hindu influence, 76
  housing, 78
  kinship patterns, 78
  language, 76–77
  local government structure, 21
  norm resistance, 156, 157, 165, 199, 200, 204–210
  religion, 76–78
  rural sample, 77
  social class, 77–78
  urban sample, 77
Intensity of reaction, 34, 38–39, 45–47, 117–122
  See also Seriousness; Seriousness scales
Iran, 85–93
  bribery, 17, 153, 160–162
  criminal law, 18, 217–219, 229, 233, 235, 238, 240, 241, 243, 245
  deviance perception, 156, 157, 159, 160, 162–164, 168–171, 174–177, 180, 184–185
    subcultural, 256–258
  education, impact on deviance control, 194, 196
  Greek influence, 85–86
  kinship patterns, 90
  literacy rate, 109
  local government structure, 21
  modernization, 85, 86, 185
  nepotism, 90, 92
  norm resistance, 156, 157, 199–201, 203–205, 207–209, 211
  peasants, 86–87, 90–91
  political structure, 86, 89
  population growth, 93
  religion, 86–90, 185
  rural samples, 92–93
  Sassainan dynasty, 86
  sex roles, 93
  Shahansha tradition, 86, 87, 92, 170, 185
  social class, 86–87
  social structure, 90–93
  socio-economic class, 91–92
  traditional class, 92
  urban/rural influence, 196
  urban sample, 93
  villages, 90–91

330

Press, social control and the, 23, 24
Pressure groups, 20–21
Prison terms
  official (*see* Official prison term)
  recommended, 230–231, 246–248
Prostitution
  decriminalization and, 1
  public attitudes toward, 44
Protest (*see* Public protest)
Public, structure of, 20–26
Public attitudes, areas of
  abortion, 44, 45, 114
  criminal behavior, 41–51
  homosexuality, 44, 45, 114
  mental illness, 36–41
  political crime, 45
  pornography, 44
  prostitution, 44
  sanctions, 47–51
  sex crimes, 44
  taking drugs, 44–45, 114
Public opinion, 18–22
  and criminal law, 1, 78, 246–248, 253,
    261, 290, 295–297
  differing structure of, 107
  See also Public attitudes, areas of
Public-opinion polls, 18–19, 33, 35, 42, 43,
  48
Public protest
  definition of act, 134–135
  deviance perception and, 115, 119,
    156–160, 162, 164, 166, 177, 182,
    184
      subcultural, 254–259, 273
  norm resistance to, 156, 157, 198,
    208–210
  preferred societal sanction and,
    141–143, 147–148
  prison term for, estimating, 244–245
Punishment, 140–146
  treatment model, 146–147
  See also Sanctions

Quasi-crimes, 17, 50, 120–122
Quasi-criminal law, 15
Questionnaire(s)
  administration of, 65–67
  construction of, 52–63
  interpretation, 67–68
  sample, 317

Relativism, 54
  cultural (*see* Cultural relativism)
  descriptive, 154, 278–280
  individual, 280–281
  normative, 282–284
  rampant, 2
  situational, 281–282

Religion
  cross-cultural studies of (*see specific
    countries*)
  and social control, 21, 23–24, 27, 138
Religiosity
  and deviance control, 188, 196–197,
    255, 259, 260
  and deviance perception, 12–13, 51,
    271–274
  and norm resistance, 199–211
  sampling and, 109
  and sanctions, 50
Research, paradigmatic origins of, 1–8
Resistance potential, 252, 253
Response bias, 65–66, 119, 155
Robbery, 5–7, 17
  definition of act, 131–132
  deviance perception and, 156–158,
    160, 161, 163–164, 166, 177, 185
  norm resistance to, 156, 157, 197, 198
  preferred societal sanction and, 141,
    142, 148
  prison term for, estimating, 229–232

Sampling, 69–112
  demographic variables, defining of,
    108–111
  methodology, 106–108
  social class and, 109, 112
Sanctions
  deviance perception and, 48, 166–169,
    172, 174, 175
  official prison term (*see* Official
    prison term, estimating)
  preferred societal, 140–148
  public attitudes toward, 47–51
  religiosity and, 50
  See also Ciminal law
Sardinia, 69–70
  deviance perception, 17, 156, 157,
    160–164, 168–172, 174–178, 181, 185
      subcultural, 265–270
  norm resistance, 156, 157
  patterns of violence, 103–105, 117,
    131
Seriousness
  deviance perception and, 117–123,
    168, 169, 171–172, 174, 175
      subcultural, 254, 256, 265–266
Seriousness scales, 121–124, 155, 159
Sex, sampling and, 109
Sex crimes, public attitudes toward, 44
Situational relativism, 281–282
Social change, deviance and, 6, 7
Social class
  deviance control and, 188, 197, 255,
    259, 260
  and deviance perception, 51, 188
  India, 79–84

331